NIGHT
AFTER
NIGHT

MAX LAMBERT

NIGHT
AFTER
NIGHT

New Zealanders in Bomber Command

HarperCollins*Publishers*

The author and publishers gratefully acknowledge the support of the Royal New Zealand Air Force Museum Trust Board.

National Library of New Zealand Cataloguing-in-Publication Data

Lambert, Max, 1936-
Night after night / Max Lambert.
Originally published 2005. This issue omits illustrations,
bibliographical references and index.
ISBN-13: 978-1-86950-644-5
ISBN-10: 1-86950-644-8
1. Great Britain. Royal Air Force. Bomber Command.
2. World War, 1939-1945—New Zealand.
3. World War, 1939-1945—Aerial operations, British.
4. Airmen—New Zealand. I. Title.
940.544941—dc 22

First published in this format 2007
HarperCollins*Publishers (New Zealand) Limited*
P.O. Box 1, Auckland

ISBN-13: 978 1 86950 644 5
ISBN-10: 1 86950 644 8

Cover design by Darren Holt
Typesetting by Springfield West

Printed by Griffin Press, Australia, on 79 gsm Bulky Paperback

Front cover photo: *Airmen prepare to board a Wellington at dusk at the start of a bombing operation.* Courtesy Air Force Museum
Back cover photo: *A lone Lancaster flies high.* Courtesy RAF Museum

For *Anna* and *Joe* and others of the new generation
so that they may know and remember.

This book is dedicated to all New Zealanders who
served in Bomber Command in World War II,
particularly the 1850 who died.

Contents

1942: A transitional year *145*

1943: Bomber Command begins destroying Germany *245*

1944: The end in sight   *389*

Acknowledgements

Many people helped me during the three years it took to research and write this book but above all I am indebted to Christchurch-based aviation historian Errol Martyn for his support and encouragement. Had he not been at the end of an email line to patiently answer my interminable questions, *Night After Night* would have been the poorer. He also made numerous valuable suggestions and read the manuscript. Any mistakes remaining are entirely my responsibility. I shall be forever grateful for his help and friendship.

An authority on New Zealand airmen in World War II, especially casualties, and honorary consultant to the Air Force Museum, Christchurch, Martyn has an unrivalled collection of information, built up by long and patient research, about RNZAF airmen — a collection of work that culminated in his remarkable trilogy *For Your Tomorrow*. Volumes I and II cover the fates of all New Zealanders who died while serving with the RNZAF and Allied air services during the period 1915–98, while volume III carries biographical data and appendices.

A number of other people assisted greatly, among them Colin Hanson, Trentham, Wellington, a retired RNZAF group captain and author of *By Such Deeds: Honours and Awards in the RNZAF 1923–99*. He generously permitted me to quote from his book, a wonderful source of names, awards, service dates, citations and other information.

I'm also grateful to Bill Simpson, Auckland, a former Mosquito pilot and founder and president of the now disbanded RAF Bomber Command Association (NZ). He supplied a membership list and steered me toward a number of men with outstanding records. He

Acknowledgements

also gave me permission to quote from BCANZ documents about Fraser Barron and from the association's oral-history project done in tandem with Auckland's Museum of Transport, Technology and Social History (MOTAT). Randal Springer, Palmerston North, president of 75 Squadron Association until just before his death in May 2004, led me to several stories, notably the one that forms the basis of my prelude.

Aviation historians Arthur Arculus, Auckland, and Harry Widdup, Matamata, were always ready to share information and provided assistance on several stories, for which I am grateful. John Best, Wainuiomata, readily lent me documents. I need to thank Ken Chilton, Dunedin, for getting and lending me the tape on which Tom Stewart talked about the Peenemunde raid. Aviation researcher Rod MacKenzie, Invercargill, put me right on several points. My thanks also to Matthew O'Sullivan, Keeper of Photographs at the Air Force Museum in Christchurch, and Defence Force historian John Crawford. Ken Turnham, a former member of a Missing Research and Enquiry Unit, kindly contacted me while visiting New Zealand and described the work of the units. Peggy Gibbons, Pauatahanui, Wellington, was ever helpful on 76 Squadron matters.

I'm grateful to Australian John Burford, whose father flew with New Zealand pilot John Lawrie. He kindly gave me permission to base my story about Lawrie's last flight on his own research and account of what happened.

Dutch researchers Co Maarschalkerweerd, Ria Schmieder, Ed Muisjers, Han Hogendijk and Hank Welting, among others, made unfailingly generous responses to requests for information and went to endless trouble for me — so typical of the Dutch. All were amazingly helpful. Hogendijk for years treasured letters he got from Victoria Cross winner Len Trent after the war but he sent them to me, a stranger on the other side of the world, when he learned I was writing about the raid on which Trent won his award. The letters and Hogendijk's own diary account of that May afternoon in 1943 have now been deposited in the Air Force Museum, Christchurch, which also has Trent's Victoria Cross.

My thanks too to Colin Armstrong, Derek Bigg, Stephen and Mary Hassall, Bob Hogg, Allan McDonald, Jean Muir, Robert Owen, Lew Parsons, Chris Pointon, Ron Rae, the Sadler family and Jock Whitehouse (England); and to Linzee Druce (Scotland), Claude Grimaud (France), Horst Ahrens (Germany) and Tom Thomson (Canada). Likewise the knowledgeable people who responded to questions I occasionally posted on the message board on Ross McNeill's wonderful website www.rafcommands.com — a treasure of information, questions and answers.

Authors Colin Burgess (Australia), Arthur Kinnis (British Columbia), Bill Chorley, Oliver Clutton-Brock, Geoff Copeman, Jonathan Falconer, Martin Middlebrook and Michael Wadsworth (England) graciously gave me their permission to quote from their books.

Thanks also to Tony Sammons and the rest of the team at Rapid Copy, Thorndon Quay, Wellington, who were always so obliging and made my life so much easier. The best copy shop in the capital.

I'm immensely grateful to the families of aircrew killed during the war or who have died since. They supplied logs, diaries, memoirs, letters, photographs and other personal information of great variety. Finally, my deep gratitude to all former aircrew I interviewed. Without exception they gave willingly of their time and welcomed me into their homes. For many, it was the first time they had talked to an outsider about their war service and some found it difficult. Some spoke about distressing experiences involving the deaths of comrades on their own aircraft, and at times I realised I was intruding into extremely private and emotional memories. I thank them all.

Abbreviations and Conversion table

Abbreviations

ASR	Air Sea Rescue
CAS	Chief of Air Staff
CGM	Conspicuous Gallantry Medal
DFC	Distinguished Flying Cross
DFM	Distinguished Flying Medal
DSO	Distinguished Service Order
HCU	Heavy Conversion Unit
LFS	Lancaster Finishing School
LMF	lack of moral fibre
LNSF	Light Night Striking Force
MB	master bomber
MBE	Member of the Order of the British Empire
MREU	Missing Research and Enquiry Unit
OBE	Officer of the Order of the British Empire
OTU	Operational Training Unit
PFF	Pathfinder Force
PRC	Personnel Reception Centre
RCM	radio countermeasures
SSC	short-service commission

Conversion table

Distance, weight, fluid volume and area are generally given in imperial units, in accordance with historical usage. This table is provided for those more familiar with metric measurements.

1 inch	2.54 centimetres
1 foot (12 inches)	30.48 centimetres
1 yard (3 feet)	91.44 centimetres
1 mile (1760 yards)	1.61 kilometres
1 pound	453.59 grams
1 stone (14 pounds)	6.35 kilograms
1 ton (2240 pounds)	1.02 tonnes
1 gallon	4.55 litres
1 acre	0.40 hectare

Preface

In the Wellington Public Library, one day in December 2000, I found an old book about World War II airmen who had won the Victoria Cross. Thumbing through it I chanced on the name of a New Zealand Lancaster pilot whose wireless operator, a Scot called George Thompson, had won a posthumous Victoria Cross on New Year's Day 1945.

Flak severely damaged Thompson's bomber on a daylight raid on the Dortmund–Ems Canal in northwest Germany, and fire enveloped both gunners. Thompson was critically burned as he pulled the men from their blazing turrets and beat out the flames. The young pilot, battling piercing cold in a shattered cockpit, nursed the crippled bomber back to Allied lines in Holland, crash-landing with great skill on a snow-covered field. All seven crew emerged alive from the wreck but Thompson and one of the gunners subsequently died.

The New Zealander's name was given as FH Denton, and the book said he came from Canterbury. Directory checks discovered a Denton with those initials in Amberley. Could it be him? Still alive? Indeed, yes — Harry Denton, DFC, 80, a retired farmer. I was working for the New Zealand Press Association in Wellington at the time and interviewed Denton by phone. A feature I wrote about him to coincide with the 56th anniversary of that harrowing flight was widely used by the newspapers and led directly to this book, for after talking to Denton I realised there must be other New Zealand bomber-aircrew veterans with stories that should be recorded before it was too late. So it proved. Their ranks are thinning quickly now but I found enough ex-aircrew with dramatic wartime tales to fill several books. I conducted interviews all over New Zealand, most face to face, some by telephone. It was a rewarding and humbling experience.

I also unearthed accounts of young men, some still in their teens, who died bravely in the service of their country. In most cases what happened to them has never been told. Theirs are deeds to make New Zealanders proud.

Since the end of the war, 60 years ago, a seemingly endless flood of books has appeared on the New Zealand Division's battles and campaigns in Greece and Crete, North Africa and Italy, and they continue to roll off the presses. Many New Zealand fighter pilots have also published books about their experiences. Amazingly, however, little has been written in this country about the several thousand New Zealanders who served with Bomber Command: only the 1950s-published three-volume official history *New Zealanders With the Royal Air Force,* a handful of personal books and memoirs, and a disappointing history of 75 (NZ) Squadron in 1991.

It's difficult to understand quite why this should be so and why, despite their significant role and achievements in Bomber Command, New Zealand aircrew have not received due credit. The big war cemeteries and memorials in Britain and Germany, sombre reminders of the sacrifice of so many aircrew, seem to be outside the ambit of New Zealand prime ministers, who so frequently pay homage to the nation's army dead on overseas trips.

Perhaps it's because Bomber Command's New Zealanders can't boast the equivalents of Crete, Ruweisat Ridge, El Alamein and Cassino, even though the skies over Germany were every bit as dangerous as those battlegrounds. The air war wasn't like the army's, with brief major battles and heavy casualties often followed by long periods of inaction. Bomber Command fought its battles every day and night of the war, and New Zealand lives bled away on a continuous but lesser scale that hasn't had the same impact on the nation's consciousness.

Bomber Command's hostile post-war press in Britain probably rubbed off on its New Zealand participants, too. The bombing of German cities, particularly the February 1945 firestorm destruction of Dresden, became hugely controversial. The arguments still rage. But bombing policy was decided by Churchill and the other Allied leaders, the War Cabinet and the Air Ministry. Bomber Command carried it out — at a cost of more than 55,000 Commonwealth aircrew lives, 1850 of them from New Zealand. Max Hastings notes in his 1979 work *Bomber Command* that the bombers' part in the war was one that many politicians and civilians would prefer to forget — 'in the safety of peace'.

The British public held a different view when Bomber Command was Britain's only offensive weapon for a couple of years after Dunkirk, alone in hitting back at Nazi Germany. Australia's official war history points out that by 1943 the British people no longer sought their heroes among the fighter pilots but among the more prosaic bomber crews. 'They followed with their prayers the receding drone of bombers heading for Germany, mourned the loss of unknown young men who did not return and proudly exulted at the mounting success of the bombing.'

The people of occupied Europe took comfort and hope from the sound of throbbing engines on British bombers overhead. One former member of the Dutch resistance wrote in a UK Bomber Command newsletter in 1988: 'For us in occupied Holland the RAF was proof of the freedom that would be regained. Without [Bomber Command] we would not live in a free Western Europe.'

One or two of the ex-aircrew I met said they felt troubled about the bombing deaths of German civilians, particularly women and children. The rest had no regrets, then or now. They still see it in simple terms, and it's hard not to agree with them and the adage that Germany began the war and reaped the whirlwind. It was nasty but it was total war. The evil of Nazi Germany had to be defeated. Bomber Command aircrew had a job to do and they did it. One may question the merits of the wholesale destruction of German cities and the deaths of 600,000 civilians, but no one may question the courage of the men who flew the bombers.

Aircrew were too busy as they approached their target to worry much about what was happening on the ground. Getting to the right place on time, dropping their bombs accurately and holding their aircraft straight and steady until the target camera took its photograph totally occupied their minds. All the while flak gunners and fighters were trying to kill them. 'Self-preservation was a major motivating force,' says Southlander Tiny Humphries, a 75 Squadron navigator.

German novelist Thomas Mann spoke from exile over the BBC in April 1942 after Bomber Command had devastated central Lubeck: 'It's my native city but I think of Coventry and cannot object to the lesson that everything must be paid for. Hitler's Germany has neither tradition nor future. It can only destroy. And destruction is its fate.'

Most of the New Zealanders killed in Bomber Command lost their lives bombing targets in Germany or occupied Europe. They were in action at the very start of the conflict and flew on the last raids a few days before peace was declared. Almost every day and night of the six years of war young New Zealanders climbed into bombers on airfields somewhere in Britain and flew off to carry the war to the Nazis. No other arm of the New Zealand services can claim such a sustained record of action.

This book recounts the personal experiences of some of the New Zealanders who flew as pilots, navigators, bomb aimers, wireless operators and gunners, with enough background to put them and their exploits into context. I was lucky enough to find and interview veterans who took part in the key raids and campaigns of the war and through them to find out what it was like to be a crewman on a bomber. Their stories are told in chronological order. Chapters on topics such as ditching and parachuting, and short profiles of several noted bomber crew, are also included.

Night After Night does not pretend to be a history of New Zealanders' participation in Bomber Command. Neither does it deal with the controversies that arose out of the bombing of Germany, nor in any detail with the technical aspects of the bombers' war. Such subjects, already discussed in countless books published overseas, are outside the scope of this volume. *Night After Night* is simply a tribute to all New Zealanders who flew in Bomber Command.

Max Lambert
Wellington
July 2004

Prelude

The stricken Stirling came down in a shallow dive, streaming fire in the late-night sky. It roared low over the small village of Vemmenaes on the east coast of Taasinge, one of Denmark's southern islands, crossed a farm, then plunged into shallow water 100 yards from shore. Flames licked high as the half-submerged aircraft burned. Distorted bits of the bomber littered the beach and nearby fields. The Stirling still carried its load of four mines but they didn't explode. Stumbling around with torches, Danish police and civilians found one dead airman floating in his Mae West and two more on the farm. At daylight they recovered another two bodies from the water and found a third lying in a thicket of whitethorn bushes on a low cliff face. That made six. Finally, the searchers located the body of the rear gunner jammed in the wrecked tail section, which had broken away from the main fuselage moments before the crash and lay 300 yards from the cliff edge.

Reverently the Danes gathered the bodies of the three New Zealanders, the three Londoners and a Norwegian in the Royal Canadian Air Force, laid them side by side in the field above the cliff and covered them with a parachute. Later that spring morning German soldiers arrived and mounted guard, shooing the locals away. For some unknown reason, the German military, normally correct and prompt in dealing with the bodies of fallen airmen, left the crew of 75 Squadron's Stirling EF137 in the field for three days before putting them on a truck and taking them away. The incensed Danes carpeted the road the Germans had to take through Vemmenaes on their way to the main highway with flowers, saluting the seven men who had given their lives in the struggle against the Nazis as they passed.

Helge Scheunchen, a young Dane who researched the crash in 1950, wrote to the widow of one of the New Zealanders, telling her a policeman called Lindtorp had conducted the first search for survivors in the early hours of 24 April 1944. 'He found your husband lying on the foreshore. He was still warm but dead, killed instantly. He lay as [if] he was sleeping, very pale, not at all bloody, cleaned by the water. His face was nice and not destroyed. Mr Lindtorp carried him in on [to] the shore.'

The New Zealanders who died in the crash at 11.23 p.m. on 23 April, not quite three hours after takeoff, were pilot Manson Lammas, 30, navigator Douglas Vaughan, 28, and bomb aimer Bob Bailey, just 20. Lammas, born in Dannevirke, was working as a share milker for his father in the Nelson area when he volunteered for aircrew in March 1941. Vaughan, a butcher, enlisted in Hamilton. Bailey, youngest of the crew by a considerable margin, was an apprentice lithographer with the *New Zealand Herald* in Auckland when he joined the RNZAF. Lammas and Vaughan were married, Lammas just before he sailed for Britain, Vaughan in October 1939.

Lammas learned to fly in New Zealand while the other two trained in Canada. They met for the first time in late September 1943 at No. 11 Operational Training Unit (OTU) at Wescott, Buckinghamshire, one of Bomber Command's big training establishments. Here they formed themselves into a crew, also taking in an English wireless operator and Norwegian gunner Ivar Larsen, 33, who had lived in Canada since he was 18. They flew twin-engined Wellingtons for several months, crisscrossing Britain day and night on training flights. When they graduated to the bigger Stirlings, with their four engines, at 1657 Heavy Conversion Unit (HCU) at Stradishall, Suffolk, the crew of five became seven with the addition of a flight engineer and mid-upper gunner. They were posted to 75 (NZ) Squadron at Mepal, Cambridgeshire, in March 1944.

They'd flown just a couple of operations together before they were killed — unlucky, perhaps, but like thousands of other young bomber crew, dying in the early stages of their tour when they were still inexperienced and at their most vulnerable. They were lost at the time when 75 Squadron was switching from Stirlings to the far superior Lancasters. They had flown the new aircraft on a conversion course but they did their ops on Stirlings and it was on EF137 that they flew their final flight. As it turned out theirs was the last Stirling the squadron lost after first flying the type in November 1942 — the last of 72 that didn't come home. The bomber was to have laid its mines in the wide bay off the important German naval port of Kiel but was intercepted before it got there.

Danish observation posts in Taasinge and nearby islands heard gunfire and saw the flaming bomber falling, a night-fighter victim, but no one will ever know precisely what happened to the Stirling, at what height it was flying when attacked or why none of the crew took to their parachutes. It may have been that the bomber fell steeply before flattening out, preventing the crew from jumping. The bodies found in the field above the sea did not have opened parachutes.

The Germans finally buried the crew in a cemetery at Aabenraa, a coastal town in South Jutland not far from the German border, on 1 May. A German army Lutheran chaplain conducted a short service and threw sand on the coffins before the graves were filled in and soldiers fired a volley of shots.

On another spring morning in 1994, 50 years to the day after EF137 was shot down, Ivar Larsen's elderly sister flew from Norway to unveil a monument to the Lammas crew in a field not far from the crash site. Four hundred people, New Zealanders among them, were present. Embedded near the top of the memorial — a massive block of unhewn stone — is a 75 (NZ) Squadron badge, cast in bronze by a Wellington foundry and donated by the squadron association in New Zealand. Below it the names of the crew are chiselled into the surface. So are the Danish words *Til Minde Om* — In Remembrance.

Beginnings

Clean sheets and pubs but the cost was high

Typically they slept in clean white sheets, ate well, drank in cosy pubs in pleasant English villages and had seven days' leave every six weeks. City life was a short train ride away. Officers had a batman, either shared or to themselves. Life on an air station was relaxed, with a minimum of spit-and-polish discipline.

What they had to do in return was climb into a bomber every three or four nights, frequently more often, and lay their lives on the line attacking targets in Germany or occupied Europe. They took off after the sun went down and flew for hours, often seven or eight, sometimes nine or ten, their bomb-laden aircraft droning through the blackness toward distant dots on a navigator's chart. For however long they flew they were assailed by the roar of engines, four of them on the big bombers. Noise was a constant, fatiguing presence. They operated in all weathers the year round. They flew through snow, rainstorms and belts of lightning, on cold winter nights when it was minus 50 degrees Centigrade outside, often battling the astonishingly quick build-up of ice on wings and fuselage that could mean disaster.

Every moment in the air they were at risk of sudden and violent death; of an unseen enemy night fighter unleashing a torrent of shells into their aircraft; of flak spitting up from radar-controlled gun batteries on the ground to smash great holes in the wings and fuselage or knock out engines and kill men; of collision with other bombers flying in the same stream; of bombs and incendiaries falling from aircraft flying overhead; of engine failure that could start a fire. They were in danger from the instant they took off, coaxing fully laden aircraft into the air, until they touched down at base at the end of the homeward trip. Enemy intruders lurking over England at night hunting unwary prey meant unflagging vigilance was necessary from the moment of takeoff to the moment of landing.

Bombs and incendiaries; hundreds of gallons of aviation fuel; hydraulic oil; fumes; ammunition for the guns — a lethal mix. When flames licked at wings or fuselage, an aircraft could explode in an instant, an enormous blast of fire that left nothing but torn bodies and twisted wreckage plunging to earth.

Bomber aircrew faced particularly violent, gruesome and sudden ends. Some fatally damaged aircraft continued to fly more or less normally for a time, allowing their crews to take to their parachutes. Some pilots even crash-landed successfully. But usually it wasn't like that. A damaged plane spinning earthwards created centrifugal forces that pinned the crew, making it almost impossible for them to move, to grab a parachute, to reach an escape hatch. A steep, straight, high-speed dive had the same effect. Even getting out of a crippled plane flying more or less level was tricky. Bulky flying suits hindered the movements of crew fighting their way in the dark along the narrow fuselage littered with sharp obstructions toward an escape hatch that might be damaged and jammed. Men trapped in blazing, falling aircraft had little chance of surviving and knew they were about to die. The final seconds of roaring engines, a flash, an awful explosion — even worse if the payload was still aboard and detonated on impact. Few aircrew were pulled alive from crashed planes.

Short-of-fuel or combat-damaged aircraft trying to reach the safety of England, their crew tossing out anything moveable in a desperate attempt to lessen the weight and maintain height, faced their own Armageddon — the terrifying North Sea, graveyard of thousands of aircraft reported 'lost without trace'. Even if they escaped from a ditched plane, men struggled to stay alive in a tossing rubber dinghy. Swimming, even wearing a Mae West, meant almost certain death. Despite the bravery of Air Sea Rescue (ASR), the chances of being saved after ditching were slim, especially at night or in winter.

Hundreds of battle-torn bombers which made it back over England were also lost, unable to stay up long enough to make their bases, or crashing because rain, cloud or fog shrouded the countryside. Weary, sometimes wounded, pilots flew into the ground while searching for airfields.

For hours, the seven-man crews that flew the heavy four-engined bombers were cocooned in their own small world, dependent on their joint skills, determination and resources to complete their mission and get home safely. Once they were in trouble they were totally on their own, a Morse key the only way to transmit a distress message, a wireless set the only way to receive a position fix or course. Other than that there was no outside help. None.

Although tours of duty varied in duration, bomber crews in the mid-war period were generally required to fly 30 operations to complete a first tour and then, after a break as instructors at an Operational Training Unit (OTU), to complete a second, shorter tour of 20 or 25 ops. This at a time when German defences against night bombing grew to their strongest and were infinitely more effective and dangerous than early in the war.

Each op was akin to 'going over the top' in World War I. Bomber Command casualty rates reached appalling levels at times; in some squadrons they were so bad hardly anyone finished a tour, and commanders screened out crews who had completed, say, 20, 22 or 25 ops, telling them their tour was over. This sustained morale to some slight degree, particularly among newcomers, who watched dismayed as crew after crew of experienced airmen failed to make it home and knew their turn would probably soon come.

90 Squadron's Stirling losses were so high in the autumn of 1943 that New Zealand wireless operator Phil Donovan suddenly found his tour over after just his 18th operation. 'They wanted a crew that had finished a tour,' he remembers. 90 lost 13 Stirlings in the two months Donovan flew ops. His crew must have been numbed by their experiences. They were attacked and hit by a night fighter over Berlin, coned by searchlights and attacked again while bombing Mannheim before crash-landing back at base, and had an engine wrecked by flak over Hanover. Donovan's logbook is signed off by the officer commanding 90 Squadron: 'First tour of operations completed 28 November 1943. No. of successful sorties — 18.'

Bill Dashwood, a 106 Squadron Hampden pilot in 1940, remembers the loss rate on his unit as 'astronomical' and says 'we often had to borrow not only 97's spare Hampdens but often their crews to make up requirements'. At that stage the two squadrons shared Coningsby in Lincolnshire.

On 17 January 1941, Jim Boyle, 26, a gunner on a 12 Squadron Wellington, wrote a letter to his mother in Featherston to be mailed if he were killed.

These days are very trying and our duties involve much risk and many chances of mishap; we cannot carry on for ever defying fighters . . . and intense anti-aircraft defences without getting scratched some time; we try not to think of it which is very nearly impossible. We never talk of it or show our feelings to one another, but we can always feel the presence of death near at hand.

Three weeks later Boyle, an only son, was dead. His bomber stalled and crashed as it came into land at a field in Nottinghamshire after an air-gunnery exercise. The Wellington dived into the ground shortly after midday on 8 February, and the grievously injured Boyle died a few hours later in hospital without regaining consciousness. The young airman had trained as a fitter with the RNZAF, then resigned and sailed to Britain in 1938. He had joined the RAF Volunteer Reserve and signed up to be a gunner the moment the war had begun. He hated the Germans and was desperate to avenge the death of his father, James, lost at Passchendaele in 1917 while serving with the Otago Regiment. He saw action on Lysanders with 614 Squadron over Belgium and France in May and June 1940 before his posting to Bomber Command and 12 Squadron in December that year.

In the face of what seemed almost certain death on operations, some crews grew weary, battle fatigued, fatalistic and pessimistic about their survival. They tallied each completed raid as another step towards the magic end-of-tour mark. They slept and ate together as small units, pretty much ignoring other crews in the squadron, feeling it pointless to make close friends of men who might well be gone by the time they got out of bed the next day, their belongings immediately swept from lockers, packed up and sent to grieving families.

Dashwood, now living in Mount Maunganui, says crews lasted an average of about four trips when he was at Coningsby. 'You never really got to know anybody except your own crew.'

The odds were not much better in the later stages of the war. Pilot Doug Hawker, survivor of a long tour of 35 ops with 630 Squadron between April and August 1944 and now living in Christchurch, remembers that new crews seemed to last about a fortnight. Because losses were so high and rapid, there was little time to get to know newcomers.

We were also very much involved with our own crews, our own aircraft. Much of the time too we were either flying on operations or sleeping. Even in the mess we dined at irregular times so overall there was little time to get to know others. A

very good friend with whom I trained at Wigram joined our
squadron, even the same flight as me, but it was a week before
I met him.

Operations placed men under tremendous strain. Auckland pilot
Pat Towsey, flying a 51 Squadron Whitley on a raid on Frankfurt
on 24–25 October 1941, watched another Whitley, riddled by
flak, go down in flames — 'the poor devil'. His own aircraft
barely escaped a similar fate, held in a cone of searchlights for
terrifying minutes, flak puffs all around. 'My God, it was a shaky
do,' Towsey wrote the next day. 'What a feeling [of relief] to get
[back] on to the ground. I've rarely felt so tired in all my life.
Mental, spiritual and physical exhaustion. Nerves like piano
wire.' Towsey kept his nerves under control to complete a tour
with 51 Squadron and another in the Middle East.

Christchurch-born and -educated Neil Blunden, 26 when he
died in icy Norwegian waters in March 1942, was one of eight
officers accompanying a big draft of sergeant pilots who sailed
for Britain in April 1941. Five didn't come home. Before his own
death Blunden watched a sad parade of New Zealand friends
and acquaintances die on ops and in accidents. Dick Austin, 21
(Pahiatua), a particular mate from his draft, lost his life in an
air-test crash in September. Three days before Christmas fellow
10 Squadron pilots Stew Beattie, 24 (Lauder, Central Otago), and
Dick Barker, 25 (Gisborne), flying as passengers, were killed in a
crash in Lincolnshire. 'Damn bad luck as both of them were the
best of chaps,' Blunden wrote in his diary. The next day he went
through the dead men's personal clothing and effects — 'bloody
awful job but one which a close friend should do I consider'.

Blunden, Dunedin pilot Jim Murray and four NCOs took the
train from their Yorkshire base to RAF Grantham, Lincolnshire,
for the funeral service. Blunden's diary entry for Monday
29 December 1941 read: 'Cold frost and ground fog. Attended

funeral in late morning. 3 chaps including Barker. Beattie being buried privately by relatives at Torquay soon.' He returned to bleak Yorkshire to continue a conversion course on Halifaxes, a course drawn out by fearful winter weather. He shovelled snow off runways and flew when he could. He had only another three months to live.

Jim Insull, then 34, was devastated when his close mate Dud Coates, 33, perished on 26 May 1943 in a 75 Squadron Stirling that plunged into the sea off the Dutch Coast. Both men were married with children and working in Napier — Insull in a bank, Coates as a linotype operator on the *Daily Telegraph* — when they enlisted on the same day in February 1942. They sailed on the same ship to North America to train as navigators, smoked fat cigars and played cards as they sped north on the railroad from San Francisco to Vancouver and then across Canada to their camp in Ontario. They graduated as sergeants on the same day in September 1942 and then had a whale of a time in New York on embarkation leave before crossing the Atlantic. They did more courses together in England before going to the same OTU to crew up and complete their training. Thereafter their paths diverged.

Health problems grounded Insull's first skipper and his second crashed their Wellington while landing. Insull survived but then suffered appendicitis. By the time he got back to OTU Coates had gone through a Stirling conversion course and been posted to 75 Squadron. Then he was killed. The news was slow reaching Insull. On 31 May he wrote in his diary: 'A letter from my old cobber Dud caught me up today. He has done one operation, in his own words, "A piece of cake".'

Two days later: 'Dud is missing. A letter . . . brought me the news today, and it has brought out the coward in me. I feel full of fear for the future.' On leave soon after, he heard that his first crew, posted to a squadron while he was in hospital, was also missing, as were three other friends. 'The news took the shine off the rest of my leave for I had a vague persistent feeling of mixed fear, indignation and resentment, and felt I wanted to get back to flying.' Coates' body was later washed ashore in Belgium and buried in Ostende.

It was only youth, generally high spirits and the belief that 'it won't happen to me' — even when they knew in their hearts it probably would — that kept many airmen going. Aucklander Bill Hickson, a Halifax pathfinder pilot shot down over Germany in mid-1943 before his 21st birthday, says: 'Subconsciously we all thought we were just about fireproof. We had to psychologically block out the losses; we'd have gone mad if we hadn't.'

Many newcomers had sobering introductions to operational life. Taranaki pilot Ian Herbert, fresh from training, arrived at 630 Squadron, East Kirkby, Lincolnshire, on 28 July 1944 to find fellow New Zealander George Joblin on the battle list for that night. 'Well,' thought Herbert as he went to bed in a Nissen hut, 'that's someone I know, someone I can ask what things are really like.' He had been at night school in Hawera with Joblin when they had both been studying for the RNZAF. At 3 o'clock the next morning he was wakened by returning crews as they stomped into the hut and began undressing. He heard one of the airman say, 'Jobby hasn't come back.' Joblin had died on his 30th op, his tour almost finished, shot down over Stuttgart, his Lancaster one of 40 RAF bombers lost that night.

Death could strike at any time — at the start of a tour, at the end or in between. 75 Squadron navigator Ted Anderson, who has lived all his life in Christchurch, notes that sometimes everybody got back, sometimes not. 'Generally one didn't dwell on the bad moments, but occasionally it hit hard.' He flew with pilot Eric Witting, a Southlander, and two other New Zealanders, one of whom was killed by German fire over Denmark in November 1943. That was the worst moment of his war, but there were other bad times.

After their tour-ending 30th raid, on Aachen, Germany, in late May 1944, he and his crewmates were back safely — finished, feeling good, happy, being congratulated. Then — two crews not in.

> One crew was piloted by 'Spanner' Fauvel, a particular friend of Eric's, and the other by Frank Scott, whom I had known all my life — our fathers went to school together — and who was my special fishing and shooting companion. Moreover, next to us they were the most senior crews on the squadron. After that night Spanner would have had only one more trip to do, and Frank only two. You could never take anything for granted.

Fauvel's Lancaster had gone down over Belgium, crashing near Ypres. No survivors and four New Zealand dead. Scott's bomber had broken up over Holland following a night-fighter attack. Scott, 28, and bomb aimer Stephen Cook, 21, a Southlander, died. Two other New Zealanders survived.

A few — a tiny percentage — broke under the strain of constant ops and danger. Sympathetic skippers and crew members, even squadron commanders, sometimes shielded fearful airmen and helped them through bad patches. But normally when an airman suffered a breakdown or simply refused to fly any more he was whisked away without sympathy and instantly replaced, his file marked LMF (lack of moral fibre). Operations had to continue, the contagion of battle fatigue could not be permitted to spread, to infect other members of a crew. Thousands of bomber aircrew, all volunteers, continued to fly despite fear and the stress of battle. Some fought personal demons of terror but still they flew, night after night. They would not let crewmates down. They had a job to do; the others depended on them. Petrified, they still flew. They were the bravest.

Pilot David Clark, a retired farmer living in Otorohanga,

often dwelt on fear and fright in the diary he kept throughout the war. On many dicey ops, he swore to himself that he was finished, that he would refuse to fly again. Of course he never did, instead winning two DFCs and in September 1944 being given command of 77 Squadron, a key 4 Group Halifax unit at Full Sutton, Yorkshire.

Clark flew two tours, the first with 419 Squadron on Halifaxes in 1943, the second mainly with 635, a Lancaster pathfinder squadron, before his posting to 77. His second DFC, an immediate award, followed a raid on the distant German port of Stettin on 16–17 August 1944. Flak knocked out one engine and damaged another, but the remaining two-and-a-half eventually carried him and his crew home. They debated baling out over Denmark or Sweden but the decision to try for England was made when the rear gunner announced, 'No, I've got a date tonight.'

In October 1944 Clark flew his 77 Squadron Halifax on a daylight attack on a synthetic-oil plant near Duisberg, in the Ruhr Valley. When he got back he wrote in his diary about watching one Halifax shot down by flak and seeing another two collide. There were no survivors among the 22 men on the doomed bombers from 78 Squadron, a nearby unit in Yorkshire. The three losses

> were so terribly realistic that they struck terror into my heart . . . There's something so final about seeing an aircraft in front of you suddenly lose a wing, and then to watch him turn slowly over on his back and dive steadily to earth. It looks almost like a fake [at the movies] but as you can see it all so clearly you can just imagine the unfortunate aircrew inside and picture the hopelessness of their plight when a wing vanishes. Possibly some of them are badly wounded, and others can't move to bale out because of the centrifugal force . . . Then you consider there are flak puffs going off all around and any one

of them might . . . hit you at any instant, and I may add that this is more than a little disconcerting to say the least.

Clark saw the collision with disbelieving eyes because there was no apparent reason for it.

There wasn't any flak to make them suddenly weave, but they just ran into one another. Mind you it isn't very surprising because there are about thirty bombers a minute traversing the same route, and they seem to fill the whole sky . . . once I got into the defences where I felt the need of weaving I was every bit as frightened of running into some one else as I was of the opposition . . . It requires constant vigilance to see where everyone else is.

The route in [to the target] was not very well selected for we were under fire [from flak] for about half the time we were over enemy territory. It shook me to the core to get shot at, at first, and as ever I made my usual resolution never to come on ops again, not even if it meant eternal disgrace. However, after the first half hour I got used to being shot at — it's curious isn't it — and even began to enjoy the trip . . . When we got to the target itself, it was bad enough, but it wasn't nearly so terrifying as the Ruhr at night. It's the searchlights and fighter flares which deter me more than anything, and of course both . . . were missing from this attack.

Some former aircrew — their memories of the conflict having perhaps dimmed — say that they enjoyed the war. Many recall the joy of actual flying. 'If you survived it wasn't a bad sort of life,' says Alister Boulton, a former navigator who baled out on a Ruhr Valley raid in 1943. Some New Zealand veterans of Bomber Command say their years in Britain were the best of their lives. Others suffered nightmares long after 1945. Each man's experiences and feelings were unique, though. Some carried scars, physical and emotional, for the rest of their lives. Service shortened the post-war lives of many New Zealand bomber aircrew. Some still suffer.

Of the 55,000 Bomber Command aircrew killed in World War II, 38,000 were Britons. Ten thousand Canadians, 4000 Australians and 1850 New Zealanders also lost their lives. More than 47,000 died on operations, the other 8000 in flying or ground accidents. Almost 10,000 became prisoners of war. Another 4000 returned wounded from raids. As many again were injured in accidents. Total aircrew casualties were 75,000, almost 60 per cent of the 125,000 aircrew who served in squadrons and other Bomber Command flying units. The casualty rate in Bomber Command was the highest among Britain's armed forces.

Of the New Zealanders lost, about 1680 were members of the Royal New Zealand Air Force or Allied air forces in RAF squadrons or units. The rest were killed while serving directly in the Royal Air Force.

The precise number of New Zealanders who flew with Bomber Command in World War II is not known. Many figures, some of them confusing, have been published, but no truly accurate tally has ever emerged. The official history says that 11,000 New Zealanders served with the RAF but doesn't break down the totals for the major commands — Bomber, Fighter and Coastal — and the other elements of the RAF; nor does it specify theatres of action.

The figure of 1850 New Zealand deaths in Bomber Command is certain, thanks to Errol Martyn's research for his trilogy *For Your Tomorrow*. Using that number and taking other factors into account, it is possible to calculate that about 6000 New Zealanders — perhaps slightly more — flew with the Command at one time or another.

The scramble to raise an air force

A few days after war was declared on 3 September 1939 the Air Department in Wellington called for volunteers for the Royal Air Force and Royal New Zealand Air Force. 'Pilots, air gunners and observers are wanted and no previous flying experience is necessary,' the national news agency reported from the capital. 'Candidates must not be less that seventeen and a half years old, but under twenty-eight years; they must be unmarried, able to pass the prescribed medical examination and educated up to the standard of the school certificate or university entrance examination. Particular emphasis is laid on the necessity for the education qualification.'

Generously, the department declared that young men selected for overseas service would be granted free passage to the United Kingdom. No recruit would have to pay to put his life in danger.

Commonwealth aircrew were volunteers, each and every one. When German guns poured flak at them or German fighters made furious attacks, many an airman, nerves taut, stomach churning, wondered why he had ever volunteered. Once in aircrew, however, there was no going back. A volunteer couldn't later decide he didn't want to fly and opt out. Until he had finished his tour or tours of duty there was no exit — short of death, serious injury, capture or the unpleasant alternative of being called a coward or, more politely, labelled as lacking moral fibre (LMF), stripped of his rank and condemned to menial tasks like cleaning toilets. But no one was ever conscripted to fly in an aeroplane.

Despite stiff selection criteria, there was no shortage of volunteers in New Zealand. As the war progressed and the demand for aircrew grew ever more insatiable, age and educational requirements had to be loosened. The Great Depression had denied hosts of academically gifted and intelligent young men any sort of a high-school education. Many more had only a bare minimum of a year or two. They simply could not meet the education standards that had been set for admission to the RNZAF. The authorities soon realised the entrance requirements were far too tough and would simply rule out hundreds of the bright prospective aircrew the air force needed. So they changed them.

Ted Caradus, senior inspector of secondary schools and education adviser to the air force, was named director of the RNZAF's education services in November 1939 and made a wing commander. He developed a brilliant pre-entry correspondence course that gave would-be aircrew, particularly potential pilots and navigators, the basic maths, navigation and science they needed before being accepted for training. Soon, by the light of candles on kitchen tables in remote farmhouses, young men itching to fly laboured over air-force papers that came by mail. Townies went home from their jobs each day to do the same thing. The material the postman delivered was full of exercises and assignments, and explanations that were simple, logical and easy to follow. The course aimed to make air-force applicants ready for camp in 21 weeks.

Sixty years later aircrew veterans still fondly remember the correspondence course, a system that developed their skills and education and gave them the chance to fly. Before he was called up for aircrew training, Trevor Dill, a decorated two-tour navigator on 75 and 7 Squadrons, did the course on his parents' property at Kaipara Hills, west of Warkworth. 'It was well set up and I did the maths with no real problems. I did it all at home, sent the assignments away and got the results back by post. It was a really good course and excellent training. It brought me up to probably sixth-form standard, which I wasn't before starting.'

In cities and some provincial towns young men went to night schools for instruction. Others packed in to telegraph offices to learn Morse code. Radio stations regularly broadcast dictation for Morse practitioners.

Vic Viggers, then 20, studied hard two nights a week to learn the course elements at Napier Boys' High School, where he and his contemporaries had raised hell just a few years earlier. 'Most of the teachers were the same masters we'd had when we were at school. They were most encouraging guys and helped us every way they could. Marvellous men.' Viggers became a wireless operator in a fine 101 Squadron crew captained by a fellow New Zealander. He survived, against the odds, flying most of the awful raids over Berlin in the winter of 1943–44 and the catastrophic operation to Nuremberg on 30–31 March 1944 — Bomber Command's worst night of the war.

By mid-1941, when the air force was regularly advertising for aircrew ('The Air Force needs pilots and observers'), the age limit for pilots had risen to 31 and marriage was no longer an impediment. Navigators, though they were still called observers, could be 32. The minimum education had been dropped to two years' secondary schooling or an equivalent standard in mathematics — which meant passing the correspondence course. To be a straight gunner was easier still — no exams.

Most young men applying for aircrew training were called in for interviews so their suitability could be judged. The selection panels obviously had wise people among their ranks. Pilot and prisoner of war Ian Herbert was an orphan by the time he was six. Raised by a grandmother and an aunt on a backblocks Taranaki farm, his very basic country-school education finished in Standard Six, when he was 12. He then went out to earn a living. He was working as a farmer and herd tester when he faced selection in Hawera. The panel astounded him halfway through the interview by asking if he would like to be a pilot. The most Herbert had hoped for was perhaps a place as a gunner.

The people on the panel said to me, 'If you do the correspondence course, you can have a go.' I succeeded but once I got to Rotorua for initial training I felt as if I'd never have a show because most of the others there were out of university or older than I was. Eventually though I got to the stage where I thought, 'Damn it, I think I'm as good as them', and I got on OK.

Herbert swept through his pilot training and was a senior pilot and flight lieutenant on 227 Squadron when he was shot down on an almost tour-ending 29th operation in early December 1944.

The Spitfires, Hurricanes and Messerschmitts of 1939 were an enormous technical advance on their fighter predecessors — a giant leap in military aviation — but bombers lagged and civil aviation was still in its infancy. Kingsford Smith had made his historic first flight across the Tasman just 11 years earlier, and Jean Batten had completed her record-smashing first direct flight from England to Auckland as recently as 1936. American heroine Amelia Earhart had disappeared on her round-the-world flight only two years before the war began. It was still an age of pioneering achievements in the air, of 'first flights'; a time when pilots were welcomed by throngs of well-wishers, who stormed onto airfields to mob famous aircraft and famous aviators. Newspapers devoted hundreds of inches of type to flyers' exploits.

Regular passenger and mail services across the Atlantic had begun in 1939. Britain's Imperial Airways and the United States' Pan Am were just reaching Australia and New Zealand. Union Airways had been flying passengers between the North and South Islands for barely four years, and Tasman Empire Airways Ltd (TEAL), the forerunner of Air New Zealand, was still to launch its flying-boat service between New Zealand and Australia. It was all so new and exciting that newspapers routinely listed passengers on arriving flights.

A generation of young New Zealanders who'd grown up worshipping World War I Royal Flying Corps heroes, reading

Biggles, following the big air races of the 1930s, attending air pageants and making model aeroplanes was swept up in the excitement. The war was a heaven-sent opportunity to satisfy the craving to fly.

Aucklander Mick Cullen, who flew a tour as a wireless operator on 15 Squadron in 1943, lived on a farm at Maungaturoto, Northland, and in his youth often lay on his back in sun-drenched paddocks watching white fluffy clouds roll across the sky. 'Periodically little Tiger Moths would fly over, going from Auckland to Whangarei, and I used to look up there and marvel at those jolly things. They gave me my passion to fly.'

Travel, adventure and excitement were also part of the attraction of the air force, while some were moved by outright patriotism. Ian Walker, an apprentice butcher in Auckland, volunteered as soon as war broke out. He felt that the Nazis had to be stopped and wanted to serve his country. 'Although it seems a bit odd these days to say things about patriotism, it did move us, there's no question about that.' The army held little attraction. Many air-force recruits had fathers and uncles who had served in the mud of the Western Front and heard the stories. 'I didn't fancy army life,' says Walker. 'The trenches had been so well described.' He liked the idea of the air force; it seemed the most adventurous of the three services. He flew as a gunner in Defiants in the Battle of Britain and then as a rear gunner on 115 Squadron until his Wellington crashed in a Belgian field one night in June 1941, shattering one of his legs. He was taken prisoner but repatriated by the Germans in December 1943, one of the first three RNZAF POWs to arrive home.

The Great War was still very real to those who enlisted in World War II. Northlander Rae Simpson, bomb aimer on a 77 Squadron Halifax flying back to England after a raid on Leipzig in December 1943, remembered something as the aircraft crossed the French–Belgian border near Lille: 'Uncle Bert from Matakohe was buried near here in 1916, a victim of the Somme battle. He lay out in no-man's land badly wounded for three days before being reached and rescued — too late.'

Jim Insull, born in 1908 and thus almost twice as old as many volunteers when he enlisted in 1942, wrote in his diary: 'I feel no burning patriotism, no desire for "fight", but confess to a deep affection for [New Zealand]. Ever since the real war started I have felt an urge to do something, and my decision to join the Air Force was never in doubt . . . it is my belief that the foundations of victory will be laid from the air.'

Others joined the air force because their mates were doing so. Frank Chunn, a gunner who knocked down three Heinkel 111s over Hull during German air raids in late 1940 and later flew on bombers, was working in his father's Te Awamutu paint and wallpaper shop when he volunteered. 'I was one of a group of young fellas who used to meet outside the Bank of New Zealand at lunchtimes, and we tossed around opinions of what service we'd go into. We decided the air force was the best and that was it. We all went in.'

Faced with the threat of growing German air power from the mid-1930s, the RAF expanded rapidly, creating new squadrons, planning and ordering new aircraft, building airfields and beginning a major recruitment drive. All this meant opportunities for New Zealanders. Some worked their passage to Britain to apply for direct entry into the RAF. Others, from 1937 on, were selected in New Zealand for short-service commissions in the RAF, their fares to Britain paid for them. Still others trained at Wigram, Christchurch, and then were posted to the RAF to take up such commissions. By September 1939 about 550 New Zealanders were serving in the RAF, mainly as pilots — with Fighter, Bomber and Coastal Commands. Just over half survived the war. By the end of 1940 almost 160 were dead, and losses rose to more than 210 over the next year. Per capita, more New Zealanders were serving in the RAF in 1939 than people from any other nation outside Britain.

At the outbreak of war two of the five Bomber Command groups were led by New Zealanders, both air vice-marshals who had fought in World War I — 2 Group's Cuthbert Maclean and 4 Group's Arthur ('Mary') Coningham, whose brilliant wartime career reached its climax with his role as chief of the 2nd Tactical Air Force in 1944–45 during the invasion of France and the later campaigns in northwest Europe. Amazingly, Coningham was succeeded by another New Zealander at 4 Group. Roderick Carr was another World War I veteran, whose term stretched from 1941 to 1944, the crucial years. He was the longest-serving Bomber Command group commander of the war. At the start of the war, Arthur Harris, who took over as Bomber Command's leader in 1942, was commander of 5 Group.

Among many other talented New Zealanders in the RAF were Andrew McKee, Cyrus Kay, Denis Barnett and Gordon Grindell — men who joined in the 1920s and early 1930s and rose to command squadrons and stations during the war and to go further still in the post-war years. And, of course, Sam Elworthy. Son of a South Canterbury farmer, Elworthy was educated in England — at Marlborough College and then Trinity College, Cambridge. He earned a BA and MA and became a barrister in 1935. He took up a permanent commission in the RAF in 1936 after earlier service with the Reserve of Air Force Officers and the Auxiliary Air Force. He commanded a squadron of Bomber Command Blenheims early in the war, earning the DSO, DFC and AFC in the first four months of 1941, and then became a staff officer.

In late October 1942, the *Daily Mail*'s aeronautical correspondent singled out four group captains he considered 'exceptional', saying, 'Watch these men. One or more will truly be great names in Britain some day.' Elworthy, one of the four, was to become Chief of Air Staff in 1963 and Chief of Defence

Staff four years later, holding the rank of Marshal of the RAF. The Mail said of the then 31-year-old: 'He is tall, fair and broad, the sort of man you would expect to find pre-eminent in any role, from that of bishop to bomber pilot.' Elworthy was the first New Zealander to become a Knight of the Garter.

Darkening European developments in the mid-1930s prompted New Zealand's leaders to build up the nation's air power. The RNZAF was hived off from army control and formally established as a separate service in April 1937, at which point it had a permanent strength of 185. This development was largely the result of a 1936 investigation into the country's air-defence requirements by RAF officer Ralph Cochrane, then a wing commander. Cochrane stayed in New Zealand for more than two years after submitting his report and became Chief of Air Staff, overseeing the rapid development of the air force. He returned to Britain in 1939 to play a huge role in Bomber Command as chief of 3 Group during 1942–43 and then 5 Group during 1943–45. New Zealand's Labour government acted decisively on his recommendations, approving a major expansion programme involving flying schools to train pilots for both the RAF and RNZAF, ground-crew training, active territorial squadrons, the construction of new airfields and much more. It also ordered 30 twin-engined Wellington bombers from Britain.

New Zealand's capacity to wage war in the air was negligible at the outbreak of hostilities, but the groundwork had been done and the RNZAF grew to be a major offensive force, with 41,000 men and women in its ranks at the peak of its effort in mid-1944.

Most RNZAF recruits wanted to be pilots, but not all. Youngsters who had huddled over home-made radio sets, earphones on as they talked to other amateur operators through the crackling ether, hankered to be wireless operators. Outdoorsmen whose passions were hunting, shooting and fishing grabbed the opportunity to become gunners. Northlander Jack Atkin stalked anything that moved when he was a youth growing up in Warkworth and loved firearms. 'I went in to be a gunner. I wanted to be a gunner. That was my whole ambition.' Atkin was in camp in Levin by January 1941 and then off to train in Canada. He was the sole survivor when his 75 Squadron Wellington was shot down near Dusseldorf in August 1942.

A few — Ted Anderson for one — wanted to be observers, or navigators as they were called from 1942. Anderson had a complete five-year education at Christchurch Boys High School, then attended Canterbury University College and was working as a tanneries chemist when he volunteered in November 1941. Because he was a whiz at maths and science he was exempted from the correspondence course but did the lessons anyway and was fascinated. 'I'd enlisted for pilot training but the more I saw of the course the more I wanted to be a navigator. So with quite a bit of difficulty I got myself remustered as a navigator. This was regarded as unbelievable, someone wanting to be a navigator.'

Pilot was the popular choice, especially among the volunteers in late 1940 and 1941, after the Battle of Britain. The exploits of The Few fired the imaginations of young men. They all wanted to fly Spitfires. The hopes and expectations of hundreds were dashed. Instructors found myriad grounds on which to fail pilots when they got into the cockpit of a Tiger Moth. Not that they deliberately sought to fail trainees. It was simply that flying an aeroplane was a business requiring many talents that not everyone possessed. Many lives depended on a pilot's skill.

Some young men were naturals in the cockpit. John Morris, a bomber pilot twice shot down and twice a survivor, came from a Waikato family involved with thoroughbreds. He rode track work and rode well. He had the hands of a jockey — the light touch, the feel and control — and applied them to the controls of an aeroplane. Not many had such a gift.

Trevor Dill set out to be a pilot —

but I had one eye they reckoned threw a bit sideways. They said I'd have difficulty landing an aircraft because of the judgment required. They were looking for excuses. Everyone wanted to be a pilot. I'd probably have killed myself if I had been one. Anyway, I wasn't, so I did the next best thing and went through as a navigator.

He was one of countless hopefuls who fell at various stages of pilot training for countless reasons. They were 'washed out', 'scrubbed', 'failed', 'thrown out' — there were lots of words.

Bill Wilson, who lives in Nelson, was driving an army truck at Waiouru in early 1942 when he decided there was no future in that and volunteered for the air force. 'They asked what I wanted to do and I suggested I could fly an aeroplane. They said, "Oh, no. We've got enough men for pilots. How about a gunner?" I said I supposed that would be all right but asked what else they had to offer. They said, "You could be an observer."' He ended up as a bomb aimer in a Halifax squadron.

It wasn't always a man's lack of skill that ended his pilot training. A wrong move in officialdom's eyes and a would-be pilot was finished. Aucklander Barney D'Ath-Weston was tossed out of training early in the war after he and a couple of other tyros flew their Tiger Moths down to sea level off New Plymouth one afternoon to have a gander at a bunch of young women bathing in the surf sans clothes. The girls waved furiously but some spoilsport phoned Bell Block. The wing commander ruled D'Ath-Weston had endangered his aircraft by flying so low. At that stage planes were more valuable than pilots. So D'Ath-Weston 'remustered' (the official term for changing 'trades' in the air force) and became a navigator, the fate of most rejected pilots — those with plenty of brains and ability but not the knack of flying a plane. It was no disgrace.

The number of trainees offering after the outbreak of war was more than the RNZAF could handle initially, but flying schools were quickly opened to supplement the one already operating at Wigram — at Taieri, Woodbourne, Whenuapai, Bell Block, Harewood, Ohakea and elsewhere — and more instructors were drafted in to cope with the influx. Inevitably there were bottlenecks, and some volunteers had to wait up to 18 months to begin training. Most of those delayed were pilots. Les Munro, one of the fabled Dambusters raid pilots of mid-1943, had to mark time until the RNZAF was ready for him. The air force gave him the option of going into camp immediately if he would train as a gunner. Thanks, no, I'll wait, he said. While waiting, some would-be pilots were called into the dreaded Aerodrome Defence Units (ADUs), introduced as a result of the fear of invasion by Japan, and spent weeks, sometimes months, patrolling airfield boundaries or huddled in machine-gun posts before being allowed anywhere near an aircraft.

South Canterbury farmer Frank Jackson was with an ADU at Woodbourne waiting for pilot training in the winter of 1942 when the authorities offered him the certainty of heading overseas by Christmas if he would switch trades and become a navigator. Jackson had always wanted to visit Canada, so took the bait and was on his way before the end of the year.

Roy Calvert, son of a Cambridge businessman and one of only two New Zealanders to win three DFCs while flying with Bomber Command, was determined to be a pilot, to have his life in his own hands. He volunteered in 1939 and while waiting for his call-up paid to learn to fly, getting a flying start as it were. He left New Zealand for Britain in June 1941, one of 10 commissioned pilots in a draft of fifty.

The first batch of pilots to leave New Zealand after the outbreak of hostilities sailed from Auckland in early December 1939. The

17 young officers, who had begun their training at Wigram before September 1939, were bound for the RAF. Leonard Isitt, acting Chief of Air Staff, gave them a pep talk. 'The service you are going to is a fine one [with] a brief but brilliant tradition. We look to you to uphold that tradition.' Seven would never come home, among them Michael Barnett, just 18 when he was killed in April 1940. His aircraft crashed and burned on a training flight out of Benson, Oxfordshire, home of Bomber Command's No. 12 OTU. Barnett, the youngest New Zealand casualty in Bomber Command, lies in St Helen's churchyard, Benson.

Among those in this little group who were to distinguish themselves during the war were Frank Denton, commander of 487 Squadron RNZAF in 1945 after flying bombers, and Jack Shorthouse, who had a fine record as a bomber pilot and formed and commanded the Lancaster-equipped 189 Squadron from October 1944 until June 1945. Shorthouse became a senior TEAL/Air New Zealand captain after the war.

So it was that trained pilots sailed off to Britain to join the RAF while the RNZAF began the rapid expansion of flying schools to meet its commitment to deliver further, large numbers of pilots. Would-be flyers began with a four-week induction course at Weraroa, Levin (Rotorua from February 1942), and then went on to elementary flying training. If they passed, they stepped up to more advanced levels. After months of hard work those who succeeded earned their wings and were reckoned fit to fly — following more training in Britain on the types of aircraft they would use in combat. From Levin, non-pilots went on to observer or wireless/air-gunnery training at Ohakea (1939–40) or Canada (from late 1940).

In December 1939 New Zealand signed up to the plan that became the hugely successful British Commonwealth Air Training Scheme. Commonwealth training had been mooted before the war, and Britain, Canada, Australia and New Zealand moved swiftly to implement the scheme in the opening months of the conflict. Huge numbers of aircrew were going to be needed, and Britain simply lacked sufficient space for the necessary training facilities. Enemy air attacks would also disrupt training. The wide-open spaces and clear skies of Canada were an ideal alternative.

The official-history volume *The Royal New Zealand Air Force* notes that more than 130,000 airmen learned their trade in Canada during the war, of whom 7000 were New Zealanders. In the six years of war 2743 pilots were fully trained in New Zealand and sent overseas to serve with the RAF in Europe, the Middle East and Far East. Before the scheme in Canada was in place, New Zealand also trained 183 observers and 395 gunners for the RAF.

In December 1939 the RNZAF operated a total of 211 aircraft. Apart from Tiger Moths, most of the types are now remembered only by old airmen and aviation historians — Blackburn Baffins, Fairey Gordons, Vickers Vincents and Vildebeests. The air force had just five of the new wooden, twin-engined Airspeed Oxford monoplane trainers, the first of which had arrived from its English makers, Airspeed, in early 1939. The Oxford turned out to be a brilliant aircraft in which thousands of Allied airmen trained, and no fewer than 8586 were built. They remained in service with the RAF until 1954. The RNZAF flew a peak number of 207 Oxfords in mid-1944. The so-fondly remembered Tiger Moths, many built in New Zealand by De Havilland after the war had begun, and the American-built Harvards, which made their appearance in New Zealand skies in March 1941, were the mainstay trainers. Both were single-engined.

To England

New Zealand delivered her aircrew to Britain and Canada by sea. They went on a variety of ships, some big, some small, some splendid, some awful. In the early stages of the war some sailed on the *Awatea* and *Aorangi*, elegant Union Steam Ship Company liners until their peacetime fittings were torn out so they could carry more men. Others went on large American passenger vessels still plying the Pacific before the Japanese attack on Pearl Harbor in December 1941. Yet others travelled on cargo ships with quarters for just a handful of passengers.

The vast majority crossed the Pacific to west-coast North American ports, en route for training in Canada or for passage by train across the continent. Most ended up in Halifax, on Canada's east coast, where they joined ships sailing for Britain in North Atlantic convoys. A few went on the largest ships. Palmerston North pilot Ian Byers was among a dozen RNZAF men among thousands of American GIs who boarded the *Queen Elizabeth* in New York in late 1943. Byers was to win an immediate DFC for his feat, in December 1944, of landing a shockingly damaged 61 Squadron Lancaster on an unlit fighter strip near Liege, Belgium.

Christchurch-born and -raised Keith Thiele, commissioned as a pilot before leaving New Zealand, sailed on the *Awatea* to Vancouver in June 1941 in the same draft as Roy Calvert. The ship carried 50 pilots and 160 air gunners from New Zealand and a host of Australian aircrew. 'It was a wild trip,' Thiele remembered years later. 'The *Awatea* was pretty much still a civilian ship then, state rooms for the officers and gin four bob a bottle.'

Wellingtonian George Hedge, an early-entry wireless operator, lived in a tent at Levin because the barracks were still being built. He was a natural for his trade having learned the compulsory Morse code while working on the railways. He was sent off to Britain in July 1940 after the RAF asked for wireless operators. 'We went on the Shaw Savill refrigerated ship *Tamaroa* all the way — Pitcairn, Panama, Trinidad, Halifax, and convoy to England. She was full of lamb. Good accommodation for 24. It was a very pleasant trip, going into the northern summer. We finished up in Manchester.'

49

Ernie Mawson left his wife and young son in Christchurch when he sailed from Auckland in November 1942 on what had been the French glamour liner *Ile de France,* launched in 1926 to carry 1800 passengers in Art-Deco luxury. Now she was on her way to North America to be turned into a troop carrier.

She was a stinking bug-infested ship; the worst sailing any of us ever had. She had been in Africa and came by New Zealand carrying about 30 German POWs, a few British guards and 25 Australian airmen. There were about 100 New Zealanders and though this enormous ship of 43,000 tons had only a handful of passengers we were stuck in a cubbyhole on E deck. They wouldn't let us use the cabins up top. Too many bugs. The food was so awful we lived mainly on biscuits and lemonade from the cafeteria all the way to San Francisco.

A few airmen never reached England. Thirty-seven New Zealand servicemen were among the 111 passengers captured when the New Zealand Shipping Company's passenger/cargo ship *Rangitane* was shelled and sunk by German raiders two days out from Auckland on 27 November 1940. Civilian passengers from the *Rangitane* and other captured ships, as well as some crew and servicemen, were later released on the island of Emirau in the Bismarck Archipelago, but 10 RNZAF wireless operators and three prospective RAF officers were shipped to Germany, where they faced four-and-a-half years of bleak POW life.

A much worse fate befell three RNZAF navigators on a Swedish motor ship heading for Britain in convoy HX168 from Halifax in the winter of January 1942. The *Yngaren*, which was carrying just three other passengers, was torpedoed at 3.00 a.m. on 12 January after the convoy she was in had scattered because of bad weather. She went down 600 miles west of Ireland. Two survivors were picked up a month later but New Zealanders Michael Angland, 23

(Greymouth), Maurice Campbell, 27 (Christchurch) and William Hewett, 29 (Roto-o-rangi, near Cambridge), lost their lives.

Five months later, on 29 June 1942, the eight-year-old Shaw Savill freighter *Waiwera* was torpedoed 450 miles from the Azores as she steamed alone for Britain. She limped around in a circle in the dark for an hour, her rudder jammed and port propeller smashed, before a second torpedo exploded in the engine room, sending her to the bottom. Eight lives were lost but there were no casualties among the 15 RNZAF pilots aboard. The airmen and the ship's company squeezed into two undamaged lifeboats and were rescued some days later by a Norwegian ship and taken to New York.

Sadly, six of the rescued New Zealanders were to die in action within 16 months, four of them captaining Bomber Command Stirlings in 3 Group squadrons: Noel Humphreys, 20 (Wellington), and Keith Shaw, 23 (Invercargill), both of 623 Squadron; Noel Rollett, 31 (Matamata), of 622 Squadron; and Norman Bluck, 22 (Otorohanga), of 75 Squadron. The other two were killed flying Spitfires.

Mothers and wives, fiancees and girlfriends watched with apprehension as the ships taking their men eased away from the wharves. For many women it was the last sight of their loved ones. Laurie Dobbin, a teacher from a small dairy farm near Opunake, and his sweetheart, Marjorie Staniland, also a teacher, hadn't planned to marry until he returned home. But they changed their minds when the *Empress of Russia* was late arriving in Auckland and were wed in a registry office on 29 December 1940. They had eight days together in the city, their honeymoon interrupted by his duties as an officer supervising a party of NCOs. Then the new Mrs Dobbin watched proudly as her husband led a column of airmen down Queen Street to the ship. She never saw him again. Dobbin died when his Wellington crashed in Holland on 12 August 1942. His widow, now 90, never remarried. 'They'll be getting tired of paying my widow's war benefit I should think [but] I'm coming near the end of it,' she says.

May Fitches was luckier. Roy Calvert bought her a two-stone diamond ring just before he sailed, and they announced their engagement at a farewell dinner with his Cambridge family in Auckland. She saw Calvert off on the *Awatea* on 18 June 1941 and waved a scarf until her arm ached and she could see him no more. Calvert wrote from England asking for the scarf. He got it, carried it with him on every one of his 56 ops and brought it home again in December 1944. His wife still has it. Calvert had something else in his luggage — another ring, with a single diamond. 'It's for you. For waiting for me,' he said. The Calverts had been married 57 years when the ex-airman died in 2002.

Margaret Hawker was lucky too. She and pilot Doug Hawker married on his final leave in Christchurch in December 1942. Hawker, a shepherd and musterer in North Canterbury, had done the correspondence course to get into the RNZAF. 'I felt that if I could become a pilot I would, to some degree, have a little control over my particular war effort,' he says. 'I told Margie she should remain free because there was a big chance that I would not come back, but she wanted to get married — and so did I.'

The new Mrs Hawker accompanied her husband on the ferry to Wellington to join his ship and they stayed with friends. Then Hawker was ordered to report to the RNZAF base at Rongotai. His bride received word too late that he was off. 'By the time I got down to the wharves the men were inside the gates and we weren't allowed in,' she remembers.

She would not see him for almost three years. They wrote regularly and she sent him parcels packed with baking and other goodies. She also read the growing casualty lists, knew other young women who had lost air-force husbands, brothers and sweethearts, and was jolted when Harold Bruhns, a close friend of her husband's who'd trained with him and been his best man, was reported missing. Bruhns, 22 (Dunedin), skipper of a 75 Squadron Stirling, was killed on a mine-laying mission over the Baltic in February 1944, his plane lost, his body never recovered.

But there came a day in late 1944 when she got Hawker's letter telling her he'd finished operations and she knew that, barring some disaster, she would see him again. In late October 1945 she stood high on the hills overlooking Lyttelton Harbour watching the *Andes* steam in. Then she went down to the railway station in Christchurch to meet his train from Lyttelton. He was home and they could begin married life.

Departing airmen fretted about their families. Jim Insull, off to Canada to train as a navigator, wrote in his diary just after his ship sailed in late April 1942: 'God protect the children [girls Robin, five, and Sue, not yet a year old] and Gwen whose anxiety is certain to be greater than mine.' Insull confided that he had been reprimanded by a friend for 'walking out on Gwen and the kids' by joining the RNZAF. 'He said it was my duty to wait until I was called up. Perhaps he was right but it would mean either the army or a ground job in the air force which I wanted to avoid.' Insull survived 29 ops to come home to his wife and daughters.

Until January 1941, New Zealand-trained airmen arriving in England went first to Uxbridge, a big RAF depot and reporting point just out of London. From there they were sent on training courses or occasionally posted directly to squadrons. New Zealanders selected at home before the war for short-service commissions and chosen to train in England reported to the Air Ministry in London, which directed them to various RAF-contracted civil flying schools for their elementary flying training. If they passed muster at these schools they were commissioned and sent to Uxbridge for a fortnight for uniform fitting and a 'discipline' course — how to behave as an officer and a gentleman.

When he was commissioned in Canada in April 1943, Ernie Mawson was told 'you are now a gentleman.' Mawson laughs about that. 'I always thought I *was* a gentleman.' The pre-war RAF was a class-ridden service, and despite the exigencies of the war and hordes of leavening 'colonials' who didn't give a toss about class, some *very* RAF types still did their best to enforce them-and-us attitudes. Officers drinking with sergeants off base was forbidden at Mawson's pathfinder squadron — 635, based at Downham Market, in Norfolk — and Mawson was hauled up by a stuffy group captain one day for daring to play tennis in the village with a WAAF sergeant. 'I was told I was a naughty boy for associating with a non-officer.' Mawson thumbed his nose at such nonsense and kept right on playing tennis with the sergeant.

After January 1941 New Zealanders landing in England reported to Personnel Reception Centres (PRCs) in large south-coast seaside hotels and apartment blocks, first in Bournemouth and later in Brighton, and continued to do so for the rest of the war except for a few months before and after D-Day, when they went to Padgate, near Liverpool, because the south coast was overrun by invasion-bound troops.

The crew and their jobs

The war turned bomber crew numbers and their jobs upside down. A Wellington, best of the early bombers, had a crew of six in 1939 — two pilots, two gunners (one in the front turret, one in the rear), a wireless operator and an observer. One pilot was the captain, the other was back-up with little to do. By mid-1942 the second pilot was gone, the RAF finally realising that every time a Wellington was lost so were two pilots. From June almost the only time bombers carried two pilots was when a new pilot arrived at a squadron. The tyro was usually given a ride with an experienced crew for one trip to get a feel for operations before flying with his own crew. It was known as a second-dicky trip. The full-time front gunner had already been dropped because fighters didn't attack from head-on at night, for obvious reasons.

Also by mid-1942, it was 'navigator', no longer 'observer'. The latter was a hangover from World War I, when little biplanes zipping across enemy lines actually carried a man who peered over the side of the plane and observed what the enemy was up to. In the early years of World War II the observer had two jobs — navigating the aircraft and dropping the bombs. As the bomber approached its target he would drop his pencils and rulers and head into the nose to squint through the bomb sight, give the pilot instructions and release the bombs. Then he would dash back to his charts to figure out the plane's new position. Sometimes he would man the guns, too.

The authorities finally recognised that the poor man had too much to do, and he became a dedicated navigator. A new crew job and a new specialty was born — bomb aimer. (The official term was 'air bomber', but most people used 'bomb aimer', and this book does too.) Navigators navigated, while bomb aimers aimed and dropped the bombs and also manned the front turret when required. Bomb aimers helped with map reading, too, and many had the job of dropping *Window* after it was introduced in mid-1943. After these changes, the five-man crew of a Wellington consisted of pilot, navigator, bomb aimer, wireless operator and rear gunner.

If the pilot was killed or incapacitated, another member of the crew usually knew enough about flying to get the plane home. A non-pilot occasionally landed an aircraft after flying it back but he usually baled out with the rest of the crew once over England.

Crew jobs were also rationalised on the four-engined heavies once they arrived. After some experimentation, the crews of the Stirling, Halifax and Lancaster settled at seven — pilot, flight engineer, navigator, bomb aimer, wireless operator and two gunners (the rear gunner and the mid-upper gunner, who operated Browning machine guns in a turret atop the fuselage behind the wings). The heavy bombers were far more complex machines than those that flew in the early years of the war, and a pilot faced a growing mass of dials and a large number of petrol tanks (six in a Lancaster, eight, 10 or 12 in a Halifax, 14 in a Stirling) whose contents needed juggling. At first a second pilot dealt with the tanks, engines and other chores, but eventually the job became one for a specialist — the flight engineer. New Zealanders trained for all aircrew trades except that of flight engineer, which was invariably a British preserve. The engineer was often the one who flew an aircraft if the pilot was badly injured. He stood or sat alongside the pilot and watched him fly so much he could almost always do likewise if the need arose.

In the latter part of the war, when most bombers carried H_2S radar, the bomb aimer's job was amended. He manned the radar set, sitting alongside the navigator for long periods, and became known as Nav. 2, especially in pathfinder squadrons. He dropped the bombs from the navigator's 'office', but if pinpoint accuracy was necessary, particularly over targets in occupied Europe, he would use the bomb sight in the nose.

An airman fresh from New Zealand was posted from his PRC for refresher or advanced training, which lasted some weeks or months, and then on to an OTU — where depending on the command he was headed for.

It was at their PRC that airmen heard whether they would go to Bomber, Fighter or Coastal Command. Most pilots hoped to fly fighters, but the need for bomber pilots was more pressing. Many crestfallen young men posted to bomber OTUs never had the thrill of whistling into the clouds in a Spitfire. They swallowed their disappointment and got on with learning to fly bombers — and eventually realised there wasn't a much bigger thrill than sitting at the controls of a giant Lancaster as four powerful, sweet-running Rolls-Royce Merlins thrust it off the ground.

In February 1941, Keith Beattie was among the first group of New Zealanders to go to Canada to learn to fly.

We trained there on [single-engined] Harvards and we all expected to be fighter pilots. But about three-quarters of us finished up on bombers. I suppose I was disappointed initially but we had no say in the matter. I had done no two-engined flying at all before OTU but I went straight on to Wellingtons there, skipping Oxfords or Ansons. I suppose it was a measure of the urgency of the times.

In the early days of the war, the RAF was desperately short of aircrew, time with training squadrons was short and rushed, and airmen were quickly posted to operational squadrons and rostered to whatever crew needed them. The days of largely settled crews had not yet arrived. Gunner Bill Smith might fly with pilot Jim Brown one night and Jack Green the next. Gradually new systems evolved, however, and in April 1940 training squadrons became part of OTUs, where complete crews were formed and trained, methodically and carefully.

When a new course began at an OTU, airmen for however many complete crews were needed would arrive from training bases all over England. Assembled in a hangar one morning, they would be welcomed by the station commander, given mugs of steaming tea and told to 'crew up'. Sometimes they were given the entire day, perhaps two, occasionally even longer. But normally the commander barked, 'You've got the morning to form a crew. If you don't do it, we'll do it for you. Get cracking. Best of luck.' Pilots in the bunch of milling airmen suddenly had to assemble a team. Navigators began looking for a likely pilot. Shy young gunners shuffled their feet, thinking 'Who'll want me?' Someone always did.

Astonishingly, this apparently crazy system worked brilliantly. OTUs flew Wellingtons with a crew of five. Often in a hangar full of men a couple of New Zealanders would spot each other and realise they'd gone to the same school. They might now be a wireless operator and a bomb aimer. They would shake hands, agree to fly together and go looking for a pilot. A New Zealand navigator might see and remember an Australian gunner he'd met somewhere in Canada and link up with him in the throng.

Navigator Alf Drew, an Aucklander who flew a tour with an English pilot on 75 Squadron before doing a second as a pathfinder on 156 with the notable Jack Wright, remembers his initial crewing up: 'The most extraordinary thing; it was like a market.'

New Zealand shoulder flashes were helpful when it came to identifying fellow countrymen. George Hedge remembers flashes first being issued not long after he reached England in the early autumn of 1940 and sitting in the sun sewing them on. 'We were pleased to have them. Until then there was nothing to indicate we were New Zealanders.'

Some New Zealanders avoided their compatriots at crewing up. They hadn't come thousands of miles to fly in an aeroplane with men from home. Many airmen considered a real mix made the best crews — a couple of Englishmen, perhaps, plus a Scot and several colonials. It wasn't unusual for a crew to be made up of three or four Britons, a Canadian, a New Zealander and an Australian. Occasionally the Canadian was an American who'd gone north to join the RCAF before the United States declared war. A good number of Rhodesians and a few South Africans, one of whom won a VC, also served with the RAF. Many small Commonwealth outposts provided aircrew, as did Anglo-South American communities. Irishmen from the republic also flew for the RAF.

In May 1943, when Christchurch navigator Ted Anderson reached No. 11 OTU at Westcott, Buckinghamshire — known as the New Zealand OTU because so many New Zealanders trained there — his group was given the luxury of two weeks to crew up. He was in the bar the first night when a bunch of pilots walked in. 'Eric Witting [from Invercargill] introduced himself. We had a couple of beers and got yarning and eventually he said, "Do you think we could make a go of it?" and I said, "Let's try." So that was a start.' The rest of the crew quickly fell into place. Anderson had already met and liked Jack Thomas, a bomb aimer from Bradford, and Witting and the Yorkshireman also hit it off. 'Then Eric found Glen Marshall and Wally Hurdle and that completed our crew.' Marshall, the wireless operator, came from Wairoa, Hurdle, the rear gunner, from Feilding.

The normal pattern was for the basic OTU five to fly their Wellington for several months in training before being posted to a squadron. If the squadron was flying four-engined bombers, the crew would receive instruction on these bigger planes before going on operations. By the time Wellingtons were phased out of Main Force bombing in 1943, a crew would graduate from an OTU Wellington to a Heavy Conversion Unit (HCU) for a short course in flying a four-engined aircraft, usually a Stirling. Lancaster Finishing Schools (LFSs) were formed in November 1943. At the HCU the crew of five would be augmented by a flight engineer and a mid-upper gunner, thus completing the seven-man crew. The two additions to Witting's crew, both English, came from the pool at 1657 HCU at Stradishall, Suffolk, and the complete crew was then posted to 75 Squadron in September 1943.

Once they had jelled at OTU, crews tended to stick together — to 'bond', in modern jargon. Of course, there were failures. Friction sometimes developed. Some men just didn't fit in. Others simply weren't up to it. Airmen who drank too much or had psychological problems caused strife. Some crew couldn't or didn't do their jobs properly. Gunners fell asleep with disastrous results. Someone would become ill, or be hurt in an accident, and so be unable to fly. Replacements were then needed. Every squadron had 'spares'. Some became permanent crew, others didn't. Last-minute replacements frequently didn't know the airmen with whom they flew — and often died. Most crews didn't like flying with replacements. A strange face disrupted routines, upset a crew's equilibrium. Old hands didn't know what to expect from a newcomer or how he would react in an emergency. But if the new man did his job quietly and efficiently and had no bad habits, he was quickly accepted.

Pilot Nick Nicklin wrote to his mother in Auckland after his Lancaster had been shot up running into Schweinfurt in April 1944 on his sixth op. Despite serious damage they had bombed their target and Nicklin said fellow New Zealander and bomb aimer Snow Baker had been as cool and composed as if he were doing a practice run on the range. Once they cleared the target, Nicklin asked Baker to go back and get the injured rear gunner out of his turret and was told, 'I'll get him' — in a voice 'I knew meant he would do so even if he had to tear the armour plate like paper with his bare hands. Snow, good reliable Snow. It's good to have a moral anchor like him in the crew.' Nicklin had praise, too, for flight engineer Geoff Copeman, who 'went on with his job as though nothing had happened. The boy has what it takes.' And there was a special word for navigator Bill Martin, 'a newcomer who had the most difficult job of all, replacing a friend and tried member of the crew. He has had his final trial now and come out tops.' Said Nicklin: 'How proud I felt of my crew. Not a sign of panic in any of them.'

Years after the war, pilot Doug Hawker wrote that he regretted never personally thanking 'members of my crew [another New Zealander and five Englishmen] for the way in which they performed their duties. I just assumed that they would always deliver 100 per cent . . . and they did.'

Pilots doing their familiarisation op with a seasoned crew often felt uncomfortable, superfluous to requirements. Much depended on the captain and his attitude. Some skippers went out of their way to be helpful, to show the beginner the 'ropes', to pass on as much as they could of their accumulated experience. Others were brusque. Jack Hardie, now living in Motueka, was shot down the night he went on his second-dicky flight. It all started badly because quite clearly he was regarded as a nuisance. Problems developed among the crew, and the Halifax strayed far off course, making easy meat for the German defences. Hardie learned a lot that night but never got the chance to put it into practice. He spent the rest of the war as a prisoner.

Many pilots were lost on their familiarisation flight. That meant a crew left without a captain just as they were about to start operations. Someone else had to be found. Hardie's 'headless' crew, given a new skipper, were all killed eight weeks later.

South Islanders Ernie Mawson and Frank Jackson, about to fly for 635, a pathfinder squadron, found themselves pilotless. Their Australian skipper became a POW on his second-dicky and they had to get used to someone else. Luckily, Emile Mange, perhaps the only Swiss pilot in the RAF, turned out to be a brilliant replacement. But losing your skipper, often already a close friend, was always traumatic. So was being left a sole survivor because you hadn't flown. On the night in March 1943 that Halifax pilot Norman Black, of Christchurch, and his 76 Squadron crew were lost without trace on a raid to Berlin, their regular navigator, Ted Strange — an Englishman — was back at base, grounded with an injured knee. He lost all his crew — six good mates.

Crews, especially those who went through a tour unchanged, forged an intense sense of camaraderie. Dependency on each other for survival created friendships that lasted a lifetime. Sixty years on, wartime crews of seven are down to just one or two men at most, but many of those who survive maintain contact. Pilot Bill Hickson, of Waikanae, and his English flight engineer, Fred

Maltas, are the only two of their 35 Squadron crew still alive. Hickson took his wife, Kath, to England in 1992 for the 50th anniversary of the formation of the Pathfinder Force and had an emotional meeting with Maltas. The two men continue to keep in touch. Says Hickson: 'Every year on the anniversary of being shot down [in 1943] I phone Freddy. It's a moving experience to renew that friendship.'

Canadian Don Smith, sole survivor of a 7 Squadron bomber downed over Denmark in April 1943, directed that his ashes be scattered on the graves of his crew in Svino War Cemetery after his death. On 4 May — Denmark's Freedom Day — 1999, when the 62 RAF bomber crew, eight of them New Zealanders, who lie in the cemetery were honoured, Smith's wishes were carried out with due ceremony.

Wounded English gunner Tom Stanley jumped from a Manchester over Holland in March 1942 and lived, while most of his crew died. After the war Stanley made a yearly pilgrimage to Bergen, where his friends were buried. After he died in 2000, his widow carried his ashes to the Dutch cemetery so he could join his crew in their final resting place. 'He was the last one to die and he does belong here,' she said. Such 'reunions' continue.

Combat turned some airmen into quivering wrecks who cried 'Enough!' Phil Langsford, now a retired Huntly farmer, was twice posted missing while flying with 78 Squadron — once after ditching in the Mediterranean, the second time after being shot down. He remembers his English navigator and how the man's nerve broke after a frightening trip when flak lopped a propeller blade off one of the inner engines. The shattered blade slashed through the skin of the fuselage not 18 inches from where Langsford was sitting at his wireless set. Vibrations from the damaged propeller almost shook the aircraft to pieces until the pilot managed to feather the blades. Flak also sliced off the Perspex astrodome cover. The Halifax strayed far off course because of poor navigation and the badly shaken crew were an hour late landing. The experience was too much for the navigator.

> When we got out to the plane for our next op Paddy the skipper and Jeff the navigator didn't arrive. Finally the WAAF who'd driven us out came back and said we had to report to the flight office. Everyone else had taken off by then. We learned Jeff had said he wouldn't go and Paddy said to us, "Well, it's over to you blokes. Do you still want to fly with me?" He thought we were losing confidence in him. I told him I was very happy to go with him. He was a fine pilot. So were the others, and he was assured of our support. We were given a week's leave and Jeff disappeared. He was just taken off the squadron. I don't know what happened to him.

Some crews flatly refused to fly with pilots they considered dangerous. The chance of death was bad enough already, never mind when flying with an incompetent captain. New Zealand bomb aimer Bill Wilson and the rest of his crew called a halt after their Australian pilot crashed twice at 1658 HCU, in Yorkshire, in late 1943. The first time he lost control on landing, the Halifax twisting around until the undercarriage collapsed. The second crash was much worse. An engine on a factory-fresh Halifax — so new the 158 Squadron letters were only chalked on the fuselage — simply fell off during a training flight, damaging the controls as it went. The pilot totally did his bun, and five miles short of base, at Lissett, the aircraft smashed through the top of a row of pines and plunged into the middle of a vast piggery where a squire bred prize animals. The Halifax hit more or less level but burst into flames and burned out. The flight engineer chopped a hole in the fuselage and everyone scrambled to safety. 'We declared we would not go up with that Aussie again. The

CO interviewed us about this and more or less suggested lack of moral fibre. He asked, "Will you fly with this pilot again?" and we said, "No."' The confrontation ended when Wilson said he would be happy to go with another pilot. So he ended up flying with the CO when he went on ops and otherwise acting as a spare. He was shot down and taken prisoner in October 1944, his tour almost over.

Most crews got on well and stuck together until they finished a tour or were shot down. Many, particularly key crews, went unchanged through 30, 40 or more ops. Mawson and Jackson sat side by side for 61 ops as Nav. 1 and Nav. 2 with 635 Squadron. Mawson did the navigating while Jackson operated the H_2S radar and dropped the bombs. Their crew became a close-knit unit under their Swiss skipper, unchanged from the time their wireless operator quit after their first op. They had to run over the target three times that night, flak was heavy, and they watched in horror as a Lancaster blew up in front of them. The wireless operator had flown in the Middle East but had seen nothing there to compare with this and wasn't a 'press-on type'. After landing he stormed into the wing commander's office and demanded out. 'They're a chop crew. They'll get the chop. They won't survive,' he predicted. Jackson says: 'I don't suppose you could blame the poor bugger. It was a pretty good baptism for us too.' The inevitable happened. The wireless operator went to another crew and perished with them three months later.

Losses on operations were heaviest among new and inexperienced crews, especially those thrown into the maelstrom of the night war at its worst in 1942, 1943 and 1944. Countless crews disappeared during their first five trips, many on their debut — after 18 months to two years of training. Wellingtonian Bruce Cunningham, downed while piloting a 514 Squadron Lancaster over Belgium in May 1944 halfway through a tour, remembers fellow POWs running a survey in his camp. The number of ops done averaged out at three-and-a-half. Crews who reached five or 10 ops had a better chance of surviving a tour than newcomers. Experience counted greatly but was no guarantee of survival. Many crews were shot down on their 29th or even 30th and last op.

Luck played its part. Some crews were lucky, others were not. Some would go through an entire tour with hardly a flak hole to show for it and never see a fighter. Others would attract trouble from the start, regularly coming home riddled with gaping holes from anti-aircraft shells or after fighting off night fighters, struggling back battle scarred on two or three engines, making crash-landings at emergency airfields.

The best crews worked hard at surviving. They trained and practised drills until everything became second nature. They knew how best to get out of a blazing aircraft, what to do without thinking if they ditched. They weaved constantly in the air to present an unsteady target for lurking fighters and to make it more difficult for ground radar to track them and direct flak onto their predicted path. They had gunners who stayed alert every second of an eight-hour trip. The best crews were disciplined crews. Everyone did his job well, everyone could rely on the other chap. There was no nonsense, no silly intercom chatter. Simply 'Captain to navigator . . .' or 'Rear gunner to skipper . . .'

In the air the pilot was the unquestioned boss, whatever his rank. Even if he were a lowly sergeant with, say, a squadron leader or a much-decorated wing commander aboard, he was in charge. He carried the responsibility of everyone's lives. In emergencies, too, he was the one who had to see, as best he could, that his men jumped before he did, to hold the plane aloft as long as possible to give the crew the chance to bale out. Only then could he try to save himself. Too often it was too late.

The bombers, night fighters, RAF squadrons and airfields

Bomber Command flew three types of 'heavy' strike bombers in 1939 — Wellingtons, Hampdens and Whitleys, all powered by two engines. When the four-engined Stirlings, Halifaxes and then Lancasters, the real heavies, began to arrive at squadrons in late 1941, the old faithfuls that had carried the burden in the opening phases of the war were downgraded to 'mediums', which is what they had really been all along. Wellingtons were still flying actively at the end of the war, although not in a Main Force bombing role, and more of them were manufactured than any other multi-engined aircraft in the British inventory — an astonishing 11,500. The Wellington was nicknamed Wimpy after the cartoon character J. Wellington Wimpy. Hampdens and Whitleys were retired from bombing ops in 1942.

At the start of the war the Command operated six squadrons of Wellingtons in East Anglia under the umbrella of 3 Group, six of Hampdens in Lincolnshire in 5 Group, and five of Whitleys further north, in Yorkshire, in 4 Group. On the Suffolk and Norfolk coasts, 2 Group had six squadrons of Blenheims, also twin-engined and rated medium day bombers. Thus, Britain began hostilities with just 23 frontline squadrons available to carry the war to Germany. Not counted were 1 Group's Battles, obsolescent single-engined aircraft designated as light bombers and based in France.

Several other aircraft featured in Bomber Command's wartime ranks, notably the Manchester and Mosquito. The first failed as a two-engined bomber but, with lengthened wings and two more engines, became the Lancaster. The Mosquito, a brilliantly versatile aeroplane built largely of wood, was used in a huge variety of roles, including bombing. The Wooden Wonder fully justified its nickname. 2 Group, which left the Command in mid-1943, flew several other types, the American-built Ventura and Boston among them.

It's worth remembering that the bombers featuring in these pages, even the wonderful Lancaster, are as remote from today's generation of jet planes as the Model-T Ford is from the latest Mercedes. Fully laden with bombs and fuel, the piston-engined, propeller-driven Lancaster strained mightily to get off the ground. Once airborne it climbed at about 500 feet a minute, taking half an hour to reach 15,000 feet. Today's Jumbos are hardly up before they achieve that altitude. A Lancaster off to Berlin with full tanks and loaded bomb bays plodded along at about 220 mph. Lacking insulation or interior linings, they were noisy — and cold away from the ducts carrying hot air from the engines. An alloy metal skin, no thicker than a matchstick, was all that stood between the crew and flak or fighter fire. The crew worked in total darkness save for the dull glow from cockpit instruments and the weak beam of a single small light in the curtained-off navigator's 'office'. He had to have some illumination to see his papers.

One Englishman who flew Wellingtons in 1943 wrote years later: 'Anyone whose sole experience of flying is confined to holiday jets has simply no idea of what it was like to fly in a wartime bomber; the numbing cold . . . the shattering noise, the constant teeth-jarring vibration, the turbulence causing the whole airframe to flex and creak; having to wear an oxygen mask which made every breath reek of wet rubber . . .'

Flying a bomber with damaged controls called for brute force. A pilot often had to call for help from other crew to manhandle the controls when his plane was in trouble. Bombers did have a rudimentary automatic pilot, known as George, but few pilots used it in flight because the seconds lost in disengaging could be fatal in an emergency, such as a fighter attack. It was also incapable of holding a plane steady when the controls were damaged.

Night fighters

Germany operated a number of different night fighters against Bomber Command but two accounted for the majority of its force — the Junkers 88 (Ju 88) and the Messerschmitt Bf 110 (Me 110). From mid-1943 the famous Messerschmitt Bf 109 (Me 109) day fighter was also pressed into a night role, particularly when the Luftwaffe adopted the tactic of fighters roaming freelance over a bombing target or in the bomber stream. The single-engined Focke-Wulf 190 (FW 190) day fighter was used in this role. The twin-engined Heinkel 219 (He 219) and Dornier 217 (Do 217) also played a part as night fighters, but the reliable and effective twin-engined Ju 88 and Me 110 predominantly carried the fight to the bombers. The He 219, or Uhu (Owl), has been described by some authorities as an exceptional machine — the best German night fighter ever built — but it was produced in only small numbers.

Squadrons

Bomber Command squadrons were numbered as low as 7 and as high as 692. At one stage or another, about 130 squadrons served during the war, some for extremely brief periods. Just two, 44 and 149, flew from the first day of the war to the last. Some were posted to the Middle East, others to India. Some were disbanded and then reformed; others became training squadrons. Many had varied careers. 104 Squadron, for example, a training outfit at the outbreak of war, was absorbed into an OTU in April 1940. Reformed as a Wellington squadron in 4 Group on 1 April 1941, it flew on ops from Driffield, Yorkshire, until February 1942, by which time most of the squadron had been posted to the Middle East.

75 (New Zealand) Squadron RAF was so named in recognition of New Zealand's gift of its 30 Wellingtons to Britain at the outbreak of war. Australian and Canadian heavy-bomber squadrons were

formed later. Canada eventually had no fewer than 14, most of them operating in 6 Group, RCAF, formed on 1 January 1943 — a Canadian group with a Canadian commander.

Many squadrons had links with Commonwealth territories. From 1942, 44 Squadron was known, by royal warrant, as 44 (Rhodesia) Squadron. It had many Rhodesian air and ground crew. 35 and 99 were both Madras Presidency squadrons, 97 was Straits Settlements. Many New Zealanders flew with 214 (Federated Malay States) and 218 (Gold Coast) Squadrons in 3 Group. Squadrons with such affiliations often had personnel from the territories concerned serving with them, or other ties. The name Madras Presidency was given to 35 Squadron in 1942 to honour the people of Madras, who raised money to pay for the unit's Halifaxes.

Surely the strangest name was 692 (Fellowship of the Bellows) Squadron, formed in 8 Group on 1 January 1944 as a Mosquito squadron in the Light Night Striking Force. It was led for a time by New Zealander Stephen Watts. According to *Bomber Command War Diaries*, the Fellowship of the Bellows was a patriotic organisation of Anglo-Argentine businessmen and families in Buenos Aires, who raised money for the purchase of aircraft for the RAF. The 'Bellows' were to 'help raise the wind'.

New squadrons snowballed later in the war as Lancasters began pouring from factories in Britain and Canada, most carrying numbers in the 600s. Many squadrons had three flights, each of eight or nine aircraft, and often an entire flight was peeled off to give a new squadron an immediate stiffening of experienced crews. It's worth noting that RAF squadron numbers didn't, and still don't, have a 'th'. Thus it is 75 Squadron or No. 75 Squadron, never 75th Squadron.

All aircraft carried three large code letters on the rear fuselage, two of them separated from the third by the prominent red, white and blue RAF roundel. The first two identified the squadron, the third the individual aircraft. Squadrons often used two, sometimes more, codes, but one was usually predominant, e.g. AA, and sometimes JN, for 75, KM for 44, OJ for 149, KC for the famous 617 Squadron. Thus AA-S identifies the aircraft as flying with 75 Squadron, with S (for Sugar) as its own particular letter and usually its call sign. The names that went with the letters of the alphabet — (A) Apple, (B) Beer, (C) Charlie, . . . — changed during the course of the war, especially after the Americans arrived on the scene in 1943, but even then there was a choice for some letters, for example Jig or Johnny. Aircraft also carried an RAF serial number — usually one or two letters and three or four numbers — on the rear fuselage.

Airmen often became attached to a particular aircraft, and crews, mainly experienced ones, got to fly the same aircraft most of the time. All squadrons had one or two planes that never lost their reputation as slow-flying clunkers despite the best efforts of ground crews. Some letters came to be regarded as lucky or unlucky. In one squadron, R (Roger) might be known as the bomber that always came back, even from the worst raids. In another it would be dogged with bad luck, plane after plane bearing that letter being lost.

Airfields

When the war began, Britain had about 170 military airfields; when the conflict ended it had an extraordinary 670. They were operated by the RAF, the 8th and 9th United States Army Air Forces, the Royal Naval Air Force and other units.

In 1945 Bomber Command operated from 135 airfields, the majority concentrated in 'Bomber Country' — eastern Yorkshire, Lincolnshire and Cambridgeshire; and Nottinghamshire, Norfolk and Suffolk. East Anglia was home both to British squadrons and to the USAAF. The bomber bases were built in the east because that was the closest point to Germany.

Most bomber fields covered about 600 acres, with runways laid out in the shape of a giant A. The main runway was 2000 yards long, the two subsidiaries 1400 yards, and all three 50 yards wide. Each field was a self-contained complex of runways, perimeter tracks, taxiways, bays for a couple of dozen or more bombers, bomb and ammunition dumps, hangars, roads and paths, a control tower and a host of ancillary buildings, plus messes and living quarters.

The pre-war airfields, with their spacious and comfortable quarters in ivy-covered brick buildings, became prized postings. Wartime fields, thrown up quickly, often provided only primitive and dispersed accommodation in Nissen huts. Jim Insull, posted to 620 Squadron at Chedburgh, Suffolk, in the summer of 1943, complained in his diary: 'Our sleeping quarters are almost half a mile from the mess, which is a good 400 yards from the crew rooms and "business" buildings that line one side of the aerodrome.' Crew walked or rode bikes between these points — no fun in winter, when wind and snow howled in from the North Sea. Insull described his Nissen hut as 'a semi-cylindrical, corrugated iron structure with a small window at each end, one door and a stove in the centre of the concrete floor. There are beds for two crews of seven men.'

Later, at the HCU at Woolfox Lodge, Rutlandshire, he found stark conditions. 'The roads are shallow rivers of mud, it is cold and bleak, and fog and mist alternate with driving rain and sleet.'

The contrast with Mildenhall, where Insull was posted in late November 1943 to join 622 Squadron, was marked. This pre-war Suffolk base was perhaps the best-known station in Bomber Command. It was here that the 1934 England–Australia air race began, and Insull luxuriated in a four-roomed flat, occupied before the war by married airmen. He and the others in the crew even had their own bathroom.

Mepal, 75 (NZ) Squadron's base for two years from June 1943, was in Cambridgeshire, six miles west of Ely, where the cathedral's spire was a welcome landmark for bomber crews returning in daylight. Built between the villages of Mepal and Sutton, the field was typical of wartime aerodromes, with concrete runways and dispersed accommodation. About 1200 people, including almost 200 WAAFs, lived and worked there.

Normally, a bomber station was commanded by a group captain. From March 1943 an air commodore, next up the ladder of seniority, controlled three adjacent stations, which made up an RAF base. Fighter squadrons were commanded by a squadron leader but, confusingly, bomber squadrons were led by a wing commander. A squadron leader was in charge of each of the two or three flights a squadron comprised. The lowest commissioned rank in the RAF was pilot officer, the steps up from that being flying officer, flight lieutenant and then squadron leader.

1939

FIRST MONTHS OF WAR,
FIRST NEW ZEALAND CASUALTIES

1939

More than 500 New Zealanders wore the RAF uniform on 3 September 1939 and they participated in the fray from day one. The first RAF officer captured by the Germans, just 48 hours into the war, was a New Zealander. Laurie Edwards, a Coastal Command pilot from Taranaki, was flying a reconnaissance patrol over the North Sea when his Anson was shot down in flames by a German seaplane. Perhaps the Germans pitied him for his long captivity, for he was repatriated to Britain in September 1944.

The first six New Zealanders to die in Bomber Command were killed over England in training crashes, and it wasn't until 14 December that the first deaths in action occurred. Twelve Wellingtons of 99 Squadron attacked German naval units near the North Sea port of Wilhelmshaven in daylight and five were shot down, none of the airmen surviving. One of the dead, Aucklander Charles Caldwell, 26, a pilot, became the first on the long, sad roll of more than 400 New Zealand names from Bomber Command on the panels of the memorial built after the war at Runnymede, near Windsor, in memory of the 20,000 Commonwealth airmen who have no known graves.

A second New Zealander became a victim of the Wilhelmshaven raid when another Wellington, Timaru airman John Hetherington at the controls, crashed on return to England. Damaged by fighters, the crippled bomber staggered back across the North Sea but then spiralled down onto a field near its base at Newmarket racecourse, in Suffolk. Hetherington, 25, had died on just his second op and was buried at nearby Mildenhall.

The action also led to the first New Zealand decoration of the war — a Distinguished Flying Medal (DFM) for Colin Knight, who flew with fellow New Zealander Andrew 'Square' McKee, both a squadron leader and the formation's leader. Knight, a member of the original RNZAF team formed before the war to ferry home the Wellingtons New Zealand had bought from Vickers, was the chief wireless operator of the attacking group. He sent a stream of messages about German ships to his base while McKee threw their Wimpy around violently to avoid German fighters. Knight was badly hurt in an aircraft accident in England in 1940 but recovered to serve for 15 years in the RNZAF. He died at 85 in 1998.

The 14 December aircraft toll was topped four days later when 12 of 22 Wellingtons were lost on a similar mission in the same area, when German fighters were directed to them by experimental radar — the first such use of this technology in the war. Losses of such magnitude could not be sustained, and these two incidents were key factors in Bomber Command's decision to suspend major daylight bomber raids.

It wasn't even as if the grievous loss of men and aircraft was balanced by bombing success. The raids achieved no tangible results. No ships were destroyed. Nevertheless, even though the chances of sinking ships protected by flak and fighters were slight, they were targets. And targets were lacking. Bomber Command could attack ships at sea but was strictly enjoined from dropping bombs over land. Industrial targets, even moored ships, were off-limits for fear of killing civilians. For the moment the RAF played by gentlemen's rules.

In 1939 the RAF didn't really anticipate night bombing. Neither did the Luftwaffe. Bomber Command's tradition, policy, training and thought were all directed towards daylight attacks. The premise was that bombers flying in close formation would provide such a curtain of fire that no fighter could stop them. They would always get through. It didn't take many raids to disprove this theory. German cannon shells blew the bombers out of the air and aircrew died in droves.

British fighters didn't have sufficient range to accompany bombers to distant targets, so Bomber Command was forced to turn to night-time operations. This posed its own problems. Little emphasis had been placed on night flying before the war, and the vast majority of training flights were undertaken when the sun was shining. When crews did fly cross-country exercises over England at night, many became disoriented or lost. Emergency landings were frequent.

War magnified a thousand times the problems of finding distant targets requiring flights over the sea. In heavy cloud, aircrew sometimes hadn't the faintest idea where they were — navigation aids were rudimentary. By day pilots and navigators could map-read, using rivers, canals, roads, railway lines and other prominent features to help guide them. At night it was different. And if crews couldn't navigate from, say, an airfield in southeast England to another in Scotland during peacetime, lights blazing everywhere, how were they to locate targets deep in blacked-out Europe on cloudy nights or when industrial haze hung heavily over the land — and bomb accurately? It was soon apparent that they couldn't.

Crews continued to get themselves hopelessly lost well into the war. In April 1942 an Australian pilot force-landed an out-of-fuel Hampden in Buckinghamshire. The crew, convinced they were in enemy territory, promptly set fire to their aircraft.

The first people Bomber Command killed in World War II were Danes, not Germans. Bombs from a Wellington, one of a number trying to hit warships in the estuary of the River Elbe, fell on a Danish town 100 miles to the north of the target area, killing two people. British bombs were incapable of sinking big naval units. Piddling 100- and 250-pound affairs, they simply bounced off armour-plated decks. Many were duds, failing to explode, and the explosive they contained was far inferior to what the Germans were using. The days of powerful and reliable bombs still lay in the future.

Wireless communications were also poor. Word on the

movements of German naval units in the first few days of the war was delayed when wireless sets on aircraft trying to communicate with base malfunctioned.

1940

75 (NZ) Squadron's beginnings

1940

The shape of the war changed dramatically in the spring of 1940. Germany struck at Denmark and Norway on 9 April and a month later her tanks and armies rolled into France, Belgium and Holland. Germany had uncorked the bottle of total war and the restraints on bombing gradually eroded.

The RAF had already lost its first aircraft attacking a German land target — a Whitley shot down in March bombing a seaplane base in the Frisian Islands. Now, as continent-based 2 Group's light bombers — Blenheims and outdated Battles — became heavily engaged in the Low Countries and France, the RAF began raids on German sea and land targets in Scandinavia, and bombers from English airfields were soon ranging into Germany trying to hit industrial targets.

While all this was going on, 75 Squadron sprang into existence at Feltwell, a pre-war base in Norfolk, and adopted the motto *Ake ake kia kaha —For ever and ever be strong*. Its badge incorporated a tiki in front of two hammers, from New Zealand's coat of arms. The squadron, which traced its roots back to 1916 when it was founded for home defence against Zeppelin airships, received its official New Zealand designation in April 1940. The nucleus of its aircrew were the men sent to Britain in 1939 to learn to operate the Wellingtons ordered by the New Zealand government and then ferry them home. The aircraft were generously offered to Britain by New Zealand on the outbreak of war — and accepted.

The squadron suffered its first loss on 21–22 May 1940, when a Wellington bombing a Belgian bridge was hit by flak at low level and crashed. Three crew survived but the captain, John Collins, 23 (Christchurch), was killed. Collins had transferred to the RNZAF from the RAF for the intended delivery of the Wellingtons.

75 operated throughout the war as the only 'New Zealand' heavy bomber squadron, first with Wellingtons, then Stirlings

and finally Lancasters. The official New Zealand war history says it flew 8150 sorties and dropped 21,630 tons of bombs. Its wartime dead of 1139 included 452 New Zealanders — almost a quarter of all New Zealand deaths in Bomber Command. It wasn't an RNZAF squadron; it was simply an RAF squadron with a large number of New Zealand aircrew and a strong New Zealand flavour that stemmed from the original gift of Wellingtons. Some New Zealanders were desperately keen to fly with 75; others weren't or didn't mind either way.

At the end of World War II, the RAF 'presented' the number 75 to the RNZAF to show its gratitude for New Zealand's contribution, and in October 1946 a new 75 Squadron was formed at Ohakea. This remained a unit of the RNZAF until it was controversially disbanded by government order in December 2001.

After Dunkirk and the surrender of France in late June 1940, the Luftwaffe began its cross-Channel assault on Britain. The Battle of Britain lasted from 10 July to 31 October, the RAF's Fighter Command emerging triumphant. Without command of the sky Germany could not invade.

History has rightly lauded the handsome, boyish Hurricane and Spitfire pilots who swarmed up from English airfields to deal an enormous confidence-sapping blow to the Luftwaffe. As Prime Minister Winston Churchill proclaimed in the House of Commons: 'Never in the field of human conflict was so much owed by so many to so few.' Although history seems to have forgotten Bomber Command's role in the battle, Churchill didn't. While praising the fighter pilots, he also declared

but we must never forget that all the time, night after night, month after month, our bomber squadrons travel far into Germany, find their targets in the darkness by the highest navigational skill, aim their attacks, often under the heaviest fire, often at serious loss, with deliberate, careful precision, and inflict shattering blows upon the whole of the technical and war-making structure of the Nazi power.

There was some exaggeration here, but Churchill appreciated what too many have since forgotten — how much Bomber Command aircrew achieved in those perilous days. By day and night they attacked Luftwaffe airfields, invasion barges in the Channel ports and river estuaries, fuel installations, docks and shipping, aircraft factories, communications and many other targets. In September 1940 Bomber Command sank so many barges the Germans had to disperse them from their choked-up assembly points. Churchill understood Bomber Command's role and value in winning the Battle of Britain.

Reviewing a book about Battle of Britain fighter pilots in 2003, English journalist Max Hastings, author of *Bomber Command,* wrote: 'It is one of life's unfairnesses that the public to this day cherishes the RAF's wartime fighter pilots . . . with an uncomplicated enthusiasm that does not extend to the bomber crews, who showed equal courage and suffered far heavier losses.'

The Battle of Britain Memorial Chapel in Westminster Abbey records the names of 537 Fighter Command personnel who died in the crucial months of 1940. There, too, are the names of 718 men from Bomber Command and 230 from Coastal Command. The New Zealand component of those numbers is 21 (Fighter Command), 37 (Bomber Command) and 13 (Coastal Command).

Apart from anything else, Bomber Command's raid on Berlin on 25–26 August — retaliation for German bombs scattered in error on London the night before — galvanised Hitler into ordering attacks on British cities, thereby switching the Luftwaffe's focus from British fighter dromes at a key moment. This disastrous policy change gave Fighter Command the vital breather it needed in the run-up to the Luftwaffe's September onslaught.

Berlin: the first raid

On the night of 24 August 1940, a handful of Luftwaffe bombers searching for targets in the estuary of the River Thames strayed off course and mistakenly bombed central London. An indignant Churchill ordered retaliation. Twenty-four hours later the RAF unleashed the first raid of the war on the German capital. But Bomber Command hadn't yet learned to concentrate its forces, and of the 100 aircraft that flew that night only half, mainly Wellingtons and Hampdens, went to Berlin.

Thick cloud obscured the target, and the best the British crews could do was drop their bombs when they reckoned they were over Berlin. Most weren't. The only bombs that fell within the city's limits destroyed a suburban summerhouse and slightly injured two people. But the raid shocked and angered Adolf Hitler. 'If they attack our cities, we will raze theirs to the ground,' he declared. 'We will stop the handiwork of these air pirates, so help us God.'

Now it was his turn. Tit-for-tat raids were on. The Luftwaffe launched a massive 1300-aircraft assault. Waves of bombers, shepherded by swarms of fighters, crossed the Channel to descend on London. Sirens wailed as the first bombs rained down, and would do so again for the next 57 nights. The Blitz had begun.

British bombers hit back several more times in the next few weeks and Berlin would soon become a regular target. But it was small-scale stuff. It would be another three years before the RAF began to fly to Berlin in great strength and with singleness of purpose.

German bombers had only to hop across the Channel to England but Berlin was a numbing 600 miles in a straight line from Bomber Command airfields and few planes flew a direct course. Aircrews faced the cold, grey North Sea followed by a long anxious flight across hostile territory. After dropping their bombs they had to do it all over again in reverse.

Wellingtons and Whitleys could manage distant Berlin well enough, but for the little Hampdens — loaded with bombs, fuel tanks brimming for the long haul — it was touch and go. If anything went wrong, they were in trouble. And something did go wrong on that first night in 1940. Homebound, the aircraft encountered strong headwinds that blew them off course and lengthened their journey. For at least five Hampdens, two of them with New Zealand pilots, it was too much. One was lost without trace, one crashed in England short of base and three ditched off the coast.

Feilding-born and -educated Nick Fawcett flew the Hampden that disappeared. His aircraft is thought to have run out of fuel and come down in the North Sea. He and his crew are commemorated on the Runnymede Memorial. Fawcett had always been keen on aviation and had given up his job with a local law firm to join the RAF, sailing for Britain in 1938. He was just 20 when he died, on his 22nd op with 49 Squadron.

In a letter to his father in Christchurch, Pat Vivian, navigator on an 83 Squadron Hampden on the same raid, said he'd been blown 120 miles north of his intended course. As a result, one of the engines had failed through fuel starvation when the aircraft was only 300 feet off the ground on its landing approach. 'Luckily I had enough time to get out of the nose and up behind the wing spar. We ran into a row of trees at 150 mph and there wasn't much of the plane left. The pilot was badly hurt . . . I came off with a cut hand and a gash on the forehead.' Vivian perished two years later, his Lancaster shot down while raiding Bremen.

New Zealander Neil Svendsen suffered the indignity of being fired on by the Royal Navy as he put his 83 Squadron Hampden down in the mouth of the Wash, off the Lincolnshire coast, at about 8.00 a.m. on 26 August 1940. As he headed for land, weary after almost 11 hours in the air, his aircraft's engines coughed, sucking the last dregs from the fuel tanks. As the bomber sank lower and lower, Svendsen spotted two ships and decided to ditch as close as possible to them.

The Navy challenged Svendsen but failed to see his reply and lobbed a four-inch shell at the bomber as it was preparing to crash-land. Luckily it missed and the Hampden stalled into the sea. 'The tail struck the water first and as the machine fell into the sea, the engines were wrenched off,' Svendsen wrote later. 'There was quite a swell running but very little water was shipped into the aircraft.'

At that time Hampden dinghies were stowed in the fuselage, and Svendsen's crew dragged theirs out onto a wing to inflate and launch it. 'The four of us stepped in without getting wet and were [soon] picked up by a boat from a naval vessel. The Hampden floated for about ten minutes.' The unit that had fired on the bomber was busy protecting a ship laying buoys. The seamen apologised and took the rescued airmen into Harwich later that day. Gave them a good time, too.

Svendsen, who was born in Pukekohe in 1915 and died in Auckland in 2003, joined the RNZAF in 1936. He was accepted for a short-service commission in the RAF and sailed for Britain in 1937. A talented pilot, he was already wearing the DFC ribbon on his tunic when he ditched. He'd been given an immediate award two months earlier for his exploits on a night mine-laying trip in German waters. A flak ship pumped a shell into his Hampden's nose, the explosion blinding the navigator/bomb aimer. Svendsen dropped the mine himself and then found his own way back to England. On the 9th op of his second tour, on 30 June–1 July 1941, and still flying Hampdens with 83 Squadron, Svendsen was shot down during a raid on Dusseldorf. He spent the rest of the war as a POW.

A gunner dies over Germany

When James Bracegirdle was killed over Germany on 6 September 1940, two months short of his 22nd birthday, he'd been gone from New Zealand less than six months. He lost his life in the climactic month of the Battle of Britain, but his death didn't rate a mention in English newspapers. He wasn't a glamour fighter pilot braving the onslaught of the Luftwaffe. He was a humble gunner, a sergeant flying in the under turret of a twin-engined Hampden. There were no decorations or honours for James Bracegirdle. He was just another airman who climbed into a bomber one night, flew away from England and never came back.

His disappearance was news, though, in Auckland, his home town. He had worked as a fireman on the railways, played for the Parnell Rugby Football Club and had many friends. The newspapers ran his photograph and reported that his father had received word he was missing. In late 1940 there was still room for extended coverage of New Zealanders lost in the skies over Europe. Soon there wouldn't be — the casualty lists would become too long.

Two months later the *Auckland Star* carried a report quoting from a letter Bracegirdle had written home just before his death about his flight to Berlin on 25 August — the first time the RAF had dropped bombs on the German capital. That was indeed news. WE WENT TO BOMB BERLIN, the headline ran. The newspapers would make one more mention of Bracegirdle. A report came out of a German prison camp the next year about the amazing parachute escape of the Hampden's navigator, and Bracegirdle's name appeared again. After that his family was left to grieve for the young man who'd gone so confidently to war and wouldn't return. His sister, Alice Harold, still mourns more than 60 years later, and she and her husband, Jack, maintain a display in honour of James in their Auckland home.

Not until six years after the gunner had been lost did the

Bracegirdles learn precisely where their son and brother had come to earth and where he was buried. RAF Missing Research and Enquiry Units (MREUs) scoured Germany and Western Europe for years after the war, looking for crash sites, searching for graves of missing airmen, conducting countless unpleasant exhumations, trying to identify complete bodies, parts of bodies and burned bodies, searching human remains for identity disks, taking impressions of teeth, noting laundry marks and rank insignia on clothing, examining the usually meticulous German records, questioning local authorities about burials, demanding answers from a conquered foe.

In October 1946, No. 4 MREU, section 20, reported to the Air Ministry in London on its hunt for the bodies of the two missing crewmen from Hampden P2087, shot down near Munster the night of 6–7 September 1940 — Bracegirdle and wireless operator/gunner William Bell, an Irishman. Both the pilot and navigator had survived. The investigating officer reported he had contacted the police chief in Gross Reken, a community southwest of Munster, where the Hampden had crashed. The policeman had been personally responsible for recovering the bodies and for their subsequent burial. 'There is no doubt that both bodies were recovered from the swamp in which this aircraft crashed. Undoubtedly, this explains the term "washed ashore" used in German documents.'

Copies of the report were passed to RNZAF Headquarters, Halifax House, London, and then to Wellington. Eventually the Bracegirdle family got their own copy, finding at last where James was buried. Later, the bodies of Bracegirdle and Bell were lifted from their graves in Gross Reken and reinterred in beautiful Reichswald Forest Cemetery, just southwest of Kleve, near the Dutch border. They lie alongside each other, the New Zealander and the man from County Antrim, in Northern Ireland, sharing their last resting place with 7576 other Commonwealth war dead,

4000 of them airmen, among them 127 New Zealanders.

Bracegirdle volunteered for aircrew in October 1939 and was in camp by mid-January 1940. He and 35 other Leading Aircraftmen were on Shaw Savill's *Akaroa* when she sailed from Lyttelton for Britain in late March 1940. Nine of them would be dead before Christmas, another 10 before the end of 1942.

On 2 June 1940, Bracegirdle reached No. 16 OTU at Upper Heyford, Oxfordshire, and, promoted to sergeant, started flying on Hampdens. In mid-July he began a three-week course at 106 Squadron, then a training establishment, and on 6 August was posted to 44 Squadron. He had a month left to live.

Bracegirdle flew the first of his handful of operations on the night of 11–12 August, his bomber carrying mines to Kiel. Then, cooped up in his awkward ventral turret manning his twin .303 machine guns, he went in quick order to five more German targets — Dessau, Luena, Frankfurt, Berlin and Stuttgart — and on another mine-laying op in Norwegian waters. The historic nature of the flight to Berlin on the night of 25–26 August wasn't lost on him. 'We went over Berlin and, boy, am I proud,' he wrote home. 'This was the first time Berlin had been raided, and though the RAF has been over since, I am able to say I went on the first raid.' He declared that when the squadron had been told where they were going and crews posted for the raid,

> we could quite easily have sold our seats to any of the boys who were not flying. One chap . . . asked me to give him the trip. But I believe it's unlucky to change jobs, so held my own seat. We had a good trip there and back. And although it was cloudy, we were able to see our eggs go off.

A few nights later Bracegirdle was killed on his eighth op. His Hampden, flown by Englishman Stan Taunton, dropped its bombs on Krefeld, on the edge of the Ruhr Valley, but on the way home took a direct flak hit. Navigator John Vollmer wrote from his POW camp about what happened and his own remarkable experience. 'Our machine was hit in the wing by an anti-aircraft shell which went straight into a petrol tank. Bell reported the starboard engine was on fire. We never heard a word from Bracegirdle . . . I think he was hit by a piece of the shell.'

Ordered by the skipper to bale out, Vollmer got to his chute a few feet away, but as he did so the Hampden began its last dive and he was thrown back into the nose cone, clutching the chute pack in his hands. 'The aircraft probably reached 400 to 500 miles per hour. It was burning like a furnace and I dimly remember the inside being full of smoke. Next there was a devil of a bang and a sort of cracking . . . the speed of the aircraft had torn a wing off.' Pinned in the nose, unable to move, Vollmer thought he would die. Suddenly, though, an explosion blew the nose off. 'I found myself hurtling through the air holding on to my parachute which was still not hooked on. I made violent efforts to do this as I fell but realising I must be nearing the ground, decided to pull the ripcord and hold on to the pack with my hands.'

In the proverbial million-to-one chance, a single hook on the pack caught and snapped on to one of Vollmer's harness clips as the chute jerked open with great force. Had it not done so, the airman would have died. It was simply impossible to hold on to a pack as the chute opened — the forces were too great. Vollmer floated safely to earth. He and the pilot, who had also parachuted, were captured next day. Vollmer was told by the Germans that Bell's body had been found in the aircraft. 'The machine buried itself and Bracegirdle might have been underneath but I never heard. They died heroes' deaths.'

The *Akaroa* draft

The war dealt harshly with the 36 RNZAF gunners who sailed on the *Akaroa* in March 1940. Nineteen dead, four POWs, others wounded, and injuries that shortened the lives of some of the survivors. One or two carried psychological scars. But whatever their problems, those who came home were alive and thankful. A few are still alive and they've had 60 years that those who died never had — marriages, children, grandchildren, careers, retirement. They survived the lottery of an air war in which, as the statistics show, the odds were heavily stacked against them. They know they were lucky.

Jack Marshall went away with that little group. He flew two tours in the rear turret of bombers, one with renowned New Zealand pilot Fraser Barron. One November day in 1940, after his Wellington had ditched at 3.00 a.m. off the English coast, he spent 15 hours in a cramped dinghy in the cold North Sea before he was rescued by a British minelayer. He fell in love with an English girl and married her in a 700-year-old Essex church in 1942. She waited out the frightening six months of his second-tour pathfinder flights over Germany, which he survived with a commission, a DFC and a citation that said among other things: 'Throughout a long and successful operational career, he has set a high standard of reliability and enthusiasm.'

In late 1943, his duty more than done, Marshall brought his wife, Mollie, home to New Zealand. The couple lived in Christchurch, producing a son and twin daughters. He ran a taxi business then worked for the Reserve Bank for many years. In 2002, still much in love, the Marshalls went back to Britain for the first time since the war. Watched by two grandsons and friends, they exchanged vows again in the church where they had wed 60 years earlier. Then they went to France and laid flowers on Barron's grave.

Why did he live when so many others died? Marshall doesn't know. 'It's very hard to understand. Why did one chap go down on his first op, another come safely through 50? It doesn't make sense.' There is no answer. Some survived, some didn't. It's what happened. Simple as that.

The RAF got its money's worth out of the young New Zealanders in the *Akaroa* draft. They flew — mostly as gunners, though some changed 'trades' after arriving in Britain — in Bomber Command, Fighter Command, Coastal Command and in the Middle East. The ones who died perished in all the ways typical of the air war: downed by fighters, knocked out of the sky by flak, killed in collisions, in training crashes and on flight tests. One was killed on flare-path duty. Others were lost at sea. Six have no known graves.

No fewer than 15 were awarded the Battle of Britain Clasp, having manned the guns in death-trap Defiants and Blenheims by day and by night as the RAF battled the Luftwaffe. Les Russell flew 73 ops on Defiants in the Battle of Britain and must have been a good shot because he was credited with an Me 109 and an He 111 plus a Ju 88 damaged. He lost his life in a Halifax over Germany in 1942. Robert Young was killed over England on the night of 8 October 1940 as the Battle of Britain still raged, but not before he had claimed one enemy aircraft and shared in the destruction of another.

John Scott, farmer and seaman before joining the RNZAF, served with 264 Squadron in the Battle of Britain. Later, during a long stint with 256 Squadron and still flying Defiants, he shot down no fewer than four enemy aircraft. He was hugely successful with his guns. He bagged a double on 3 May 1941 — a Ju 88 and a Dornier bomber. He was commissioned and decorated with the DFM by the king, his citation noting his 'conspicuous success during night fighting operations'. He got back to New Zealand in late 1943, having survived the Germans and a crash that fractured his spine and put him in hospital for five weeks.

After the Battle of Britain, the survivors of James Bracegirdle's group went in many directions. Bill Burns flew with Coastal Command, manning the Leigh light on the first aircraft equipped with the new weapon — a searchlight designed to illuminate and surprise U-boats on the surface of the sea at night. He then did 65 trips with a Hudson squadron. He died in Auckland only four years after the war.

Cliff Emeny, who died in 2000, was credited as a night-fighter gunner with one German bomber and another probable before he turned to navigation. Later he trained in Canada as a pilot and was posted to Burma. He was shot down while flying a Mosquito in late 1944 and taken prisoner by the Japanese. He distinguished himself in POW camp. After the war he became a well-known public figure in New Zealand — a passionate lobbyist for constitutional rights, a farmers' spokesman and a parliamentary candidate.

Bill Murland was another who served with 264 Squadron on Defiants. Later he flew as a gunner on Wellingtons, Stirlings, Blenheims and Mitchells with five different squadrons, completing 52 ops. He died in Wellington in 1978.

Apart from Marshall and Scott, three others in the group were decorated. Peter McLaren, Punch Marusich and Keith Street all won DFMs. McLaren was killed when his bomber crashed into the North Sea, shot down by a night fighter in 1941. The other two survived the war. Marusich flew with 75 Squadron then went to the Middle East with 37 Squadron. He was hit by shellfire while attacking a Libyan airfield on the night of 5 September 1941. According to his citation, though 'suffering severely from pain and loss of blood, [he] made light of his injuries', thus permitting the rest of the crew to get on with the bombing run. Repatriated in May 1942, he served as a gunnery instructor in New Zealand until 1946. He died in 1987.

Street, who flew with 44 Squadron like Bracegirdle, was given an immediate DFM for his part in a low-altitude night attack on the battle cruisers *Scharnhorst* and *Gneisenau* at Brest in March 1941. While his pilot defied intense flak and blinding searchlights to plant a bomb on one of the ships, Street, under gunner on the fragile Hampden, laid into the searchlights, destroying many of them with streams of machine-gun fire. He later flew on a 90 Squadron Fortress, one of the few New Zealanders to do so while the RAF was evaluating the American aircraft, and then flew a tour on Stirlings with 199 Squadron before returning to New Zealand. He died in 1994.

Ian Walker came back to New Zealand on a hospital ship just before Christmas 1943, repatriated from a German POW camp two years after he had ended up in a Belgian field with a shattered leg. He earned the right to wear the coveted Battle of Britain Clasp by flying 15 night missions in 600 Squadron Blenheims trying to destroy German aircraft around London. But even when the plane's primitive radar latched on to enemy machines the Blenheim was too slow to catch them. At the end of 1940 Walker went north with 600 to Yorkshire, for rest, conversion to Beaufighters and radar training. 'It's silly, looking back on it,' he says, 'but a group of us got fed up not doing anything and decided we would transfer to bombers.'

Walker's application to join Bomber Command was approved, and after converting to Wellingtons he found himself at Marham, Norfolk, with 115 Squadron. His first op — to Wilhemshaven — was on Anzac Day 1941. By the time he crashed in Belgium he had flown 15 ops — half a tour. Mannheim turned out to be his final mission, in early August. The bomber never reached its target. An engine that had caused problems from takeoff failed, and the RAF pilot ordered the bombs dropped on what looked like a bridge over the River Rhine and then turned for home. Walker recounts:

We flew on, having gone down to perhaps 3000 feet to avoid the lights. Everything seemed to be set for a journey back on one engine until suddenly I heard front gunner Ted Lambert calling agitatedly for someone to open the bulkhead door behind his turret and let him out. The pilot hadn't said that anything was wrong but I could hear Ted shouting. The next thing I knew we hit the ground . . . suddenly just a rending crunch and we were down.

The Wellington had crashed through the tops of tall trees and onto a field. The front turret was smashed off on impact and rolled 50 yards with Lambert still inside. He emerged without a scratch and raced round to the rear to check Walker. The New Zealander screwed his turret round manually, opened its doors and got out. For a few seconds he didn't realise he'd been hurt, but he fell over as he tried to stand and felt excruciating pain in his left leg. Shattered bones penetrated the flesh — a compound fracture.

Nearby villagers carried Walker and the unconscious navigator to their homes. They had no option but to call the Germans, and the two men were taken to hospital in Louvain. There an Austrian doctor, who whispered one day that he was not a Nazi, looked after Walker superbly, setting the smashed bones and applying plaster. The gunner was cared for by the hospital nuns for several weeks before being transferred to a Brussels hospital and finally, after a bad spell in an Antwerp prison, to a POW camp in Germany.

One day early in his camp stay he was examined by Red Cross staff, who found his leg hadn't healed well, and his name was put on a list for repatriation. Months later, still in captivity, he decided the limb had improved enough for him and a British soldier to seize a chance to escape. They made a successful break one afternoon, melting into nearby woods. Sleeping by day and walking by night they made 60 miles west in seven days, heading for Belgium. Then the soldier became ill and Walker's leg started playing up. They surrendered.

Though Walker was now a classified escaper his name was still on the repat list and the Germans let him go with other sick and wounded in late 1943. The party was taken by train south through France to Marseilles, on to Barcelona by ship, and transferred to a freighter that took them across the Mediterranean to Egypt. There they boarded the hospital ship *Oranjes* for the trip home.

When he got out of the air force, Walker took up an adult apprenticeship in furniture upholstery and worked in this field until he retired. Today he lives in Mairangi Bay, on Auckland's North Shore — one of the lucky ones who had another 60 years. He doesn't really mind that his left leg still aches sometimes.

The toll of war

The 19 deaths among James Bracegirdle's draft of 36 amounted to a 53 per cent loss — an unexceptional figure. Another four of the men on the *Akaroa* spent long years in POW camps. Many other drafts of young aircrew volunteers suffered similarly. Those who died are listed here as one small example of the sacrifice a generation made.

Some of the dead changed trades after leaving New Zealand, retraining — or 'remustering' — to become navigators or bomb aimers. Those for whom no trade is given were killed as gunners with Bomber Command. The 19 are listed in order of date of death.

1940

14 August **Sgt John Edward Fuller, 24 (Wellington).** 15 OTU, Harwell, Berkshire. Wellington. Killed in a training crash at the mouth of the Bristol Channel. Commemorated on the Runnymede Memorial, at Runnymede, Surrey.

21–22 August **Sgt Jack Stephen Brennan, 22 (Auckland).** Battle of Britain Clasp. 23 Sqn, Fighter Command, Wittering, Northamptonshire. Struck and killed by a landing aircraft while on flare-path duty. Buried at Wittering, Cambridgeshire (formerly Huntingdonshire).

1–2 September **Sgt Thomas Chamberlain Molineux Browne, 19 (Featherston)**. 37 Sqn, Feltwell, Norfolk. Wellington. Killed on fifth op. His aircraft apparently crashed in the sea on the way home from a raid on Hanover. Commemorated at Runnymede.

6–7 September **Sgt James Bracegirdle, 21 (Auckland)**. 44 Sqn, Waddington, Lincolnshire. Hampden. Killed on eighth op. Shot down over Germany while returning from a raid on Krefeld. Buried in Reichswald Forest Cemetery, Germany.

8 September **Sgt John Bernard Philpott, 30 (Wellington)**. 82 Sqn, Watton, Norfolk. Blenheim. Aircraft lost without trace on a cross-Channel photographic reconnaissance flight. Commemorated at Runnymede.

23–24 September **Sgt Alfred Frederick Blatch, 26 (Te Anau)**. 83 Sqn, Scampton, Lincolnshire. Hampden. Killed on 10th op. Shot down by flak on raid to Berlin. Buried in Becklingen War Cemetery, Germany.

8 October **Sgt Robert Bett Mirk Young, 22 (Palmerston North)**. Battle of Britain Clasp. 264 Sqn, Fighter Command, detachment at Northolt, Middlesex. Defiant. Crashed on a night patrol over England. May have been shot down by an enemy aircraft. Buried at Northwood, near Northolt, Middlesex.

28–29 October **Sgt Arthur Fraser Dallas, 22 (Hunterville)**. 105 Sqn, Watton, Norfolk. Navigator. Blenheim. Killed on 15th op. Crashed in England on return from a raid on Mannheim. Buried at Great Bircham, Norfolk.

22–23 December **Sgt Alfred Henry Ritchie, 22 (Auckland)**. 75 (NZ) Sqn, Feltwell, Norfolk. Wellington. Killed on seventh op. Brought down over France during a raid on Mannheim. Buried at Therouldville, France.

1941
10–11 May **Sgt Eric Russell Lucas, 26 (Waitara)**. 15 Sqn, Wyton, Huntingdonshire. Stirling. Killed on 29th op. Shot down over the Netherlands by a night fighter during a raid on Berlin. Commemorated at Runnymede, Surrey. (His body and the remains of other crewmen were recovered by a Dutch team from the buried wreckage of the aircraft in late 2003 and buried at Opmeer, near the crash site, in May 2004.)

23 May **Pilot Officer Stuart Charles Niven, 25 (Wellington)**. 45 Sqn, Fuka, Egypt. Middle East Air Force. Navigator. Blenheim. Lost during a raid on Crete. Commemorated at El Alamein, Egypt.

28 May **Sgt Gerald Bruce Johnson, 21 (Auckland)**. Battle of Britain Clasp. 23 Sqn, Fighter Command, Ford, Sussex. Havoc. Crashed during mock dogfight near Manston airfield. Buried at Clymping, Sussex.

26–27 June **Sgt Peter Victor McLaren, 21 (Auckland)**. DFM. 97 Sqn, Coningsby, Lincolnshire. Manchester. Killed on 33rd op. Crashed in the North Sea off Germany during a raid on Kiel. Commemorated at Runnymede.

22 July **Sgt Ivan Norton Robinson, 20 (Auckland)**. Battle of Britain Clasp. 96 Sqn, Fighter Command, detachment at Squires Gate, Lancashire. Defiant. Crashed near Chester during a night-flying test. Buried at Byley, Cheshire.

1942

10–11 January **Sgt Harry Chapman Downs, 22 (Wellington).** 82 Sqn, Watton, Norfolk. Navigator. Blenheim. Shot down by flak during an intruder raid over the Netherlands. Buried at Oud Leusden, the Netherlands.

19–20 May **Flight Sgt Leslie Plimmer Russell, 25 (Marton).** Battle of Britain Clasp. 35 Sqn, Linton, Yorkshire. Halifax. Killed on a raid to Mannheim on his 82nd op, 73 of them on Defiants with 264 Sqn. Buried in Durnbach War Cemetery, Germany.

28–29 July **Flight Sgt Alan Campbell, 22 (Hawera).** Battle of Britain Clasp. 75 (NZ) Sqn, Feltwell, Norfolk. Bomb aimer. Wellington. Killed on 52nd op. Crashed in Germany during a raid on Hamburg the night 33 New Zealanders died — the most of any night or day of the war. Buried in Becklingen War Cemetery.

13–14 September **Pilot Officer Patrick Aylmer Vivian, 21 (Christchurch).** 1654 Conversion Unit, Wigsley, Nottinghamshire. Navigator. Lancaster. Killed on 32nd op. Shot down over the Netherlands during a raid on Bremen. Had previously completed a tour with 83 Sqn on Hampdens. Buried at Nieuwehorne, the Netherlands.

5–6 December **Flight Lieutenant Robert Ian McChesney, 29 (Auckland).** Battle of Britain Clasp. 488 Sqn, RNZAF, Fighter Command, Ayr, Ayrshire. Navigator. Beaufighter. Killed on 94th op. 71 ops as a gunner on Blenheims and Defiants. Killed when two of the squadron's aircraft collided while on exercise in Scotland. Buried at Ayr, Ayrshire.

Out of fuel and down in the sea

Flying to Italy in the early stages of the war was not for the faint-hearted. Turin, Milan, Genoa — the big-city targets in the north — involved long, tiring, dangerous trips, mostly in Whitleys. The Alps barred the way, and foul weather, primitive navigation aids and fuel problems contributed to the loss of many aircraft. Whitleys were poorly heated, and crews suffered cruelly from the cold.

Bomber Command first sent aircraft to Italy on the night of 11–12 June 1940, a day after Italy had declared war on Britain. Thirty-six Whitleys took off for Turin but only 23 even reached Italy, and just nine delivered their bombs. One crashed in France while homebound, its crew perishing.

The first New Zealander killed on operations to Italy was pilot Ian Parsons, 27 (Christchurch), his 10 Squadron Whitley hit by a night fighter over Turin on the night of 13–14 August 1940. He nursed his damaged aircraft back to the English coast but while trying to make an emergency landing on a Kent beach crashed a mile offshore and died. His body washed ashore in France.

In November 1940 two 77 Squadron Whitleys captained by New Zealanders ditched on return from Italy, both out of fuel. Hugh Miller and Rob Bagnall joined 77 at Linton-on-Ouse, Yorkshire, at the height of the Battle of Britain. The day he reached Linton still sticks in Miller's mind. He spent all day on a train that stopped countless times as it chugged north. 'I was dead tired when I reached the base but I flew on ops that night because they were so short of crew. We bombed invasion barges at Calais.'

Miller, a teacher at a Hamilton boys' school before the war, was granted an RAF short-service commission in 1939 and reached England three days before the outbreak of war. He flew 10 ops as a second pilot with 77, the most memorable to Krefeld, on the outskirts of the Ruhr Valley, with a pilot who dived to avoid searchlights.

'When we flattened out we were at 30 feet. It was absolutely terrifying. The aircraft was right down among the chimneys. I don't know why we didn't get written off. I've been back to Krefeld since and I'm horrified at the thought of what we did.'

Miller also flew a trip with 77's commanding officer, Ashburton-born Wing Commander Geoff Jarman, who'd joined the RAF in 1930 and was to become an air commodore later in the war.

I went to Berlin with Jarman. We got into some real flak over the city and were diving around . . . a shocking trip . . . I was in the nose and a small piece of flak came through my window and I went up and said to the skipper, "Hey, you know this is getting a bit rough", at which he pointed to a big hole in his windscreen. A piece of flak had come through, hit his glove and gone on and landed on the navigator's table. It was still smoking . . . We got out of it all right and got back. I learned an awful lot from him that night.'

Miller made his first flight as a Whitley captain in late October 1940, and then on Guy Fawkes Night took off for Turin. He sat in his pilot's seat for 12 hours and 50 minutes, numbed by the cold and worried all the way home about their location. Few aircraft did longer trips in World War II.

'As we flew back the bad weather turned appalling and we knew later the wind pushed us to the east. We couldn't see the ground and the radio wasn't functioning so we couldn't get bearings or fixes. We had nothing — not a thing.'

As the hours wore on Miller and his navigator realised they had no idea where they were. When they finally emerged over water and spotted islands as the sky began to lighten, they reckoned they had found the Channel Islands, out from France's Cherbourg peninsula. In fact they were Dutch islands, far to the northeast. Instead of crossing the Channel they were flying straight up the

North Sea, next stop the Arctic Circle. But they didn't know that then and were hopelessly lost. Come dawn they could see nothing but ocean rollers.

'Finally I said, "Let's turn northwest and see if we hit something that way." That's what got us home. Otherwise we'd have been down in the North Sea and no one would have known where we were.'

The fuel should have run out but Miller kept finding a little more in the tanks and still the motors purred. The crew threw out everything moveable to lighten the load. It was the rear gunner, kicking out the back door in readiness for ditching, who spotted a little vessel on the heaving sea. None of his crewmates believed him but as the Whitley wheeled they all saw it.

Miller made an amazing landing near the craft, a navy patrol boat, touching down perfectly in waves up to 10 feet high. A wall of water washed over the Whitley as she hit but the pilot had got her down tail first. Nose first and she would have gone straight under. The second pilot and the other three crew, all at ditching stations aft, got the dinghy out and made it safely aboard the patrol boat. Miller escaped through the hatch directly above his seat, walked down the top of the fuselage and stepped onto the little craft without getting his feet wet. Picked up by a larger vessel a short time later, the airmen learned they had ditched just outside a minefield off England's northeast coast.

Two weeks later, Rob Bagnall had a similar experience which ended in tragedy. He was the only survivor. Recording in his log what happened on 23–24 November 1940, he wrote simply, 'Alighted on sea, shortage of petrol.' Later, before he died in Auckland in 1996 at the age of 85, he wrote a fuller account.

Bagnall flew his Whitley to a field in Norfolk on the afternoon of take-off to reduce the flight time to Turin and top up with petrol. 'I watched the refuelling carefully to see that all tanks were quite full.' Deep into French airspace, Bagnall lifted the bomber to 17,000 feet to clear the Alps but was already anxious. 'We had not seen Geneva when we expected to, and if we were not lost, at least we were not sure exactly where we were ... we saw nothing of the Alps . . . when the navigator said we should be safely over we came down and looked hopefully for some help in the way of better visibility, searchlights or AA fire.'

They found a large, lit-up town beneath them just when they should have been over Turin. They flew east to look for the Po River, which should have been there but wasn't. Then west, only to find water. 'Obviously our navigation, using forecast winds which we had been unable to check, was sadly out and we were on the west coast of Italy.' Bagnall guessed they were over Genoa, but they had no maps detailed enough to make certain.

> We flew round and round the dock area at 2000 ft dropping flares and could see the docks and railways perfectly. No one fired a shot or took any notice of us. Three or four other aircraft were dropping flares too, and some of them dropped bombs . . . starting large fires. With such a long trip we couldn't spare much time so I thought "we can't all be mistaken", dropped my bombs in the same area and departed.

Homebound over the Alps the plane developed an engine fault, and Bagnall responded by cutting revs and flying slowly — at about 110 mph.

> We flew on and on for hours and when we reached our estimated time of arrival at the French coast we obtained some wireless fixes, but these disagreed so hopelessly with our dead reckoning position and with one another that we couldn't rely on them. Then the rear gunner thought he saw through the clouds that we had just left a coast behind us and were over sea. Another wireless fix tended to confirm this.

Bagnall drove the bomber, now desperately short of petrol, down through the clouds. They *were* over the sea. The wireless operator transmitted an SOS. On and on they flew, still with no sign of England. Fuel tanks empty, Bagnall turned on the navigation lights, spotted smoke ahead and landed in the water, one engine dead, half a mile from what turned out to be two naval launches. As he climbed out on top of the Whitley it was obvious something had gone badly wrong. The crew were splashing into the water without a dinghy.

> It was no time to ask why, so I yelled to them that there were ships not far away and devoted my energies to signalling with my torch. The ships approached within sight as the aircraft sank. For a moment or two I saw something of my crew in the water and then I was too busy trying to get rid of my boots and some of my heavy clothing.

Barely kept afloat by the inflatable collar on his parachute harness, Bagnall struck out for one of the launches, and after a few minutes was picked out by a searchlight. Now began a grim struggle for survival as he grabbed the lifebelt thrown to him.

> They tried to pull me aboard but I had over estimated the strength left in my hands — the water was very cold and I'd been flying for nearly 12 hours — and I slipped back into the sea. The next half hour was a sequence of nightmarish failures to get me aboard. The vessel had a freeboard of perhaps ten feet and was rolling violently. They had no small boat, the sea was too rough to allow any of the crew overboard, I was getting rather weak and with all my waterlogged clothes must have been very heavy indeed. Finally two boathooks caught firmly in my clothing and I was hauled aboard.

The other launch searched desperately but fruitlessly for Bagnall's crew. All four sergeants were lost. Bagnall learned he had been picked up in the Strait of Dover three miles from land. Petrol for another two minutes' flying would have put the Whitley on shore in Kent.

'Happy birthday, you old bastard'

Stirlings flying to Italy had their own particular problem — altitude. With petrol and bombs weighing them down, the four-engined aircraft had trouble getting above 13,000 feet — the height of the Alps. Most managed somehow. Some didn't and flew into mountainsides.

An exceptional navigator helped Nick Williamson safely over, or through, the mountains on the night of 23–24 October 1942. Williamson, a Gisborne man all his life, was to become a squadron leader and flight commander on 75 Squadron in 1944, but on this trip to Genoa he was still in the early stages of his first tour with 214. So were the other New Zealanders in his crew — navigator Archie Davis, bomb aimer Ron Florence and wireless operator Keith Neilson.

'Luck was on my side when I crewed up with Archie,' Williamson says.

> He was big and a big-hearted decent guy. I always wished I'd had a brother, and in Arch I virtually had one. He had sailed in the Hauraki Gulf and taught himself astro-navigation. He had marvellous star-recognition techniques, and with his astrograph he could tell me our location precisely if he could see a star. The two of us had a simple arrangement. He guaranteed to tell me where we were and where we had to go, and I guaranteed to fly his courses with absolute accuracy.'

Williamson had implicit faith in Davis, an Auckland accountant who, at 32, was eight years older and the granddaddy of the crew.

Williamson remembers Florence and Neilson fondly too, particularly the latter, a farmer from Waverley. 'He was a lovely guy, fearless, totally unflappable and innovative.' The flight engineer and mid-upper gunner were English, and the rear gunner was Rhodesian. Neilson was shot down with another 214 Squadron crew in 1943 and captured. Florence was the only one of the New Zealanders who didn't survive the war, losing his life with 617 Squadron in late 1943.

A snowstorm raged over the Alps the night they flew to Genoa, 50 Stirlings struggling to clear the peaks. 'We were at 13,100 feet and I couldn't see a thing,' recalls Williamson. 'I asked Arch for the height of the mountains and he said 13,300 feet. But he said there was a pass, fractionally over 13,000 feet, and he would lead us to it. Sure enough he did and we broke out into clear air on the other side.'

Flying home over France, the mountains behind them, Williamson heard the intercom click on. 'I thought, "Oh Jesus, here we go, night fighters." Instead it was "One, two, three — happy birthday to you, happy birthday to you, happy birthday, you old bastard, happy birthday to you."'

The crew had remembered Williamson's 24th birthday.

1941

DEAD RECKONING AND BLIND HOPE

1941

Late in 1940 the British government determined to smash Germany's industry and oil refineries, but Bomber Command simply didn't have the capacity to do so in 1941. The number of squadrons and aircraft had scarcely increased from a year earlier, and the Wellingtons, Hampdens, Whitleys and Blenheims were still inadequate for the job. Better aircraft were arriving but it would be some time before they could make a significant contribution. The Lancaster was still more than a year away from squadron operations.

Bomber Command continued to bleed squadrons to other theatres, notably the Middle East, and squadrons were routinely detached for Atlantic patrols from Coastal Command's southwest bases to help combat the U-boat menace. The attack on Germany was further weakened as Bomber Command was increasingly drawn into the offensive against the enemy's submarine bases on France's Atlantic coast, and the ports where submarines were built and assembled. The arrival in Brest at the end of March 1941 of the battle cruisers *Scharnhorst* and *Gneisenau*, joined later by the heavy cruiser *Prinz Eugen,* signalled the start of a long succession of raids which damaged the ships and confined them to port until their escape up the Channel in early 1942.

All this was vital work, but it meant Bomber Command could not get to grips with what it saw as its prime task — hitting Germany. When it did mount operations into the enemy homeland it was confronted by stiffening defences. In the early phases of the war Germany had no night fighters: just as the RAF didn't expect to be out in the dark, the Germans didn't expect to be bombed at night. German targets were well defended by flak batteries, but RAF bombers didn't have to contend with night fighters on an organised basis until the second half of 1940.

It's generally accepted that the first Bomber Command victim of a night-fighter attack was a 49 Squadron Hampden shot down on a mining operation near Sylt, in the German North Frisian Islands, on 25–26 April 1940. The bomber was claimed by the pilot of an Me 109 from a day-fighter unit which was, according to *Bomber Command War Diaries*, 'scattered along the German coast in small detachments to act as night fighters'.

It wasn't until June 1940 that the first designated night-fighter unit was formed, but thereafter the night-fighter group expanded quickly to meet the threat of Britain's bombers. It blossomed into a major arm of the Luftwaffe, with hundreds of fighters employed in the defence of Germany. By the start of 1941 it had several operational units, each more than 140 strong. The Luftwaffe's biggest and most important base was built from scratch at Venlo, in Holland, and opened by March of that year. On the Dutch–German border, it lay virtually on the bombers' route to the Ruhr Valley, and its aircraft made an incalculable number of kills.

Night fighters claimed about 40 bombers in 1940 — 15 per cent of Bomber Command's losses to enemy action. The following year the numbers rose sharply to 420 bombers and 55 per cent, and continued to rise.

German night-fighter forces were led by the dynamic Josef Kammhuber, who established a line of searchlight, flak and radar stations from Denmark to southern Holland, a defensive barrier that became known as the Kammhuber Line. Bomber Command crews had good reason to fear the defences they had to cross on their way to targets in the enemy's heartland. The night-fighter war, the development of German defences, British countertactics and the technological advances and wizardry on both sides are fascinating subjects that have been explored in many books.

The first of Britain's four-engined heavies began to make their presence felt in 1941. The giant Stirling was delivered to 7 Squadron in August 1940, followed in November by the Halifax. However, continuing technical problems with the new breeds of big aircraft took months to overcome and, coupled with the slowdown in operations during the harsh winter of 1940–41, delayed their bombing debuts until 1941. 7 Squadron's Stirlings flew their first raid on 10–11 February, and 35 Squadron unveiled the Halifaxes on ops a month later. The Halifaxes' debut ended tragically when one was shot down by an RAF fighter over the Hampshire–Surrey border coming back from Le Havre.

The twin-engined Manchester, first flown operationally by 207 Squadron in late February 1941, was bedevilled by its two unreliable Rolls-Royce Vulture engines and ended up on the scrap heap of aviation history, a failure. But with four Rolls-Royce Merlins and other modifications, Avro's brilliant designer, Roy Chadwick, performed the fairy godmother's pumpkin–gold-coach trick, turning a dud into the Lancaster. The bomber *par excellence* began arriving at 44 Squadron at Scampton in late December 1941.

Early production of Stirlings and Halifaxes was agonisingly slow and well short of target levels. But that was only one of Bomber Command's worries in 1941. Bravely, the crews did their best but many still found it difficult to reach and identify their targets, and when they did much of their bombing was still ineffective. Damage to industrial plants and important railway junctions was frequently slight and quickly repaired.

Crew shortages continued to hamstring operations. The scarcity of navigators was brought home to RNZAF pilot 'Tinny' Constance when he joined 408 Squadron in mid-1941. The Canadian unit was still waiting for its Hampdens, so Constance was shuffled off to 83 Squadron for some action. The commander there told him, 'You'll have to do two trips as a navigator.' Given three days to nut out the intricacies of a new and baffling craft, Constance was then ordered to find his way to Kiel on a night operation. He watched the runway disappear, directions ringing in his ears: 'Before you get there, you'll see the canal. Kiel's on the left . . .'

Somehow Constance guided his skipper to the target and back despite a flak shell which blew out the cockpit windows and carried his navigation papers out of the aircraft, leaving him a pencil and a weather report written on thick cardboard. When they landed the pilot ordered, 'Get all your gear, your maps, your log, that sort of thing. We've got to go to debriefing.' Constance confessed he had nothing. The pilot squinted at him and said, 'I *thought* you were guessing.'

New Zealander Keith Beattie, who went on his first operational flight as second pilot on a 115 Squadron Wellington in September 1941, remembers the horrors of his fifth op, to Nuremberg, the following month — the second 'major' raid on Nazidom's citadel. The mission should have taken about seven-and-a-half hours. Instead, Beattie's Wellington landed back in England, desperately short of fuel, nine hours and 20 minutes after takeoff. Icing, thick cloud and strong, unpredicted winds had caused havoc.

We flew in cloud, couldn't see the ground and couldn't take a star sighting by sextant. It was all dead reckoning and blind hope. We eventually found a target when some flak came up, sometime after our ETA at Nuremberg. There's a note in my logbook which says 'Bombed Mannheim', but I'd say that was just a guess. Anyway, we set off for home and when daylight came up we were still over land, which turned out to be France. We started to see other aircraft, late getting back like us. The wireless operator told us England was saying 'Just keep going, keep going.' Some aircraft turned back thinking they were over Ireland or the Irish Sea or the west coast of England. That's where we might have been on the length of time we had been flying. A lot of aircraft thought they'd overshot and turned around. But we kept going. We were just about out of gas when we landed.

Bomber Command War Diaries says only three groups of bombs landed on Nuremberg, injuring six people.

Beattie's Wellington often carried empty beer bottles. So did many other aircraft in the early days. 'They made a bit of a whistling noise when going down from a great height. The belief was the Jerries would think they were being bombed and start shooting. I think it was an old wives' tale but we shovelled them out when we didn't know where we were to try to stir things up.'

It was all hit and miss. Crews decided their own courses, flew at a height that suited them, and pretty much did their own thing. Bomber Command sent crews here, there and everywhere on the same night. As a result, damage to German targets was sometimes light, even non-existent. The practice of concentrating bombers on one target in one stream on a set course at a set height was yet to come. In 1941, crew reports of bombing success often bore no relationship to reality. Crews with faint hearts dropped their bombs short of the target and returned to base. Some off-loaded in the North Sea, stooged around to make up the mileage and then flew home. Even dedicated crews — and they were a majority — who pressed on to the target were never sure where their bombs went. The programme to install cameras in every aircraft to take automatic photographs of bomb loads exploding proceeded slowly.

Growing concern about the accuracy of the bombing campaign led to a detailed analysis in mid-July of bombing photographs. The disturbing conclusions in the famous Butt report of August 1941 shocked everyone. The summary showed that of those aircraft recorded as attacking their targets, only one in three got within five miles. Over Germany the proportion was one in four; over the Ruhr in particular it was one in 10. Doubts were voiced in high places as to the wisdom of the bombing offensive against Germany, but there was no other option and the air chiefs held firm. However, disastrous losses during a raid on Berlin on 7–8 November and the onset of winter led Churchill to order a slowdown in bombing until new navigation aids and Lancasters appeared.

The ice saved their lives

George Hedge owes his life to the thick ice on Holland's Ijsselmeer, formerly the Zuider Zee, when he crashed there on the night of 10 February 1941 — and swapping places with a fellow crewman. In summer the aircraft would probably have plunged straight to the seabed. Instead, nose down and trailing flames after a fighter attack, it hit the frozen surface, bounced high, then smashed down and slithered over the ice for three or four miles before dragging to a stop.

The New Zealander had taken over as wireless operator after changing places with Glyn 'Taffy' Reardon so the Welshman could man the front guns. The two men were both wireless operators/air gunners and shared duties. Reardon was the only fatality on the Wellington, perhaps killed by German gunfire but certainly trapped and crushed as the front turret shattered and compacted in the hard landing.

Born in 1920, Hedge was odds-on to become a wireless operator in the RNZAF. He had joined New Zealand Railways in 1936 and even though he worked in stores had had to learn Morse code. When war came he joined up almost immediately, early enough to be among the first intake at Weraroa, near Levin, in January 1940. Then he was plucked out of the wireless school at Wigram in July 1940 as New Zealand answered an urgent call from Britain for wireless operators, especially those who could teach the craft.

He was soon in England, posted first to 75 Squadron and then to 40 at Wyton, Cambridgeshire. Wyton was hit by flu in late autumn 1940, and Hedge flew on operations as a spare on Wellingtons to replace sick aircrew. On his first trip, in late

October, the squadron dropped bombs by night on invasion barges in Antwerp. Hedge sat in the front turret manning the twin machine-guns. He'd done no gunnery training but by watching and listening had learned to use the weapons. 'I never fired a gun on the ground but I did in the air. Don't forget these were early days. The RAF was really just getting under way.'

Posted next to 15 Squadron, Hedge crewed up with Bill Garrioch, a volunteer from Dublin. Second pilot Bill Jordan was English, as was navigator Bill Beioley. Reardon and a Scot, rear gunner, Jock Hall, completed the crew. Garrioch, Beioley and Reardon had already flown 12 hazardous ops together on Blenheims. The six sergeants worked well as a team and by the time they were shot down had bombed Antwerp, Leeuwarden (a major German air base in Holland), Hanover and Hamburg. Hedge had manned the guns several times but on their last op Garrioch okayed Reardon's request to switch places with Hedge.

They were homebound from Hanover again when they were attacked over Holland just before midnight. Hedge remembers:

> We were well on the way, stooging along at about 10,000 feet, when Jock shouted suddenly, 'Fighter, right on our tail.' The moment he got the words out the port motor was hit and went up in flames. Shells flew down the fuselage. One went by the top of my head, blowing up the transmitter in front of me and hitting the armour plate behind Bill's seat. Another cannon shell almost severed one of Jock's legs in the turret.

In his combat report, Walter Ehle, the German night-fighter pilot who shot them down and was to prove the nemesis of a number of New Zealanders in the years ahead, said he had spotted the Wellington below him in the moonlight while patrolling around a radio beacon at 11.35 p.m. He had dropped his Me 110 down to the bomber's level and closed in from behind. 'When I was at about a distance of fifty metres, I was fired on by the rear gunner. I then gave a short burst of fire and shot the left engine of the aircraft [setting it] on fire . . . the firing of the rear gunner stopped. The Englishman pushed off in a steep glide to the Zuider Zee.' Ehle reported firing 560 machine-gun rounds and 100 cannon shells.

Inside the smoke-filled Wellington, Garrioch sent Beioley back to prise Hall out of his smashed turret while Jordan opened the forward escape hatch and tried to get Reardon out of the front turret. The Welshman, probably hit, was moaning feebly.

Port motor and wing flaming, the bomber lost altitude. Hedge, standing alongside the pilot and clinging to the instrument panel, says the crew knew they were over the Ijsselmeer but didn't realise it was frozen. 'Bill levelled out and said he would try to pancake. Then we hit nose down and she bounced, 30 or 40 feet perhaps, and came down on her belly. I remember watching the props bending under as we crashed, and I don't mind admitting I prayed.' The impact tore the bomb bay doors off, crushed the underside fuselage and killed Reardon — if he wasn't already dead. The bomber didn't explode but skidded several miles across the glazed 30-inch-thick surface before sliding to a halt on thinner ice, burning furiously. Water and chunks of ice began flooding in through the escape hatch in the floor.

The crew got the badly injured Hall up and through the cockpit escape exit and lowered him to the ice. They failed in their desperate efforts to break into the front turret to get to Reardon, who wasn't moving. The aircraft was sinking nose first as it burned, melting the ice around it. Unable to reach the Welshman, the survivors backed away as the plane blazed and ammunition exploded.

Now the five men, one of them with a leg hanging by a thread, were alone on the ice. Their heavy fur-lined flying suits and boots would save their lives in the sub-zero temperatures, but they couldn't stay where they were. Garrioch used his scarf as a tourniquet on Hall's leg while the others wrapped the injured gunner in a parachute and used a chute harness to pull him along.

They set off, one man walking in front to test the ice. The strong wind whipped up icy spindrift, making progress difficult. Scott-of-the-Antarctic stuff. They stumbled on for hours, a glimmer of light in the far distance their only guide. At one point they came across an open channel cut by an icebreaker. 'We had fun and games trying to drag ice floes together so we could get across to the other side,' Hedge says. 'It took us about an hour.'

As a wintry dawn broke, the bedraggled little party neared shore, where the ice turned to slush. The waiting Germans finally sent out a small boat to pick them up, and an ambulance arrived for Hall. 'Jock never really lost consciousness. He was warm inside his suit and parachute, and the chute kept him off the ice. Just the same, I think the cold froze him up, helped stop the bleeding.' Hall's leg was amputated below the knee by German doctors, and 18 months after the crash he was repatriated. The other four faced four long years in prison camp.

In 1967, a farmer turning a field in East Flevoland, a polder reclaimed from the Ijsselmeer, hit something hard with his plough. He investigated and found he had struck the tip of an aircraft's tail fin. The Royal Netherlands Air Force uncovered the wreck and from serial numbers easily identified it as the Wellington flown by Bill Garrioch and his crew. The remains of Taffy Reardon, still in the aircraft, were recovered and buried with due ceremony in a Dutch military cemetery.

Father and son — casualties of war

When he sailed for the Western Front in 1917, Alexander Mee, a private in 2 Battalion, Otago Regiment, carried a pair of handsome hairbrushes in his kit. On each brush was a silver shield bearing the engraved legend 'AM 23.2.17'. Mee was killed on 12 October that year, cut down at Passchendaele.

His name is on the Tyne Cot Memorial to the Missing, one of many New Zealanders recorded there. Before he went to war, Mee had married Jessie Coutts, who came from a farming community north of Dunedin. His new wife was pregnant when he bade her farewell, and she bore a son just eight days after he fell. She eventually remarried but died in 1929, and Alexander Coutts Mee was then brought up by his maternal grandmother.

A bright youngster, he was educated at Otago Boys' High School, joined the Civil Reserve of Pilots in 1939, enlisted in the RNZAF in February 1940 and learned to fly at Taieri and Wigram before sailing for Britain eight months later — taking with him his father's hairbrushes. He trained on Wellingtons in Scotland and was then posted to 75 Squadron. He was happy. Among his few surviving letters is one he wrote on 7 April 1941:

> I am now with the New Zealand bomber squadron and it's the best there is. Absolute minimum of rot like parades and clean buttons. Just suits me down to the ground. So far I have done only two raids but hope to get a lot more in soon . . . Well, I have an appointment with some German docks so must away and get ready.

Mee was flying with fellow New Zealander David Nola, who at 26 was three years older. Nola was the eldest child of a hard-working Dalmatian couple farming at Tatuanui, near Morrinsville, where some of the family still live. Ivan Nola arrived in New Zealand around 1900 and worked on the gumfields around Dargaville until he had saved enough to go home to find a bride. Ivan and Kate Nola returned to New Zealand about 1912, and four years later bought the property at Tatuanui. They were a novelty, the only Dalmatians in the district.

David Nola spoke no English when he started at the local school but soon picked it up and eventually taught his father to read. When he was 11 he took the train to Hamilton every day to attend school and then boarded at Auckland's Sacred Heart College for four years. After that he did a year at university and worked on the side, emerging as a fully fledged accountant. Not long before the war he joined the Audit Department in Wellington, and in his spare time learned to fly at Rongotai, the capital's airfield in the southern suburbs. He volunteered as soon as war broke out and two months later was training as a pilot.

Mee flew his first op with 75 Squadron on 12 March 1941, quickly learning how things could go wrong. Six days later he had to parachute over England after a raid on Kiel with a skipper called Collins. Something must have gone radically wrong with their navigator's reckoning because when the crew abandoned their aircraft they were near Leeds, Yorkshire, half the country away from Feltwell, Norfolk, and probably out of fuel.

It was after this unnerving experienced that Mee joined Nola as his back-up pilot, and together the two men flew to Berlin on the night of 9–10 April. A newspaper photographer took a picture of 75 Squadron aircrew togged up for the mission, some already in the back of the crew truck. 'Berlin Boys' the caption said when the photograph was published. 'Here are some of the RAF flyers who battered the centre of Berlin for three hours . . .' Nola sent a copy to Tatuanui with arrows and names scrawled on the page to indicate his crew.

They got back safely that night, but less than a month later all but one of them were dead. On 6–7 May the Nola–Mee Wellington was one of 115 aircraft detailed to attack Hamburg. Stronger winds than forecast evidently drove the bomber off course on its homeward run, for its position was pinpointed off the mouth of the River Humber just before 5.00 a.m. The plane turned south for Feltwell but then struck one, maybe two, steel cables on barrage balloons and plunged into the sea near Trinity Sands, a few miles from Grimsby — the only Bomber Command loss that night. The RAF rear gunner was the sole survivor. Nola had completed at least 16 ops; Mee was on his eighth. Both New Zealanders are buried at Grimsby.

The heirloom brushes were again returned to New Zealand with a dead man's effects. Mee's cousin, Ronald Mulligan, who also became a wartime pilot, has them now at his home at Waikanae. They were given to him in 1943 by his grandmother when he visited her on final leave. 'She formally presented them to me. I took them and I still have them, but given their history and given also that even in 1943 the way ahead might not be without hazard, I thought it best to leave them at home for when I got back.'

Jimmy Ward, VC:
the man who fought a fire on a wing

The day Jimmy Ward took off on his final flight from an English air base, the Chief of Air Staff (CAS) in New Zealand approved a proposal to bring the Victoria Cross winner home. Documents in Ward's file in Archives New Zealand show that on 12 September 1941 the New Zealand liaison officer at the Air Ministry in London suggested to Wellington that 'you might consider his return to New Zealand for employment under [the] Empire Training Scheme. Suggest his presence in New Zealand would be useful propaganda and might assist recruiting. Would appreciate your comments.'

CAS Air Commodore Hugh Saunders, RAF, wrote on the message: 'Discuss with Air Ministry and if they are prepared to release Ward we will have Ward back. He can be employed in a GR [General Reconnaissance] squadron or on one of the AT [Advanced Training] squadrons.' He added his initials and the date — 15 September 1941. A message was transmitted to London at 9.30 p.m. telling the liaison officer to discuss the proposal with the Ministry and saying 'if Ward can be released posting here can be arranged. Advise result discussion.'

Ward surely would not have known such a plan existed, but had he done he would almost certainly have rejected it out of hand. He had done nine flights as a second pilot, had just been given command of his own crew and aircraft on 75 Squadron and had flown one successful trip to Brest as captain. It's hard to imagine he would have wanted to do anything other than continue operations. He wasn't the sort of character to take an easy option like a return to New Zealand.

But such considerations are academic. Ward and his crew flew from Feltwell, Norfolk, at 7.45 that night bound for Hamburg. Their Wellington was set alight by a night fighter on the outskirts of the city after they had dropped their bombs, and went down in flames. The Canadian navigator and English front gunner were the only two who jumped. The other four, including Ward, were killed.

It has often been written that Ward's bomber was hit by flak over the target, but after the war the Canadian, Lloyd Peterson, made an official statement to the authorities in which he said the plane had been caught by searchlights just as the bombs were being released.

There was no flak so we knew there were night fighters. About 15–20 miles out of Hamburg a night fighter attacked. One member of the crew, Sgt Gordon Sloman, RAF, second pilot, saw the fighter, which . . . attacked from port with cannon and .303 [sic]. Aircraft was immediately a mass of flames and Sgt Ward . . . was hit but how badly I do not know. I also got hit in the left hip, and opened the door for [the] front gunner, and he and I baled out by parachute. While I was coming down I saw the aircraft go down and hit the ground, in flames. The Germans claim that four bodies were in the aircraft.

After the war an MREU exhumed several bodies in Hamburg's Ohlsdorf Cemetery and positively identified Ward's remains. His body was reinterred in the same cemetery.

Ward perished barely two months after he had won the Commonwealth's highest gallantry decoration, the first of three New Zealand airmen to be awarded the VC in World War II. The others were Leonard Trent, also of Bomber Command, and Lloyd Trigg, killed sinking a submarine while flying a 200 Squadron Liberator from a West African base in August 1943. Ward was to have had the medal pinned on his breast by King George on 23 September 1941. Instead, it was presented later to his parents in Wanganui.

Ward's astonishing act of bravery on the night of 7–8 July when he was flying as second pilot to Canadian Ben Widdowson is almost beyond comprehension. Thousands of feet over Holland's Ijsselmeer, he climbed out onto the wing of a Wellington to try to extinguish a fire started by a night fighter. Homebound from Munster, the Wimpy was attacked from below by an Me 110. The fighter raked the plane with fire but as it swept past it filled 19-year-old New Zealand rear gunner Allan Box's gun sight and he got a long burst into it. The Messerschmitt rolled on its back and disappeared, but cannon shells and incendiaries had wrought major damage.

'We were pretty badly shot up,' navigator Joe Lawton, 22 at the time, recalled in 1991. 'The starboard engine was damaged, the hydraulics went, the bomb doors flapped open, the wireless and intercom were shot out and wireless operator, Taffy Evans, was wounded.' Smoke filled the plane and flames, fed by petrol from a fractured line, spurted near the starboard engine, threatening to engulf the entire wing. 'The fighter was gone but it looked to me as if we might blow up at any moment. We had to try to do something about that fire. Ward and I chopped a hole in the fuselage over the wing and used the fire extinguisher, even threw out coffee. Of course nothing worked. The wind whipped everything away.'

Widdowson, nursing the aircraft over the Dutch coast out over the North Sea, ordered the crew to don parachutes. Ward had other ideas. 'I think I might be able to do something about that fire,' he told Lawton, an Aucklander. When he explained what he proposed Lawton was aghast, but Ward was determined. He squeezed through the astrodome, the aircraft's dinghy line tied round his waist. Half stuffed into his jacket was a canvas engine cover with which he planned to smother the fire. Lawton had at least persuaded him to wear his parachute.

As the howling wind clawed at Ward, the young pilot kicked holes in the aircraft's tough fabric skin for hand and foot holds and gradually worked his way down the fuselage to the wing three feet below. Then he was lying flat on the wing, feet securely in holes he had punched, hands gripping metalwork and other holes. Once the wind threw him back against the fuselage but his feet held.

The official war history quotes Ward himself: 'It was just a matter of getting something to hold on to. It was like being in a terrific gale only worse than any gale I've ever known.' He tried to shove the cover down through a hole torn by one of the fighter's shells to smother the leaking pipe and fire. But the wind kept lifting him up and the cover nearly dragged him off the wing. He tried again and finally managed to stuff the cover down into the hole, only to see it blown back out and whisked away before he could seize it.

'After that there was nothing to do but get back,' the history records. 'This was worse than going out as Ward was now almost exhausted. The navigator kept a strain on the rope as Ward slowly pulled himself along the wing and up the fuselage to the astro-hatch where Lawton finally dragged him in.' Lawton: 'He was totally done in.'

The cover had gone but Ward had been successful. He'd ripped away the fabric near the seat of the fire, and with less to feed on the flames gradually died. Widdowson piloted the damaged aircraft to a brilliant landing in England, sans flaps and brakes. He and Box were decorated immediately, and Ward's VC was announced on 5 August.

Both Box and Lawton survived the war, Lawton navigating the aircraft that took CAS Leonard Isitt to Japan as New Zealand's representative at Japan's formal surrender in 1945. By the time he retired in the early eighties he was Air New Zealand's navigation superintendent. Somewhat surprisingly he missed out on a decoration for his role in events the night Ward won his VC but was awarded an Air Force Cross in June 1945. Widdowson's flight report, on which the recommendation for Ward's VC was based, specifically mentioned Lawton for 'a very fine job in navigating us back solely by astro-navigation as the radio was destroyed during the attack'.

Ward, born in Wanganui on 14 June 1919, was a teacher when he enlisted in the RNZAF in July 1940. He learned to fly at Taieri and Wigram and sailed for Britain in February 1941. His No. 3 course also included outstanding bomber pilots Fraser Barron and Jim Starky.

Hugh Kimpton, who lives in Feilding, flew Wellingtons and Stirlings with 149 Squadron and was at 20 OTU at bleak Lossiemouth in northern Scotland with Ward and Barron. He'd been on No. 2 course in New Zealand but there was some overlapping and he'd got to know and like Ward. Pilots from Ward's course caught up with Kimpton's group at Lossiemouth because bitter weather in the winter of 1941 halted a lot of flying training. In the spring and early summer they all finished and prepared for postings to squadrons.

'Came the crucial day and there was one posting for 75 Squadron at Feltwell,' Kimpton remembers. 'Jimmy wanted to go to 75 and so did I. The CO said, "Right, there is one place at 75 and two New Zealanders. Who is it to be?" We tossed a coin. Jimmy won.'

The 408 Squadron pilots

In a photograph of pilots taken in the summer of 1941 at No. 16 OTU at Upper Heyford, northwest of London, eight of the 12 pilots were New Zealanders, the rest Rhodesians. Just three of the New Zealanders — original members of 408 (Goose) Squadron, Royal Canadian Air Force — survived the war. In fact all three were still alive when the writing of this book was finished in mid-2004 — Phil Farrow, 85, Bill Houghton, 90, and 'Tinny' Constance, 91.

Farrow escaped death by a whisker during a raid on Bremen in January 1942 when a night fighter poured fire into his aircraft and fatally wounded two of the crew. In the last year of the war on another squadron, he got out of a Mosquito as it broke up in the air and became a POW. He completed 77 ops and came home with a DFC and a DFM.

Houghton's Hampden was caught by searchlights on the way back from Essen in November 1941 and shot to ribbons by a fighter. Somehow he crash-landed in the dark on Dutch soil, and although the bomber slammed into a tree as it careered along the ground everyone got out safely to become POWs.

Constance was one of the Hampden pilots who braved the massed fire of the battle cruisers *Scharnhorst* and *Gneisenau* and their escorts as they dashed up the English Channel in February 1942. His little aircraft was pockmarked by a storm of flak as he dived to drop his bombs, but he made it back to base and finished a tour with a DFC to his name.

Farrow and his younger brother, Ralph, were working for the Forest Service in Rotorua when war broke out. Both signed up for the RNZAF immediately but had to go to night school before the air force would have them. The elder Farrow got the call first and was a course ahead of his brother, who also trained as a pilot and was killed on one of the thousand-bomber raids in 1942.

Napier-born Houghton was one of Union Airways' early employees, working as a maintenance engineer in Palmerston North, where the airline began life in the mid-1930s. He was number two in Gisborne when Germany invaded Poland, and figured that if he didn't act quickly he'd never get out of what would be a reserved occupation. So he and friend Merv Warnock, killed in England in a crash in April 1942 while instructing, drove over tortuous roads to Wellington in a rickety Austin to plead their case. A fortnight later Houghton was ordered to Levin for induction training.

When Delwyn Stanley Norris Constance first went to school in Dargaville, he was called Little Tinny because for some reason an older brother was known as Tinny. The nickname stuck, eventually minus the 'Little'. The Constance boys' father had fought in the Boer War and been badly knocked about in World War I. 'He came home on a hospital ship and wasn't able to do much afterwards. Of course my mother didn't want me to go but she accepted the situation and waved me off on the *Awatea*.'

By mid-May 1941, Farrow, Houghton and Constance were at Upper Heyford flying Ansons — 'the nicest and kindest little aeroplane I ever flew,' Farrow says — then Hampdens. By late July the three of them, and other New Zealanders from the OTU, had been posted to 408, the second Canadian squadron in Bomber Command. When they arrived at 408's airfield at Syerston, Nottinghamshire, the ground crew were there but the squadron's Hampdens weren't. While they waited for delivery of the aircraft, they spent time at other Hampden squadrons gaining operational experience, Houghton and Constance at 83, Farrow at 50. Guy Gibson, later the first commander of the Dambusters, was a flight commander with 83 at the time.

The young New Zealanders soon learned that they were engaged in a grim struggle for survival. Three of their fellow countrymen at Upper Heyford were dead within three months. Don Brook, 26 (Lower Hutt), was lost in the North Sea on the night of 30–31 July, and Stuart Beedie, 23 (Dannevirke), and his crew disappeared without trace raiding Karlsruhe a week later. Both were flying 144 Squadron Hampdens. In October the first 408 Squadron New Zealander was killed. Des Bradley, 22 (Waipukurau), died when his Hampden, back from a raid, crashed short of the runway.

Houghton's war ended on the night of 8–9 November 1941. The Hampden was picked up by searchlights over the German–Dutch border area and a fighter closed in. 'We went straight down the master beam firing everything we could lay hands on but the fighter followed us, knocked off most of one rudder, shot up the dashboard and set an engine on fire.' As the bomber plummeted in a high-speed dive the burning engine was torn from its mounting. The plane was almost unflyable, and the crew had no show of using their chutes. Houghton figured their only chance was a crash-landing, and somehow he managed it, flattening out and skidding, wheels up, across a field and into a tree somewhere northeast of Eindhoven. A broken leg suffered by the navigator was the worst injury. The crew all became prisoners.

Farrow's decorations were both immediate awards. He won the DFM on the night of 21–22 January 1942 on his 21st op, a raid on Bremen, when his Hampden was hunted by two night fighters as it headed away from the target. 'We should have been shot down that night,' he says.

They came at us from both sides and I put the aircraft over and dived. As I did, the German on the starboard opened up with a terrific burst of machine-gun and cannon fire, which caused us severe damage and hit the other three crew. But Bill Millward [wireless operator/gunner] got the fighter on the port side. I saw the aircraft go down and explode on the ground. He got the DFM for that and saved us. Had he not shot down that plane, I wouldn't be here. The other fighter gave it away then. We were sitting ducks really but there were no more attacks.

The Hampden was down to perhaps 1500 feet when Farrow got it back level and realised the second fighter had gone. But now he didn't know whether his crew were alive or dead, or whether they were even in the aircraft. (The pencil-slim Hampdens were a tight squeeze, and the four crew positions were virtually isolated from each other.) He'd ordered them out but the intercom had been blasted in the attack, so he didn't know whether they'd heard him or not, and thought he might be the only person left in the aircraft. The fighter had caused massive damage to the tailplane, and fire sprayed along the fuselage had smashed Farrow's instrument panel, leaving him with almost nothing but a compass. Amazingly both engines ran sweetly. 'I had no maps of course, but thank God I had the compass, and I set a course for home.'

A weary Farrow flew across the coast of England south of London and alerted observers on the ground that he was in trouble by flashing SOS with his ID light on the bottom of the fuselage. Searchlights laid a path for him to follow to West Malling, Kent. Wheels up because his hydraulics had been destroyed, he put the Hampden down on the snow-covered field, sliding and slowing gently to a stop. It was then that he found the other three crew were still aboard and alive, but the under gunner, with a cannon shell through his liver and colon, died the next day, and the navigator, a bullet in his lungs, lasted only two days. The wireless operator, hit in one leg by a cannon shell, was taken to hospital for treatment. 'I went back to my airfield by train, carrying my navigator's bloodied bag. I was a bit distraught about that. I was just given a rail ticket and told to find my way home.'

Constance's encounter with German naval fire occurred on the afternoon of 12 February 1942 as the *Scharnhorst* and *Gneisenau*, accompanied by the heavy cruiser *Prinz Eugen*, steamed up the English Channel in filthy weather — just what they wanted — thumbing their noses at the British. The Channel Dash, as it became known, was one of Britain's most embarrassing moments of the war. The big ships had been at Brest for months, pounded relentlessly by aerial attacks. They had been damaged but not destroyed. Now, ordered home, their break-out caught the British navy and air force napping. The ships slipped out of Brest under cover of darkness just before midnight on 11 February 1942. They were missed by patrolling RAF aircraft and not spotted and identified until 11 hours later, by which time they were entering the Strait of Dover.

British attempts to sink or cripple the warships as they steamed at high speed through the strait and into the North Sea, making for Wilhelmshaven and Kiel, were uncoordinated, delayed and ineffective. Bomber Command's main attack, late in the afternoon when the ships were off the Hook of Holland, was unsuccessful and cost 16 aircraft, including no fewer than 10 Hampdens. Two New Zealanders lost their lives: navigator Alex Abbot, 23 (Wellington), and pilot George Harris, 28 (formerly of Wellington), by then an RAF squadron leader. Harris' remains were washed ashore on the Dutch coast four months later.

Constance was fortunate not to be blown out of the sky, as so many of the Hampdens were that day. 'We were having lunch in the dining room when someone put his head through the door and yelled, "They're out! They're out!" The ships were well up the channel, it was panic stations, and we piled into the trucks to take us out to the planes.'

The bombers had little chance of finding the battle cruisers in the impossible conditions — thick low cloud, with only an occasional break and storming rain showers. Constance knew he was close to his target when he saw flak coming up through the clouds and put his nose down. At about 1200 feet the aircraft was hit, losing its port aileron to a shell.

I couldn't do anything else but keep going down. Then there was another big bang and the control stick was wrenched out of my hands. The wing was hit, six feet of metal torn up. We went into a spin but I got a hold of her again. Then we were out of cloud momentarily and suddenly I got glimpses of the ships. They'd disappear and then I'd see them again as we went in and out of cloud.

Streams of coloured tracer bullets hosed up as the Germans saturated the sky with flak. Constance went for one of the ships, either the *Gneisenau* or the *Prinz Eugen*, managed to get the bomb doors open, dropped his load and was in cloud again immediately. 'I can't remember now whether we had four 250-pound bombs or two 500 pounders, but they wouldn't have done any damage anyway. The bombs we had wouldn't have smashed a fly.' He clawed back height to about 700 feet and turned for home. The flak-riddled Hampden made it back to base safely, where everyone came out to see the damage.

News reports of Constance's close shave trickled back to New Zealand, and thus it was his mother learned he was no longer at a training base. 'She took me to task in a letter for not telling her, but she was a sensible woman and finished by saying, "Well darling, be good, be brave."'

The enemy ships vanished into the black of night at 6.00 p.m., and the British set about totting up the day's casualties. One destroyer had been badly damaged and the RAF had lost 37 aircraft — bombers, Swordfish torpedo bombers, and fighters. The German ships reached port early next day, although not without cost. Mines, put down a few days earlier by Hampdens, proved the ace. Steaming up the coast the *Scharnhorst* struck two, the *Gneisenau* one. The explosions halted the ships only briefly but the long-term consequences were severe. The *Scharnhorst* was under repair for almost six months, while her sister ship never fought again. A British bomb crashed through the *Gneisenau*'s foredeck in Kiel two weeks later, touching off fuel fumes and igniting a major fire. She was towed east to Gdynia to have a new forepart fitted, but the work was never completed and she was scuttled in March 1945. The *Scharnhorst* was trapped and sunk by the Royal Navy in the Barents Sea on Boxing Day 1943.

Farrow and Constance finished full tours with 408 Squadron, Farrow first because Constance became a flight commander and squadron leader, taking over the flight when its previous leader was killed, and duties that came with this kept him from flying as often. He remembers the night Farrow took off for his last op — his 34th — to make up 200 hours (the duration of a tour at the time).

> He wasn't in my flight but he came into my office; he was quite tense. He'd sit down, stand up, go out, come back. He had every right to feel that way about his last op. I finally took him out to the plane for takeoff, said cheerio and told him, 'Don't be late getting home.' Well, he was, and it was my turn to be tense and jittery. I phoned up all round the place to see if Phil had landed somewhere else. He hadn't. I was in the control tower when he finally called up ready to land. I was very pleased to see him.

In 1943 Constance graduated from the Empire Central Flying School as an instructor with a distinguished pass. Later he formed and commanded the Transport Training and Conversion Flight at RNZAF, Hobsonville, and was CO of 14 Squadron, RNZAF, from 1949 to 1951. Farrow instructed for 20 months and then began flying Mosquitoes with 692 Squadron, of the Light Night Striking Force, in March 1944. Houghton saw out the war in POW camps.

Attacking the big ships at Brest

The *Scharnhorst* and *Gneisenau* were recurring Bomber Command targets for much of 1941. The sister ships reached Brest, the naval port at the tip of France's Brittany peninsula, on 22 March 1941 after a mildly successful convoy-raiding mission in the North Atlantic. They put in for end-of-voyage refits and provisioning but were to remain bottled up until their audacious break-out through the English Channel in February 1942.

The two big ships, joined by the *Prinz Eugen*, which scurried into Brest after the loss of the *Bismarck* in May 1941, posed an enormous threat, and Bomber and Coastal Commands went to great lengths to try to sink them. They failed, but their terrier-like attacks wrought considerable damage and the battle cruisers were not ready for sea until the end of the year.

Operations to Brest drained Bomber Command's precious resources but the big ships were accorded priority status. The bombers often flew by day because the chances of hitting the vessels in the dark from great heights were slim.

The long series of attacks cost the lives of 17 New Zealanders serving with Bomber Command. The first casualty occurred on a night raid, on 10–11 April, when the RAF planted four bombs on the *Gneisenau*, killing 50 sailors and causing damage that took until Christmas to repair. Gunner Tahu Dabinette, 21 (Ashburton), was lost with the rest of his crew when their 218 Squadron Wellington plunged into the sea off Brest.

The toll of young New Zealanders rose as attempts to destroy the German warships intensified over the summer months. Seven were killed in two days in late July when the RAF mounted daylight raids on the *Scharnhorst*, which had moved a short distance south to La Pallice for trials, and the other two ships at Brest. On the evening of 23 July six 15 Squadron Stirlings from Wyton, Huntingdonshire, attacked the *Scharnhorst* at her new anchorage. The bombs missed, and one badly damaged aircraft came down in the sea with the loss of all her crew, including navigator Donald Lewis, 23 (Levin), who was nearing the end of his tour.

Early reports, later corrected, had the Stirling crashing 50 miles off the southwest tip of Wales, at the entrance to the Bristol Channel, and some records still say that's what happened. In fact the Stirling crashed in the North Sea, and it's possible the crew — or at least some of them — got into their dinghy after ditching. If they did, they perished. All that's known is that the sea yielded up Lewis' body — the only one found — about three weeks later on the island of Amrum, off the coast of Germany near its border with Denmark, 400 miles from England.

On 24 July 15 unescorted Halifaxes returned to La Pallice, landing five armour-piercing bombs on the *Scharnhorst*. Several failed to explode, drilling holes straight through the ship and letting in several thousand tons of water. Fighters and flak knocked down five aircraft and damaged the rest. One 76 Squadron Halifax put down off La Roche, the first Halifax to ditch successfully. The German navy decided La Pallice was too exposed and sailed the *Scharnhorst* back to Brest for repairs.

Earlier the same day, Bomber Command mounted a major raid on the *Gneisenau* and *Prinz Eugen*, using mainly Wellingtons and Hampdens escorted by Spitfires. The Germans must have sensed what was coming because the attack was met by heavy fighter opposition, and 10 Wellingtons and two Hampdens were lost. Six New Zealanders were among the dead — in Wellingtons of five different squadrons.

Two of the six, both pilots, were at the end of their tours. Mervyn Evans, 25 (New Plymouth), who had joined up in 1939, was killed with the rest of his 40 Squadron crew when their aircraft, hit by ground fire on its bombing run, caught fire and exploded. Evans, still a sergeant, had only just been awarded a DFM, his superb flying allowing his rear gunner to destroy an Me 110 near Rotterdam. 101 Squadron Wellington skipper Fred Craig, 26 (Hastings), was on his 31st op when he died. Two of his crew baled out over the sea and were picked up after the Wellington was attacked by fighters in the target area, but of Craig and the others there was no trace.

The four other New Zealanders killed that day were also experienced aircrew, men the RAF could ill afford to lose. 75 Squadron pilot Don Streeter, 24 (Wellington), and his front gunner Graham Walker, 25 (Te Kuiti), were both on their 20th op. Hit by flak while approaching the target, their Wellington dropped out of formation. Thus exposed it was hammered by a fighter and dived vertically into the sea. No one survived. Also attacked by fighters, the 103 Squadron aircraft on which Ed McDonald, 21 (Bucklands Beach), served as a gunner was last seen losing height with an engine out. One body was later washed ashore but it wasn't McDonald's. The fourth New Zealander killed was pilot Morrison Jolly, 23 (Wallacetown, in Southland), who perished when his 218 Squadron Wellington crashed into the sea near Brest. He and McDonald were both on their 22nd op.

English wireless operator John Knott and Canadian navigator 'Jake' Jacobsen were the only two survivors from Jolly's crew. Knott kept a diary and later wrote an account of what had happened. He doesn't mention Jolly, who must have been fighting to keep the fatally damaged Wellington airborne so his crew could escape.

A good run up to the target . . . flew in V-formation in the first three. Ack-ack intense. Bombs dropped with flak thudding underneath aircraft. Saw target through bomb aimer's window.

Having survived such an onslaught met by German fighters — about fifteen 109s around us with our rear gunner letting loose. He gave a running commentary over the intercom. Time about 1530 [3.30 p.m.]. While this was going on knelt down because of bullets from fighters . . . clipped chute on. Second pilot tapped me on my back. Rear of aircraft on fire. Opened door to bale out. My ripcord was pulled and the chute opened in the plane. One of the cords caught on hook on door. Lifted cord off and gathered the chute in my arms. Jake had dropped out by this time. I was next to go. Dived out.

Knott was buzzed by a low-flying Me 109 after dropping into the sea and thought it was about to fire at him but found out later it was indicating his position to those ashore. He and Jacobsen were hauled from the water by a French trawler 20 minutes after jumping, and then a German boat came out for them. 'I thought it was wonderful to be alive after such an ordeal. Reached beach to be greeted by dozens of French girls, who were sunbathing, and some German officers.'

War has many surreal moments and this was one. Life in occupied France, even close to a heavy air attack, went on much as normal. Young women frolicked on the beach while men fought in the air above and plunged to their deaths in flaming aircraft.

Knott was given lunch by the Germans in a chateau overlooking the bay where his friends had died. An officer 'loaned us his binoculars so we could see the large German machine searching for survivors. He told us that one of us had dropped about a third of the distance before the chute opened . . . Estimate that I baled out at some 8000 feet.' The aircraft had crashed two miles offshore; Jolly was never found.

Don Streeter's lost Wellington was one of six put up by 75 Squadron from Feltwell that day, their pilots including such notables as 'Popeye' Lucas, Artie Ashworth and Ivan Breckon.

57 Squadron, which shared Feltwell with 75, contributed another six. The group, flying in four three-plane Vs, was led by Wing Commander Trevor Freeman, one of New Zealand's best World War II pilots. Freeman, born in Lawrence, Central Otago, in 1916, flew fighters with the RAF before the war, was a founder member of the New Zealand bomber squadron, flew 58 ops in two tours and commanded 115 Squadron during 1941–42. He returned to New Zealand in 1943 and was appointed commander of the RNZAF fighter wing on New Georgia, in the Solomon Islands. He was killed leading Warhawks against the Japanese at Rabaul in December 1943.

One of the 57 Squadron pilots on the Brest raid was Palmerston North-born Jock Stanford, who had an eventful air war that ended in a POW camp. He finished a tour with 57, instructed for a while and then went back on ops with 115 Squadron. He ditched in the North Sea early in his second tour before being shot down over Duisberg in mid-1942. He was awarded a DFM in November 1941, the citation noting the Brest raid in particular. 'Throughout the whole attack and in the face of intense and accurate anti-aircraft fire, Sergeant Stanford flew in close formation with his leader, presenting such a determined front that the enemy did not dare attack.'

Stanford, one of Freeman's wingmen, remembers the formation closing up tightly to present a united defence as they approached Brest and saw fighters coming up toward them. Over the target the flak was heavy and more worrying than the fighters. 'After bombing we ran through fighters again going out but we were lighter now and picked up speed. Fortunately we came out of it okay and got back more or less unscathed. That was probably because I was among the lead planes.'

Stanford joined the RAF after the war and was a squadron leader by the time he retired in 1963. He returned to New Zealand to be near family in 2000, settling in Christchurch.

A grand life in the RAF

> We've been shot up once or twice . . . but we've always managed
> to make a safe landing. Once, coming back from Bremen, a Jerry
> fighter knocked us about a bit and wounded the rear gunner
> and we had to land at the nearest aerodrome we could find
> in the south of England . . . [but] . . . there has been nothing
> particularly eventful about my bombing career.

So wrote Russell Orchard in a script for a wartime BBC talk he
gave near the end of his short life. Still only 21, he had done 25
ops on Whitleys with 58 Squadron but was destined to complete
only two more. He was killed on his 28th on 19–20 September
1941 in an attack on distant Stettin, now Szczecin, in Poland. His
was one of just two aircraft lost on the raid.

It's not known whether Orchard's Whitley was a victim of flak
or a night fighter, or even if it was brought down while heading
for Stettin or homebound after bombing. All that is certain is that
the aircraft crashed near Rostock, on the Baltic coast 140 miles
west of Stettin, and that all five aboard perished. The men's bodies
were buried locally but reinterred after the war in Berlin.

Orchard was killed five days after VC-winner Jimmy Ward but
his death didn't make the same impact. His name appeared in a
list of missing but that was about all. Orchard was a late and only
child and had few relations. When his parents died no one claimed
his scanty papers — his wartime logbook, his photograph albums
— or his DFC and the medals he had won as a crack secondary-
school shooter. Eventually these items were gathered up by the
woman who had nursed his mother during her last years and sent
to his old school in Christchurch — St Andrew's College.

There they were found in a shoebox by Jan Hampton when
she was appointed curator of the school's museum some years ago.
They fired her imagination and she determined to find out all she
could about this young man who had died decades before. The

result is a showcase of carefully mounted material honouring one of the school's old boys.

Orchard attended St Andrew's between 1932 and 1935, developing a passion to fly. 'I made up my mind when I was at school that one day I would be an airman,' he said on the BBC. As soon as he was old enough, in late 1937, he sought a short-service commission in the RAF and sailed the following year with 17 other young New Zealanders in the *Remuera*.

Orchard was rated above average by his flying instructors in England, and after war broke out was posted to a fighter squadron in Scotland, where he flew not Spitfires or Hurricanes but Defiants and Blenheims. At some stage in 1940 a flying accident in the north landed him in hospital, and later he was transferred to bombers.

> There is really no comparison between flying a light, dainty fighter and a big bomber, or in the kind of life you lead. With the fighters there were quick periods of excitement, followed by long waits for something to turn up, then going into the air at a few minutes' notice. But with bombers I found there was plenty of time to plan out what you were going to do, and you were up in the air so much longer.

Orchard also enjoyed the comradeship and crew spirit on bombers — 'often it's a lonely job in a fighter'. He also enjoyed the travel! 'You get about a good bit. I'd never been to Germany, for instance, until I joined a bomber squadron. Now I've been plenty of times . . . to Berlin, Hamburg, Kiel, Cologne, Mannheim, Frankfurt and the Ruhr Valley.'

He finished his BBC talk with the words: 'So far I've had a grand life in the RAF, and I've never regretted the decision I made at school to become a flying man. I hope I'll be able to fly back to New Zealand after the war.'

Survival against the odds

Someone was looking after rear gunner Norman Bidwell when his Whitley was attacked by a night fighter over Hamburg in late 1941. An armour-piercing bullet bored a huge hole in his chest and then the aircraft's two pilots leapt out, leaving the other three crew to fend for themselves. Remarkably, the wireless operator and navigator managed to keep the bomber in the air despite few of the controls still working and made a perfect crash-landing.

When German soldiers picked up Bidwell and carried him away he was so badly wounded they thought he was beyond help and deposited him in a local barracks. He was still alive next morning, so they took him to a hospital. It was months before he was fit enough to be moved to a POW camp for airmen, but he had survived and continues to do so.

Born in Christchurch in 1921, Bidwell has lived in the southern city all his life except for the war years, and only recently gave up his accountancy business. When war broke out he volunteered for the RNZAF and sailed through selection for pilot training, but the air force couldn't fit him into a course until early 1941. In July 1940 he was called up by the army. 'I wrote to the air force and said if they wouldn't take me I'd have to go with the army. The response was that I could go into camp the following month if I'd go as an air gunner. So I did.'

Bidwell sailed on the *Aorangi* in October 1940, one of 70 young men destined to train in Canada as gunners. They were the first group of New Zealanders to go to Canada under the Commonwealth training scheme. Twenty-nine would die serving their country. Bidwell and four others would become POWs.

Their training complete, the airmen sailed for Britain on an armed cruiser, in May 1941. When the British learned the German battleship *Bismarck* was prowling the Atlantic, the cruiser was diverted to Iceland, where the young men stayed until it was deemed safe to continue their voyage. Bidwell and 12 of his mates were posted immediately to Kinloss, in northern Scotland, to train on Whitleys. Bidwell had three particular friends there from barracks days in Levin: Omer Bishop (Norsewood); Geoff Carman, who had migrated to New Zealand from England; and Arthur Evans (Hawera). All three would be dead inside a year. 'Bishop slept next to me in the barracks because the alphabet determined that, Carman was down the row a bit and Evans was opposite. Geoff was a good bit older and called us the Three Musketeers. He introduced me to my future wife, Wilma, at a dance near Kinloss.'

Bishop, 22, was the first to die, posted to a Blenheim squadron and killed during a suicidal daylight low-level attack on Heligoland on 26 August 1941. Five aircraft took off, one of which turned back early. The other four, easy targets, were shot down by fighters, none of the 12 crew surviving. Carman, 31, was killed less than two weeks later in a Whitley on a raid over Germany. Evans, 23, perished in a Halifax attacking the *Tirpitz* in a Norwegian fjord in April 1942.

Two more of the gunners who'd been on the *Aorangi* with Bidwell died on the same raid as Carman. Pine Takarangi, 23 (Putiki, Auckland), was on his first op, Richard Minnis, 27 (Wellington), on his seventh. Both were also flying in Whitleys. Minnis, a married man with a five-year-old son, had been 1939 national amateur wrestling champion.

Bishop's parents suffered another cruel blow when a second son — Leon, 21, rear gunner on a 207 Squadron Lancaster — was lost without trace with his entire crew during a raid on Dusseldorf in June 1943. Both brothers are commemorated at Runnymede.

Bidwell is fortunate he doesn't feature on a roll of honour too. Posted to 58 Squadron at Linton-on-Ouse, Yorkshire, in the first week of September 1941, he completed just six missions and was lucky to get that far. On his second, a gruelling 10-hour flight to Nuremberg, his Whitley eluded an attacking Ju 88, but when the bomber arrived back over Yorkshire, almost out of fuel, much of the county was hidden by thick fog. The circuit over Pocklington, the base to which they were diverted, was packed with aircraft. Landing, they flew in over a crashed and burning Whitley from their own squadron, and in the morning found they didn't even have enough fuel to start the engines.

Bidwell's last flight, starting in the dark on 30 November, began badly when navigator Joey Deane couldn't get his chart table to stay up as the Whitley, flown by a Canadian with an RAF man as his second pilot, prepared for takeoff. Delayed by repairs they were late getting away, and the night continued to go wrong, an engine supercharger giving trouble.

> We were last in over Hamburg in bright moonlight and got coned. The heavy flak was coming up to 20,000 feet, our maximum, and we couldn't shake the lights. And then I spotted an Me 110 coming in from behind and above. He let go at me and I had a go at him. He came in quite close, about 250 yards, then went on his back and dived down. I don't know if I hit him.

Two minutes later the Whitley was attacked again, this time from beneath and probably by the same fighter. 'We stayed up there where we were silhouetted. We should have gone down.' The fighter poured machine-gun fire into the Whitley, setting an engine on fire and doing other major damage. Bidwell was hit by a stray bullet. 'It was just as if someone had punched me in the chest: no pain, no sensation other than that clout.'

An armour-piercing bullet, copper-covered on the head, spreads on impact, allowing the core to drive on. The one that hit Bidwell smashed into his chest just above the heart on an upward path, dragging bits of flying suit, battledress and shirt up through his body. It lodged under his right collarbone, somehow missing the big arteries and windpipe.

Despite a gaping wound two fingers wide and blood that soon soaked his uniform, Bidwell didn't lose consciousness. But he couldn't raise anyone on the intercom and didn't know that up front Deane and wireless operator Freddy Ivins had suddenly discovered the escape hatch in the floor open and both pilots gone. The pair had heard no order to bale out and were astonished to find themselves alone when they crawled into the cockpit. Though neither man could fly, they had watched pilots at their job and knew vaguely what to do. The fire in the engine had gone out and the Whitley seemed to be flying level enough as the two settled into the pilots' seats, but the aircraft was sluggish and difficult to control.

Several times in the next half-hour the bomber seemed about to stall but the airmen wrestled its nose down to increase speed. However, they continued to lose height and by the time the coast appeared they were down to a couple of thousand feet. Ivins and Deane knew they had no chance of getting home so chose to turn and crash-land.

In the rear of the plane, Bidwell knew what was coming even though he didn't yet appreciate the circumstances. The intercom was out and the two men in front thought he was probably dead.

> I was aware we were going down gradually, and as we got close to the ground I could identify things. I couldn't move my right arm but held on tight with my left, though I pictured myself being shot out of the turret when we crashed. I braced myself for the impact, and the next thing they did a wheels-up landing in a field that was a credit to anyone.

After Ivins and Deane had got Bidwell out of the aircraft they fired rounds from the plane's Very pistol into the fuel tanks to start a fire to destroy the Whitley. German soldiers from a nearby camp swarmed around them. They could see Bidwell's heart beating through his awful wound and gave him up for dead. He spent the night in a navy barracks, and it wasn't until next day that he was taken to a hospital in a camp for navy and merchant-navy prisoners, where a Yugoslav surgeon removed the bullet. The anaesthetist was a New Zealander Bidwell now remembers only vaguely as a Dunedin man called McDermott.

The pilots who quit the Whitley were killed. The Germans found their bodies and buried them in Hamburg. Exactly what happened will always remain a mystery. One account suggests the men were not wearing parachutes when they were found, but Bidwell rejects this. 'My view is that when the night fighter hit us from below, things moved pretty quickly. I think the pilot saw the situation as desperate and jumped. The second pilot must have followed him out. And I'm pretty sure they went with chutes. Airmen aren't going to jump from a plane without them, are they?'

1942

A TRANSITIONAL YEAR

1942

The war was half over before Bomber Command became truly effective, capable of delivering devastating night attacks on Nazi Germany. It took until late 1942–early 1943 to overcome the factors that so limited its early performance. Three long years were needed to equip enough squadrons with enough four-engined heavy bombers, particularly Halifaxes and Lancasters; to create the Pathfinder Force and give it the target markers and other tools needed to do its job efficiently and accurately; to develop powerful and reliable bombs; to train crews properly; to coordinate main-force bombing streams; to pass those streams over a target in the shortest possible time to swamp the defences; and, most importantly, to develop a range of navigation aids to enable aircraft to find and pinpoint targets hundreds of miles from home.

Bomber Command essentially improvised for the first two years of the war, and it wasn't until 1942 — a transitional year — that increasing numbers of new aircraft with bigger payloads and more powerful bombs enabled the RAF to strike telling blows against Germany's industry and cities. The appointment in early 1942 of Arthur Harris, known to his crews as Butch, to head Bomber Command was a key step. He was to infuse the command with energy and a sense of direction, and to unleash his squadrons on Germany with a single-minded belief and determination that the bombers could end the war unaided. He thought his fleets could pound Germany into submission. They couldn't, but by God Harris and his gallant squadrons tried.

Shorten the war they did. The invasion of Hitler's Fortress Europe in June 1944, a near-run thing, succeeded largely because of pre-landing bombing by the RAF and USAAF. The bombers dealt devastating blows to northwestern Europe's rail network, stifling the movement of German troops and equipment. They delivered constant and effective attacks on German forces preparing to resist the invasion and on their fortifications. Following the invasion the bombers worked closely with the Allied troops on the ground, wreaking havoc on Germany's supply lines, unleashing heavy attacks on her armies and strong points and raiding the refineries and synthetic fuel plants that kept those armies — and the Luftwaffe — on the move.

The bombing campaign of 1940, 1941 and, to an extent, 1942 was really an amateur affair compared with what was to come from 1943 on. Countless brave men, among them many New Zealanders, died for little apparent effect during those early years. Yet every raid, whatever its calamities and losses, was part of the experience Bomber Command had to amass before emerging as the powerful force it eventually became. The aircrew who died early on paved the way for later success.

When the first bombers winged off over Germany the night war was declared — to drop leaflets, not bombs — no one could foresee the shape the bombing campaign would assume over the next six years. At its climax in late 1944 and early 1945, Bomber Command regularly dispatched fleets of 1000 four-engined bombers to German targets. The world had never seen anything like it, and never would again. It was a oncer. The weight of bombs dropped on Nazi Germany grew exponentially. In the last nine months of the war the RAF dropped a greater tonnage than in the previous five years combined. By the end of the war Germany's cities were rubble, utterly destroyed from the air.

Whatever their problems, operations in the early years were a vital part of learning, and Bomber Command learned a little every raid. And there is no doubt that the bombing, erratic as it was, hurt Germany. In the wake of the disasters that led to the evacuation of Dunkirk in June 1940 and subsequent defeats in other battle zones, Bomber Command's attacks on Germany were an enormous morale-booster for the beleaguered British people. Standing alone in 1940 and 1941, Britain was still hitting back, and Bomber Command was doing the hitting. The bombers were the country's only offensive weapon. Luftwaffe boss Herman Goering had once bragged that no enemy bomber would appear in the skies over Germany. He had long since regretted his foolish remark.

Britons living in East Anglia, the Midlands, Lincolnshire and Yorkshire listened night after night to the sounds of straining engines lifting bomb-laden aircraft into the night skies. They were comforted and warmed knowing that Bomber Command was taking the war to the enemy, dishing it out to the Germans. So were the captive peoples — the Danes, Belgians, Dutch and French — who cheered to themselves and wished the bombers Godspeed as they droned overhead on their way to Germany. It was not surprising that RAF graves in occupied Europe were tended with an open devotion that infuriated the Germans.

Down in Denmark

Pilot Bill Dashwood was still only 20 when a failed engine abruptly finished his war. He parachuted at low level over Denmark on a freezing winter's night in January 1942 and spent more than three years in captivity. What made his long incarceration in miserable German POW camps all the worse was knowing that he might have got back to England if he'd gone to the right people in Denmark — the police.

Dashwood, who now lives in Mount Maunganui, joined 106 Squadron on Hampdens at Coningsby, Lincolnshire, in July 1941. He remembers the grim attrition rate during his time there. 'The average crew lasted about four or five ops, so one or two of us who had a good number up were considered to have fairly charmed lives.' On his 23rd op the night he didn't get home, he was beginning to think he might even reach the magical 30 mark and finish his tour.

Because Dashwood and his crew were an experienced team,

they were among the four chosen to act as 'firelighters' for the 15–16 January 1942 raid on Hamburg, flying in advance of the attack force with a full load of incendiaries to start fires that would act as aiming points for the aircraft following them. In effect they were pathfinders, such experiments paving the way for the development of the Pathfinder Force later that year.

Dashwood was near Wilhelmshaven when his port engine suddenly burst into flames for no apparent reason. He hit the extinguisher and the fire died, but the motor was finished. On one engine, the Hampden immediately began losing height, and clearly there wasn't the slightest chance of getting home. 'It was a question of "What the hell do we do now?" Sweden [a neutral country from which RAF flyers were normally quickly returned to England] was fairly close, so the navigator and I decided we'd head north for the Danish coast, swing east over Denmark and try for Sweden.'

The crew dumped incendiaries, guns, ammunition, radio — the lot — to lighten the aircraft and did well to get substantially north of the Danish–German border and turn right for Sweden. However a few miles northeast of Esbjerg it was obvious the Hampden wouldn't make it. 'She was losing height constantly, and at about 1500 feet the wireless operator and gunner called out, "We'll lighten her a bit more", and jumped.' At under 1000 feet a few moments later, the navigator and Dashwood followed. All four survived.

Dashwood was on the loose for four days with his navigator, moving by night, sleeping in stock-filled barns by day. Farmers fed them but were anxious for them to move off their properties. Finally, one jittery farmer lost his nerve and called the local German outpost. Dashwood woke to find a bayonet point on his throat.

The irony was that when they were lodged in police cells at Grindsted they were told by the Danish cops, 'Sorry, we can't do anything for you now but you should have come to us in the beginning.' Dashwood: 'They said they could have got us back to the UK with the help of the local fishing fleet. Apparently escapees were taken to sea by the fleet and contact made with a Royal Navy submarine. How lovely to know this when too late to take advantage.'

The raid on Hamburg cost 11 aircraft, the majority in dreadful weather on returning to England. Six of the 33 RAF aircrew who lost their lives were New Zealanders. *For Your Tomorrow* notes the circumstances: 'Encountered a snow storm and crashed in the Cheviot Hills'; 'Presumed to have crashed into the North Sea off the Yorkshire coast'; 'Passed over the base preparatory to landing but a few minutes later crashed and caught fire'; 'While returning to Yorkshire . . . struck the side of a hill about five feet below its summit'; 'Lost without trace.' All six were in the early stages of their tours. The youngest was 20, the oldest 30. Hamburg reported 36 fires, three people killed and 25 injured, but no major incidents. The city's apocalypse was yet to come.

Lubeck burns

The opening blow in the strategic air campaign against Germany's cities was delivered by Bomber Command against the ancient Hanseatic League port of Lubeck, near the Baltic coast, on the night of 28–29 March 1942. More than 230 bombers — Wellingtons, Hampdens, Stirlings and Manchesters — were mustered by the RAF in what was the start of so-called area bombing — systematic attacks on the Reich's towns and cities.

Gone now were the old rules under which bomber crews were briefed to aim only at industrial and military targets. The general population of Germany, in homes, offices, shops and other workplaces, was now also fair game.

The policy of area bombing was not, as is often claimed, developed by Arthur 'Bomber' Harris, named Command-in-

Chief, Bomber Command, on 22 February 1942 in succession to Sir Richard Peirse. It was handed down in a July 1941 Air Ministry directive, reinforced a week before Harris was appointed and awaited the new boss at his High Wycombe headquarters 30 miles west of London. From now on the primary objective of the bombing campaign was to be the destruction of the morale of the German civilian population, industrial workers in particular. Helpfully, the ministry provided a list of targets.

Harris, who so ably led the command until the end of the war, embraced the policy with enthusiasm and never deviated from it except when he was ordered to do so. He believed the levelling of Germany's cities would bring her to her knees, and anything other than area bombing he regarded as a mere sideshow to Bomber Command's main role.

Harris and his crews did not bomb Germany into submission, but Bomber Command played a key role in the Allies' victory. Without its strikes in the spring and early summer of 1944 it is possible to argue that the Allied invasion forces would have been thrown back into the sea in June that year.

Albert Speer achieved miracles of war-materiel production despite the devastation wrought by Bomber Command, and by the Americans from 1943. It's easy to imagine what he might have achieved had there been no bombing. Speer called the assault Germany's greatest lost battle and wrote that it opened a second front long before the invasion of Europe.

Late in the war Germany employed one million fighting men to man the anti-aircraft guns that tried to ward off the bombers. Flak batteries fired millions of rounds of ammunition from thousands of the fabled 88-millimetre guns that would have had an enormous impact had they been used as artillery or tank busters against the Allied ground troops on the Eastern and Western fronts. This enormous force of men, equipment and ammunition was tied down in defence of Germany — by Bomber Command. Without the bombing the war would have gone on much longer.

When Harris chose Lubeck, on the River Trave near where it flows into the Baltic, as the first objective of the new campaign, he chose well. The ministry directive had recommended the fullest possible use of incendiary bombs, and Harris approved of that too. The raid's aiming point, the historic centre of Lubeck, was choked with narrow streets and wooden houses. It would burn easily. Harris wrote later: 'Lubeck was not a vital target but it seemed to me better to destroy an industrial town of moderate importance than to fail to destroy a large industrial city.' He also wanted his aircrews to have a taste of success for a change. Until now the bomber squadrons had been committed piecemeal — five aircraft here, 10 there. The results had been minimal and discouraging, considering the effort and the loss of valuable aircrews. The men needed results and a victory. They got both at Lubeck.

Later in the war, when enormous fleets of aircraft dealt death and destruction to Germany night after night, Lubeck tended to be forgotten. But this was a key raid in Bomber Command's history, a signpost to the future. An almost full moon helped crews find the target, and because the city was only lightly defended, many aircraft flew low to attack. Three waves of bombers unloaded 400 tons of bombs, two-thirds of them incendiaries. Two hundred acres of central Lubeck were devastated and the city's industrial capacity badly damaged. More than 300 people died. It was one of the few occasions so far when German casualties exceeded those of the attackers. Shaken, German propaganda chief Joseph Goebbels confided in his diary that the city's Nazi chief had told him this had been the worst raid of the war and that conditions in parts of Lubeck had been chaotic: 'Eighty per cent of the old city must be considered lost.'

Another of our Wellingtons is missing

Lubeck rated as a huge success but the attackers paid a price. They always did. Fifty-nine aircrew killed, another 20 POWs. Thirteen aircraft lost, 5.5 per cent of the attacking force of 234. Wellingtons made up two-thirds of the force and suffered proportionately, with eight shot down. Three Stirlings, one Manchester and one Hampden were also lost. The Stirlings all belonged to 7 Squadron and not a single man from the three crews survived.

During the evening of 28 March 1942, ground control staff at Feltwell waved off 10 of 75 Squadron's Wellingtons to join the Lubeck-bound force. It was two years and a day since the squadron's first mission of the war, and now the New Zealanders were a well-tried, well-regarded unit. 75 was one of Bomber Command's premier heavy-bomber squadrons, flying to all the tough, well-defended targets. It was always involved in the action but German flak and night fighters had exacted a toll. In two years 75 had lost 34 bombers, mostly over Germany. Another 20 had come home with dead or wounded crew, crashed on return or been abandoned over England.

And 75 lost another Wellington on the Lubeck raid. Maurice Bell's bomber was brought down over or near Kiel. No one has ever pinpointed its precise crash point and it isn't known whether the Wimpy was on its way to the target or homebound when it was knocked out of the sky. All that's definite is that the Germans found the wrecked bomber and buried the dead crew in the naval garrison cemetery in Kiel. Later, the bodies were reinterred in the adjacent Kiel War Cemetery, laid side by side in their graves, together in death as in life.

Taranaki-born and -raised Bell, 26, was on his 13th trip when he and the other five aboard, two of them also New Zealanders, were killed. Frank Cran, 21 (Invercargill), was the second pilot and Claude Harris, 31 (Helensville), was navigating. The other three were Britons — Tom Cross, Jim Hinton and Ron Allen. Cross, at

35, was the oldest, and he and Hinton were both married.

Though Lubeck was an easy target, the city was not far from Kiel and Hamburg, both heavily defended, and the air corridor between them crossed the flak-infested Kiel Canal. Aircraft in this area always got a hot reception.

Jim Robinson, who now lives in Sydney, finished a tour with 75 Squadron in June 1942, but was a new boy on only his fourth trip when he went to Lubeck. His aircraft was coned by about 20 searchlights over the canal and the skipper dived from 10,000 feet to 3000 feet to get out of them.

> I was in the bomb aimer's position, dropping the load, when suddenly there was a smell of burning aircraft. I thought we had been hit. Simultaneously the rear gunner yelled over the intercom that we were on fire. The second pilot discovered that a flare had gone off and was burning in the aircraft. He set about the most difficult and blinding job of dislodging it. I got back to the navigator's table to see the wireless operator and the front gunner trying to get the fire extinguisher going. Glare and smoke were terrific and the captain gave the order to abandon the aircraft. He dived the aircraft again to keep the flames from the tanks, and by sheer determination the second pilot managed to force the flare out of the fuselage. The skipper had given a second order to bale out and we were making preparations for an exit when the rear gunner called out the blaze was almost under control.

The crew had fought the blaze for 15 minutes, and Robinson says that without the second pilot's frantic efforts they would all probably have been POWs in Germany. The fire left a 'devilish' hole in the aircraft's belly. The Lubeck trip and the one after, when the plane was held by a host of searchlights over Frankfurt and shot full of holes, were the worst of Robinson's tour.

Another bomber that ran into trouble over the Kiel Canal during the Lubeck operation was a 218 Squadron Stirling flown by Aucklander Arthur Humphreys. He distinguished himself by getting his bomber out of a tight spot and earned an immediate DFC. Several night fighters speared in to attack, their fire slashing through one wing, wounding the gunners and damaging their turrets. The Stirling was down to near ground level before it shook off the fighters.

Humphreys had flown a total of 53 ops, half with 75 Squadron, the rest with 218, before he was shot down on a mining, or 'gardening', trip over Denmark in mid-May 1942. Several of the crew were wounded by shrapnel as they floated to earth, one later dying from a stomach wound. Although Humphreys was not hit he suffered medical problems in POW camp and died in 1959 as a result of his war service, leaving a young family.

Maurice Bell and his two brothers were reared by their widowed father, George, on the family farm at Tuna, near Stratford. When war came Maurice joined the air force and Bill the army (to be captured in the North African desert). Third brother Jack stayed home to run the farm. Bell reached 75 Squadron in early October 1941 and was immediately on operations — over Cologne, Nuremberg, Dusseldorf, Mannheim and Antwerp.

As friends and acquaintances failed to return, Bell quickly learned that life with a bomber squadron was frequently short. Aucklander Trevor Robertson, another newcomer, was lost over Cologne on his second op; Fred Spark, from Dunedin, went down a week later during a raid on Mannheim — his first trip. Both were 26, and Spark left a widow. 'Pilot Officer Robertson, the fellow who trained with me, did not return,' Bell wrote in a letter to fiancee Thelma Dandy in Wanganui. 'The pilot Robbie flew with last night had need for a second pilot. His usual had frost-bitten hands and Robbie volunteered to take his place.'

In another letter he wrote: 'Saw two machines go down in

flames, a most awful sight. The first appeared to explode after going down flaming. The second was one huge glowing mass and appeared to float down slowly.' Bell didn't underrate the enemy, writing in his diary: 'The Germans are certainly well organised; they have been adding considerably to their defences and we have to pass over miles of searchlight belts to get to our targets. Our losses are considerable.'

Bell was hurt during a raid on Hamburg in late October 1941. As he struggled to release a flare down the chute in the fuselage it exploded, breaking his collarbone and knocking out several teeth. While he was stumbling around dazed, the Wellington was caught by searchlights and dived steeply to escape, dropping from 15,000 feet to 3000 feet. The bomber got back to England, desperately short of fuel, and headed for the first available airfield. As one motor failed, pilot Ken Climie, 25 (Lower Hutt), crash-landed. It was only later the crew learned they had hung-up bombs in the bay. An ambulance took Bell to hospital.

In the dreadful winter of 1941–42, the squadron flew few operations and the assault on Germany wasn't renewed until March. Bell was promoted to flight sergeant on 1 December 1941 and by the time of his last flight was a pilot officer and skipper of his own aircraft. Before he took off for Lubeck, he made his last diary entry: 'Tested my machine in the morning. Received letters from Thelma. Briefed 1530 hrs. Target — Lubeck. Commission has come through.'

Augsburg: the Lancasters fly to Germany by day

A New Zealander drew up the battle plan for what developed into one of the most celebrated raids of World War II — the 17 April 1942 daylight attack by 12 Lancasters on the Augsburg diesel plant, deep in southern Germany. Sam Elworthy wrote operation order No. 143 at Bomber Command headquarters just nine days before the mission and stamped it 'Most Secret'. Elworthy, then a wing commander, was destined to become Marshal of the Royal Air Force and Britain's Chief of Defence Staff in 1967.

Quickly approved by higher authority, the Augsburg plan was passed to 5 Group's 44 and 97 Squadrons, the only two in the RAF equipped at that stage with the new four-engined Lancasters. The crews chosen for the daring flight were not told their target until the day they flew, but had been practising formation and low-level flying and knew something special was on.

The Admiralty sought the raid. The war news in early 1942 was not encouraging, especially in the Atlantic, where U-boats were wreaking havoc on Allied shipping. The Admiralty knew that diesel engines for submarines were manufactured at the huge Maschinenfabrik Augsburg-Nurnberg (MAN) plant in Augsburg and believed that if it were destroyed or damaged, Germany's submarine-building industry might be disrupted. Bomber Command was therefore asked to attack the plant, where diesels had been built for 50 years, ever since genius Rudolf Diesel had invented his reliable heavy-duty engine.

The decision was made to attack the sprawling engine-assembly headquarters in daylight because no British bomber could hit such a target in the dark at that stage of the war. Elworthy and other staff officers were aware of disastrous raids early in the war that had shown the defensive firepower of bombers, even in close formation, was no match for fighters in daylight. But old beliefs die hard and Elworthy clearly thought Lancasters might prove more effective, writing: 'Operating in daylight, the firepower of a section of three . . . is such as to deter all but the most determined of enemy fighters'. The reality proved otherwise. Apart from the famous October 1942 attack on the Schneider armaments factory at Le Creusot, in France, Lancasters would not fly major daylight raids again until mid-1944, by which time the Allies had mastery of the skies and long-range escort fighters.

Elworthy also argued in his 1942 plan that the German day-fighter force on the Western Front was weak and thinly spread, having been drained by the demands of the Eastern Front, and that the Lancaster's qualities, combined with well-coordinated diversions, should enable the force to cross the French coast at a soft point and penetrate deep into enemy territory without meeting serious opposition.

Six Lancasters of 44 (Rhodesia) Squadron and six of 97 (Straits Settlements) Squadron took off from their Lincolnshire bases at 3.00 p.m. They were to cross the French coast between Cherbourg and Le Havre, sweep across France into southern Germany, then dog-leg across the northern tip of Lake Constance and on to Augsburg. It would be a testing 1250-mile round trip, the bombers targeting the MAN works in the last of the sunshine and flying home in the dark.

John Nettleton led the two 44 Squadron three-plane Vs, Ginger Garwell as his port wingman, George Rhodes to starboard. Nick Sandford headed the second group, a quarter of a mile behind, John Beckett and Herbert Crum on either side. John Sherwood and David Penman commanded the 97 Squadron formations, which flew independently and some distance away. Each aircraft carried seven men: skipper, second pilot, navigator/bomb aimer, wireless operator and three gunners. Specialist flight engineers and bomb aimers were about to be introduced for the new breed of heavy bombers but for now the second pilot acted as flight engineer, watching the engine gauges, fuel tank dials and other key instruments. The navigator, still officially 'observer', would also drop the bombs.

Two New Zealanders flew with 44 — Lawrence Baxter as second pilot with Rhodes, and Frank Kirke as Garwell's navigator. There were none with 97. Baxter, 23, who'd been working for the New Zealand Dairy Company in Hamilton when he enlisted, had joined 44 in February 1942. It's thought he'd done only one raid before being rostered for Augsburg. On the other hand, Kirke, 25, was vastly experienced and held the DFM. He'd enlisted in the RNZAF in October 1939, and by May 1941 had flown 34 ops on Hampdens, 25 with 83 Squadron, the rest with 61 Squadron. He'd been decorated after all that, the citation saying his navigation 'has been of the very highest order'. After five months instructing he was posted to 455 Squadron, RAAF, also on Hampdens. He did four trips with 455 before surviving a nasty crash on Guy Fawkes Day 1941, which left him with a fractured skull and burns. Recovered after four months, he joined 44, completing three ops on Lancasters before the Augsburg raid.

As planned, diversionary raids on 17 April drew German fighters away from the corridor through which the Lancasters thundered into France at chimney-pot level, but by cruel misfortune an enemy fighter returning to its base spotted Nettleton's group halfway between the coast and Paris and gave chase, calling in aid. The bombers were slightly off course, and Messerschmitts pounced as Beckett broke radio silence to announce, 'Thirty 109s eleven o'clock high.' Despite the talk of defensive firepower, the Lancs had little chance against the fighters, their machine-guns outranged and outpowered by the enemy's cannons. The Germans picked off the rear three one by one, Beckett first, next Crum, then Sandford. Crum managed to put his stricken Lancaster down in a brilliant crash-landing that the seven crew survived. The other two bombers plunged to the ground in hideous gouts of flame, fuelled by bombs and full petrol tanks. Fourteen men died instantly.

Then an Me 109 darted at Rhodes' Lancaster, flying just behind Nettleton. The guns on all three turrets were silent, apparently jammed. Unopposed, the attacker closed in, firing bursts into the bomber's engines. The bomber reared, slewed to port, stalled and crashed in another enormous fireball, Baxter among the victims. No one had a chance.

The attack ended as suddenly as it had begun, the Germans

short of fuel or out of ammunition. The two surviving Lancs flew on, their crews appalled by what they had witnessed and still three hours from their target. Meanwhile, the 97 six were unmolested and unaware of 44's disaster. Elworthy had been half right. They had slipped through. But it does seem surprising that the small force, rumbled by the Germans, was left totally alone for the rest of the trip.

Nettleton reached Augsburg as the sun was beginning to set and easily picked out the distinctive factory he was seeking. No fighters were present, but flak crews, alerted, were waiting. Despite a torrent of fire as he roared over the city at 300 feet, Nettleton planted his bombs and got away safely, the crew watching the blasts after 11-second delay fuses had functioned. Garwell's aircraft was hit badly in the fuselage as it ran in towards the target, but Kirke, lying face down over the bomb sight in the nose, coolly directed his pilot. The aircraft lifted as its bombs went but it was streaming fire and doomed. A couple of miles out of the city Garwell found an open field and accomplished a masterly crash-landing. Four of the stunned and shaken crew, Kirke among them, stumbled from the blazing wreck. The other three died. The survivors were captured. When 97's aircraft came in a few minutes later on the same path of attack, the Germans had depressed their flak guns to fire almost horizontally and shot down another two bombers. The only survivor among the 14 crew was Sherwood — catapulted, still in his seat, from the crashing plane into a clump of trees.

Five Lancasters straggled home to acclaim. Prime Minister Winston Churchill called the raid an 'outstanding achievement', and the British press lauded the flyers and their bravery. Nettleton was awarded a Victoria Cross, Sherwood a DSO. Nettleton continued to fly bombers until shot down and killed in July 1943. Among other decorations awarded was a DFC for Kirke when it became known he was a POW. The first member of the RNZAF to wear the dual ribbons of the DFC and DFM, Kirke remained in the RNZAF after the war but died prematurely in 1957.

The cost of the raid was high — seven of the 12 aircraft and the lives of 37 crewmen. The Lancasters' bombs wrecked their target but the damage was repaired quickly and the long-term effect was negligible, for it was learned later that five other plants were also making diesel engines for U-boats. The real significance was the chilling realisation among Germans that no corner of the Reich was now safe from RAF attack.

The thousand-bomber raids

New Zealand bomber aircrew flooded into Britain in late 1941 and early 1942 as the Commonwealth training scheme, fully into stride, began churning out thousands of men for the RAF. Many of their logbooks show the targets of their first raids as Cologne, Essen or Bremen, sometimes all three, in May and June 1942. Scores of these young New Zealanders were still under training, not really primed for operations. But ready or not, they flew to those big German cities, pressed into service to make up the numbers in what became known as the thousand-bomber raids.

Conceived by Arthur Harris and approved by Winston Churchill, the raids were designed as a master propaganda stroke to demonstrate the hitting power of Bomber Command: one thousand aircraft flying over one target in a short time, swamping civilian and military defences, dealing death and destruction.

Harris and his lieutenants scraped up every serviceable plane and airman they could find for the first strike, and when naval chiefs went sour on the big operation and pulled out 250 Coastal Command aircraft, they went round the airfields and training stations once more, roping in incompletely trained crews in clapped-out planes. In the end Bomber Command put 1047 aircraft into the air on the night of 30–31 May for the opening thousand-bomber blitz. Bill Chorley in *Bomber Command Losses* says 678 were from Main Force bomber squadrons and HCUs, the rest from the bomber OTUs and sundry training units — 'all crewed by a rich mixture of "old hands" and trainees in the final stages of learning the bombing trade'. Hamburg was the favoured target, but in the end weather forecasts dictated that Cologne, Germany's third-largest city after Berlin and Hamburg, would be the objective.

When crews learned they would be concentrated in a stream from which they were not to deviate, they voiced concerns about the danger of collisions. The authorities were ready, and at briefings airmen were told experts reckoned only two aircraft would be lost to collisions — which led to the famous crack by one wit, 'Yes, but which two?' In the event the experts were right. There was only one collision.

The raid proved an outstanding success. About 890 aircraft in three waves actually reached the city, on the Rhine south of the Ruhr Valley, passing over in a record short time of 90 minutes and dropping almost 1500 tons of bombs, two-thirds of them incendiaries. The city did not burn as Lubeck had for it was more modern and its streets wider. Just the same, immense damage was done, upwards of 500 people were killed and as many as 150,000 fled.

Chorley puts British losses at 27 Main Force and 12 OTU crews plus one or two others, including a Blenheim intruder from 2 Group's 114 Squadron, shot down while attacking a German night-fighter airfield. The plane was flown by New Zealander John Fox, 24, on just his third op. He died in a hospital from injuries on 1 June, leaving a widow in Wellington. Eight other New Zealanders lost their lives on this big raid, five of them still under training and on their first operation. At the other end of the scale were two highly experienced pilots, both of whom had completed tours and held the DFC. Harold Blake, 24 (Christchurch), was called down from Lossiemouth in the north of Scotland, where he was instructing, to fly a Wellington with a crew in training from an airfield in Warwickshire. His aircraft crashed near Dusseldorf and although his body was recovered it could not be located after the war and he is commemorated at Runnymede. Donald Harkness, 25 (Midhirst, Taranaki), a squadron leader on 158 Squadron, had completed at least 34 ops when he lost his life on the Cologne raid. He had sailed to England in late 1938 to join the RAF.

Among several New Zealanders who became POWs on this raid was Geoff Gane from Blenheim, known to everyone on 12 Squadron as the Kid because he looked so young and cherubic. He acquired the name at No. 1 Bombing and Gunnery School at Jarvis, Ontario, in 1941, and when he graduated in late May a Canadian newspaper trumpeted that the youngest airman was 'Geoff Gane, a 17-year-old New Zealander. Gane will be 18 next month. He's one of the youngest flying members in the Commonwealth Air Training Scheme.' Another report said he'd 'got into the New Zealand air force and out of the country before anyone found out his age'. Gane was delighted to have fooled the newspapermen. He was in fact a month past his 21st birthday.

Gane was posted to 12 Squadron at Binbrook, Lincolnshire, just before the Cologne raid. He flew that night deeply pessimistic about his chances of survival and felt he wouldn't come back. He'd watched friends die — gunner Peter Gennon, 25 (Granity, West Coast), whose plane had crashed into the Channel on his first op, and close mate Eric Inder, also from Blenheim, killed while they were still at OTU. Inder was older than Gane — at 29 — but the two men had gone through training together. Inder had also been lost on his debut trip, an OTU leaflet raid over France. Killed with Inder was another wireless operator/gunner, Wilf Mutton, 21 (Wellington). The loss of Inder had unsettled Gane: 'We were waiting for their Wellington to come back about 2.00 a.m. because we were going up on the same aircraft on a cross-country flight.

They didn't come back and so we trudged off to bed.' He wrote later: 'I knew we had a hard, even hopeless task, to come through alive.' Gane, Gennon and Inder had been among the first batch of New Zealand gunners sent to Canada for training.

Near Cologne Gane's Wellington, flown by Australian Bruce Shearer, was trapped by a blue master searchlight and quickly coned by others. They escaped the lights with a violent stall turn but as they got away their port engine started spitting sparks — 'most uncommon for a Rolls Royce to catch fire, I thought', says Gane. He watched embers streaming back past his turret. 'They got bigger and bigger. Not much smoke but a hell of a lot of embers, and I thought, "Now that's not right," and I started to feel around for my parachute. When the skipper said "Bale out", I was more than ready.' He was captured next morning.

Another New Zealander who fell into German hands was navigator Doug Cookson of Christchurch, a member of a settled 158 Squadron Wellington crew halfway through a tour. Suddenly he was shuffled into a scratch team on a 1652 Conversion Unit Halifax and off to Cologne. Not quite 22, he was at Driffield, near the Yorkshire coast, on the eve of the raid when he and a crewmate, wireless operator Jack Tavener, were called in and told 1652 needed two crew for a Halifax — 'you and you'. They packed overnight bags and later in the day their raid pilot, Englishman Stan Wright, flew his Halifax into Driffield, picked them up and winged back to 1652 at Marston Moor, west of York.

Plucking two men from Driffield at a moment's notice to fly with people they'd never met in a crew of just five in a plane that normally carried seven indicates the extreme measures taken to get 1000 bombers into the air. The particular model of Halifax Cookson and Tavener found themselves on, one of just a handful, had no dorsal turret. Instead it had Vickers guns in beam positions — without gunners. Cookson was expected to drop the bombs as well as navigate. He was introduced, shook hands and said hello to the inexperienced flight engineer and rear gunner before takeoff, but that was the extent of the men's knowledge of each other. Wright had a DFC and a tour behind him but hadn't flown ops for some time.

Cookson, used to flying with a top team, felt uneasy.

Our 158 pilot always moved the plane about on ops so we didn't make an easy target and I'd got used to that. We flew straight and level to Cologne. When I went down into the nose to fuse the bombs as we neared the target, I felt very uncomfortable. The engine exhausts weren't shielded properly and were glowing red for everyone to see. I just didn't like the feel of things.

Then it happened. Tracer poured past from behind and the Halifax shuddered under the blows of a fighter's cannon fire. 'The rear gunner never fired a shot and was probably killed outright before he could react. The fighter must have been right behind and shot away the controls at the rear. I think one engine was on fire.'

Wright ordered the bombs jettisoned and told the crew to prepare to jump but Cookson couldn't get the escape hatch open as the plane tipped over into a spin and centrifugal force pinned him down. 'This was the end, I thought. I just sat there waiting for it.' But Wright managed to wrench the Halifax out of its death spin and fly level again. Desperate, they got the hatch open and the four men still alive jumped. All became POWs.

New Zealand pilot Roy Calvert eluded the clutches of the Germans by a whisker, skilfully flying his 50 Squadron Manchester back to England on one engine. He was at the start of a distinguished career that was to bring him a DFC and two bars. He'd been on a leaflet raid, a mining op as second pilot and then another leaflet drop on his own before taking off for Cologne as skipper on his first bombing trip.

We made our run-in at 9000 feet and had no difficulty identifying the target as the whole city was alight. We could see the Rhine clearly, even the Cathedral, which was close to our aiming point though we had been instructed not to destroy it if at all possible. Terry Taerum, my Canadian navigator [later to fly with Guy Gibson on the Dambuster raid] called 'Bombs gone', but as I closed the bomb doors a burst of flak hit us and the starboard engine burst into flames.

Engine feathered, the flames died out, and Calvert evaded the searchlights clamped onto the crippled bomber. He turned for England and began a long battle to keep the aircraft in the air. The bomber started to lose height and the crew heaved out all the moveables. Calvert unfeathered the crippled engine to see if it would run but the moment the engine began turning flames erupted, so he had to feather it again. The Manchester was down to 100 feet as it crossed the Dutch coast and flew out over the North Sea.

Trying every trick he knew, Calvert found that by closing the radiator flaps and using maximum revs he could get the Manchester up to 200 feet.

The engine then overheated so I opened the flaps and reduced revs and we sank back gradually to 100 feet. I kept on repeating this process until we saw the English coast ahead.

As the hard-working engine ate up fuel, the plane became lighter and easier to handle, and uplift over England took the plane to 800 feet. The damaged bomber landed at Tempsford, Bedfordshire, where the crew found shrapnel had burst the engine coolant pipe.

For 'Tinny' Constance, the Cologne raid was the last operation of his tour as a Hampden pilot with 408 Squadron, RCAF. When

New Zealand High Commissioner Bill Jordan visited the squadron just after the raid, Constance told him it had been so bright over Cologne it had been just like daylight. 'We stooged around for a good look and then flew straight across the target and dropped our bombs in the middle. We were held by searchlights for five minutes, but only because I was a chump and remained looking at the fires. But we escaped safely.'

Fellow New Zealand pilot Bill Gould said: 'We saw Cologne's fires when crossing the Dutch coast [about 150 miles away]. They glowed like a cigarette butt.' Gould, then a sergeant, had been commissioned and promoted to flying officer by the time he was killed three months later over Saarbrucken on his 25th op.

The second thousand-bomber raid, to Essen on 1–2 June, was much less successful than the Cologne operation. Bomber Command managed to raise only 956 aircraft, and haze or cloud shrouded the city, making it difficult for crews to find the target. Bombs fell all over the Ruhr and more people were killed in Oberhausen and Duisberg than in Essen. Thirty-one bombers were lost and five New Zealanders were among the dead aircrew.

The final thousand-bomber raid, on Bremen on 25–26 June, saw a record attacking force in the air and also the greatest loss of RAF aircraft so far. Bomber Command mustered 960 planes of every type in service: 472 Wellingtons, 124 Halifaxes, 96 Lancasters, 69 Stirlings, 51 Blenheims, 50 Hampdens, 50 Whitleys, 24 Bostons, 20 Manchesters and four Mosquitoes. According to *Bomber Command War Diaries*, which gives these totals, never before had such a mixed force been dispatched, and never would be again. At Churchill's insistence Coastal Command sent 102 Wellingtons and Hudsons, and Army Co-operation Command put up another five, making a total of 1067 aircraft. Forty-eight Bomber Command and five Coastal Command aircraft were lost. Though Bremen was cloud-covered, leading crews dropped their bombs accurately, beginning fires which many of the following crews then bombed. The damage inflicted was much greater than at Essen but the results were not as good as those at Cologne.

Thirteen New Zealanders died on the Bremen raid, bringing the total of those killed on the three big operations to 27. 75 Squadron put up a record 23 Wellingtons for Cologne and 20 for Essen and Bremen. Only one aircraft was lost on the three raids — a Wimpy on attachment from a gunnery school — and no New Zealanders were aboard.

Almost all the New Zealanders killed on the Bremen raid were from OTU crews. One of two exceptions was Ralph Farrow, a Lancaster pilot from 83 Squadron at Scampton, Lincolnshire. Farrow had flown 495 hours and was on his 22nd operation yet was still four months short of his 21st birthday. He and his older brother, Phil, both flew on the Bremen raid. By the time of the thousand-bomber raids, Phil had finished a tour at 408 Squadron and was instructing. He was called in to pilot a Wimpy to Bremen. He got home to find his brother missing. Devastated, he was given time off and went to Scampton. 'I spoke to the CO and said, "Well, let's hope — he may be a POW." The CO looked at me for a minute, then shook his head and said, "No show." Someone had seen him go down.' Farrow's Lancaster crashed near an ammunition dump about 20 miles from Bremen. All seven crew lie in Sage War Cemetery.

75 Squadron suffers attacking Hamburg

Bomber Command's twin attacks on Hamburg in the late summer of 1942, one on 26–27 July, the other two nights later, were mere pinpricks compared with the great firestorm raids on the city exactly one year later, when countless Germans died. But the opening strike, the first in three months on Hamburg, proved significant in its own way. It caused major damage and for the first time the city's fire department had to call in outside help. About

340 people were killed and another 1000 injured. The second attack, flown in poor weather, was much less successful, the RAF losing more than 150 aircrew killed for only 13 Germans dead on the ground. Some aircraft were recalled, others turned back and only 68 of the 256 dispatched actually bombed the target. Aircraft losses were high on both occasions — eight per cent of the force on 26–27 July, almost 13 per cent on 28–29 July. In 3 Group, to which 75 (NZ) Squadron belonged, the second-night loss rate reached 15.2 per cent.

From a New Zealand perspective the two raids proved disastrous. No fewer than 31 New Zealanders lost their lives in the first attack, and two more on support operations were also killed, making a total of 33 — the most in a single night or day of the entire war.

Hamburg cost 75 Squadron dear too. On the first night the squadron lost two Wellingtons and 10 men. Two nights later six of the 17 Wellingtons the squadron dispatched were downed and 21 men killed. When deaths in other squadrons are taken into account, the two Hamburg attacks claimed 45 New Zealand lives. Another 14 New Zealanders became POWs.

New Zealanders died in 18 separate aircraft on the two Hamburg raids — 15 Wellingtons and three Stirlings. The planes were downed by flak, destroyed by night fighters or lost without trace. One casualty was the result of collision. A 101 Squadron Wellington carrying RNZAF wireless operator Robert Stubbings, 22 (Reikorangi, near Waikanae), had been in the air only 15 minutes after taking off from Bourne, Cambridgeshire, when it collided with a Stirling from the same squadron's conversion flight flying from nearby Oakington. The Wellington ripped off most of the Stirling's port tailplane but the Stirling's crew all leapt out successfully before the aircraft crashed. No one in the Wellington survived.

New Zealand navigator Eric Yates, 21 (Auckland), was brought

home dead on a 142 Squadron Wellington. He was killed by a
night fighter as the bomber approached Hamburg, dying in the
first blast of fire, which also wounded the pilot. The wireless
operator baled out by mistake. Helped by the gunner, who shot
their attacker down, the pilot nursed the crippled plane back to
England. Yates is buried in Grimsby.

A good number of homebound bombers crashed into the
North Sea off Germany, among them Charles Croall's 75 Squadron
Wellington. It went down in the early morning of 29 July without
warning. One moment, despite a few shell holes, it was flying
normally, the next it was in the water. Four of the crew of five
survived the impact in shallow coastal water to become POWs
but the young rear gunner died.

Sixty years after the event Croall is still unsure what happened.
'I suddenly had no control,' he says. 'It just wasn't responding. To
this day I don't know what happened but I think the tail fell off.'
He and his men had endured a tough time over Hamburg and the
Kiel Canal but didn't expect to end up in the ocean.

> The master searchlight found us at Hamburg and then they all
> coned us after we dropped our bombs. We had to dive almost to
> ground level to shake them off, but we weren't hit and began to
> climb as we pulled away and headed for base. We got back up
> to about 12,000 feet but as we crossed the canal we were caught
> by the lights and coned again. The Germans began firing and
> shells started going through the plane. They weren't exploding
> so obviously they hadn't got our height correct. They weren't
> set to explode at our level. But they had us in their sights so I
> dived for the ground again. We went down to about 1000 feet,
> lost the guns and flew on.

But somehow the heavy flak shells, knocking holes in the frame,
had done unseen mortal damage. Ten minutes after clearing the

canal Croall flicked on the intercom and announced, 'It's time to climb and fly home.' With that, the aircraft simply crashed. 'The control column came loose and we hit the water in a matter of seconds.'

Croall was strapped in his seat as the Wimpy plunged into the sea. He remembers little of the next few minutes except that suddenly he was out of the aircraft and floating. Navigator Ron Harvey, from Christchurch, and front gunner/bomb aimer Bill Bright, from Auckland, popped up alongside him. Amazingly, Croall could see wireless operator Jimmy Gratton, an Australian living in New Zealand when he enlisted, standing in the opened astrodome, the observation bubble atop the fuselage.

The water was only about 14 feet deep where the Wellington had gone in, nose down at an angle of 45 degrees, in a wide bay offshore from the town of Tonning, not far from the German–Danish border. A good part of the fuselage was exposed and even in the dark the survivors could see the tail had gone. There was no sign of rear gunner Tom Crarer, who came from Wairoa. Shocked and stunned by the suddenness of it all, the survivors splashed about in their Mae Wests calling for the 21-year-old. There was no answer. The sea was chilly but mercifully flat calm. The dinghy had popped out of its wing compartment automatically and inflated, and the four men dragged themselves aboard and began paddling.

'We could see a vague outline of the coast and I guess we were about a mile out,' Croall remembers.

I thought the shore was lined with trees and figured a forest would be good for hiding up. The dinghy had holes in it, started filling, and we weren't making much progress. So a couple of us got out and pulled the dinghy along as we swam. Then I got tired and let my feet drop. They touched bottom and we waded ashore.

The forest wasn't forest, it was grass. And the Germans were waiting, spaced out along the shoreline. 'We walked up to one of them and that was that.' Crarer's body was found by the enemy and buried in Tonning before later reinterment in a cemetery near Hamburg.

Jack Moller, who now lives in Whakatane, has stark memories of July 1942. As bomb aimer and front gunner, he was a key member of Terry Kearns' crew, which was to complete a tour with 75 Squadron and then, without pause, another with 156 — one of the first four pathfinder squadrons. Kearns, one of New Zealand's top World War II bomber pilots, flew three tours, his last with 617, the Dambusters.

The crew teamed up at 11 OTU, Bassingbourn, Cambridgeshire, in early 1942 – Kearns (the West Coast), Moller (Hawera), navigator John Barclay (Dunedin), wireless operator Morrie Egerton (Winton) and rear gunner Buck Price (Waianiwa, Southland). Egerton, at 26 the oldest in the crew, was married — the only one in the crew who was — with a son born after he'd left New Zealand. All survived the war, all were decorated.

The Kearns team flew both Hamburg raids, their 14th and 15th ops. Moller, a youthful 19, had the time of his life the first night. Their Wellington — in the first wave with a load of incendiaries for starting fires to light up the target for the follow-up bombers — was coned by searchlights over the city. Kearns dived steeply, down to rooftop level, before flattening out. At one stage they were so low they roared under high-tension cables strung between pylons. Moller laughs as he remembers. 'As we went under, Terry lifted the nose so the big tail would drop and not snag the cables. We got through OK.'

As they flew off, Moller and Price fought an exciting and exhilarating private battle with searchlight crews. The Germans depressed their lights, looking for the cheeky bomber they could hear but not see. Whenever they got a chance — and there were plenty because the city was studded with belts of lights — the gunners turned their barrels down the beams and clattered off hundreds of rounds. Says Moller:

> When we hit them, the lights exploded with a brilliant flash of whites and pinks and went out. The ones I missed, Buck got from the rear turret. I think we shared seven lights between us that night. It was very satisfying. We were young and shouted out when the lights blew up. We were like kids who do wheelies today. Something in our systems we had to get rid of.

Moller and his mates exulted again when they knocked out a machine-gun post firing at them from alongside a searchlight. Moller took aim and cut down a German who jumped out of the gun pit and dashed across a paddock: 'I gave him a burst and bowled him over.'

But Moller grieves when he remembers the high price 75 Squadron paid on the second night. 'It was a real balls-up; we lost so many guys I'd trained with in New Zealand, Canada, OTU. We'd expected another saturation raid over Hamburg but the other groups were cancelled and some planes didn't make it. We saw them being shot down around us . . . they just picked us off . . . like ducks in a shooting gallery.'

Another 3 Group squadron that suffered severely on the Hamburg raids was 115, which always had a good sprinkling of New Zealanders — 67 of whom were killed during the war. Flying Wellingtons, it lost four aircraft on the opening raid and two on the next. Remarkably, all the first-night losses went into the North Sea. One of three Wellingtons ditched skilfully by their captains was flown by Jim Howells, who died in Auckland in 1995. On his first trip as captain, Howells had dropped his load of high explosives and incendiaries and was flying straight and level to get a good target photograph when flak smashed the port motor. The bomber immediately began to lose height, and by the time it crossed the coast getting home was out of the question. The crew all made it into the dinghy only to find the flares package defective. With no way of attracting aircraft flying overhead they drifted for three days before being spotted and picked up by a German seaplane from the air-sea rescue base on Norderney, one of Germany's East Frisian Islands.

Two New Zealanders from another 115 Wellington also owe their lives to a Norderney rescue plane after 38 hours in the water. Navigator Barney D'Ath-Weston, now a spry 91-year-old Aucklander, was nearing the end of his tour when he took off from Marham, Norfolk, on the first raid. Three of the four other crew, including pilot Jim Burtt-Smith, were English, but Canterbury farmer Bill Frizzell was in the rear turret. 115 Squadron, equipped with the new *Gee* radar navigation aid, was among the first over Hamburg, dropping flares and their 4000-pound bombs to guide the other squadrons to the aiming point — the job the new Pathfinder Force would be doing when it began operations the following month.

A night fighter attacked as they began their long flight home, and D'Ath-Weston thinks flak also thudded into an engine, which spurted flame. Burtt-Smith got the fire out but the motor was finished. 'The Wellington was supposed to fly on one engine but I'm damned if ours could and we began to lose height,' D'Ath-Weston says. Moonbeams playing on the water and a calm sea helped the pilot land safely, and the Wimpy floated for about 20 seconds, enough time for all five crew to get out. When day came the sun shone and dried the men's sodden uniforms. They hoped for rescue by their own side but the Norderney seaplane found them first.

> It landed in the water, came up to us and by accident or design one of the floats got under the dinghy, lifted it up and dumped

us in the water. It worked well for them. They fished us out
on the end of a boat hook and dragged us onto the pontoon,
spluttering, wet again and what have you. They frisked us for
weapons and then put us in the rear of the plane and flew us
to Nordeney, one of them holding a revolver on us.

Following the Hamburg raids, many New Zealand families were
shattered by the arrival of condolence telegrams. For two of
them, Hamburg meant a second bitter blow. Mervyn Lund, 23,
whose parents Gustaf and Mary lived in Mt Eden, Auckland, had
died on 25 July 1941 as captain of a 103 Squadron Wellington
that had exploded and fallen in flames over Holland. The next
night George Wells, 23, navigator on a 10 Squadron Whitley, had
been lost in the North Sea. His parents, George and Ada, lived
in Feilding. Now, unbelievably, over Hamburg on 29 July 1942,
a year later almost to the day, the airmen's brothers — Clarence
Lund, 26, second pilot on a 7 Squadron Stirling, and Charles
Wells, 28, bomb aimer on a Stirling flying with 1651 Conversion
Unit — were among the dead.

Four other New Zealand families who grieved over the loss
of sons on the Hamburg raids were to lose a second son later in
the war.

Death in the Ijsselmeer

A 75 Squadron Wellington shot down in the Ijsselmeer during
the second Hamburg raid unwittingly provided some of the most
poignant photographs of the entire air war. Four of the crew were
New Zealanders — pilot John Gilbertson, 22 (Waipawa), navigator
Martin Byrne, 32 (Auckland), wireless operator Ron Callaghan,
22 (Gisborne), and bomb aimer/front gunner Alan Rutherford, 33
(Auckland). The rear gunner was Englishman Bill Titcomb, 21.

What happened to this aircraft was first disclosed by writer
Roy Nesbit, himself a wartime RAF navigator, in Britain's

Aeroplane Monthly in December 1988. According to Nesbit's account, Gilbertson's plane was homebound after dropping its incendiaries when it was attacked by a night fighter. Both Rutherford and Titcomb were keeping a sharp lookout from their gun turrets as the Wellington beat its way over the northern part of the Ijsselmeer, Callaghan providing another pair of eyes as he stood in the astrodome. Gilbertson weaved slightly, but this routine and the three watching crew didn't help. Unseen, an Me 110 flown by Wolfgang Kuthe, 35, from the big German airbase at Leeuwarden, pounced from beneath at 3.05 a.m. on 29 July, apparently having spotted the bomber on his Lichtenstein interception radar set. Cannon and machine-gun fire sprayed into the bomber, wrecking the electrical cables and preventing the power-operated turrets from turning. But when the fighter appeared in Titcomb's arc of fire, the Englishman opened up. Hearing him, Gilbertson asked over the intercom for instructions. 'Dive starboard, dive starboard,' Titcomb shouted. 'You're in charge. Over to you,' the pilot called back. Those were the last words Callaghan heard from Gilbertson. The plane was falling fast as the wireless operator clawed his way forward toward the cockpit. Byrne, wounded in the back, lay on the floor, parachute on. Gilbertson had blood on his right temple but was still trying to control the Wellington. Rutherford had come up from the nose. Then the plane hit the water.

Callaghan and Rutherford were the only survivors, apparently floating free from the fuselage as it broke in two. Held up by their Mae Wests they bobbed about in the water for two hours until a searching launch scooped them up. Their German rescuers treated them well, dressing gashes, handing them warmth-giving tots, drying them off and replacing their sodden uniforms with fresh, warm outfits. Rutherford walked ashore with support, Callaghan was carried. Before they were shunted off to Dulag Luft for interrogation some days later, they were taken out to a beer garden for drinks by friendly German officers. Nesbit says it's almost certain one of these was Kuthe. The Messerschmitt pilot had eight victims to his credit when he was killed, his plane flying into the ground at Leeuwarden in 1944.

Gilbertson's Wellington had crashed in the Ijsselmeer near a seaplane base, and a salvage vessel moved quickly to lift the wreck in the Germans' continuing search for new specialist equipment installed in RAF bombers. As the crane on the ship hoisted the crumpled forepart of the bomber to the surface, wings still attached, Gilbertson's body was exposed. The cockpit around him had shattered but he was still strapped into his seat, looking as if he were merely asleep. His hands were clasped together as though still holding the control column. Byrne's body was also in the aircraft. Titcomb's washed ashore some days later.

Nesbit first became aware of the Gilbertson story in 1986 when he unwrapped a set of photographs of the salvage operation from a German source. An unknown photographer had taken shots of the two survivors, the salvage operation and the destroyed Wellington. Nesbit quickly traced the aircraft by its serial number — BJ661, clearly visible in one of the photographs of the fuselage. He found out the names of the crew and contacted Callaghan and Rutherford, then still alive in New Zealand, for details of what had happened to the bomber in its death throes. The Gilbertson family gave permission for the photograph of their dead son to be published.

Like a bit of netting going through the air

Like many bomber captains, New Zealander Laurie Dobbin gave his life trying to save a crewman. Wireless operator and fellow countryman Jim McQueen and two others baled out of their 75 Squadron Wellington over Holland on 11–12 August 1942, and there was time for Dobbin to follow them. But the bomb aimer, another New Zealander, had opened his chute in the aircraft and refused to jump. Dobbin wouldn't leave the youngster and died trying to crash-land. Shot up by a fighter, on fire, bombs still aboard, the Wellington fell near Vaals, a small town in the finger-like extension of Dutch territory at the country's southern extremity, between Belgium and Germany, in the wooded foothills of the Ardennes.

Counting Dobbin and his bomb aimer, 10 New Zealanders died that night during a raid on Mainz, a city on the west bank of the Rhine just below where the river hooks southwest before straightening to flow north toward Cologne. Three of the 10 Wimpys 75 Squadron sent failed to return, and seven of the 10 casualties were in these aircraft.

By chance, the rear gunners on all three Wellingtons lived, two of them sole survivors. One of the two was New Zealander Jack Atkin, who emerged from the flaming wreck of his bomber on the ground near Dusseldorf, astonished he wasn't dead. The other, an Englishman, parachuted over land just before his crippled aircraft, piloted by George Bradey, 25 (Maharahara, Hawke's Bay), who'd been severely wounded by flak over Cologne, plunged into the sea. Atkin and McQueen, imprisoned in the same barracks in POW camp, became close friends — a friendship that endures today.

McQueen had a short war. Southland-born and -raised, he was an Invercargill bank clerk when he joined the RNZAF in late 1940. He trained in Canada and crewed up in England with an all-New Zealand team posted to 75 Squadron in early July 1942. But the crew's navigator, Phil Spittal, 26 (Christchurch), was killed over Hamburg on 26–27 July, and two nights later skipper Ken Westerman, 24 (Hastings), flying as a second pilot for experience, and rear gunner Jack Savage, 33 (Christchurch), died when 75 lost six aircraft on the second of the Hamburg raids.

That left McQueen, 21, and Aucklander Red Jury, 20, the only original crew, and McQueen had yet to do an operation. The pair joined Dobbin, also new to the squadron, and two Englishmen, one of them gunner Bert Elson. They were all happy to fly with Elson, who had already completed a full tour. He gave them confidence.

At 29, 'Dobby' was older than the others and had more than 720 flying hours to his credit. Born on a dairy farm in Taranaki, he'd worked hard during the Depression to put himself through university and teacher-training college and was working at Wairoa District High School when he enlisted in June 1940. He rated above average as a pilot and was commissioned in New Zealand. He reached Britain in February 1941 but once there was held back as an instructor. He had one op to his credit when he joined 75 — one of the thousand-bomber raids of mid-1942.

Dobbin, McQueen and the others flew one complete mission together on 9–10 August, to Osnabruck. Two nights later they were still a long way from Mainz when they were hit by a night fighter. The starboard engine began burning and oil ran into the bomb bay, producing choking smoke. Dobbin called for the bombs to be jettisoned but for some reason they couldn't be. Then he ordered the crew out. The aircraft had dived steeply but he'd got it under control and McQueen jumped from the rear. Later, Elson, who'd gone up front, told him what had happened next. Part of Jury's chute had billowed out of the open front hatch but together they had wrestled it back from the grasp of the slipstream and Jury had wrapped his arms around it.

> Bert urged Red to jump but Red wouldn't go so Bert went himself. There was nothing else he could do. He told me there was nothing to stop Laurie jumping other than leaving Red behind. He wouldn't do that and obviously tried to crash-land. We reported this at our debriefing back in England in 1945. We considered Laurie deserved a posthumous decoration but we didn't hear any more about it.

McQueen landed unharmed in a field and walked into Belgium, where he was soon picked up by a German patrol.

A mechanic by trade, Jack Atkin grew up in Warkworth and now lives in Kawakawa. He joined the air force as a gunner. 'I wanted to be one, that was my whole ambition.' As a young man he was happiest when he was out shooting — 'rabbits, pigs, anything'. He remembers the Mainz trip, his ninth, as the best bombing run the crew had. 'I was sitting in the back turret and knew the bombs had gone. I counted each one as it went off. We dropped them in a stick, in a line.'

His Wellington was homebound when hit by box-barrage flak near Dusseldorf.

> The starboard engine caught fire. I could see it from the turret. I think the other poor bastards in the aircraft were dead actually. We were so riddled by shell holes we were like a bit of netting going through the air. I yelled out that the engine was on fire and then there was just one ungodly bang. From what the Jerries told me later, we must have dropped a wing; and they said we struck a house. Whether that's true I don't know. Then the plane hit the ground.

Atkin was knocked out by the impact, and when he came to and realised he was on the floor and alive, he also realised the Wellington was burning. 'How I got out I don't know to this day, because I couldn't open the turret door. But somehow I pulled myself free. The heat and flames were starting to melt the turret Perspex, and when there's fire around you you've got massive strength.'

Stunned, badly cut, pouring blood and shattered by the crash and the death of his crew, Atkin was picked up by the 'brown-shirt bastards', bandaged and thrown in a jail, where he was left alone for two days. The Luftwaffe found him, apologised for his rough treatment and took him to hospital, where he was put between white sheets and his injuries treated. When he was taken by train to Dulag Luft for interrogation, however, he still couldn't walk, and lay stretched out on a seat. 'I was black and blue with bruises everywhere. You'd think I'd been in a big fight.'

The worst six months of the war

The lives of New Zealand aircrew in Bomber Command haemorrhaged in terrible numbers in the second half of 1942. July to December that year was the worst six months of the war for deaths, with more than 360 killed and many taken prisoner. *For Your Tomorrow* notes that those 360 were more than all wartime RNZAF deaths in the Pacific. Large numbers of New Zealand airmen reached Britain in late 1941 and early 1942 as the full effects of the dramatic increase in training programmes were felt. After that the war in the Pacific, where New Zealand was directly threatened, began to drain away men who would otherwise have gone to the European theatre. Growing numbers were recalled to New Zealand after training in Canada, some even returning from Britain.

In both percentage terms and absolute numbers the tally of New Zealanders in Bomber Command began to peak in the second half of 1942, and the casualty figures reflect this. Bomber Command was also suffering greater casualties from stiffening German defences as 1942 wore on. Over the whole year, one in every 25 aircraft dispatched from England failed to return — a record four per cent average loss. As *For Your Tomorrow* observes: '1942 ... was by far the grimmest for bomber crew survival.'

The worst one-night toll of New Zealanders was the 33 killed in the 28–29 July raid on Hamburg, but night after night groups of New Zealanders died in blazing bombers over Europe: in August, 10 on the night of the 11–12th, 13 on the 27–28th, 10 again the next night; in September, 11 on the night of the 6–7th, 19 on the 10–11th, 17 a few nights later. So it went on, raid after raid. Fifteen on 17–18 December, a week before Christmas. The long casualty lists in newspapers, with their frightening 'Missing On Air Operations', spread desperate anxiety into many New Zealand homes.

Raids with only one or two casualties were just as sad for individual families. June Jamieson of Palmerston North remembers how her father's hair went snow white overnight when his only son, Arthur, was reported missing after an attack on Aachen, Germany, on 5–6 October. At home in Woodville, 'He used to listen to the radio in the hope that Arthur would be mentioned, that his name would come over but it never did.' News about missing servicemen and those in POW camps, as well as snippets of information from the Red Cross and other sources, was regularly broadcast by radio.

Twenty-year-old Arthur Schaw was on his 13th op the night he was killed. Seven of the eight men on the 102 (Ceylon) Squadron Halifax parachuted successfully. Schaw may also have escaped the plane. June Jamieson: 'I think Dad had a letter from his wing commander saying his parachute didn't open or that he was hit by flak as he jumped.'

Some aircrew — a few — floated serenely through an entire tour, even in the worst of times. Others, like Schaw, attracted trouble for reasons known to no man. They were simply on the wrong side of the odds in the air. Schaw got into real problems one night in August 1942. Attacking Bochum, in the Ruhr, his Halifax was hit by flak as well as cannon fire from a Ju 88. Shells burst across the bomber's wings, hitting the port outer engine, damaging the fuel tanks and tearing the starboard rudder and elevator to pieces. The aircraft fell 6000 feet in a few frightening seconds before Schaw regained control. Then it turned for home but was in trouble as it crossed the Norfolk coast. As Schaw later told a reporter:

> The starboard outer began to splutter and when all the three remaining engines packed up, I gave the order to abandon the aircraft. The navigator, wireless operator and flight engineer jumped. At 800 feet we were too low for anyone else to jump, but suddenly the port inner picked up and I was able to guide

the aircraft between two trees, the wings hitting the branches.
I landed in a turnip field.

Later the same month, Schaw brought back another flak-damaged
Halifax, crash-landing in Suffolk a few minutes before one of his
crew, hit by flak splinters, died from his wounds. Six weeks later
Schaw himself was killed.

Wireless operator Doug Giddens had a close call over Belgium
on the same raid that claimed Schaw. Homebound, already
damaged by flak, with an engine on fire and losing height, his
103 Squadron Halifax was polished off by an Me 110 that attacked
from behind and below at about 4000 feet.

'I never saw the fighter that did us in, but imagine being in
a tin can; it was something like that. Rattle, rattle, bang, bang,
bang.' The Messerschmitt sprayed cannon shells into the bomber
all along its fuselage, hitting the rear gunner and causing more
damage. Splinters whammed into the back of Giddens' right leg,
but despite his injury he went to check on the gunner. The man
was dead.

Giddens struggled back along the fuselage, the pilot yelling at
him to jump. The plane was virtually out of control, the port wing
afire and the ground close. Giddens noted that the altimeter read
900 feet as he leapt below and out the escape hatch, second to
last to leave. One crewman broke his legs and another died after
exiting the plane. The pilot was still aboard when the bomber
exploded on the ground a quarter of a mile from where Giddens
landed, stunned, on a road that he'd seen glistening in the wet
as he'd floated down. He became a POW.

Gravel on a tin roof

Roy Calvert had one close brush with disaster on the Cologne
thousand-bomber raid at the end of May 1942, and a second five
months later when he flew to Hamburg. On the first occasion he

struggled to get a Manchester home on only one engine, barely keeping it out of the sea. On the Hamburg op he had to wrestle a flak-damaged Lancaster back to England. 50 Squadron was still flying the Manchesters when Calvert was posted there but he had only five operational flights on them before the squadron was re-equipped with Lancasters.

The pilot from Cambridge enjoyed flying Manchesters despite their unreliable engines, but he liked flying Lancasters even more. 'It was love at first sight,' he wrote long after. 'To me the Lanc was like a good well-mannered horse — comfortable to ride, easy to manage and it did everything you asked of it.'

On 9–10 November 1942 Calvert flew R5702-S (Sugar) to Hamburg, almost at the end of his first tour. He and his crew had a rough trip to the target, hitting towering cloud as they approached Denmark, cloud that lasted into Germany, gave them icing problems and was so thick they could see nothing that would help identify their position. He turned south to run to the target by dead reckoning. As navigator John Medani told him the ETA on target was up, Calvert spotted a large blue light through a break in the clouds, thought 'railway marshalling yards' and swung to starboard, telling the bomb aimer to get ready. His memoir discloses what happened next:

> There was a crack off our port wing tip and we were sprayed with shrapnel — it sounded like a handful of gravel thrown on to a tin roof. In the cockpit a top forward panel of Perspex and the starboard blister [lookout window] were shattered and our intercom went dead. Then another shell burst on our port, closer this time. Poor old S (Sugar) shuddered violently and we were sprayed with shrapnel once again.

Deadly shell splinters from the second blast scythed through the Lancaster's thin skin, killing wireless operator Lewis Austin outright and smashing Medani's left elbow. Fragments of Perspex peppered Calvert's face and a flak splinter smacked into his left arm. Medani gave his pilot a course for home before collapsing, blood pouring from his wounded arm.

The badly damaged bomber, its radio and most of its navigation aids out, flew left wing low, aileron trim and rudder bias unserviceable. A freezing wind shrieked through the holes in the cockpit and Calvert went down to 1000 feet, where it was warmer and they were less likely to be found by fighters. He struggled to control the bomber and found that if he flew at more than 190 mph it vibrated alarmingly, so they scrambled home at 180 mph, coming in over the coast where river junctions indicated Harwich, in Essex. Because of heavy cloud to the north, Calvert turned south, spotted a cone of three lights and found a flare path. Fog then obscured the lights, but suddenly the runway was in front of him.

> We were a shade too steep. I opened the throttles, pulled back on the stick, then cut the throttles. The wheels hit and collapsed and we skidded along on our belly, gradually turning to the right . . . until we slid on to the grass and stopped. I switched everything off. We were home! On my way out I said goodbye and thanks to Lewis, my friend and wireless operator for many trips.

They had landed at Bradwell Bay on the Essex coast.

After a short stay in hospital Calvert returned to the airfield 'to pay my last respects to poor old S (Sugar). She was a sad sight, splattered all over with shrapnel. The elevator and rudder control rods were three quarters shot through in three places, but she hadn't let us down for twenty-four ops over France, Germany and Italy, surely reason enough for my love of the Lancaster.'

Calvert didn't know until long after he had retired that Sugar hadn't been scrapped as he'd imagined. By late August 1943 she'd been repaired and flew again with 100 and 625 Squadrons. She was on her 43rd operational flight, to Berlin, on 15–16 February 1944, when she was shot down over Denmark with only one survivor. An aviation historian was given remnants of the aircraft by Danes living near the crash scene in the late 1980s, and a small piece of wing tip arrived in Calvert's Cambridge letter box one day in 1996.

Both Calvert and Medani were decorated after the Hamburg raid, Calvert receiving a bar to the DFC awarded earlier in his tour, Medani a DFM. Calvert, flying again a month later, finished his tour on 2 January 1943, instructed for a year and then flew a second tour at East Kirkby, Lincolnshire, with 630 Squadron. When he finished in July 1944, his operational tally at 59, he was acting CO of the squadron. His wartime service ended with a third DFC.

Calvert's 630 crew was a nicely balanced Commonwealth mix — himself, two Australians, a Canadian, a Yorkshireman, a Lancastrian and a man from England's West Country. Bomb aimer Bob Hogg, the Yorkshireman, remembers Calvert as a 'superb pilot' and a good friend. 'It was my good fortune having Roy as my skipper. He instilled confidence with his calm approach . . . during rather frightening times when we felt very vulnerable, and he could handle the aircraft with great skill.'

It was fun — sometimes

Bomber operations were life-and-death struggles, fraught with deadly danger. Occasionally, though, they were plain good fun, and some skippers and crews seemed to get more than their fair share of such romps over enemy territory. Nick Williamson, who flew with 214 and 75 Squadrons, had many tough trips, but sometimes he and his crew hugely enjoyed themselves. For a short period in late 1942, the Williamson team, which included another three New Zealanders, had a whale of a time on 214.

They rained down incendiaries on a German factory from a mere 50 feet in the dead of night, flew so low they got a piece of tree through the nose of their Stirling, shot up trains in the dark and exchanged fire with flak and searchlight batteries. 214 historian Jock Whitehouse calls the Williamson team 'brave and skilful', a 'fantastic crew' who proved exceptional practitioners of the art of low flying into and out of the target zone. 'Their gunnery was exceptional as was the bomb aiming, but to allow this to happen the pilot had to be one of the very best.'

Williamson, born in Gisborne in 1918 and still living in the house where he grew up, flew Stirlings with 214 with navigator Archie Davis (Auckland), wireless operator Keith Neilson (Wanganui), bomb aimer/front gunner Ron Florence (New Plymouth), and two top-class specialist gunners — Englishman Cliff Passingham up top and Danny Gaunt, a Rhodesian, in the rear turret. They did 23 ops as a team before they went different ways in the spring of 1943. Williamson, Davis and Neilson were all commissioned when they arrived at Stradishall to join 214. Florence, already there, was happy to crew up with the other three when they found they needed a new bomb aimer.

The crew's most memorable outing was just before Christmas 1942, to Damme, a small place 25 miles north of Osnabruck. 'The idea was for Stirlings to fly on moonlight nights and go in low, really low, below 100 feet, tree-hopping,' says Williamson.

> We entered into this with relish, practising over the Wash and nearby land, disturbing the stock. Low, low, low, with the farmers in the paddocks shaking their fists at us. The target was a factory making some sort of component. We flew in over the Zuider Zee [now the Ijsselmeer] and here's this destroyer sitting in the middle of it. Keith's got his trailing aerial out with lead balls on it. We went over between the masts of the destroyer

and pulled off the ship's aerials. The ship starts shooting but Danny at the back fired right back.

The Stirling careered across northwest Germany, Davis navigating by the stars. 'We found the factory and attacked from 50 feet, sprinkled a couple of cans of incendiaries on it, went around again and approached from another direction and sprinkled more. It was burning nicely when we left.'

As the Stirling swung away, extremely low, the branch of a tree crashed through the nose of the aircraft, narrowly missing Florence. The tree also damaged other parts of the aircraft, which was suddenly almost uncontrollable. Williamson wrenched her back up as one wing tip almost scraped the ground. Just how close to disaster the plane had come was clear next morning, when ground crew found bits of shrub embedded in the wing tip and declared, 'This is carrying low flying too far.'

Homebound, Williamson manoeuvred the Stirling, despite difficulties, to give his three gunners maximum opportunity to shower fire on two trains steaming across the countryside, all lights on in the certain knowledge no English bomber would be that low at that time of night. The gunners blazed away, setting the trains alight from end to end, the Stirling close enough for its crew to see Germans leaping from carriages. 'One of the trains stopped as it approached a station, where the platforms were alive with people. Not all of them were alive when we finished. The eight Brownings fired off hundreds of rounds. They were pretty lethal at only 300 feet.'

The crew's time together ended in the early spring of 1943. Williamson was needed as an instructor and Davis was posted to 3 Group headquarters, where his incomparable navigational abilities were employed until the end of the war. The skipper left 214, now at Chedburgh, a Stradishall satellite, with a DFC and Florence with a DFM. Davis got a DFC later. Only Neilson went unrewarded. Wireless operators were so often overlooked. He stayed on at Chedburgh acting as squadron signals officer. He was on duty on the night of 25–26 June when a wireless operator reported sick at flight time for a raid on the Ruhr and he volunteered to fly in the man's place. He parachuted into a Dutch cornfield when his Stirling was shot down, one of only two survivors, and spent the rest of the war in prison camp.

Florence instructed at an OTU for three months then went to 617, the Dambusters squadron, flying with Ted Youseman. On 16–17 September 1943 his Lancaster was part of a small force that flew to Cannes for a low-level attack on the Antheor Viaduct, which carried the coastal railway to Italy. No direct hits were scored. A repeat attack on 11–12 November after high-level training with the new Stabilised Automatic Bombsight was no more successful.

Instead of returning to England direct as usual, the Lancasters flew on to Blida, in Algeria, and then to Rabat, Morocco, preparatory to the flight home. Late on 17 November Youseman's aircraft lifted into the night sky and turned north, routed along the Iberian Peninsula and across the Bay of Biscay. It was never seen again. The entire crew and three army men thought to be passengers perished.

New Zealander Les Munro, flying one of the other 617 aircraft that night, describes conditions on the flight as the worst he ever encountered. 'We flew about 7000–8000 feet under a front the whole way and I was airsick at the controls for the only time on my service overseas. The weather was violent and there was a lot of electric stuff.'

Is it possible Youseman's plane was hit by lightning and exploded? Perhaps — but at one stage Munro saw a brief flash in the sky about 15 miles ahead that didn't look like lightning. 'It might have been a Jerry night fighter but I don't know what he'd be doing out there [in the Bay of Biscay].'

After 15 months as a Stirling instructor, Williamson joined 75 Squadron as a flight commander in mid-1944 and flew another 20 sorties. On the last day of June he became an instant celebrity — the man who landed a Lancaster on a fighter strip in the Normandy beachhead — the first heavy bomber to touch down in France since the invasion three weeks earlier. He was flying a daylight mission to Villiers-Bocage, a crossroads close to the fighting, where German armour was massing to attack.

> We were approaching the target and in among the flak when Pat McDevitt, the engineer, came up and stood beside me. As I leant forward to do something a shell exploded very close and a piece of flak the size of an apple went between my back and the seat. I sat back and there's McDevitt with the white bone of his knee exposed and blood pumping out. He just looked at me. I can still see his eyes, like a spaniel asking for help.

The crew couldn't stem the blood, and moments after bombing Williamson decided to land and seek medical help. He'd spotted the fighter field on the way in and turned for it now, peeling away from the bomber stream. 'The closer I got, the smaller it got, and I had to land downwind because of heavy German ground fire.' He just cleared a boundary fence, stall-landed from about 10 feet and got the tail wheel down to help the drag. Even so, the strip disappeared in a flash, the Lanc stopping with a gentle ground loop in an overrun area. The injured engineer was rushed to a field hospital while the commander of the squadron operating from the strip wagged his finger at his pilots: 'Don't complain to me about this strip. If a Lancaster can get down then you should have no trouble, blah, blah, blah.' The fighter boys made rude gestures in Williamson's direction.

The New Zealander now had a problem though. He hadn't done a formal conversion course on Lancasters and had no idea about the sequence for starting the engines. He had to wait two days until the engineer recovered well enough to instruct him. It seemed to Williamson that the entire British army lined both sides of the runway when B (Beer) prepared for her historic takeoff. 'Bomb aimer Graham Coull [from Christchurch] held the throttles back while I revved her on the brakes and then let her go. By God, those Rolls Royce Merlins were magnificent bloody engines. We cleared the fence and she was up.'

Williamson's crew trooped off the plane at Mepal wearing German helmets, waving swastika flags and bearing copious amounts of wine and cognac. Williamson even carried a souvenir Spandau machine-gun, which he eventually presented to High Commissioner Bill Jordan.

Almost a Victoria Cross

New Zealand pathfinder pilot Frank Watkins was just short of his 21st birthday when he was killed in December 1942, giving his life in a vain attempt to save a close friend — and earning a recommendation for a Victoria Cross.

A member of Watkins' crew, held in a POW camp in Germany, revealed the pilot's heroism, and the commanding officer of 156 Squadron urged the award be made, strongly supported by pathfinder chief Don Bennett. The head of Bomber Command ruled against an immediate VC on the grounds of insufficient supporting evidence, but Arthur Harris suggested further investigation when POWs were repatriated at the end of the war. However, when peace came the authorities reduced the proposed award to a mention in dispatches, the only other allowable posthumous honour, for 'gallant and distinguished service'.

The young man who acted so nobly was born in Dargaville in March 1922 and grew up in Ruawai, a small farming community a few miles away. He did well at the local district high school before moving to Wellington, where he was working for the Native

Lands Office when he enlisted at the age of 18, on 1 December 1940.

Watkins sailed for Britain in June 1941, flew five ops on Manchesters with 106 Squadron, one with an OTU and then 21 on Wellingtons with 150 Squadron, based at Snaith, Yorkshire. He was chosen for the recently formed pathfinders in late 1942, joining 156 Squadron on 1 December, by now an experienced and capable pilot.

He flew twice to Turin that month as the RAF continued to pound Italy following the invasion of North Africa, and then just after 6.00 p.m. on 20 December, two days after his commission had come through, he lifted his Wellington off the runway and headed for Duisberg, in the Ruhr. The Wimpys, increasingly easy pickings for night fighters, were doing almost their last ops with 156; the squadron got its first Lancasters on the final day of 1942.

Flying with the New Zealander as his navigator was John Carter, a squadron leader with a DFC. Writing from Stalag Luft III on 5 January 1943 to 156 CO Tommy Rivett-Carnac, Carter described how they'd taken a direct flak hit over the target, bomb aimer Bill Brooke-Norris being severely wounded. The bombardier had flown with Watkins for some time and the two men had become close mates. Carter said they'd intended to inject the wounded airman with morphine and then launch him from the aircraft by parachute but while getting him ready they'd been coned and hit again and suddenly the aircraft was too low and out of control. The rest of the crew had already jumped when Watkins ordered Carter out and said he was staying.

> Had he not been so devoted to his friend he could have saved his own life by leaving the dying [bomb aimer] to his fate. Yet he refused to do this and attempted the alternative crash landing . . . his life was forfeited in the crash ... He

willingly and selflessly gave his life in a forlorn effort to save his friend . . . his actions were the most outstanding example of . . . sacrifice. I am inspired by his memory.

Recommending a VC for Watkins, Rivett-Carnac wrote: 'This final record of his unquestionable and unequalled courage in the face of death is considered worthy of the highest award that can be made by His Majesty the King . . . It would appear that at no time did the question of his own safety enter Watkins' mind.' The recommendation was endorsed by the station's group captain ('This act of unselfish sacrifice, cool devotion to duty and astonishing courage') and Bennett ('The manner in which [he] went to his death is an outstanding example of heroism and self-sacrifice'). A VC, Bennett said, would be a lasting tribute to Watkins' memory as well as to the memory of the many other captains who had sacrificed their lives under similar circumstances. Harris sent the recommendation to the Air Ministry for further investigation when POWs were repatriated, 'as I consider that the supporting evidence is insufficient at present'. Carter and the rest of the crew might have been interviewed after the war, although this isn't known. Whatever happened, the outcome was a mention in dispatches, gazetted in June 1946.

Watkins and his bomb-aimer friend, found in the crash remains in the target area, lie together in Reichswald Forest Cemetery.

Thomas Fredrick Duck

Nick Carter believes a nightmare debut operation in mid-1942 taught his crew a lesson that helped them survive the war. They'd crewed up in England in the early spring of 1942, five young New Zealanders on a Wellington: pilot Jack Wright, 28, who'd been a clerk in a meat works near Hamilton; navigator Charlie Kelly, 21, a porcelain enameller from Christchurch; wireless operator Carter, 20, a telegraphist from Hastings; front gunner Podge Reynolds, 23, who'd worked in his father's Lower Hutt grocery store; and rear gunner Bruce Neal, 19, not long out of school in Warkworth. Posted to 75 Squadron they flew together on ops for the first time on the night of 20–21 June to Emden, a port on Germany's northwest coast.

'It was a bright moonlight night, [a] fairly short trip,' Carter remembers.

> We'd bombed and were back over the North Sea when Bruce yelled suddenly, 'Dive port, dive port!' I was standing in the astrodome. Everything went haywire and we fell into a huge dive. Banging and flashing and lights. I thought to myself, 'So this is how you die.' And then we pulled out, just above the water. Bruce got a squirt at the fighter, claimed him as a possible. The German had been stalking us.
>
> The entire side of the aircraft where I was standing was just about ripped right out — one big hole. We were unzipped back to the tail. When I stood up again I found my head out in the open. The astrodome cover had been blown right off. And there were half a dozen holes over Jack's head in the cockpit. A real mess at the back, hydraulic oil everywhere and Bruce cut off in his turret. We finally landed after a fair bit of trouble. Bruce said he wouldn't fly again but the group captain told him, 'Yes, you will,' and he did.

The crew learned a great deal that night.

> I think it was the best thing that ever happened to us. We never relaxed after that. No talking, no skylarking. We stayed alert from the moment we took off until we got down again. It's probably what kept us alive. A lot of young guys thought it was a big adventure. They all got in the aeroplane carrying on, yapping away, and before

they knew where they were they were shot down.

Wright's crew needed a replacement aircraft and were given D (Donald). After a while they decided they needed some artwork on the nose. Donald Duck was chosen as a subject and a talented ground-crew artist drew him to the crew's specifications — wearing helmet, goggles, earphones and New Zealand wings and sitting in an egg shell. The mascot, painted on a piece of the fabric used on the Wimpys and doped onto the frame, proved a lucky talisman. The Wright crew survived while all around others in 75 were falling from the sky. In July and August 1942 eight Wellingtons went down in two nights on Hamburg, three on Mainz, one on St Nazaire, one on Kassel and another two on Nuremberg. Fifteen in four weeks. Only half a dozen crews came through that bad period.

Wright's men did the last ops of their first tour from Mildenhall, Suffolk, where 75 was stationed from August to November 1942, and it was there that D (Donald) and its nose art met their end. On a wet day with mist almost down to ground level, airmen on the station heard an aircraft circling. A bomb-laden Boston came in, overshot, crashed and exploded in flames, killing its crew. One flaming motor landed in the bay where D (Donald) stood and the Wellington burned out too.

Their tour finished, Wright's crew — minus Neal, who was posted to a gunnery school — went together to instruct at an OTU at Lossiemouth, in northern Scotland, where they endured a miserable winter. 'Terrible place,' says Carter. When they had completed their 'rest' tour, the four crewmen volunteered for pathfinders. They'd have taken Neal too but the youngster had died in a training crash on 30 March 1943.

Posted to 156 Squadron on Lancasters, they needed another three crew. 'We wanted a bomb aimer/nav,' explains Carter, 'and Kelly said, "What about Alf Drew?" He said he knew where he was and sent him an SOS.' Drew, 27, a linotype operator on the *New Zealand Herald* before the war, had flown a tour on 75 with English pilot Neville Hockaday in F (Freddy) at the same time as the Wright crew had D (Donald), and

Freddy had always parked alongside Donald at dispersal.

Drew jumped at the chance. Now five, the crew became six with New Zealand rear gunner Ken 'Ring-the-Bell' Crankshaw, 22, and English flight engineer Harry Holland made it seven. West Coaster Crankshaw, a motor-garage storeman before he enlisted, was well known to the others. A top-class gunner, he was already at 156, having finished a tour (and won a DFM) at 75 ahead of the others. He'd flown with many 75 pilots, including flight commanders Ray Newton, later to lead the squadron and lose his life doing so, and the renowned Artie Ashworth.

Crankshaw flew his last 17 ops at 75 with extrovert Australian Frankie Curr, a stockman from Queensland who wore brown cowboy boots that he told dress-conscious RAF types were Australian air-force issue. Curr and his crew were doing ops in the days before the strict control of routes and tactics and the discipline of staying in the bomber stream, and Curr liked attacking searchlights. 'When he saw lights coming out of a target,' Crankshaw recalls, 'he'd say, "Let's go down and get the bastards," and if things were a bit quiet over the target he'd tell us, "I think I'll put my nav lights on to see if we can get a bit of flak."'

The New Zealander acquired the nickname Ring-the-Bell while in Curr's crew. He purloined a handbell from the kitchen of a stately home where crews were quartered and from then on carried it in his turret, ringing it into his microphone over the target as the bombs went. Via the transmitter, the sound was boomed out over the airwaves to the accompaniment of the song *Oh, the Bells of Joy Go Tinga-linga-ling* — a 75 Squadron trick to convince the Germans a new secret weapon had arrived.

Crankshaw went to 156 with Curr in early 1943 and did two ops before the Australian was posted elsewhere. He then flew 10 with Terry Kearns, another newly arrived New Zealander from 75. Kearns was to go on to complete a distinguished wartime flying career with the Dambusters squadron, first on Lancasters and then on Mosquitoes with fellow countryman John Barclay, marking targets at low level.

Crankshaw missed going to 617 with Kearns because he was in Scotland on leave when the pilot moved.

At this point the Wright crew arrived and Crankshaw joined, manning the rear turret for the rest of his tour. Reynolds swapped his bomb-aiming and front-turret tasks in the Wimpy for the mid-upper turret of the Lancaster. As they began their operations as pathfinders, they decided they needed a mascot on the Lanc, so a similar but bigger Donald Duck was painted and applied just below the cockpit. D (Donald) was in the past; the team was flying T (Tommy) now. But nostalgia and the fact that newcomer Drew had been closely associated with F (Freddy) at 75 were taken into consideration before the crew voted to name their emblem 'Thomas Fredrick Duck'. It satisfied everyone. 'It sounds a bit childish now,' says Carter, 'but it meant a lot to us then.'

T (Tommy) carried the crew safely through easy trips and tough trips, through storms of flak and fighter attacks, and through the Ruhr campaign, Hamburg and the first big raids on Berlin in the autumn of 1943. And it carried them through their final op — just. One engine failed on the long run to Leipzig in eastern Germany on 20–21 October 1943, the first major attack on the city. Says Carter:

> We were late when we got to the target and couldn't get above about 11,000 feet, and the main force above was dropping all sorts of stuff around us. To make matters worse some of the bombs held up and Alf and I had to chop away at the floor with an axe to get at them. Even then we couldn't get rid of them all.

A second engine packed up after the plane headed for home. The crew discussed the situation over the intercom, thought about trying for neutral Sweden (much closer than England), then decided to have a go for base. T (Tommy) lumbered along slowly on two engines but she got them back. They came in low, hedge-hopping as dawn broke, more than two hours late and posted missing. Everyone on the station had gone to bed.

Jack Wright died in 1956, Podge Reynolds in 1991 and Charlie Kelly in 1995. The other three New Zealanders are still alive, 60 years after they flew T (Tommy) in the dangerous skies over Germany — Nick Carter in Hamilton, Alf Drew in Auckland and Ken Crankshaw in Australia. And Thomas Fredrick Duck lives on. Their tour finished, Carter ripped the painting off the plane, rolled it up and brought it home. It gathered dust on a shelf in his wardrobe for more than 40 years. No longer. It now hangs in honour on a wall at the RNZAF Museum at Wigram, Christchurch.

Fraser Barron

No New Zealander flying in Bomber Command matched Fraser Barron's row of ribbons. When he died in a collision over Le Mans, France, in May 1944 he had a 'full house' — DSO and bar, DFC and DFM. Only 55 members of the RNZAF won the DSO in six long years of war. Barron was one of four of those awarded a bar to that medal, and the only one in Bomber Command. Had he lived there might have been a Victoria Cross as well. Barron was the standout New Zealand bomber pilot of the war.

The man and his record were widely known and admired when he was alive, yet 60 years later he is a largely forgotten figure in his homeland. Quote his name to people outside the circle of aircrew vets, aviation historians and others with an understanding of New Zealand's participation in the 1939–45 air war and you will receive blank stares.

It's partly due to the fate that has befallen Bomber Command and its 55,000 dead, the fate that followed the post-war denigration of the long bombing campaign by people who lay safely in their beds while aircrew flew into the faraway night skies over Germany to take the fight to the Nazis. Fraser Barron deserves better. He should be remembered as a national hero, ranked alongside Fighter Command's New Zealand aces and soldiers like Charles Upham. One day perhaps a New Zealand prime minister will lay flowers on Barron's grave.

Barron was on his 79th op and third tour the night he was killed. He was one of those airmen who seemed to have no fear and didn't know when to call it quits. He chafed whenever he was away from ops. He was bored by between-tour periods as an instructor, forever anxious to get back to the fray. Anyone who flew so many missions survived because they were superb pilots with skilled crews — and incredibly lucky. But the odds finally turned against Barron.

He often wrote to his parents saying he was about to finish ops. On 21 September 1942: 'I am back on ops for a short while . . . please don't worry as I shall probably be finished by the time you get this.' 4 December 1942: 'I've done fifty-three raids now and I'll soon be coming off night bombing for good.' 6 March 1943: 'I have finished ops and this time I'm afraid at least for a year or two. I did sixty-one raids altogether and was about to do the sixty-second when the wing commander [Arthur Harris] said I had done enough and wasn't to do any more.' But he wangled his way back on to ops in early 1944, and on 30 March that year, six weeks before his death, wrote: 'I've done thirteen on this tour now and I shall be doing another eight.'

Barron, born in Dunedin on 9 January 1921, was an average academic student at Waitaki Boys' High School, and at just five feet six inches in height and slightly built was one of the school's lightest rugby players. In 1939 he was working in Wellington as a cadet in the Mines Department. War was much more exciting than shuffling paper. He enlisted in June 1940 and went through training at Taieri and Wigram with Jimmy Ward, who was to win the Victoria Cross. They sailed together on the *Aorangi* in January 1941 and were both stationed at 20 OTU Lossiemouth, Scotland. Training complete, Barron was posted to 15 Squadron, Ward to 75 (NZ) Squadron.

15 was one of the first squadrons equipped with the giant Stirlings and it was on these that Barron flew his initial tour, his first 10 ops as a second pilot and lowly sergeant in the spring and summer of 1941. His

experience and confidence grew quickly as op followed op. He endured fighter attacks, pastings by flak, the attention of searchlights, hung-up bombs, fires in his aircraft, dangerous landings, dead engines, long, numbingly cold trips over the Alps to Italy, and the threat of ditching.

Promotion to flight sergeant ('pay now 15/6 a day') and then pilot officer was rapid, and in May 1942 he won his first decoration, the DFM — basically an end-of-tour award. Thirty ops was the standard first-tour tally, but Barron's was an astonishing 42, 39 straight with 15 Squadron plus another three tacked on with 15 — two of them the thousand-bomber raids on Cologne and Essen — while he was nominally instructing.

Barron much preferred operational flying and got himself posted to 7 Squadron, a founding pathfinder unit, in September 1942, a month after the pathfinders had been established. He flew with the squadron's A Flight, whose leader was the legendary Hamish Mahaddie. By December 1942 he was writing home, 'I think I could get back to New Zealand if I wanted to but I wouldn't like to leave England while the war was on as I would feel out of things.'

The decorations and promotions continued: the DFC ('courage, skill and determination') and first DSO ('exceptional gallantry and devotion to duty'), flight lieutenant (skipping the rank of flying officer) and squadron leader, the latter when he was at an OTU again after finishing his second tour, by order of Bomber Command headquarters, at 61 ops.

He told his parents, living in Palmerston, and only sibling, sister Patsy: 'I got the DSO for a trip to Cologne [defying searchlights and concentrated flak to make two bombing runs], and I really thought they had me that night.' He lauded his crew as the 'most wonderful chaps in the world . . . the only thing I was frightened of was that some day I might let them down and not be able to bring them home. The navigator got the DFM, the engineer the DFC, and rear gunner Jack Marshall from New Zealand has been recommended for the DFC.' Barron's DFC was gazetted on 8 February 1943 and his DSO three weeks later. At the end of May he collected both from Buckingham Palace.

The New Zealander was dedicated to flying and not much else, but when he went back on ops for the last time, with 7 Squadron again, in January 1944, he admitted to his parents:

> I've never had a great deal of time to worry about girls since I've been in the air force . . . but when I was instructing I met a girl I liked very much. This was about ten months ago and I've been very friendly ever since. She was a WAAF at the camp, and we used to see quite a lot of each other on duty. Her name is Marie and her home is in London.

One New Zealander who flew with Barron briefly wrote of him years later:

> I think that he was a virgin but was very understandable of the insatiable biological urges of the rest of us. One night we had been wishing the tail wheel of the Stirling good luck [bomber crews habitually had a final pee on the wheel before boarding for ops] and all of us went into the aircraft except [one crew member] who was having his way with his girlfriend, the WAAF driver . . . The side cockpit window slid back and Fraser said, 'Are you finished yet?' 'In a few seconds Fras.' 'Well, don't be long, I'm waiting to start the engines.'

The same man said Barron was a

> straight and level merchant [while flying] and I wondered at times how he managed to survive for so long — a little gentle weaving over the target but no more. Tubby [another pilot] was different. He and we believed in the maxim that straight and level you were dead, so all I can remember is going up, down and sideways like a ride in a New York elevator.

In early 1944 Barron flew the tough trips that were costing Bomber Command so many casualties — Berlin, Leipzig, Schweinfurt, Stuttgart. Writing home again:

> The Leipzig trip was the only one I did not enjoy much. We lost seventy-eight of our bombers. There were hundreds of night fighters up against us, and it was pretty solid going all the way. I almost forgot to tell you I've been promoted again and am now a wing commander. I never thought I would get as high as that.

On 30–31 March 1944 Barron flew to Nuremberg on the raid that cost the RAF its worst losses of the war, but he had a soft trip. 'It was the quietest op I've ever been on. I seem to be having the most amazing luck.'

Six weeks later he was dead, killed on the night of 19–20 May while acting as master bomber, directing an attack on railway yards at Le Mans by 112 Squadron Lancasters. What exactly happened is still debated but a collision with his deputy's aircraft is thought most likely. The 15 men on the two 7 Squadron aircraft were killed and so were another eight on a Lancaster from 115 Squadron that might also have been involved in the disaster. Among the dead was Barron's New Zealand wireless operator Jack Walters, who'd worked for the post office in Napier before the war. He'd done a tour with 75 Squadron before joining Barron and was on his 51st op the night he died.

Barron rose from the rank of sergeant to wing commander and CO of a major pathfinder squadron in less than two years, and when he reached that position he was barely 23. It's not surprising he was known widely as 'the boy' wing commander. He wasn't the youngest of that rank in the war, indeed wasn't even the youngest New Zealand wing commander. But he was a giant by any measure.

In 1985, in a tribute to Barron compiled by New Zealand's Bomber Command Association, former 7 Squadron navigator Trevor Dill wrote: 'To me [he was] New Zealand's greatest bomber pilot. Quiet, slight, fresh complexion, looked about eighteen. Our crew was operating from 7 Squadron when Fraser was wing commander and we were honoured to fly twice as deputy Master Bomber with him. A wonderful chap who kept on keeping on just that bit too long.'

Bomb aimer Ron Mayhill, destined to serve with 75 Squadron, was at 11 OTU, Westcott, at Christmas 1943 when Barron was there instructing. Baron impressed Mayhill with his charm and modesty as much as his row of medals. 'No VIP table for him. He joined us at our table and instantly made me feel at ease.'

David Mercier joined 7 Squadron after Barron's death but had also met him at OTU. He wrote: 'Of all the good types to meet and serve with, he was a great fellow — my hero. The pinnacle of everything a New Zealander could and should be. I still recall the shock and dismay that went around 3 Group when he was lost and that was nothing compared with the feelings on 7 Squadron.'

Mercier, who now lives in Blenheim, attended the formal dinner marking 7 Squadron's 70th anniversary in England in 1984, the only New Zealander present. He says Barron was warmly remembered that night and that Group Captain Mahaddie said publicly that had Barron lived he would have recommended him for a Victoria Cross at the end of his tour.

Keith Thiele

When distinguished New Zealand pilot Keith Thiele declined a posting to 617 Squadron, the Dambusters, in mid-1943 he may have turned down command of the squadron. Christchurch-born Thiele, 22 at the time, already a squadron leader and the holder of a DSO and DFC and bar after completing two tours, was asked one day to go to see Guy Gibson, VC, the man who'd led 617 on the May 1943 raid that blew the Ruhr dams. A few weeks after that famous operation Gibson had been called in by 5 Group chief Ralph Cochrane and told he was being taken off operations. He had done enough and was not to fly again. The search was on for a successor.

Thiele says he got a message that Gibson wanted to see him at Scampton, in Lincolnshire.

> I didn't know what it was all about but I got in the Tiger Moth [every squadron had one] and flew over there and went in to see Gibson. He was in the mess surrounded by WAAF secretaries and letters congratulating him on his VC. The first thing he said to me was 'When are you coming over?' I replied, 'What do you mean?' and he said, 'Well, I thought you were coming over.'

The conversation didn't advance much further because Thiele, with more than 50 ops behind him, had had his fill of bombers and was desperate to fulfil his ambition to fly Spitfires. He says he hadn't heard anything about going to 617 and told Gibson so. He also informed the Englishman he didn't want to appear ungrateful but disclosed he had all the wheels rolling to go to a unit flying experimental Spitfires as a step out of Bomber Command. 'Gibson was quite reasonable. He said, "I don't blame you. I wouldn't mind doing that myself. I don't know why you'd want to come here." So I knocked it back — whatever was being offered.'

Thiele says now he's not sure precisely what Gibson meant that day, whether he was being offered the squadron, a job as a flight commander or a posting just as a squadron pilot. He wishes he had asked but he was so keen at the time to switch to fighters he wasn't interested in 617. He was never specifically offered command of the Dambusters and wasn't called in by group headquarters for discussions.

All the same, it's a fair assumption that Thiele had been picked out by group HQ as a likely successor to Gibson, for he was a brilliant pilot and leader with the grit and mana to run 617. He held the same rank and was more highly decorated than the man Cochrane eventually settled on, Squadron Leader George Holden, DSO, DFC.

As it turned out, Thiele made the right choice. He had nothing to prove. He already had a dashing record — and it was going to get better. Holden lasted only a short time. The night of 15–16 September, 617's first significant raid since the dams trip, ended in disaster. In a suicidal low-level attack to drop Barnes Wallis' new 12,000-pound thin-case blast bomb on the Dortmund–Ems Canal at Ladbergen, five of 12 Lancasters were lost, among them Holden's. His aircraft was knocked down by light flak on the run-in, hitting the ground in a tremendous explosion that gave the crew not the slightest chance of survival.

Gibson might have sympathised with Thiele's decision not to join 617 in any capacity but 5 Group didn't, taking a dim view and giving him the word that he wasn't going to fly Spitfires. The man who had flown 56 ops, first with 405 Squadron, then 467 Squadron, was banished, posted to a transport squadron and then almost immediately to the trans-Atlantic Ferry Command to fly Canadian-built Lancasters to England.

But Thiele had no intention of being sidelined. He spent three months in Canada, flew one of the first Canadian-built Lancs to England, then pulled strings to get, finally, to a Spitfire conversion unit in early December 1943. 'I loved that aeroplane. God, it was a beautiful thing. The first time I ever got in one, I climbed up high and did some cloud-chasing around the tops. Wonderful.'

Thiele flew Spitfire XIIs and Tempests from Tangmere with 41 Squadron, served with 486 (NZ) Squadron, also on Tempests, from Volkel, Holland, then joined 3 Squadron, in the same wing, at the same base flying the same fighters. He became 3's commanding officer in January 1945. He shot down two German aircraft before flak got him at low level over the Ruhr on 10 February 1945. Burned by the flames from his engine, he parachuted safely but was nearly lynched at a railway station by the German crowd that had been waiting for the train he had attacked. He was taken prisoner in the nick of time by the flak crew that had shot him down. Eventually Thiele and another airman walked out of an open POW camp and got back to Allied lines five weeks before the war's end. In May 1945 he was awarded a second bar to his DFC, making him one of New Zealand's most highly decorated airmen and, it's believed, the only one to win the DFC as both bomber and fighter pilot.

Thiele, working as a cub reporter on Christchurch's *Star-Sun* when war was declared, itched to fly fighters from the moment he made his first flight in the air force in 1941. He was good, too, and one of just 10 commissioned pilots in a group of 50 who left for England in June 1941.

On the train steaming south from Liverpool, Thiele spotted his first Spitfires and was more than ever convinced they were for him. At the reception centre he was asked to state his preference. He confidently wrote 'fighters' and was promptly posted to a bomber OTU. Six weeks on Wellington ICs with Pegasus engines and Thiele was on his way to 405, a Canadian squadron at Pocklington, outside York.

This was before the process of crewing up had developed and airmen were simply posted to squadrons individually and assigned to whichever crew needed personnel. Flying Wellingtons, Thiele did the usual few trips as a second pilot, then was given command. His first mission as skipper, to Cherbourg, France, was almost his last. On return he got the green light to land but as he touched down was confronted by another aircraft looming out of the dark. The two planes collided engine to engine, ripping their wings off. Recalls Thiele: 'He had been doing takeoffs and landings and was taxiing back up the runway. A good start to operations. Two wrecked planes. But the court of inquiry absolved me.'

These were still early days in Bomber Command's attack on Germany. Raids were not yet concentrated, a few planes went to many targets, navigational aids were nonexistent, communications were primitive and studies showed few pilots dropped their bombs anywhere near their targets. 'We probably killed as many cows as anything else,' Thiele reckons.

At that stage of the war the hundreds-strong Main Force bomber streams, precise bombing instructions and pathfinders lay some distance in the future. Pilots did their own thing. Thiele developed his personal technique for ops. He flew between the flak bands — light stuff up to 6000 feet, heavy from around 12,000 feet — bombed at about 7000 feet and then flew home 'on the deck'. It was a good way to evade fighters, although dangerous in the inky blackness. Good or bad, it worked for Thiele as he roamed all over Germany. He also took part in the thousand-bomber raid on Cologne, in a Halifax (405 having by now switched planes), and finished his first tour with 32 ops to his credit — and his first DFC.

Thiele went straight from pilot officer to flight lieutenant, skipping the intermediate rank of flying officer, and then to squadron leader in the space of a few months. 'The early promotions were mostly stepping into dead men's shoes.' The body of one superior who didn't come back was eventually washed ashore and cremated. 'We took up his ashes in a small canister carried by the padre, all robed up. We should have put the ashes out the flare chute but I didn't think and opened a window in the cockpit. The airstream blew them back everywhere.'

The New Zealander hated every minute of the short time he instructed during his 'rest' spell and dropped in rank from squadron leader to flight lieutenant to get back on ops with newly formed 467 Squadron flying Lancasters. 'They were beautiful aeroplanes, so manoeuvrable and nice to handle. No vices at all. Strong and well performed.'

Thiele joined the Australian squadron at Bottesford, Leicestershire, at Christmas 1942 as Bomber Command was expanding rapidly and suffering heavy losses. Morale was bad, too many crews were aborting missions and the number of LMF cases was increasing. In this atmosphere, Thiele's determination to get to his target and back was welcomed by the higher-ups. 'They appreciated anyone who did anything out of the ordinary or "pressed on regardless", as the saying went.' Thiele certainly fell into that category.

One night, set to fly deep into Germany, one of Thiele's engines failed just after takeoff. He flew on, intending to drop his bombs over the English Channel. But the aircraft seemed to perform perfectly well on three motors and he went all the way to the target and back.

Thiele performed sensationally late in his second tour, twice bringing home Lancasters missing both starboard engines, each time knocked out by flak. On 14–15 April 1943, returning from Stuttgart, he touched down on one wheel without flaps after the hydraulics failed. One wheel was down and couldn't be retracted, the other wouldn't go down. In a masterly landing, Thiele held the aircraft steady as the wing minus undercarriage sank slowly to the ground. The bomber was almost stationary before the wing tip touched the earth.

The following month he came in on two engines again. Coned by searchlights over Duisberg on the night of 12–13 May, on one of the heavy raids during the Battle of the Ruhr, his Lancaster was badly damaged by flak. He brought the crippled bomber back to a safe crash-landing at Coltishall, Norfolk. 'That made about five aircraft I'd wrecked in two tours,' Thiele jokes.

Australia's official war history saw it differently. It said of his Stuttgart epic:

> This difficult feat, which succeeded only because of Thiele's cool airmanship and the engine power, manoeuvrability and rugged construction of the Lancaster aircraft, gave new confidence to crews of his own and other squadrons facing the ever increasing gun defences of the Ruhr.'

Thiele's inspirational flying was why he got the DSO and another DFC in quick succession on his second tour. The DSO was announced on 12 May 1943 and the bar to his DFC on the 25th of the same month.

After the war, Thiele flew for years as a senior captain for Qantas, later built and operated a marina in Sydney, and sailed his own yacht across the Tasman to see New Zealand's first America's Cup defence when he was 80. He still lives in Australia.

John Fabian

Wellingtonian John Fabian was a navigator — a good one — posted to 15 Squadron as nav leader for his second tour in 1944. But he distinguished himself in other ways, too. He returned to New Zealand with a double DFC, both awards earned at moments of great crisis in his aircraft and both immediate. Few navigators were so decorated.

Born in 1909, Fabian was a barrister and solicitor working in the capital when he enlisted in mid-1941. Trained in Canada, he reached 75 Squadron in the autumn of 1942, making his operational debut on 16 October. He was halfway through his tour when he won his first DFC on a Hamburg raid on 3–4 March 1943. More than 400 aircraft bombed Germany's second city that night and 10 were lost. Fabian's Stirling could easily have been the 11th.

A news report says the aircraft was hit badly by flak and went down out of control:

> Only the combined efforts of the captain, the wireless operator and Fabian all pulling together on the dual controls brought the Stirling out of the dive when it was only 1000 feet from the ground. Fabian's navigational instruments had been flung all over the aircraft during the dive but he guided the Stirling out over the North Sea, obtained an astro fix and set an accurate course for his base.

Fabian crewed with noted pilot Dick Broadbent for the second half of his first tour. Broadbent, who now lives in Kerikeri, enlisted in November 1939, did 34 ops on Wellingtons with 40 Squadron in 1941 and then, after instructing, joined 75 at Newmarket as C-Flight commander in April 1943. He linked up with Fabian and the two men flew together at the height of the Battle of the Ruhr, bombing Duisberg, Bochum, Dortmund, Dusseldorf and Gelsenkirchen, before Fabian was chosen for a specialist navigation course.

The 25 June raid on Gelsenkirchen, Fabian's last flight with the squadron, was a good one for the crew because the gunners combined to shoot down an attacking single-engined fighter. That night Broadbent was piloting BK778-U (Uncle), as he did on every one of his ops during his eight-month tour with 75. He flew BK778 for the last time on 20 October, when its camera took the widely published photo of Mepal, by then 75's station in Cambridgeshire. This particular Stirling's luck ran out with Broadbent's departure, for it was lost over Denmark early the following month with all its crew, four of them New Zealanders, including skipper Bill Masters.

When Fabian went back on ops in April 1944 it was with 15 Squadron at Mildenhall, Suffolk, in charge of the squadron's navigation. He was on just the third trip of his second tour on 22–23 April when he won his second DFC — and was lucky to escape with his life. His log tells it starkly: 'Shot up over target — Me 109 and predicted flak. Bomb aimer killed and wireless operator fatally injured. 2 motors u/s [unserviceable]. Crash landed at Woodbridge. Great effort by Brooks [pilot].'

The Lancaster was over Dusseldorf when its crew suffered this double whammy. Seconds after Canadian bomb aimer Allan Gerrard released the bombs he was hit by shrapnel from a shell bursting under the fuselage and was dead within three minutes. Fragments from the same shell almost removed one of wireless operator Bob Barnes' legs. The Londoner succumbed on the way home, the crew unable to stem the blood pumping from severed arteries. At the moment the Lancaster was struck by flak a fighter attacked from the rear, knocking out two motors and setting one of them on fire. Shredded by the twin hits, the bomber fell 8000 feet from 22,000 feet before Oliver Brooks could get it under control. Barely airborne, with two engines out and great jagged holes in the fuselage, the Lancaster was in dire straits. Flames in the fuselage, eventually extinguished, created more problems.

The bomber laboured out over the North Sea at 2000 feet and about 100 mph, Brooks just able to keep it from stalling by slowly but surely losing height. While he struggled to maintain speed and altitude, Fabian and the surviving crew threw out everything they possibly could.

Ditching was not an alternative — the dinghy had been shot out of the wing. The plane's height stabilised at about 400 feet, even rose fractionally as the pilot closed on Woodbridge, the big emergency landing field near Ipswich.

Like many another crew, the men on the Lancaster were grateful that April night for lifesaving Woodbridge. Brooks crash-landed the plane, wheels up and bomb doors down — no hydraulics to move either. Despite the terrible damage, he put it down safely and they were home. He and Fabian were given immediate DFCs, a flight-sergeant member of the crew a DFM. The citation lauded Fabian's skill, coolness and determination.

Fabian completed his tour and after the war became a partner in a Napier law firm. He was appointed a stipendiary magistrate in 1968 and served in Wanganui and surrounding areas for 10 years. He died in 1981.

Woodbridge

Built on flat East Anglian land almost on the coast, Woodbridge opened in 1943. It had a heavy-duty runway oriented east–west to take damaged or fuel-short bombers on a straight-in approach from the North Sea. The runway was 4500 yards long and 250 yards wide — twice as long as normal and five times as wide — giving bombers without brakes enough room to roll to a stop and still have hard ground beneath them. The runway actually consisted of three strips side by side. Which an aircraft used depended on the degree of damage it had suffered. The field was stacked with ambulances, medical teams, fire engines, trucks and cranes, as well as bulldozers that could shunt crashed aircraft aside.

Because they were on the coast, Woodbridge and two other emergency fields — Carnaby, in Yorkshire, and Manston, in northeast Kent — were usually fog free. They also had *FIDO* — petrol-fuelled burners beside the runway to heat the air and dissipate fog. *FIDO* stood for either Fog Investigation Dispersal Operation or Fog, Intensive

Dispersal Of. No one was quite sure which — everyone simply used the acronym.

The three emergency fields gave the crews of planes struggling home a sense of security: quick straight-in landings and all the help in the world; no circling fog-shrouded home fields waiting for permission to land.

'Speedy' Williams put his badly damaged 7 Squadron pathfinder Lancaster down at Woodbridge the night of Bomber Command's first raid on Schweinfurt, 24–25 February 1944. As the plane banked to port after dropping its load, two 30-pound incendiary bombs slammed into it from an aircraft above. One ripped a gaping jagged hole in the starboard fuselage behind navigator Trevor Dill, smashing part of his seat, bursting open his parachute and destroying the flight engineer's panel. The other lodged in the inner-starboard engine's nacelle. Dill remembers:

> I could see right out along the starboard wing, the incendiary burning on the engine and the flames streaming back. How it never got into the petrol tanks I don't know. It was pretty hectic for a few minutes. Speedy put it into a screaming dive and we plunged down to 10,000 feet in a few seconds. The slipstream sucked the flames off the wing and then we flattened out.

The damaged Lancaster headed out over Lake Constance into Swiss territory, the starboard inner dead and the outer slowly fading to a stop too. But both port Merlins still throbbed powerfully and they brought the bomber home safely, if slowly, long after Main Force had touched down. 'Speedy flew for five hours across Germany, occupied France and the North Sea with aching arms holding up the dead wing, and made a diving, very fast landing [at Woodbridge] to keep the plane straight.'

Another 7 Squadron pathfinder pilot, Alan Speirs, remembers Woodbridge fondly. He put his Lancaster down there on Anzac Day 1944 after being shot up by a fighter on the way to Karlsruhe. Short of fuel, he zeroed in on the emergency facility. 'It was an amazing field; the runway seemed to go on forever. There was no nonsense about doing a circuit.' The Lanc's hydraulics had gone and Speirs had no brakes. 'We landed, rolled and kept going until we stopped.'

Robin Craw was yet a third 7 Squadron New Zealander grateful for Woodbridge after his Lancaster, homebound following a raid on a flying-bomb site in France's Pas-de-Calais in July 1944, was attacked and damaged by a Ju 88. The unseen fighter set one engine ablaze. Craw feathered the prop and extinguished the fire while taking such violent evasive action the ammunition for the rear guns fell from its feed trays.

'Ground staff accused us of looping the bomber,' he recalls. 'I knew there was low cloud over Oakington [the squadron's Cambridgeshire home base], I didn't fancy circling on three engines and I didn't know whether the wheels under the shattered engine were damaged or not. So I decided to land at Woodbridge. That's what it was there for. It was all lit up and we landed safely.'

Craw, a farmer from Little Pigeon Bay on Banks Peninsula, did 19 ops on Stirlings with 199 Squadron from Lakenheath, Suffolk, before he and his crew, two compatriots among them — navigator Ron Johnson (Scargill, North Canterbury) and bomb aimer Gordon Gibson (Wellington) — were tapped for pathfinder duties with 7 Squadron. They transferred to Oakington and flew another 31 ops between 1 May and 18 August 1944 for a final tally of 50. All three New Zealanders were awarded the DFC at the end of their tours.

Gordon Cochrane

One day in the early 1920s when he was a small boy, Gordon Cochrane watched pioneer aviator George Bolt land a seaplane on the Hokianga Harbour at Rawene. That huge event in the remote little settlement determined Cochrane's destiny. From then on he was determined to fly, and war gave him the opportunity. Backed by glowing references, including one from the district high school's headmaster, Cochrane was accepted for pilot training. He left Rawene, where he worked in his uncle's general store, and enlisted in September 1940.

He ended the war an acclaimed pathfinder captain with 156 Squadron, three tours and no fewer than 88 ops behind him, and the ribbons of a DSO, DFC and two bars on his tunic — a brilliant and apparently fearless pilot. Cochrane was among the most highly decorated New Zealand bomber pilots and, uniquely, his DSO and second and third DFCs were immediate awards in a brief period late in the war. After the war he remained in Britain, joining BOAC, the forerunner of British Airways. He flew Yorks, Hermes, Stratocruisers and Comets before becoming a Boeing 707 captain in 1964. When he retired at the end of 1971 as a senior captain after twenty-five years' service, an executive said, 'He has served British aviation well in military and civil capacities.'

Cochrane's wartime-operations tally on bombers ranked among the highest of New Zealand pilots in non-Mosquito squadrons. He did his opening tour on Wellingtons with 150 Squadron from November 1941, completing 33 ops, including the three thousand-bomber raids, and was awarded an end-of-tour DFC. After attending an instructors' school, he spent 18 months teaching others how to fly multi-engined aircraft and was then posted to 156 Squadron, beginning operations again in June 1944. Over the next 11 months he flew two tours for a total of 55 ops on Lancasters and was frequently the master bomber, directing the markers and Main Force aircraft as he circled the target, often at low level — one of the most dangerous occupations for bombers.

Michael Wadsworth in *They Led the Way*, the story of 156, says the MBs and their deputies were required to display a great deal of precision while flying over the target. 'Again and again, these skilled and courageous captains and crews came from 156.'

Cochrane won the DSO at the end of his second tour in November

1944, the citation praising his 'accurate and determined bombing in the face of concentrated anti-aircraft fire'. Wadsworth says the DSO was recognition of a 'brilliant operational career with the squadron'. Ten days after it was announced, Cochrane had his second DFC, won the day before Christmas 1944 during a daylight raid on a Dusseldorf airfield. He was over the target seven minutes before the main stream and was hit by flak. A lump of iron burst through the nose of the aircraft and ricocheted around the interior but somehow missed him and his New Zealand bomb aimer, Keith Dee. Despite this he continued to direct the attacking bombers for another seven minutes before turning for home.

Cochrane's third DFC was won in even more stressful circumstances on the night of 7–8 February 1945, when he controlled the bombing of two fortified towns standing in the path of British troops massing to cross the German frontier. The citation says that soon after reaching the target his port wing sustained severe damage and part of it fell off. 'Undeterred, Squadron Leader Cochrane, with superb airmanship and courage, continued with his task.' The citation doesn't disclose that it was a near-death collision with another Lancaster that ripped some of the wing off. Cochrane himself wrote some years later: 'It was a dark night and the pilots had only a fleeting glimpse of the other aircraft as they were banking . . . but in that split second they managed to avoid a fatal accident.'

Another scary moment occurred on 2 November 1944, when his Lanc 'crashed' on its takeoff run at Upwood, 156's Cambridgeshire airfield. The circumstances made the accident one of the most celebrated of the war. As the bomb-laden Lancaster surged down the runway, Cochrane began urging it on as usual: 'Up, up, you bastard, up you bastard,' he roared. A new flight engineer sitting beside Cochrane obeyed instantly, jerking the undercarriage up. The bomber smashed down onto the concrete, careering along the runway in a shower of sparks. The crew, petrified their 4000-pound cookie would explode, leapt from the still-skidding plane and ran for their lives. Amazingly, no one was hurt and the bomb didn't detonate. *Bomber Command Losses* puts the cause of the crash succinctly: 'Premature retraction of the undercarriage.'

Cochrane died in England in 1994.

The men who manned the turrets

> It takes guts to be a gunner, to sit out in the tail
> When the Messerschmitts are coming and the shells begin to wail.

Anonymous gunner

No aircraft, friend or foe, ever approached our tail without Jamie spotting it. The intercom would click on and then the quiet voice would say, 'I think something is wandering about behind us. I've got him covered, be ready to corkscrew.' At no time did I ever think we would be shot down by a fighter. The only one that ever got near was shot down by Jamie and Johnny Keen, our mid-upper gunner.

So wrote Englishman Ron Rae in 2002 of coolly efficient Rex Jamieson, one of the best New Zealand gunners of the air war. Blessed with great vision, quick reflexes and an unerring eye, Jamieson knocked down three German night fighters, scored another probable and damaged several others in the course of two tours, one with 75 Squadron, the other with 149 Squadron. He got two of his victims within a few minutes one night over Berlin in late 1943. He had more 'kills' than many RAF fighter pilots, and his fine shooting was recognised with a DFC.

Rae, a former bomb aimer who served with Jamieson in 149, remembers him as a 'superb rear gunner, a quiet man who never got excited' — and never talked about his successes. Rae wasn't flying the night in July 1944 that Jamieson and Keen got the Me 109 that attacked their Stirling during a supply-drop operation to the Maquis in northern France, but navigator Derek Bigg, another Englishman, was.

He remembers the fighter was first sighted at 600 yards, Jamieson giving their skipper instructions to corkscrew to port and then opening fire with a three-second burst. As the Messerschmitt broke away without hitting the bomber, Jamieson's guns jammed. 'The enemy aircraft, now on fire, started to attack again from port-beam level and Jamie promptly handed over fire control to Johnny, who opened up with a two-second burst at 400 yards. The Me 109 blew up and fell to earth.'

Waitara-born Jamieson, almost 21 when war broke out and working for biscuit manufacturers Bycroft in Auckland, enlisted in November 1941. He trained in Canada, crewed up with pilot Don Whitehead, navigator Peter Dobson and bomb aimer Maurice Parker, all New Zealanders, and joined 75 Squadron in March 1943. A hunter with a rifle from the age of 16, he was a natural with a gun, a crack shot. He once told an interviewer that hitting night fighters was like hitting rabbits.

His first taste of success was over Duisberg on the Whitehead crew's fifth op on 26 April, when he hit a Ju 88. 'It was pretty well illuminated with searchlights and was coming right in at us. I just opened fire and he sort of turned over and went down with smoke pouring out of him. So it was put down as damaged and possibly destroyed.' Jamieson was given a 'probable' credit for another Ju 88 while raiding Dusseldorf in June.

His big night was 23–24 August 1943, in the opening raid in the Battle of Berlin. Jamieson covered his startling success with just five words in his log: 'Shot down two enemy fighters.' Many gunners never came near shooting down a night fighter. Two in a night. Some shooting. Years later Jamieson elaborated a little on his log entry.

We were approaching the target and there was another Stirling coned in the searchlights, and this Me 109 made an attack on that, and as he went past us I opened fire on it and just shot it down; it went down in flames. And about, oh, I'd say somewhere about 10 minutes later, after we had dropped our bombs and were making our way to the first turning point on the return journey, there was a Ju 88 ... dropping . . . some form of illumination where the bombers were altering course . . . I shot that down. He had a light showing, a slick of light, must have been the light in the cabin; well I just aimed there and down he went, smoke belching out.

Jamieson finished his tour with Whitehead, instructed for some months and then was posted to 149 Squadron. He was almost up to 50 ops and the end of his second tour when his war ended abruptly. Flak burst near his Lancaster during a daylight raid on a refinery in Homberg on 2 November 1944 and shrapnel hit him in one shoulder. It wasn't too serious but 149's wing commander wrote in Jamieson's log: 'Certified 2nd operational tour completed comprising 24 sorties and one Air Sea Rescue.' Jamieson died in Auckland in 1999.

A rear gunner bade farewell to his mates when the crew climbed into their aircraft and normally didn't see them again until after touchdown on their return. He squeezed into his own little world — isolated, lonely and cold — at the tail end of the plane. The intercom and a system of lights were his only contact with the others up front. For numbingly long hours, he scanned the black sky for the slightest hint of movement — movement that could mean a lurking night fighter. The mid-upper, with his two guns, played his part too, but the rear gunner was better placed to spot an attacker approaching from behind.

Gunners wore layer upon layer of clothes and several pairs of gloves to try to keep out the cold of high altitude, especially in winter. Many made their unheated turrets even colder by removing the central Perspex panel to give clearer vision.

Four .303-inch Browning machine-guns were mounted in the rear turret of a Lancaster, fed by belts of ammunition in trays running down the side of the fuselage. Each gun could fire 2500 rounds. Late in the war, turrets with .5-inch guns were developed but for most of the conflict RAF gunners had .303s. Hydraulically powered from the engines, the turret moved through a wide arc both horizontally and up and down so the gunner had a broad field of fire. The Brownings could deliver a mixture of tracer, ball, armour-piercing and incendiary bullets at a rate of 1150 rounds a minute, but such sustained fire was rare. Guns usually fired in short bursts of a few seconds. The .303 bullets could damage an adversary at 600 yards and were lethal at 400. The shorter the range, the better the results. The Brownings were popguns compared with a night fighter's cannons, so theoretically a fighter could stand off and destroy a bomber. But that didn't happen often, German pilots preferring close range so as to wreak greater damage and to be sure of hitting their target. When they closed in, however, they became targets themselves. Both sides played deadly games to get the upper hand.

Until the Germans began installing upward-firing *Schrage Musik* in their fighters in autumn 1943, and attacking bombers from their blind spot underneath, almost all attacks came from the rear. The Germans knew that a knocked-out rear turret and a dead or grievously wounded rear gunner left a bomber pretty much at their mercy. The mid-upper gunner was equipped with gear that prevented his fire striking any part of his own aircraft, so couldn't hit a fighter coming in from dead astern and below. Even after the introduction of *Schrage Musik*, a bomber's rear continued to be the prime strike area.

The rear gunner normally ran the show when a fighter attacked from behind, warning his skipper and then giving him instructions on evasive action — usually a corkscrew, so called because that was its effect and what it looked like from behind. The manoeuvre was designed to keep the bomber out of the fighter's line of fire, make it a difficult target and give its gunners a shot at the fighter.

Rear gunner Jim Kirk, from Christchurch, whose 75 Squadron Lancaster was shot down by flak over France in July 1944, says that when the order 'Corkscrew port, go, go' or 'Dive port, go' was given, the pilot would roll off to port 500 feet then change direction and fly down to starboard for another 500. He'd then roll the bomber and climb

500 to port, then change direction and fly another 500 to starboard to complete the manoeuvre and regain his original course and altitude. 'The skipper would complete the corkscrew and repeat the dose for as long as it took to destroy the fighter or shake him off.'

Corkscrews could be extremely violent depending on the degree of danger or the imminence of attack and how the pilot threw the aircraft around. Pilot Doug Hawker, also from Christchurch, performed the ultimate corkscrew one night in 1944. Flying to Brunswick on just his third trip with his own crew on 630 Squadron — 'it was very scary until you had a bit of experience' — the rear gunner forgot to turn on his intercom and Hawker learned they were under attack only when he heard the guns chattering. When the rear gunner finally switched on he shouted that the fighter was coming in on another attack. 'I was looking around to port when the gunner yelled, "Starboard, go." I kicked the rudder and rolled over to starboard and tipped the damn thing upside down.'

The Lancaster had been flying for several hours at 18,000 feet in temperatures of minus 50° C, and when it plunged into warmer air a film of ice instantly spread over the cold windscreen, windows and everything. Hawker couldn't pick up his horizon, and upside down most of his instruments were useless, though the airspeed indicator showed 400 mph, roughly twice the standard cruising speed with a bomb load. He fought a life-and-death struggle to pull the plane out of its dive, and when he succeeded the bomber had so much speed on it zoomed way up again. 'I got myself under control as well as the aircraft, and we flew straight and level.' Then he worried about the fighter. Was he still sitting on their tail? He wasn't. 'He had decided he couldn't compete with that sort of flying.'

Hawker dropped his bombs and had a good trip home, which was just as well because the ammunition for the guns had fallen from the feed lines while the Lanc had been inverted, putting the weapons out of action. Getting through the upside-down experience helped Hawker's confidence but it also made him understand why most crews didn't last five trips. He survived 35, ending up a flight commander with 630, taking over from brilliant New Zealand pilot Roy Calvert, who was promoted to take over the squadron after the death on operations of the wing commander. Hawker had gone from raw pilot officer to veteran flight lieutenant in nine weeks.

Corkscrewing was an effective defence against fighters but it wasn't foolproof and a lot depended on the skill of the pilot, the advice of his gunners and the teamwork of the three men. Night-fighter crews faced with a corkscrewing bomber often went in search of easier prey, but some German pilots viewed the manoeuvre as a combat challenge and clung to a corkscrewing bomber like glue. The longer combat continued, the greater the chances perhaps of a bomber winning. Fighter pilots, particularly the inexperienced or rash, often made mistakes that presented bomber gunners with tempting targets.

Thousands of gunners defending their bombers made the ultimate sacrifice in World War II, especially rear gunners. Many a bomber came home with rear turrets, tailplanes, fins and rudders devastated by machine-gun fire and cannon shells. And often inside those destroyed turrets were the torn remains of gunners. The grim phrase 'They hosed them out' was too often true.

Ted de Joux knocked down three Me 109s in one firefight in 1941 and another two fighters on later occasions, to end the war with a tally of five. He was one of the top-scoring rear gunners of the war, his skill and results recognised by a CGM and DFM, the rare CGM for his brilliant shooting over a long period. He bagged his three Messerschmitts during a daylight raid on 18 December 1941 on Brest to attack the warships *Scharnhorst* and *Gneisenau*. His 7 Squadron Stirling was turning away from the target when seven yellow-nosed fighters pounced.

In a BBC broadcast in 1942 de Joux said: 'When I saw them coming, I expected to be killed. I couldn't see how we could possibly get out of it. They had apparently worked out their tactics before they took up positions in a well-conceived plan.'

One by one the first three came in to attack and one by one de Joux destroyed them.

> I opened up at 400 and got him with a burst . . . he fell away in flames . . . I opened up again and got him too with my first burst . . . [the third] fired and missed because our skipper turned away at exactly the right moment. I opened up on him at 200 yards, and got him at once. He turned over on his back and went down in flames.

The mid-upper forced one beam attacker away but an Me 109 from the opposite side raked the Stirling with cannon shells, destroying the hydraulics which operated the rear turret. Working his guns by hand, de Joux warded off the sixth attack, the German smoking as he broke away. The seventh Me 109 fled.

'Because I could count absolutely on [the pilot], I knew the exact instant to open fire. The fraction of a second I gained each time because of good teamwork made all the difference between whether we would get the fighter or he would get us.'

Ted de Joux later downed a night fighter that swooped on his Halifax over Germany, and then got his fifth kill, the satisfying destruction of a Ju 88 intruder flying over his home base. A battle of wits ended with the German pilot making a fatal mistake and de Joux pouring shot into him.

75 Squadron bomb aimer Ron Mayhill tells a nice story about de Joux in his book *Bombs on Target*. At an OTU in January 1944, he listened to a lecture given by the gunner, in which de Joux told his audience about firing techniques and was surrounded by admirers during the break. Questions tumbled out. Just how did he have time to work out the deflection shots? How many aircraft lengths did he aim ahead of a fighter? 'He looked around to see where the top brass were. "Oh, forget that bull. I just pulled the trigger and hose-piped the bastards."'

Born in Scotland, the son of a New Zealand soldier married there after World War I, de Joux arrived in New Zealand as a small boy and grew up in Temuka and Timaru. He returned to Scotland in the 1930s to live with his grandmother and go to school, and enlisted in the RAF in 1940, transferring to the RNZAF in January 1944. After the war he moved to Australia but died in Timaru in 1983 while visiting his sister.

Among many mid-upper gunners who distinguished themselves was New Plymouth-born Saville 'Micky' Moon, who enlisted in the RNZAF in April 1941. He finished with a DFC but was extraordinarily fortunate to survive, twice suffering savage wounds. He was mid-upper on the flight that won him a DFC on 156 Squadron in 1943 but began his war as rear gunner on a 101 Squadron Wimpy. He was on only his third op, to Kassel on 27–28 August 1942, when his bomber was hit by flak and mangled by a fighter. The plane struggled back to England, crash-landed and burned out at a base on the Suffolk coast. Moon, suffering from severe cannon-shell wounds, was taken to hospital. His injuries were so serious he took nine months to recover. When he was fit again he was posted to 156.

Moon tallied up another 20 ops with the pathfinder squadron before, on the night of 20–21 December 1943, 650 bombers raided Frankfurt. Sitting in the mid-upper turret he was shockingly wounded once more as a fighter attacked the Lancaster. His citation for an immediate DFC says he was badly hit early in the fight, a bullet penetrating his back and emerging through his chest to cause paralysis in his left arm and side. 'Nevertheless, displaying fine spirit, he refrained from reporting his injury and tried as best he could to bring [his] guns into action.'

Michael Wadsworth's history of 156 Squadron says the bomber was attacked three times and both gunners 'performed valiantly in driving off these attacks'. The pilot 'hurled his aircraft all over the night sky in a skilful evasion routine, and nursed the badly damaged Lancaster to Warboys, landing brilliantly, burst tyre and buckled wheel notwithstanding'. The pilot and rear gunner, like Moon, were decorated. But only Moon survived to receive his medal from the king. Twelve nights after the Frankfurt trip, while Moon was still in hospital, his crewmates were shot down and killed over the French–Belgian border while homebound from Berlin. The scarred Moon never flew again and was repatriated. He died in Montreal in the mid-1960s.

On 17 March 1944, navigator Jim Insull, recuperating in an annex to the RAF hospital in Ely, wrote about Moon in his diary.

A fellow Taranakian arrived here the other day, Pilot Officer Micky Moon. He is convalescing from a bullet wound in the chest. The front has healed but the back won't — the bullet went right through him. He is, however, quite mobile, and last Sunday he and I accepted an invitation to spend the day at the home of one of the ladies of the Red Cross who visit us.

A large, highly polished car, complete with chauffeur, called for us and we settled in the back like a brace of VIPs. We sped majestically along for a few minutes until Micky said, 'Don't look so snooty. It isn't so very long ago that you and I were delivering papers for the *Taranaki Herald*.' And he was right. But I countered, 'Please don't call the chauffeur Dig!'

Down in the sea

Bill Chorley's *Bomber Command Losses* lists enormous numbers of aircraft and crews as 'lost without trace'. In most cases the missing planes simply plunged into the sea on their way to or from targets in Germany and occupied Europe. They and a myriad others known to have crashed at sea took the lives of thousands of young airmen, many New Zealanders among them.

All too often men and women listening on distress frequencies in England heard faint signals from aircraft calling for help, sometimes with position plots — then nothing. Another bomber down at sea. Air Sea Rescue (ASR) aircraft, routinely airborne at first light each day, scoured the endless grey sweeps of the North Sea, the English Channel and the Bay of Biscay looking for missing airmen in rubber dinghies. Squadrons mounted searches for their own aircraft. Fighters returning from patrol, light bombers on daylight missions, Coastal Command aircraft — everyone — searched the sea for dinghies. Seamen scanned the ocean for signs of life. Sometimes the hunt for survivors was successful; often it was not.

When ditched airmen were found, ASR made desperate efforts to save them. Larger dinghies were airdropped while aircraft flew protective patrols and directed ships to the rescue. Fishing trawlers, minesweepers, minelayers, patrol boats, dedicated RAF High Speed Launches (HSLs) — every conceivable small craft was pressed into service to save downed airmen. The brave men of the life-saving service launched boats from dozens of towns around Britain. The Walrus, an ungainly seaplane but the backbone of the ASR squadrons, rescued hundreds.

The fact that such an enormous rescue organisation would do everything possible to try to find and then save aircrew down in the sea was a huge morale booster for bomber crews.

Ditching a bomber successfully demanded great skill of a pilot, even in daylight. At night, when most aircraft ended up in the sea, it was doubly difficult; in stormy seas virtually impossible. Moonlight made it fractionally easier. A pilot had to judge his approach just right, hit first with the tail, then let the plane settle. A nose-first landing usually signalled disaster. The plane dug in and kept going, taking everyone with it. A wing touching first could mean a cartwheel and certain death. Crews of battle-damaged bombers flying with impaired controls had little chance of surviving an impact in the North Sea, especially in winter.

Even if an aircraft floated briefly, allowing the crew, or some of them, to scramble into the dinghy, survival was touch and go. Immersion meant almost certain death — within a few minutes in winter. The best bomber crews practised ditching drills over and over. They knew that a familiar routine in which every man knew his job and could do it without thinking was vital to survival.

In the early years of the war, Whitley and Hampden crews had to physically launch rubber dinghies from the rear door or cockpit. In later machines, dinghies that popped out and inflated automatically when an aircraft hit water were stowed in the wing close to the fuselage. Crews of aircraft shot up by fighters or crippled by flak and about to hit the cold sea prayed that bullets, cannon shells or shrapnel hadn't shredded the dinghy.

Ditching was a traumatic experience, more so if an aircraft was carrying wounded. Getting a man torn and bloodied by enemy gunfire out of an aircraft that was awash and clearly sinking was appallingly difficult in daylight, terrifying in darkness. Some aircraft floated a long time, others went down in seconds. Often crew scrambled clear of a sinking plane only to find someone missing. Men risked their lives going back in a bid to save mates — or jumping into the water to do the same. Sometimes men trapped in tangled wreckage couldn't be freed. Shocked airmen watched, appalled, as sinking aircraft carried them down.

A full crew in a small round dinghy found themselves tightly packed together, with no room to move and usually wet and cold. Airmen had to hope their dinghy had been serviced properly and came with rations — and flares that could attract passing ships or aircraft. Sometimes they found themselves totally without equipment or food. The little craft didn't carry radios although small transmitters were among the gear crews took with them into their dinghies if they could.

Men bobbing on the waves hoped for a quick rescue. Every hour spent at sea diminished their chances of rescue. They hoped, first, that they would be found; second, that they would be found by their own side. The Germans, like the British, had an effective search-and-rescue service and plucked many downed British flyers to safety — and captivity.

Sixty-odd years after ditching in the North Sea, Neil Guymer is still angry. Not about the ditching itself but about the stupidity of sending his 15 Squadron Stirling all the way to Berlin in summer when the hours of darkness were short and with a scratch crew, most of them without experience. The 'raid' of 25–26 July 1941 was absurd in other ways, too. Just nine aircraft — seven Stirlings and two Halifaxes drawn from at least three squadrons — were dispatched. It was asking for trouble. Two Stirlings and one Halifax were lost, one-third of the force at a time when German night-fighter and flak defences were still relatively weak and heavy bombers in short supply.

Guymer, a rear gunner, had clocked up 30 ops, but just as he and his crew were about to leave 15 to join Coastal Command a rear gunner failed to return from leave and he was called in as a sub on the Berlin trip. The New Zealander had flown with the skipper but the other five and a second pilot along to learn were on their first op. Guymer scoffs at reports in official records that say the Stirling was badly shot up by a Ju 88, sustaining damage to the fuel tanks.

> A pack of lies. There were simply two navigation errors which put us way off course and cost us fuel. The second brought us out at the coast over what I have always believed was Rotterdam. The anti-aircraft fire was intense, with the result the necessary evasive action cost us more fuel. I have also always thought that but for this latter mistake we had a good chance of making it home, or close to it.

The fuel ran out 20 minutes short of England and the Stirling went down on a dead-flat sea. Stirlings had a poor reputation when it came to ditching, but Guymer's pilot landed the big plane well and it floated for three hours. The crew clambered into the dinghy and five days later, hungry and wet, were washed ashore near Flushing, Holland, greeted by a German officer who uttered the famous words 'Hands up.'

Despite everything Guymer was lucky. The names of his friends who went to Coastal Command are on the panels at Runnymede. Guymer came home after the war, worked in the fruit industry and in 1959 was posted as deputy London manager of the old Apple and Pear Marketing Board. By 1970 he was European manager, and in 1982, nominated by growers, he was honoured with an OBE for the difficult job of negotiating entry of New Zealand apples into Europe after Britain joined the EEC. He lives in England.

Angus MacKenzie survived two ditchings in the North Sea within two months but died when he went down a third time. The 29-year-old was working for a Wanganui motor firm when he enlisted, arrived in England in July 1941 and was posted to 58 Squadron at Linton-on-Ouse, Yorkshire, in late September that year.

MacKenzie had hardly settled in before he was in the water as second pilot on a Whitley that ditched off Skegness, Lincolnshire, at 8.25 a.m. on 10 October. It's not known why the bomber went down but it had been flying for almost eight hours. Everyone was picked up three hours later by the Skegness lifeboat, but it was late in the year and cold and MacKenzie was taken to hospital suffering from exposure.

On the first day of December he was down again. Returning from a raid on Hamburg, his aircraft splashed into the sea short of Grimsby. A passing trawler rescued the entire crew. Few bomber airmen lived through two ditchings but MacKenzie had become a twice-over member of the Goldfish Club in a matter of weeks. He was posted to 35 Squadron, also at Linton, in May 1942, skippering his own aircraft, but lost his life on 8–9 June on an operation to Essen. The bomber was shot down off the Dutch coast.

A year later the pilot's mother and father grieved afresh for younger son Donald, born eight years after Angus. A Lancaster pilot with Australia's 467 Squadron, he was shot down over Germany on the last operation of his tour and killed with his entire crew on 11–12 June 1943. He had a DFC and a Battle of Britain Clasp, having flown fighters before, unusually, switching to Bomber Command.

The MacKenzie family was touched by death a third time when Wanganui woman Jane Winstone, 31, an Air Transport Auxiliary (ATA) ferry pilot, was killed in Britain. She was Angus' fiancee and learned he was missing just before she left Wanganui in June 1942. Winstone, who had learned to fly in the early 1930s, was killed on 10 February 1944 when the Spitfire she was piloting crashed after engine failure on takeoff. She was one of five New Zealand women flying at the time for the ATA, an organisation that flew service aircraft from airfield to airfield and between squadrons and maintenance units.

When wireless operator Maurice Robison finished training on Whitleys at Kinloss, Scotland, in late April 1942, he was posted to 51 Squadron at Chivenor, north Devon, where the unit was on secondment to Coastal Command operating anti-submarine patrols over the Bay of Biscay. Robison, who came from the East Coast, flew most of his 23 patrols with a crew skippered by New Zealander Ron Cook, who completed 39 sorties with 51. (Cook was drowned in a recreational boating accident in Scotland in May 1943.) They had a narrow squeak in August 1942 when three Ju 88s swept in, guns blazing. The Whitley jettisoned its depth charges and found sanctuary in a fortuitous cloud as the rear gunner kept the fighters at bay. 'We circled around for a while and when we ventured out, the Ju 88s could not be seen,' Robison wrote later. Cloud was about the only thing that could save a lumbering Whitley from 88s.

Beaufighters, long-range fighters brought in to counter the Junkers, weren't around on the afternoon of 28 September. Carrying a different crew, Robison's Whitley was confronted by another trio of enemy fighters and this time there was no cloud. Pilot Harold Sullivan took the bomber down toward the sea. 'The 88s attacked in line astern, raking us from tail to nose,' wrote Robison. 'Canon and machine gun fire hit the cockpit area . . . the rear turret took a lot of cannon hits and was a shambles.' Rear gunner Bill Green lay dying. Second pilot Paddy Shaw was slumped over in his seat while Sullivan had a bullet in his back. Robison clamped his Morse key down to send distress signals automatically, then dragged Shaw from the cockpit to the crash position aft while Sullivan, despite his wound, readied the Whitley for ditching.

'With Shaw leaning against me . . . a sustained burst of fire tore through the fuselage . . . I could hear the strikes all around us . . . another burst. I saw a bright flash, then blackness ... and found I could only see from my right eye.' Navigator George Bushell was now also badly wounded.

Sullivan made a superb landing and the uninjured front gunner tossed the dinghy from the rear door. 'I got Bushell and Shaw over to the door and we put them in the dinghy. Returning to the aircraft I found Green dead.' As the dinghy drifted off, the seriously wounded men were given morphine and their comrades did their best to dress their wounds. Robison assessed his own injuries — an eye full of shrapnel, a piece in one ear and three minor punctures in his right hip. He spat blood for an hour.

The dinghy had drifted perhaps a hundred yards when suddenly the depth charges on the sinking Whitley exploded, showering the survivors with water and bits of aircraft. The men used their flying boots to bale out and plugged shrapnel and bullet holes in the leaky craft with bungs from a kit. 'Sullivan and the gunner baled while I pumped on the small hand bellows to keep the air pressure up.' Robison couldn't see over the swell but the weather was good, with brilliant sun.

At sunset, 120 miles from land, they were rescued by a French fishing boat whose crew had heard the depth charges go off and were looking for U-boat survivors. The French sailors, with families ashore, had no option but to take the airmen back to port and captivity. Five days after the ditching the fishing boat was back in Les Sables-d'Olonne, too late for Shaw and Bushell, who died on board. As well as going into a POW camp, Robison lost his left eye. A powerful magnet removed steel shrapnel but the device had no effect on a tiny sliver of copper, which triggered infection.

Sheer determination on the part of searchers — their refusal to give up
the hunt — often saved airmen in dinghies. Thus New Zealander Pat
Towsey found his mate and fellow countryman Reg Coates in the cold
Atlantic in late 1942 after persevering for many hours in the air. Both
men, experienced pilots who'd been together in 51 Squadron, were
flying 10 OTU detachment Whitleys on anti-submarine patrols out of
St Eval, Cornwall, at the time.

Engine trouble forced Coates down into the sea on 31 October, but
not before a distress message had been transmitted and picked up. The
five men on his aircraft made it safely into their dinghy, then began
the anxious wait for what they hoped would be rescue. Towsey was
soon flying towards the lost Whitley's plotted position, firmly resolved
to find his friend. He returned to base two or three times to refuel and
gulp down food. Then he was in the air again and out over the Atlantic,
scouring the ocean.

Towsey's dogged persistence was rewarded late the next afternoon,
when he finally spotted the dinghy, joyfully radioed its position, began
circling and directed a destroyer to the rescue. Coates and his crew had
spent 31 hours on the water. Towsey's DFC citation 10 months later
mentioned, among other things, his prolonged search for the missing
crew. Coates' DFC, awarded about the same time, also noted the same
event and the 'great fortitude' he showed while afloat.

When Towsey met Coates' parents after the war they presented
him with a framed photograph of their son in uniform. Attached to the
frame was a small silver plaque inscribed 'We thank you, Pat'.

Coates lost his life in July 1947 with the RAF's Transport Command.
He was piloting an Avro York which collided with a Scandinavian Airlines
System DC6 in bad weather over Northolt airfield, near London. All
seven in the York and all 32 in the airliner were killed in what was then
Britain's worst civil-air accident. Towsey, a talented musician, died in
Auckland in 1998.

Wireless operator Phil Langsford's first operational flight with a frontline bomber squadron ended in a ditching in the Mediterranean of all places. The pilot of his Yorkshire-based 78 Squadron Halifax made a perfect landing on a flat sea off the coast of Spain after a raid on Genoa. The 7–8 November 1942 op began badly when the plane wouldn't start and the replacement turned out to be a lemon. It had got to only 12,000 feet crossing the French coast, and flak shells exploded uncomfortably close. Pilot Paddy Dowse, an Irish volunteer with a DFC and a full tour to his credit, persuaded the bomber up to 15,000 feet to clear the Alps but as the Halifax flew into Italy one motor, its radiator apparently damaged by flak splinters, had to be switched off. The plane began to lose height and was at 5000 feet over Genoa. Getting back to base was impossible.

Langsford says the crew chose to head for Gibraltar, although they had insufficient fuel to get that far. 'We didn't have maps for further southern travel but there was no blackout in southern France and Spain so we cruised along the coastline a few miles offshore, using the lights as a visual aid.' Off Valencia, halfway down the Spanish east coast, at 3.00 a.m., the engines soaked up the last fuel and Dowse decided to put the plane down outside the three-mile limit.

'We waited tensely for we'd not done this before. I was aware of the attitude of the plane as Paddy groped for the sea in the dark . . . with landing lights switched on, he eased down . . . I could feel the tail lowering until the tail wheel thumped through the waves.'

The Halifax was down safely at 100 mph, virtually undamaged and with no one hurt. A calm sea, no wind and it wasn't cold. The crew scrambled clear and into the dinghy and were picked up by a customs boat five hours later. The largely undamaged Halifax stayed afloat for 10 hours.

The crew was interned in Spain, living comfortably in inland hotels, before transfer to Gibraltar and repatriation to England. Langsford, an Aucklander, spent his 21st birthday in Gibraltar.

The last casualty suffered by 2 Group before leaving Bomber Command was New Zealander Alan Wood, 20, who died on 31 May 1943 in the group's final operation. Trapped, he went down with his aircraft after it had ditched. He declined to have his foot cut off, a move that might have saved his life.

Vic Viggers, who lives in Napier and flew on the same operation, tells the story. He and Wood, an Aucklander, trained together in Canada, Viggers becoming a wireless operator, Wood a gunner. In England they converted to American twin-engined Mitchells. Viggers was posted to 98 Squadron, Wood to 180, both flying from Foulsham, Norfolk.

On 31 May each squadron provided six aircraft for an attack on the docks at Flushing, in Holland. They took off in the late afternoon and were back within two hours — all except Wood's bomber. Hit by flak, FL198 was forced into the sea off the East Anglian coast.

Viggers: 'Everybody got out except Wood, who was trapped. They just couldn't free him. Dobbie [the RAF pilot] told us he said to Wood, "I can save you if I chop your foot off," and offered to give Wood a jab of morphine before doing so. How the hell he was going to hack it off I don't know.'

But Wood, a tall handsome man and a fine dancer who lived for the dance floor, shook his head. Viggers quotes Dobbie as saying Wood was adamant that he'd rather go down with the plane than be a cripple. That's what happened. The aircraft sank, taking the young gunner with it. Dobbie and the others watched distraught from their dinghy. 'It was terrible stuff . . . and Wood was such a corker guy.'

Twenty-two-year-old pilot David Aubrey sacrificed his life trying to save his rear gunner in the sea off France in 1943. The Wanaka man's 192 Squadron Wellington ditched because of engine failure 30 miles from Brest on the night of 15–16 August while flying radio counter-measure duties. Only two men survived to be taken prisoners six days later. After the war one wrote that Aubrey was safely into the dinghy when he'd heard the gunner, a non-swimmer, flailing around in the water crying for help.

They couldn't find anything in the dinghy to tie to Aubrey so he went over the side without a lifeline.

Aubrey kicked off his shoes, asked us to try to follow him and dived into the water. Our attempts to follow him proved too much in the heavy seas. We kept contact by shouting, and after some time we cried to him to come back. But he continued to cry "come on". This was repeated a number of times until we received no answer.

Aubrey, remembered at the Runnymede Memorial, was honoured by a mention in dispatches in the 1946 New Year's honours when authorities learned details of his selfless act.

Pilot Nick Nicklin put his Lancaster down successfully in a rough North Sea on the shortest night of the year in 1944 — quite a feat, and one that saved himself and all his crew, among them fellow New Zealander Snow Baker, the bomb aimer. The 57 Squadron aircraft's engines quit one after another during the homeward journey after an attack on a synthetic-oil plant in Wesseling, 15 miles south of Cologne. The fuel lines to the engines were damaged by a rocket that exploded under the aircraft just after the bomber had left the target, and flight engineer Geoff Copeman couldn't get the 600 gallons in the main tanks to any of the engines. The Lancaster went down 60 miles short of the coast of East Anglia between 2.00 a.m. and 3.00 a.m. on 22 June.

The crew were at ditching stations, escape hatches in the roof of the fuselage open, as Nicklin, alone in the cockpit, guided ND471-A (Able) toward the sea, with no engine power to help him. Copeman wrote about their ordeal in his 1996 book *Right-Hand Man*:

The last engine had now stopped and the only sounds were the rushing of the wind over the open hatch above and Nick's voice in my headphones as he read off the decreasing height: 'One thousand feet . . . eight hundred . . . six hundred . . .' At last, 'two hundred feet' and I pulled off my helmet and shouted, 'Brace for impact!'

For never-ending seconds we hung on; then, with a crash that flung me upwards and banged my face against the roof, Able hit the North Sea. There was a rending screech, accompanied by the hissing of air and oxygen from broken pipes . . . we had been told that aircraft usually bounced when they hit the sea, so we held on tight for the second impact; this time it was surprisingly gentle.

Nicklin's head hit the Perspex above him so hard during the first crunch he smashed a hole big enough for him to climb through, the blow cutting his head and face open. All the crew emerged from the aircraft into the dinghy. 'We soon drifted clear and watched in silence as the mid-upper turret disappeared and Able was gone to her resting place in seventeen fathoms. Thus she ended her fortieth operation and I think we all felt a little sad.'

The seven men, seasick in rough, white-capped waters, endured several hours of pitching around in the dark until daybreak. The sea gradually calmed and they were spotted at 11.30 a.m. by Wellingtons searching on a grid, and picked up by a rescue launch late in the afternoon. Nicklin needed 26 stitches to close his wounds.

Nicklin and Copeman got back to their station — East Kirkby, Lincolnshire — to find how extraordinarily lucky they had been. Of the 133 attacking Lancasters, 37 had been lost — a staggering 27.8 per cent. Only slight damage had been done to the Wesseling plant.

Six 57 Squadron bombers were among the casualties, and 630 Squadron, which shared East Kirkby, had lost five. 'Of the crews, only we seven and six members of a 630 crew — they lost a gunner — got home.'

Nicklin and his crew ditched on their 24th op. A month later they were back flying and by late August they were finished, their tour over. Nicklin was awarded a DFC, and Baker, later commissioned, a DFM. Baker died in Manaia in 1981, Nicklin, a farmer after the war, in Whangarei in 1993.

New Zealander Bill Barnett joined 627 Squadron, a 5 Group pathfinder Mosquito unit, in November 1944, finally achieving his ambition to get on operations. He had been in England almost three years but because he rated highly as a pilot had been used as an A category instructor.

Barnett was shot down into the North Sea the night of 27–28 March 1945 after planting mines at low level in the Elbe estuary in an attempt to block the port of Hamburg. The special mines needed to be placed with pinpoint accuracy.

Barnett let his first mine go, swept round a bend in the river, released the second and ran straight over a flak ship. A hail of shells set the port engine on fire. The Mosquito pulled away in a long climbing turn, the fire went out and the aircraft had managed to reach the coast at 600 feet when the starboard engine stopped. Barnett used a moon path on the water to help him ditch. The tail struck first but the aircraft bounced 300 yards before shuddering to a stop. Barnett was knocked out, coming to when the nose-heavy Mossie was well down with water up to his face in the cockpit. Deep gashes on his head streamed blood. He had a tough struggle to get out of the aircraft and inflate his one-man dinghy.

Barnett then discovered his Australian navigator, Johnny Day, sitting on the wing of the slowly sinking aircraft minus his personal dinghy, now under water in the nose. The automatic release for the two-man aircraft dinghy was disconnected and the manual release out of reach under water.

I tried to support both of us on my dinghy but it was no use so [Day] got back on the remains of the aircraft. He was feeling very cold but there was nothing we could do. I must have lapsed into unconsciousness for the next thing I knew it was daylight and I was in my dinghy full of water and just buoyant, floating in a rough sea with nothing in sight.

Day had perished.

For three full days Barnett drifted, half in and half out of his water-logged dinghy, without fresh water and desperate for a drink. On the morning of the fourth he woke to find the dinghy bumping up and down alongside a six-foot sea wall. It had reached the tiny island of Hooge, one of Germany's North Frisian group. Painfully, Barnett struggled up the wall, crawled 100 yards to a dwelling and hammered on the door for help. The elderly woman who opened up screamed. Barnett had four days' growth on his face, angry head wounds and blood on his forehead, and was coloured deep yellow all over from marker dye.

When the Germans got over their fright they treated Barnett well, tending his injuries. The head of the family who did most for him said in a letter after the war: 'My wife fetched a buddle of rum, at first you wouldn't drink but when my woman's father had drunk a bit, you did it and nearly the half buddle.'

Planting vegetables in the garden

Mine laying from the air, or 'gardening', had a language all of its own. Bombers tending their gardens 'planted' mines, or 'vegetables', in areas code-named after vegetables, flowers, shrubs, trees and fish — Broccoli and Carrots for the Great and Little Belts in Danish waters, Forget-Me-Nots for the Kiel Canal, Oysters for Rotterdam, Beech for St Nazaire . . .

Bomber Command planted mines all the way from Norway and the Baltic Sea to the French–Spanish border in the Bay of Biscay — in coastal waters, straits, rivers, canals and ports. Begun in 1940, the operation was considered one of the command's most successful. Mines destroyed thousands of tons of enemy shipping, hindered ship and freight movements, and tied up fleets of German minesweepers and thousands of flak guns. Hampdens and Wellingtons were used at first, but from 1942, as mining intensified, Stirlings, Halifaxes and Lancasters, with their bigger payloads, were employed. Most mines looked like elongated 44-gallon drums and were dropped on parachutes.

New crews often did mining on their introductory op and some veterans were inclined to look on it as 'easy' work. Perhaps it was, in comparison to the searchlights, flak and night fighters encountered over Germany, but it was far from a picnic, as countless airmen found to their cost. Until the introduction of onboard radar, or H_2S, in 1944 gave crews the ability to identify dropping areas accurately and enabled high-level mining, most mine-laying aircraft had to find their targets visually. This meant flying low, especially in cloudy weather, and bombers on their final run-in to the target area, flying straight and often slowly, were easy targets for any guns within range.

The Germans placed flak ships in favoured 'gardens' or on approach paths, packing guns on hulks, fishing boats and other craft. One hulk, a former light cruiser, carried five huge 105-mm guns. One shell could blow a plane apart. Most flak batteries had lethal quick-firing 20-mm or 37-mm light flak guns.

Pilot Lin Drummond and wireless operator Bill Harvey won immediate decorations after a mining trip in the Bay of Biscay in mid-February 1943. Drummond defied searchlights and flak in a low-level run to place his mines accurately and then flew his damaged Stirling home. Harvey, streaming blood from a deep head wound, ignored his injury to get radio fixes to guide the aircraft back to England.

The two New Zealanders came from opposite ends of the country, Drummond from Auckland, Harvey from Dunedin, and from opposite ends of the social spectrum. The captain was a solicitor when he joined the RNZAF, Harvey a labourer when he enlisted. But social differences didn't matter a damn in an aircrew in which every man depended on his mates. Harvey came up trumps for his skipper when flak knocked out their compasses.

Drummond and Harvey were on their 22nd op, well into their tour on 149 Squadron, when they were briefed to lay mines in the Gironde estuary, the long gash in the French coast leading to the port city of Bordeaux. Drummond, born in 1913, still remembers that night. Piloting just one of four aircraft on the operation, he was to go in at 800 feet to drop his load in the middle of the estuary.

> We got down there OK and went in at low level. It was a clear night and easy to see where you had to drop the mines. But I would have been pretty visible too. Various shore batteries and perhaps those on the estuary as well opened up and got us. Three of the crew were hit, Bill quite severely in the scalp — blood was running into his eyes. The aeroplane wasn't too badly damaged and we didn't get any shells in the tanks. But they knocked out our compasses and though Bill was badly wounded he stayed at his post and operated the wireless to get fixes, enabling the navigator to give me the courses home.

The navigator that night was another Dunedin man, George Patrick, a clerk before the war. He and Drummond started and finished their first tours together and Patrick was awarded a DFC at the end of it, the citation noting that his 'determination to reach and bomb his target in the face of the heaviest opposition has set an outstanding example to the rest of the squadron'. Patrick went on to become the mostly highly decorated RNZAF navigator of the war, winning a bar to his DFC at 109 Squadron, a pathfinder Mosquito squadron, and then a DSO after a third tour with 35, a pathfinder Lancaster squadron. He flew a total of 118 ops. After the war the talented Patrick became a pilot, flying for years with BOAC, forerunner of British Airways.

Drummond remembers Patrick as a first-class navigator. 'He was very skilful and never had any navigation problems. He would say to me,

Training for war. *Pilot Alan Speirs, then 18, at Wigram, Christchurch, in the spring of 1941. He was the sole survivor when his Lancaster was shot down over France in 1944. He came home with a DFC and a Pathfinder's badge. The aircraft here is a twin-engined Airspeed Oxford.*

ANNE DAVIS

England bound. *Laurie Dobbin leads a column of sergeant pilots down Queen Street,
Auckland, to join the* Empress of Russia *in early 1941, eight days after he was married.
He was killed when his Wellington crashed in Holland in 1942.*

Leaving New Zealand. *This group of pilots and gunners on the deck of the* Akaroa *before sailing from Lyttelton in March 1940 suffered cruel losses. Seven of the 11 pilots — those in front wearing flat caps — were killed, all but one while flying bombers. Another two became POWs. Nineteen of the 36 gunners died.*

Final leave. *Geoff Gane on the front steps of his parents' Blenheim-area farmhouse just before sailing for Canada to train in October 1941. A rear gunner, he parachuted from a stricken Wellington over Germany on his first raid.*

New Zealand's first Victoria Cross winner of the air war. *Jimmy Ward stands in the opened cockpit of a 75 Squadron Wellington in August 1941 after the award was announced. He was killed a month later, his bomber shot down over Hamburg.*

Survivors. *Just three of the eight New Zealand pilots in this photograph, taken in the summer of 1941 at an Operational Training Unit, survived the war. Phil Farrow (extreme left, front row) was one. The other two sit together at the far right of the same row — Tinny Constance (flat cap) and Bill Houghton.*

16 O.T.U.
UPPER HEYFORD

Collision peril. *This 75 Squadron Wellington was damaged in a mid-air collision with a Blenheim immediately after rear gunner Davenport Brown shot down a German night fighter in April 1941. The bomber landed safely. The Blenheim crashed.*

DAVENPORT BROWN

'We should have been shot down.' *Rear view of Phil Farrow's crippled 408 Squadron Hampden after a wheels-up crash-landing on a snow-covered Kent fighter field in January 1942. Two of his crew died from injuries inflicted by a pair of German night fighters but his wireless operator-gunner got one of their attackers. Farrow was decorated for getting his bomber home.*

PHIL FARROW

Death in the Ijsselmeer. *Pilot John Gilbertson looks as if he is asleep but is in fact dead in the wreckage of his 75 Squadron Wellington as it is hoisted from the water by a German crane in Holland's Ijsselmeer (Zuider Zee). The bomber was shot down by a night fighter homebound from Hamburg the night of 28–29 July 1942.*

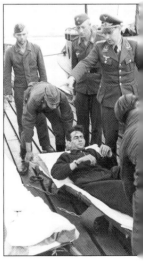

Prisoners of war. *Fellow New Zealanders Ron Callaghan and Alan Rutherford somehow survived when Gilbertson's aircraft plunged into the shallow Ijsselmeer. The remaining two crewmen died. Here a heavily bandaged Callaghan is helped ashore from a rescue boat while Rutherford is placed on a stretcher.*

Prisoner of war. *Pilot Keith Gregory was shot down when his Halifax attacked the battleship* Tirpitz *in a Norwegian fjord in April 1942. Plaster on his cheek and forehead bandaged, Gregory is disconsolate at being in German hands. This photograph was first published in a German magazine.*

Flak damage. *Roy Calvert's Lancaster was riddled with flak by close shell bursts over Hamburg in November 1942. A splinter killed the wireless operator; others wounded Calvert and his navigator.*

Night-fighter attack. *Enemy fire from astern killed the rear gunner and shredded the turret, rudder and other parts of this 75 Squadron Stirling in April 1943. Young pilot Peter Buck won an immediate DFC for getting the bomber home, crash-landing at Newmarket. Here, 75 flight commander Dick Broadbent (left) and visiting New Zealand fighter pilot ace 'Hawkeye' Wells inspect the damage.*

German propaganda. *The Luftwaffe put the wrecked fuselage of New Zealander Terry Taylor's Ventura light bomber on display in central Amsterdam to show off their success against the RAF. Taylor crash-landed his aircraft during an attack on a power station by 487 Squadron on 3 May 1943 and became a POW. This was the day Len Trent won his VC and 487 lost 10 Venturas, a disaster for the RNZAF squadron.*

"This is the course," and that was that. He would expect me to follow it. There was no dithering with him. He knew what he was doing and where he was going.'

Bill Harvey was killed 11 months after the Gironde trip. By the time he got out of hospital, Drummond and Patrick had finished their tours so he didn't fly with them again. Instead, he was posted to a conversion unit as an instructor. Late in the year he went back on operations, flying Lancasters with 514 Squadron. He had done 25 ops when his aircraft was shot down during a raid on Brunswick in January 1944. The entire crew is buried in Hanover War Cemetery.

Drummond instructed during his 'rest' tour and hoped then to go on pathfinders. But he was asked to join 75 Squadron as a flight commander, and did. He flew another 20 ops, four on Stirlings, the rest on Lancasters after the squadron converted in May 1944. He was hit in the leg by flak the first time he flew a Lancaster operationally and spent 10 days in hospital. Otherwise he came through unscathed and returned to New Zealand to see out the rest of his working life as a partner in an Auckland law firm.

Bomber Command laid more than 47,000 mines during the war, almost 7000 of them in Danish waters. The biggest operation was mounted the night of 28–29 April 1943, when almost 600 mines were planted in various vegetable patches in German and Danish waters. The cost was high. Of the 207 participating bombers, 23 — 11 per cent of the force — were shot down by flak ships, shore-based guns and night fighters. 75 Squadron lost four of the eight Stirlings it dispatched, a horrific 50 per cent loss, and there were no survivors among the 28 aircrew. It was 75's worst gardening trip. The night cost 145 lives, just four men surviving from the 23 lost bombers. Twelve New Zealanders were among the dead, 11 from the 75 Squadron planes, the other from a 158 Squadron Halifax lost without trace.

75 Squadron was assigned the Radish area — the Fehmarn Belt, the narrow strait between Germany and the Danish island of Lolland.

Three of the 75 aircraft were brought down off Lolland, two of them by naval gunners within a quarter of an hour. The fourth was lost without trace.

One of the four 75 Stirlings that made it back to Newmarket that night carried a crew on their debut op. The core, four New Zealanders, all sergeants at the time, were to weld into a standout group of airmen over two tours, the second on pathfinder Lancasters with 7 Squadron — pilot Hilton Williams, navigator Trevor Dill, bomber aimer Adrian Carson and rear gunner Ivon Kaye. Williams was known to everyone as Speed or Speedy. Dill came from a farm west of Warkworth, in Northland. Carson, called Shorty for obvious reasons, grew up in the Wanganui area but before the war managed a sheep station in the Chatham Islands. Kaye, of part-Chinese descent, was from Marton. Delivering the eulogy at Williams' funeral in Warkworth in 1999, Dill remembered his skipper as a handsome young man with sandy hair, blue eyes and a steady gaze, telling mourners that during their training in England in the winter of 1942–43 they had soon realised they had an exceptional pilot.

> He made good decisions in foul weather, was a good captain of crew, didn't get rattled and seemed able to handle all types of aircraft. When finally posted to 75 we were a well-knit crew thanks largely to Speedy's insistence on everyone knowing his job backwards and strict discipline in the air. We became very close friends, flying and drinking at village pubs together.

Three of the four survived. Cruelly, Carson was killed in a crash while training, two days before the crew's last op.

The Williams' crew returned safely from its shakedown op dropping mines but the loss of four aircraft was a rude awakening. Says Dill:

> It was supposed to be easy, this gardening, but it wasn't. It was dangerous. We were in big lumbering Stirlings flying low, 1000 feet

to 1500 feet, and the Germans had flak ships anchored out there. If you happened to fly over one, they'd just stay quiet until you were there and then, whoomph, and you'd had it. Four missing. A bad night for our crowd.

1943

Bomber Command begins destroying Germany

1943

The tide of war turned irrevocably against Nazi Germany in 1943. Frozen, starving and encircled by Soviet troops, the Sixth Army capitulated in the snow at Stalingrad; the Allies drove the Afrika Korps out of North Africa; and Italy surrendered after the Allied seizure of Sicily. By the end of the year German U-boats had lost the Battle of the Atlantic.

1943 was also pivotal for Bomber Command. Everything that had gone before was the curtain-raiser to this year. Now grown vastly stronger with an ever-increasing force of Lancasters and Halifaxes, the RAF began in March to seriously damage the industrial cities of the Ruhr Valley in a long successful campaign that included the stunning dams raid in May. Then followed the firestorm hammer blows on Hamburg in July, the strike at the rocket-research establishment at Peenemunde the following month, and the beginning of the Battle of Berlin, a series of attacks that extended into 1944.

Bomber Command wreaked havoc on Germany as 1943 wore on, its attacks made more potent by the pathfinders, introduced in late 1942. H_2S, the first navigation and bombing radar set, appeared in January 1943, and improved flares and target markers dropped by the pathfinders indicated more clearly to Main Force crews where to bomb.

The British also unveiled systems to counter German radio and radar signals, prominent among them being *Window* — foil-backed paper strips which fogged German ground radar screens with millions of images, first used over Hamburg in July 1943. The jamming of German signals by the RAF and the enemy's responses to this became a battle of wits and technical innovation.

Volume IV of *The Strategic Air Offensive*, Britain's official war history, tells a nice story about *Corona*, the codename for British ground stations broadcasting bogus instructions in idiomatic German to enemy night fighters. *Corona* caused utter confusion on its debut in October 1943. The broadcasts enraged the German controller, who began swearing. *Corona* then remarked, 'The Englishman is now swearing.' The German retorted hotly, 'It is not the Englishman who is swearing, it is me.' The enemy introduced female controllers. The RAF countered with German-speaking WAAFs. The electronic war had its lighter side, but it was deadly serious. Countless lives were at stake.

The Luftwaffe fought fiercely to defend Germany's cities and industries, committing more and more fighters to the night battle and devising new strategies and weapons to combat the RAF. One weapon was unveiled the night the British attacked Peenemunde. *Schrage Musik* — twin upward-firing cannons mounted at the rear of a night-fighter's cockpit — added a frightening dimension to the night war. The guns enabled a German pilot to slide his aircraft unseen under an unsuspecting bomber and pour fire into the wing fuel tanks, setting the wing alight and dooming the aircraft. Fighters armed with *Schrage Musik* rarely aimed at the bomb bays, for exploding bombs posed an immense danger at close range. The night-fighter pilots also preferred a wing fire because it gave bomber crews a chance to escape. An element of chivalry survived in the air war, but hundreds of bombers and men would be lost to this weapon.

The night skies became ever more deadly during 1943 and Bomber Command certainly did not have it all its own way. It is sobering to reflect that, as *Bomber Command War Diaries* notes, a Lancaster lost over Hanover on the night of 18–19 October 1943 became the 5000th bomber lost on air operations.

Hitler's homeland faced more than the bombs of the RAF now. The first Fortress units of the 8th US Army Air Force, the 'Mighty 8th', had arrived in England in early 1942 to bolster the bombing attack. But the American build-up was slow and it was well into 1943 before the 8th could commit serious numbers of bombers for strikes on Europe. For many months the Americans were confined to targets in France and on the fringes of Germany; they didn't begin deep-penetration raids until the second half of 1943. They suffered grievous losses in the process, losses that continued until early 1944 and the arrival of the superb Merlin-engined Mustang fighter. With drop tanks Mustangs could accompany the bomber fleets on long-range missions. It was then that serious round-the-clock bombing could begin — the 8th by day, the RAF by night.

Happy Valley: the Battle of the Ruhr

Aircrew called it Happy Valley, a flippant name if ever there was one for such a killing field. Halifax pilot J Alwyn Phillips described it much more aptly in the title of his 1992 book — *The Valley of the Shadow of Death*. Bomber Command's assault on the Ruhr Valley, Germany's industrial heartland, lasted almost five months. Two-thirds of the major raids mounted against Germany in this period targeted the cities lying in and around the valley. 'Bomber' Harris called this offensive the Battle of the Ruhr.

It was a battle won by Bomber Command and signalled the start of the heavy, intensive attacks that would lay waste to Germany by war's end. Yet it was not a one-sided contest. German flak and night fighters exacted a heavy toll. Officially the campaign lasted from 5 March to 24 July, the day Harris switched his focus to Hamburg. In that time Bomber Command lost 1000 aircraft, the equivalent of 40 squadrons of 25 planes each, and an estimated 5500 aircrew were reported dead or missing with another 1200 taken prisoner. The battle cost the lives of 150 New Zealanders.

Grievous losses of men and machines did not deflect Bomber Command from its purpose. Aircrew from the Commonwealth training scheme continued to pour into Britain, and British industry more than replaced crashed aircraft. *Bomber Command War Diaries* notes that Harris began the Battle of the Ruhr

with 600 bombers. Despite heavy losses he was able to bomb
Dortmund in late May with more than 800, four-fifths of them
four-engined planes carrying the heaviest bomb loads so far. In
a single mid-February raid Bomber Command dropped a record
1000 tons of bombs. More than 2000 tons fell on Dortmund on
23–24 May.

The time was right for the raids. Heavy bombers were available
in large and growing numbers, the pathfinder techniques had
been refined, and the Ruhr was now within range of the new
Oboe radar equipment fitted to fast and high-flying Mosquitoes
of the Pathfinder Force. *Oboe* was to improve bombing results
significantly, its signals indicating the precise moment to release
flares or bombs as primary target markers. Pathfinder Lancasters,
Stirlings and Halifaxes then followed up by dropping target
indicators on the markers.

The Ruhr, in west-central Germany, was one of the closest
German points to England and was thus the best target for the
shorter nights of spring and summer. Berlin, too distant for
Oboe because the radar beams could not bend round the earth's
curvature, was better left for the longer nights of autumn and
winter.

The 1300 square miles of the east-west Ruhr Valley was
bounded by three rivers — the Ruhr to the south, the Lippe
to the north, the Rhine to the west — and, to the east, the city
of Hamm. Within its boundaries lay such targets as Duisberg,
Mulheim, Essen, Oberhausen, Bottrop, Gelsenkirchen, Bochum
and Dortmund. Krefeld lay just southwest of the valley limits,
and Dusseldorf and Wuppertal were a little further away to the
south and southeast. Cologne, with its majestic Gothic cathedral,
was more distant, on the Rhine. The fact that these latter cities
were really outside the Ruhr was of little importance to bomber
crews. They were all in the great conglomeration that made up
Happy Valley, all heavily defended, all part of the great industrial

complex, based on bountiful coal deposits, that powered the German war machine.

Essen, at the heart of the Ruhr and destined to become the most heavily bombed German city of the war, was the opening objective of the battle on 5 March, the raid counting as a major success. 109 Squadron Mosquitoes marked brilliantly, slap on the great Krupp works, the pathfinders followed and then Main Force rained down bombs and incendiaries. The raid inflicted immense damage, and 30,000 people, most of them Krupp workers, lost their homes.

A follow-up raid was called off because of bad weather but Bomber Command then made damaging attacks on Nuremberg and Munich, thus keeping up the pressure outside the Ruhr as well. A less than successful raid on Stuttgart followed. For the first time, the Germans, masters at countering British tactics, used fires and flares outside the city as dummy target indicators, and most of the RAF bombs fell in the open countryside as a result.

Wellingtonian Maurice Marment, then still a flight sergeant, won an immediate DFM for bringing his crippled bomber back safely from Stuttgart. He was homebound when the 408 Squadron Halifax was attacked by a night fighter, whose fire damaged the propellers. One engine quit immediately, a second failed later and a third ran roughly. The crew heaved out anything moveable while Marment, later cited for his 'great skill', kept the bomber airborne. He was over the Midlands, making for Leeming, 408's Yorkshire base, when he hit foul weather and had to land at the first airfield he could find. As the Halifax skidded to a halt at Langar, in Nottinghamshire, the engine giving trouble fell out of its nacelle.

On 16–17 April Bomber Command turned its sights on the twin Rhine cities of Mannheim and Ludwigshafen and the Skoda armaments factory in Pilsen, western Czechoslovakia. On a bright moonlit night fighters fell on the attackers as they winged home from this distant target, and 18 Lancasters and 18 Halifaxes were downed — 11 per cent of the force. All up losses of 54 for the night were the highest of the war so far.

In Auckland a day or two after the Pilsen mission, wireless operator Phil Langsford's parents received the telegram that all families with sons serving in the air force dreaded: 'Regret to inform you that your son Sgt Phillip Langsford has been reported missing on air operations . . . The Prime Minister desires me to convey to you on behalf of the Government his deep sympathy with you in your great anxiety. Letter following. F Jones, Minister of Defence.' It was the second such telegram delivered to the Langsfords, the first having arrived after their son's November 1942 ditching in the Mediterranean. He had survived that, and although his parents didn't know for some time, he had survived again, this time as a POW.

For most families like the Langsfords the long, dreadful wait that followed the 'missing' telegram was in vain. Next came 'missing, believed killed', and then, months later, the awful and final words 'now presumed dead'.

Langsford was posted 'missing' in an air-force casualty list published in New Zealand newspapers on Saturday 29 May, along with Donald Atkinson, 20 (Rotorua), Kevin Debenham, 26 (Oxford), John Fitzgerald, 22 (Hastings), and Robert Milliken, 31 (Springfield). With the exception of Langsford and Fitzgerald all were dead, killed on the Pilsen–Mannheim raids, as were three other New Zealanders — Ronald Anderson, 19 (Christchurch), Kelvin Groves, 30 (Masterton), and Ronald Stone, 26 (Auckland) — whose names for some reason did not appear on that particular list.

Langsford had returned to 78 Squadron in March after his ditching. With the same skipper, Irishman Paddy Dowse, and the same crew he did four more ops before the Pilsen trip — to

Duisberg, Berlin, Essen and Kiel. They were shot up over Duisberg on 26 March and flew back to base on three engines, and were badly knocked about on the Berlin flight the very next night, an op that put their navigator over the edge, frightening him so much he refused to fly again.

Homebound from Pilsen their Halifax was hit without warning by an Me 110 near Geislingen, southeast of Stuttgart, as they headed for France across southern Germany. 'I'm sure no one saw it,' Langsford says. 'There were no shouts, just suddenly cannon shells and explosions and the starboard wing on fire. There were flames in the fuselage too, I think from an auxiliary fuel tank we were carrying for the long flight.'

Bomb aimer Eddie Thompson and Langsford got out of the front hatch, though Thompson pulled his cord too early. The chute snagged on a tail fin and ripped. The Englishman fell to earth much more quickly than he should have done, suffered compound fractures of both legs as he landed in a vineyard and impaled a thigh on a metal stake. German doctors amputated one leg, and when the airman was repatriated several months later RAF surgeons had to take off the other.

Everyone got out of the doomed aircraft except Dowse. He held it up long enough for his crew to escape but was still aboard when it exploded in mid-air. His body was blasted out of the Halifax before the wreck hit the ground and recovered fairly complete.

Fitzgerald, a rear gunner on a 90 Squadron Stirling after completing a tour with 15 Squadron, survived a crash-landing in France northwest of Reims while homebound from Mannheim. The bomber flew to the target at 500 feet and was doing the same on the way back when it was caught by light flak over an airfield. It flew on, two engines knocked out, but then a third failed and the pilot had to put her down in the countryside. A full moon helped and, amazingly, everyone emerged alive from the burning wreck.

'We seemed to be rushing into eternity,' Fitzgerald wrote years later of the approach to the ground. 'Suddenly a tearing crash, a flash of blue flame. We had cut a high tension power line. A second crash, heavier than the first, and then the whole world seemed to explode into a deafening roar, mixed with crazily spinning lights and then a terrible silence.'

The injured pilot was handed over to the Germans for treatment but the rest of the crew evaded capture with the help of the Resistance, slipped across the Pyrenees into Spain and got back to England. Fitzgerald reached London on 1 August, his 23rd birthday. A smashed eardrum, sustained in the crash, ended his war and he was invalided home to become a gunnery instructor.

Gunner Alastair Warne cursed his ill luck when he learned the 431 (RCAF) Squadron Wellington from which he parachuted on the 23–24 May raid on Dortmund had got home safely. When Warne was captured and reached Dulag Luft interrogation centre, he met fellow countryman Ron Marquet, who had been there since the previous year. Most prisoners stayed at the centre only briefly before being shipped off to a POW camp, but the Germans had discovered that Marquet was a whiz on the piano and delayed his departure because music was considered good for the prisoners' morale.

Marquet kept a small notebook in which he invited arriving New Zealanders to write a line or two about what had happened to them. It's a little treasure of a volume with its comments, some quite bitter. Warne wrote philosophically: 'Hit by flak, plane out of control. Fell out of turret, crew got back. Unlucky me.' Which was true as far as it went, but the fact that Warne baled out and became a prisoner while his Wellington flew back to England almost certainly saved his life.

The 22-year-old from Whangarei had done well at OTU, where

he had been crewed with Wing Commander John Coverdale. The two men went from OTU to 431 Squadron, which was formed in November 1942 but didn't become operational until March 1943. Warne flew with Coverdale when the wing commander took part in ops but otherwise he and his crew acted as spares, going with other pilots. On his ninth op, his captain was a man called Hall. Their aircraft was battered by flak over the target and fire broke out in the rear fuselage. Warne heard a bale-out order just as the intercom failed. He rotated his turret and fell out backwards as trained to do. He was taken POW soon after getting down safely.

Later, Warne learned his plane had got home without a pilot. Hall, not waiting for the rest of his crew to jump first, left through the cockpit hatch, leaving the bomb aimer, navigator and wireless operator in the crippled bomber. The fire went out and bomb aimer Stewart Sloan, 19, somehow got control of the Wellington and turned it for home. He'd done a little flying when allowed by pilots and had badgered link trainer instructors for tuition. Now he flew the Wellington back to base, put it down safely and climbed out a hero. He was awarded a CGM, commissioned and sent off to become a pilot. The other two crewmen went back to flying with Coverdale — and death. A month later, the three men disappeared without trace on another Ruhr raid. Had Warne been around to go with the wing commander he'd have been dead too.

The night Bill Hickson was shot down and reached the ground in Holland, suddenly very lonely as he listened to the bomber stream going home, he vowed never to volunteer for anything again. 'When I got home and rejoined the Post Office I never turned down any task. I always did what I was asked to do but I never volunteered for anything.' Wartime cured him of that. He'd volunteered for aircrew and volunteered again for pathfinder service with 35 Squadron. The fact that he never once put his hand up after the war didn't hinder his career, for he was appointed director-general of the New Zealand Post Office in 1979.

Seven hundred and five bombers took off from England on the shortest night of 1943, June 21–22, their target Krefeld. Hickson's Halifax and 43 other aircraft didn't make it home. It was a bad night for both sides. More than six per cent of the attacking force was lost, 224 Allied aircrew were killed and 63 were captured. The centre of Krefeld was devastated by fire, more than 1000 Germans died and 72,000 people were burned out of their homes.

Moonlight helped the defenders, and night fighters took a heavy toll of the pathfinders. 35 Squadron lost six aircraft, its worst single-night tally of the whole year. 7 Squadron had four shot down, 83 two and 156 one.

Hickson says Pathfinder commander Don Bennett told him years later that he always remembered Krefeld because that night he had been over the Ruhr too, in a Mustang, watching the raid to gauge the work of his crews. 'He flew back to Graveley [35's station] and was marching up and down waiting for the captains to come in to tear a strip off us for opening the attack late. None of us came back and he said he felt terrible.'

35 spearheaded the raid, and Hickson's Halifax and two others were scheduled over the target at zero hour minus three to put down markers. All three planes were hacked down before reaching Krefeld. Hickson's bomber was at 18,000 feet and closing on the aiming point when it was attacked. Fighter fire slashed into the port inner and flames sprouted. Hickson feathered the props and used the extinguisher but the fire continued and began eating into the wing.

'I did what I had to do and gave the bale-out order. My navigator, down below me and not seeing the flames, came on the intercom saying, "Skipper, do you mean it?" He couldn't believe I'd given that terrible order. Someone down there kicked out the escape hatch and they began to go.'

All but the rear gunner of Hickson's crew of four Britons and two Canadians parachuted safely, but a second casualty was an Australian pilot riding with them for experience. He jumped first but was killed when his chute failed to open. Hickson himself got out just as the flaming port wing snapped off. 'The plane was starting to disintegrate and spin. I was very lucky to make it. It was all just a lottery, absolutely. The chop rate was so high. I've been on borrowed time since 1943.'

Aucklander Gordon Cammell, captain of a 115 Squadron Lancaster, was the sole survivor of his crew on the night of 27–28 May 1943, when Bomber Command went to Essen again. The bomber was hit and exploded as it approached the target, and Cammell was blown clear. The six others on board died and now lie in Reichswald Forest Cemetery. Among them: New Zealander Halford Pye, 23, eldest of Doug and Gwen Pye's seven children and named after his father's close friend Ralph Halford. The two men stood shoulder to shoulder in the trenches of World War I.

'My father had fought in that ghastly war,' says Pye's sister Madelyn Bruce, who lives in Wellington. 'He thought it was the war to end all wars and he was furious about his sons having to go overseas.' A second son served with the RNZAF in the Pacific.

Hal Pye grew up on a dairy farm by the sea in the Bay of Plenty and caught the train to school in nearby Katikati every morning with his brothers and sisters. He was good at sport and captained the district high school's first XV. Madelyn Bruce recalls:

As a youngster he was mad keen on model planes and he used to fashion propellers too. We'd hold them out the carriage window and as the train went along the wind would make them go fast. He'd make bigger and bigger ones and we'd have to hang out further and further so that they would go and then there was a tremendous row because some of us of course were hanging out dangerously. Hal was the ring leader.

Doug Pye delivered the news to his family that his son was missing. He had joined the RNZAF as a physical-training instructor and was working in Tauranga when he got word. Madelyn Bruce again:

Dad wasn't due home so when he came walking up to the house that day and mother saw him she said, 'It's Hal, or Dad wouldn't be returning.' He was the big brother, our hero. We couldn't believe that he couldn't be alive and we were like that for a long time until his death was confirmed. Mum didn't think that. She told us she always had the feeling that he wouldn't return. She said, 'I certainly loved all my children equally but I had the feeling he was a little more precious because I wasn't going to have him all the time.'

The raid on Wuppertal on 29–30 May 1943 was an awful night for the RNZAF, among the worst of the war over Europe. Twenty-one dead on 11 aircraft — terrible losses on an attack that *Bomber Command War Diaries* ironically calls the 'outstanding success of the Battle of the Ruhr'. The strike devastated the Barmen half of Wuppertal, knocking out 80 per cent of the built-up area, wrecking 4000 dwellings and hundreds of businesses and killing about 4300 civilians. *War Diaries* says a fire in the centre of the old town was so severe that the 'first, small form of what would later become known as a "firestorm" developed'.

Alister Boulton, a 218 Squadron navigator from Christchurch, flew that night on just his second op. He still remembers the briefing, the intelligence officer tapping the map and saying:

'Tonight we're going to Wuppertal . . . a lot of the people who work in the Krupps steel plants live there. We're going to get them. They're in the war just as much as you and I. They're making the shells and bullets that are going to get you so you've got to get them.' What he said shocked some of the fellas but it didn't worry me. That's war.

Boulton's Stirling got back that night but was brought down over the Dutch–German border four weeks later.

Thirty-three bombers were lost on the Wuppertal raid, 4.6 per cent of the force. 75 Squadron flew a record 20 Stirlings and lost four, only the fourth occasion at that time that four or more squadron aircraft had been brought down on a single operation. Twelve New Zealanders died on those four bombers and only seven men parachuted safely.

Pat Middleton and Alan Davidson were two of the lucky ones. Friends for 60 years now and living near each other in Tauranga, they survived by a slim margin because they acted quickly. As the plane went down, rear gunner Middleton threw himself out of the back of the Stirling. Navigator Davidson dived out of the front while two other crewmen stood there thinking about it. Both got out at low level moments before the bomber, its load still aboard, exploded. The English flight engineer also landed safely but their skipper, Ray Bennett, 29 (Otahuhu), and the others were killed. The pity of it was that Bennett, Middleton and Davidson were all on their 25th op so had nearly finished their tour. Two or three weeks more and they'd have been on leave and off to instruct. Were they anticipating the end? 'Oh yes,' says Middleton. 'We had all sorts of ambitions.' Davidson: 'Only one crew finished a tour while we were on the squadron. We would have been the second to finish. I think about 200 men were lost or went missing in that period.'

Middleton and Davidson, both born in 1917, came together and found Bennett at 11 OTU at Oakley. In that New Zealand way, Davidson already knew Bennett. They'd played first-grade rugby against each other in Auckland. The three men crewed up, joined by another New Zealander, who couldn't cope and returned home, replaced about halfway through the tour by wireless operator Stan Kavanagh, 24 (Dunedin).

The original threesome nearly got themselves killed on their first op, a mining trip in December 1942. They survived two close encounters with enemy fighters, the first with an Me 110, the second with two Ju 88s, and twice flew over flak ships pumping up shells. The mid-upper gunner and Middleton exchanged fire with the fighters and the Stirling was forced down almost to sea level. But a good pilot and good gunnery saved them and eventually the bomber found security in a thin layer of cloud. 'This is considered a shade steep for a first trip as captain,' Bennett wrote in a report quoted in New Zealand newspapers.

The Bennett crew, still before Kavanagh's arrival, were fortunate again on 5 March 1943, the opening night of the Ruhr campaign, when they crashed on takeoff from Newmarket. 'We were lucky to get out of that one,' Davidson remembers. Says Middleton: 'If it hadn't been for Ray, we wouldn't have. A couple of the motors packed up as we got off. We were up about 500 feet. Ray put the nose down and drove her into the ground, a ploughed field. If the nose had been up we'd have stalled and been goners.'

Stirling BK776-B (Beer) began her last flight with five New Zealanders aboard: Bennett, Davidson and Middleton, plus Kavanagh and pilot Ray Norman, 23 (Winton), along for his second dicky trip. None of them knew Norman.

Davidson recalls:

We had a marvellous trip and got there a bit early, waiting for the pathfinder target flares to go down. We hadn't dropped the bombs when we were hit by flak at about 10,000 feet and started to burn. I can remember telling Bernie [Harrison, the flight engineer], 'There's petrol pissing out; I can see petrol pissing out of the tanks.' Ray said he'd dive to try to put the fire out. Then Pat [Middleton] called up and said, 'I'm off,' and I replied, 'Hooray.'

Davidson then dived out after getting Bennett his chute. 'I just went straight out. We were told to count to 10 and pull the cord. I counted one and pulled. The canopy billowed and then the plane blew up overhead, the others still aboard.'

RNZAF pilots and POWs Charlie Chambers and Stan Brown grew up in rural Canterbury but didn't meet until after the war at an air-force function in Christchurch, where they discovered some quite astonishing coincidences. Both had been shot down within a few minutes of each other on the same night, 12–13 June 1943, during the same raid on Bochum — and, so they discovered later, by the same German pilot. Both men were flying 4 Group Halifaxes from Yorkshire bases, Chambers with 51 Squadron from Snaith and Brown with 158 Squadron from Lissett. Both bombers crashed near the Dutch town of Oldenzaal, almost on the border with Germany. There the coincidences ended: Chambers was the sole survivor, Brown got out with his entire crew.

Chambers, born on the West Coast in 1918, grew up on a farm at Motukarara. He learned to fly at Harewood and Wigram, like Brown, who was born in Oxford in January 1921, one of the first babies delivered in the small town's new hospital. Brown's father had fought on the Western Front in World War I, suffering a wound that caused permanent damage to his left hand. He owned a butchery in Oxford and leased a couple of small farms. The young Brown worked in the shop and slaughterhouse, drove a tractor and learned all about engines. Like many other New Zealand pilots with a mechanical background, he understood his aircraft's engines and nursed them carefully, and they never let him down. He got his wings in December 1941 and had his 21st birthday on his final leave

Chambers and Brown both flew OTU Whitleys on secondment to Coastal Command from bases in southwest England hunting submarines. Chambers actually spotted a U-boat on the surface one day but it had vanished by the time the slow old plane reached the spot. Brown never saw a U-boat.

> We'd load up with depth charges and go stooging off into the Atlantic. We'd take off at 4.00 a.m. and be out there for 10 or 11 hours; low-level stuff, under the clouds and pretty boring for everyone except the navigator and me. The Whitleys were nice to fly but underpowered and slow. And cold, but we had sandwiches and Thermoses of coffee so we were OK.

Chambers was posted to 51 Squadron in Yorkshire in May 1943 and was shot down the following month on just his third op. He was flying his Halifax home over the Dutch–German border when the attack came.

> The rear gunner comes on the intercom and says flak's coming up on the port side so I swung her over to avoid that, only it wasn't flak at all. It was a bloody night fighter. He hit us all over the place and knocked out the intercom. I couldn't talk to anyone. We were on fire and I went down the steps to where the navigator and wireless operator sat, virtually under me. The nav knew we'd been hit pretty bad and motioned that the bomb aimer had been killed. He was trying to open the escape hatch but couldn't. I got it open and the nav went. I said to the wireless operator, 'Come on, get going. We're not staying here.' He told me to go first because he hadn't got his chute on yet.

The wireless operator evidently followed Chambers but his chute didn't open. Chambers got an enormous thump on his head leaving the aircraft, and was more or less unconscious in a German hospital for four or five days. When he was shifted out he was given underpants to put on. They bore an English name on the laundry mark: A Trott. Arthur Trott, 21, had been Chambers' navigator. The shocked New Zealander learned Trott had died of injuries two days after the crash.

Brown was happy to get to 158 Squadron and delighted to be given a shiny new Halifax. 'She weighed 32 tons and was beautiful to fly. I loved flying that machine. I got so good with landings that we were often down and rolling to a stop before some of the crew knew we were home.'

The night they were shot down they were on their 16th op. They were hit at 20–21,000 feet.

Barney [the navigator] and I had worked out a good system for getting home. We stayed way up where the ground speed was higher because of the thinner air. At a given point I'd put the nose down, keep the power on and scream home. We always turned in to the coast abeam of Grimsby Light and were almost always first down.

Not this night.

We were cruising along after dropping our bombs and just as Barney said 'Fifteen minutes to the coast, skip', enemy fire started coming up from an Me 110 below us. The German radar was better than we ever knew and the night fighter must have been sent in our direction by ground stations who had detected us.

The fighter then homed in on the Halifax with its own radar.

'Cannon and machine-gun fire knocked out both starboard engines and the wing began blazing. We were a flaming mess in no time, a sheet of flames streaming away from us. Five or six of the tanks were on fire.'

Brown feathered the two props, put full power on the port engines and ordered his crew out, knowing the wing would burn through and fold up soon. Wireless operator Sid Holroyd reported the rear gunner and all the rest gone and followed them out.

> I was left, dead scared she was going to blow. It was no place to be. The Perspex on the cockpit canopy was beginning to melt. She kept steady as long as I kept my foot down hard on the left rudder but when I released the pressure and got out of the seat she fell off to port and began to spin. I had great difficulty backing down the ladder to the escape hatch.

The man who shot down the two New Zealanders was 22, like Brown. Hans-Heinz Augenstein, a skilled pilot, had 46 bombers to his credit when he was killed over Munster on 6 December 1944, victim of an RAF Mosquito. Remarkably he got Chambers and Brown within about five minutes and then claimed a third Halifax, a 10 Squadron machine from which there were no survivors.

3 Group's 149 Squadron suffered the lowest percentage loss rate among Bomber Command squadrons operating continuously from 1940 until the end of the war, but like all squadrons it had bad nights, and 28–29 June, toward the end of the Ruhr campaign, was one. Three 149 Stirlings failed to return from Cologne. Of the 21 men aboard only two survived, one of them a wireless operator, Aucklander Ivan Mears. Four New Zealanders were among the dead.

Mears escaped with his life because he acted decisively and quickly. That didn't always guarantee an airman lived but it increased his chances and worked for Mears. Homebound, his Stirling was jumped by a night fighter, which ripped the length of the aircraft's underbelly with fire. The German pilot was Walter Ehle, who had shot down George Hedge's Wellington over the Ijsselmeer more than two years earlier. The Stirling was Ehle's 30th victim, but there weren't to be many more. The German ace was killed on 17 November 1943 while trying to land at a Belgian airfield, his tally by then 35.

Mears was galvanised by an instinct for self-preservation.

> Shells just raked us from underneath from stem to stern. They marched along the fuselage and didn't miss me by much. Suddenly we were on fire. I didn't hear a bale-out order because the intercom had failed, but I thought, 'This is no place for me,' grabbed my parachute, ducked down to the escape hatch, kicked it open and rolled out. She was on fire . . . burning round me . . . the whole plane was on fire.

The English navigator and flight engineer also got out before the Stirling flipped and crashed in flames in the backyard of a house in the small Belgian town of Houwaart, about 25 miles northeast of Brussels. The navigator died soon after landing but the engineer survived, coming down in a village with Resistance cells. He was quickly spirited back to England.

The bodies of the navigator and two other crewmen found near the crashed Stirling were buried in a Catholic churchyard at Houwaart, but no remains of the pilot or bomb aimer Bruce McCallum, 34 (Auckland), were found.

Mears landed in a fruit tree in the village of Teilt Winge. When the branches stopped cracking and shaking it was so quiet he could hear the ticking of a clock through the open windows of the dwelling in whose garden he'd fallen. He was given help but by morning people were peeping at him through the windows of the place where he was being sheltered and he knew he had to give himself up. 'It was a small place and too many people had seen me. The Germans weren't too choosy about who they shot when Allied flyers were helped.'

The 19-year-old who got his bomber home

Peter Buck was just 17-and-a-half when he enlisted in the RNZAF in June 1941, and was still only 19 years and five months on the night of 26–27 April 1943, when he won an immediate DFC for getting his heavily damaged 75 Squadron Stirling back to base after a night-fighter attack over the Ruhr. His bomb aimer, Englishman Philip Sadler, recalled 60 years later: 'It always struck me as odd that my pilot was a young man of only 19 who couldn't drive a car but who could fly a four-engined bomber and its crew to Berlin and back.'

Despite his youth, Buck was a highly experienced pilot when his Stirling fell victim to a fighter over Duisberg. Already on his 26th op, he needed all his experience and youthful reflexes to evade the enemy and then raw strength to get his plane home to England. The attack, as they ran in to bomb, mortally wounded the rear gunner, shredded his turret and shot the tail fin and rudder to pieces. No one saw the fighter flash in from astern, and the first Buck knew of the attack was a cracking 'whoompf' that seemed to come from under the tail. He thought it was flak but it was in fact cannon fire into the rear turret. A few seconds later more fire hit the wings and mid-upper turret.

Buck dumped his bombs and incendiaries, the latter on fire as they fell away. He could get no answer from the rear gunner on the intercom so sent Sadler and the Canadian wireless operator back to check on him. The two men struggled desperately to get the gunner out of his wrecked turret and give him first aid while Buck threw the aircraft around as he took evasive action. 'The gunner was clearly very badly hurt and in great pain and distress,' Sadler says. 'We eventually managed to get him out and into the fuselage but he died almost immediately.'

Buck was quoted in a news report at the time as saying:

> Without rudder control it was difficult to turn the aircraft and we seemed to be in a right-hand spiral turn for hours and fell from 15,000 feet to 12,000 feet. The second pilot [on his familiarisation trip] and I had to use all our strength to hold the aircraft but we managed to set off for England. Just after we had turned for home the starboard outer packed up — the oil pipes had been cut by bullets — and we began losing height steadily. I thought we might have to crash in the Channel as we kept losing height and the Stirling kept turning to starboard. The crew jettisoned everything moveable and fortunately we managed to reach our home base safely.

Despite the problems with the Stirling's controls, Buck managed a perfect crash-landing on three engines to end an op that Sadler remembers as a 'nerve-racking and frightening experience'.

A couple of days later the crew went to London for the funeral of their gunner, Brian Rogers, and then 75 Squadron's CO said the young New Zealander and his crew had done enough and ruled their tour finished. Buck then served as an instructor and later in the war flew another 18 ops on Mosquitoes with 487 Squadron, RNZAF, based in France. After the war he joined National Airways Corporation, ferried the airline's first Fokker Friendship to New Zealand from Amsterdam in 1960 and jointly delivered the first Boeing 737 in 1968. He was domestic operations director with Air New Zealand when he retired in 1979, by which time he'd flown a total of 16,341 hours. At his funeral in Wanganui in 1992 he was saluted by an air-force fly-past.

'The pain of losing him is still there'

The night Peter Buck struggled back to England from Duisberg, another New Zealand pilot, 13 years older, was killed on his way to the same target. Gordon McNab, 32, died with his entire 76 Squadron crew when their Halifax, loaded with incendiaries, was shot up by a fighter and crashed in the centre of Amsterdam. Trailing flames, the stricken plane plunged into the back of the Carlton Hotel, setting the entire block on fire.

As it came in over the coast McNab's aircraft was attacked by night-fighter pilot Heinz Vinke, the German pouring a lethal stream of cannon shells into the bomber. Vinke had been vectored to his target by a ground station at Leeuwarden, a major German air base in Friesland, in northwest Holland. He had shot down 54 British bombers by the time he was killed 10 months later. Dutch aviation historian Co Maarschalkerweerd, writing about the crash in an article in 2002 for the English magazine *After the Battle*, says Vinke let out a triumphant shout of 'Sieg Heil, Halifax!' as his fire blasted the bomber.

The plane is said to have gone into a steep dive, but McNab must have managed to gain some semblance of control over it because it was next reported on fire and flying low over the Nordzee Canal, which runs the few miles between Ijmuiden, on the coast, and Amsterdam. It isn't known what happened aboard the doomed aircraft for there were no survivors and no one baled out. Alive or dead, all seven crew — McNab, a Canadian and five Britons — were still inside when it crashed.

The aircraft was apparently finished off by flak from German batteries stationed near the hotel. Maarschalkerweerd quotes eyewitness Peter Saul, who lived close by the hotel:

That night was like so many others in the early months of 1943 when night after night we heard the sounds of aero engines overhead. On that particular night our sleep was also disturbed by the firing of the anti-aircraft guns. I saw a British bomber caught in the searchlights getting coordinated fire from guns in different locations. All were concentrating on that one aeroplane — the noise was incredible. I remember the bomber was in great distress. It was on fire with one or two engines out. The cockpit area seemed free of flames but as it flew overhead I could see straight through large parts of the wings and fuselage. Burning fuel and molten metal were falling down on the streets and houses, and it was so low I could feel the heat as it passed over our house. It was a most frightening sight and I was shocked, unable to move, wondering how the crew could possibly keep their crate flying for so long. It was almost unbelievable that it was flying at all.

The noise awakened a teenage Jewish girl hiding from the Nazis in a building in the centre of Amsterdam. Anne Frank, 13, wrote next day in the diary that was to become famous after her death in Bergen-Belsen concentration camp in March 1945:

> The Carlton Hotel has been destroyed. [A British plane] loaded with incendiary bombs fell right on top of the officers' club. The whole corner of Vijzelstraat-Singel [Canal] burned down. The air attacks on German cities have been increased from day to day. We do not have a good night of rest any more, and I have black circles under my eyes due to lack of sleep.

The Halifax slammed down on the hotel at 2.34 a.m., hundreds of gallons of aviation fuel and incendiaries igniting the biggest fire ever seen in Amsterdam. The hotel guests had long ago been kicked out by the Germans, who had taken over the building as the Luftwaffe's Holland command centre. At that hour of the morning most of the offices were deserted but the blast of the crash and the subsequent fire killed three Germans. The hotel was gutted and next door a historic building used by the Germans as a courthouse was destroyed. Seven Dutch civilians lost their lives and 22 houses were burned out. One hundred and fifty firemen and 30 engines fought the blaze.

McNab, an accountant in Timaru when he enlisted in September 1941, was on just his fourth raid when he was killed, still settling into the routine of bomber operations. Prior to taking off on that final flight, shortly before 1.00 a.m. on 27 April 1943, he wrote in the last of his almost daily letters to his wife in Timaru: 'I have just about 10 minutes before we get cracking so I'll post this on the way. There is nothing to report except that I love you.' He did tell her he had lost 31 'bob' (shillings) that morning to his gunner on the rifle range, beaten in a shoot-off, then added: 'Well my dear, we are on the job so all my love . . . things are going all right. We should get leave at the end of this week so I'll have something to write then. Goodnight my dear and once again all my love.'

Joan McNab has been a widow now for 60 years. She was a nurse, a sister at Timaru Public Hospital, when she married Gordon in Wellington on 9 April 1942 at the church where her grandparents had worshipped when they had first arrived in New Zealand from the Shetland Islands. The couple had just nine weeks together before she bade him farewell at the railway station as he boarded a train heading for Lyttelton. She took no time off from her nursing duties when her husband was reported missing, nor later when he was confirmed dead. Other staff had husbands, brothers and fiances overseas too, and she was needed. She continued to work at the hospital until retirement age and to live in Timaru.

In 1954 Joan and her sister-in-law, Nancy McNab, visited Gordon's grave in Amsterdam. A Dutch woman whose doctor husband had worked in the underground took them to the graveside. Before they left Amsterdam their Dutch host arranged for their attendance at an international memorial service in the city's cathedral for Allied war dead. Wreath after wreath was put on a black catafalque, and then Joan and Nancy McNab were called. They proudly laid their own flowers for a New Zealand husband and brother.

Joan McNab: 'The pain of losing him is still there, but we were so close I felt that he was still growing older with me, still living and influencing me, part of the fabric of my being.'

Joan McNab died in Timaru on 24 July 2004, after this book was completed.

Trent VC and the unsung heroes

Jack Sharp still remembers the shocked voice of his navigator, Paddy Gibson, that day in 1943. 'Christ, look at this,' he said, pointing down. Sharp, at the controls of a Ventura, saw a cluster of powerful stubby-nosed Focke-Wulfs climbing to attack in the late-afternoon sky. The Ventura had come in over the Dutch coast a few minutes earlier, headed for Amsterdam, and was now flying past Haarlem with Schiphol airfield off to starboard. Sharp barely had time to alert his two gunners before the fighters pounced, pouring in fire from behind and below. Tail-end Charlie of the group of 11 aircraft, his is thought to have been the first picked off by the Germans.

'The starboard engine caught fire and then there was attack after attack,' Sharp says. 'In a matter of moments both engines were dead and belching flames.' Fire flared in the nose, and flames streamed back through the instrument panel. The control column flapped uselessly. Neither of the English gunners answered Sharp's urgent cries to bale out, probably dead already. As Gibson, a Belfast man, headed back to jump from the door behind the cockpit, Sharp clipped on his own chute. Now the flames roared aft, fed by the draught through the open doorway, and Sharp knew he couldn't get out the same way.

He stood up and got his head and shoulders through the escape hatch above his seat but couldn't seem to wriggle further. The plane was falling steeply. 'From then on I can't remember what happened. I don't know.' His best guess is that he pulled the rip cord while still partly in the aircraft and that the opening parachute yanked him free. The dazed pilot landed among cowpats in a farmer's field near Haarlem. His aircraft, trailing smoke and flames, crashed nearby, the gunners' bodies in the wreckage. Gibson had jumped but was dead.

Sharp was not the only one shot down during this disastrous 3 May 1943 raid when New Zealander Leonard Trent won his Victoria Cross. Twelve twin-engined Ventura light bombers from 487 Squadron, RNZAF, took off from Methwold, Norfolk, just before 5.00 p.m. on a sparkling afternoon to attack a power station in Amsterdam. One turned back, its escape hatch gone, just after the formation had left England. Only one of the 11 that reached the Dutch coast returned to Methwold. The other 10 were gunned down one after another in one of the heaviest single-action, single-squadron losses of the entire war.

The sky over Dutch soil became a whirling mass of German crosses and swastikas as the fighters ambushed the Venturas. Spitfires detailed to protect the sluggish and vulnerable bombers at high level had arrived early and already left, low on fuel. But they had been spotted on enemy radar, and the Germans were up and waiting, or climbing, as the Venturas headed for their target. The close-support RAF fighters were outnumbered and the Venturas were pretty much on their own, unprotected prey for the FW 190s and Me 109s.

Aircrew losses on the Venturas were heavy. Twenty-eight airmen, seven of them New Zealanders, died. Six New Zealanders were among the 12 who survived to become POWs. Killed were pilots Tom Baynton, 27 (Dunedin), Andrew Coutts, 27 (Whakatane), Stuart McGowan, 22 (Hastings), and Rusty Peryman, 21 (Christchurch), gunners Des Goodfellow, 23 (Auckland), and

Tim Warner, 25 (Motueka), and wireless operator/gunner Cyril Smith, 29 (Miller's Flat, Otago). Captured were pilots Trent, 28 (Nelson), Sharp, 23 (Wellington), Terry Taylor, 28 (Christchurch), and Owen Foster, 22 (Omihi, North Canterbury), navigator Tom Penn, 29 (Christchurch), and gunner Ivan Urlich, 20 (Hawera).

The late-afternoon massacre virtually destroyed 487 Squadron, which had to be brought up to strength again with replacement aircrew and planes. The squadron's diary commented, 'It's a very bleak day . . . everyone is dazed by the news.' Formed as an RNZAF squadron in England on 15 August 1942, 487 was a light day-bomber unit flying the American-designed and -built Ventura, a derivative of Lockheed's civil transport, the Lodestar. It was an unsatisfactory aircraft, and after 487 left Bomber Command at the end of May 1943 the squadron was re-equipped with Mosquitoes.

Numerous New Zealand aircrew and some ground crew served with the squadron but it was not exclusively a New Zealand outfit and had a good Commonwealth mix. It flew its first operation on 6 December 1942, taking part in the famous raid on the Philips radio works at Eindhoven, Holland. The only casualty that day was the squadron's CO, Wing Commander Frank Seavill, a 32-year-old New Zealander in the RAF. He was shot down by flak and killed. Fellow New Zealander Gordon Grindell, who succeeded him, did not fly on 3 May 1943.

Trent's Victoria Cross wasn't announced until almost a year after he'd arrived back in England from a POW camp in May 1945. A pre-war RAF officer, he wanted to remain in the service and did not return to New Zealand immediately. He was on a Transport Command squadron when he learned on 1 March 1946 that he'd won the VC. His career in the RAF was assured with such a decoration and he finally retired as a group captain in 1965.

The *London Gazette* notice announcing the award cited Trent's 'outstanding leadership', adding, 'Such was the trust placed in this gallant officer that the other pilots followed him unwaveringly. His cool unflinching courage and devotion to duty in the face of overwhelming odds rank with the finest of these virtues.'

The citation indicates Trent's Ventura was the last in the air over the target that day, and most accounts of the action agree. Not so, according to Owen Foster, who lives in retirement in Christchurch. Foster was in the six-plane A-Flight behind the five aircraft of B-Flight led by Trent and watched as other Venturas disappeared in flames. One disintegrated in front of him, showering his aircraft with wreckage. Foster's A (Apple) was also under constant attack from flocks of fighters and soon lost an engine. Foster wrote in a family memoir that gunner Tim Warner appeared in his cockpit, blood running from his mouth. 'He said "Goodbye skipper" and slumped down on my seat and died.'

As Warner fell, Foster was on his bombing run, Tom Penn huddled over the bombsight calling instructions. Australian Russell Mann's .5-inch machine-guns were still hammering away. 'While this was going on the remaining plane up in front disappeared. I saw it turn over and dive straight down. I believe it was Trent's plane. Now we were on our own, the last of the twelve. We were still going on one engine, trying to keep up and start our bombing run when he was shot down in front of us.'

Suddenly the Ventura's bombs had gone and Penn came up from the nose to debate who'd let them go prematurely, just short of the target. Neither man had. Attack damage had triggered their release. That moment a shell set off the plane's front ammunition containers, the explosion knocking off the nose of the aircraft. Had Penn still been there he would have gone with it. As it was his back was showered with shrapnel.

Foster slammed the bomb doors shut and put the plane into a steep dive to escape the fighters, before levelling off and heading down the canal linking Amsterdam to the sea. Once over the water and clear, he turned for England. But the Ventura was finished, its fuselage full of holes, its port fin and rudder partly shot away, both wings holed, the nose shot off, the starboard motor stopped and pointing skywards, petrol pouring from holed fuel tanks. Suddenly the port engine quit and the plane smacked into the sea, 15 miles off the Dutch coast.

Somehow Foster, Penn and Mann emerged from the water-filled aircraft. Their dinghy had been riddled by German fire, so they floated about in their Mae Wests, each waging his own private struggle for life in the cold choppy water. A fishing boat rescued them two hours after they'd ditched. Warner's body washed ashore later and today lies in Bergen-op-Zoom Cemetery.

There were many remarkable tales of heroism that afternoon, and all the airmen who flew on the mission deserve a share in the tributes subsequently lavished on Trent. He is rightly lauded for his 'press-on' attitude, but at the preraid briefing the participants were told that that was what was expected of them all, and they were ordered to press home the attack regardless of opposition. That's exactly what most of them did, many paying with their lives. Sharp says he was surprised when he heard Trent had been awarded the VC. 'The citation said he carried on regardless. Well, that was done every night by bomber pilots. If they got smacked up a bit they still carried on. I didn't think it worthy of a VC but it was awarded so they must have thought otherwise.'

Foster reiterated in an interview in 2001 that his had been the last Ventura to remain in the air. 'I was the only aircraft left. We were behind Trent. He couldn't see what was going on behind him.' When Foster and Penn met Trent at Stalag Luft III, Trent took them aside and told them he had been last down. Foster's response: 'I said, "No, that's not true", but [after that] we let it go and never bothered about it. After the war when we were back here and heard that Trent had got the VC, we couldn't believe it.'

A plot of the known Ventura crash sites shows Trent's aircraft closest to the power station, in the northern suburbs of Amsterdam. The wrecks of the McGowan, Peryman and Baynton aircraft are not far away. Those three pilots pressed on to the point of death. McGowan's gallantry was never recognised. He and Canadian navigator Ernie Thornber saved wounded gunner Ivan Urlich. The time they took doing so probably cost them their own lives.

Urlich, the only survivor of the four on his aircraft, told NZPA correspondent Alan Mitchell when he got back to England from POW camp that he owed his life to McGowan and Thornber. He was hit in both legs in a succession of attacks, and then the Ventura was battered again from the front by a fighter.

> He really smashed up [my] turret. I got nicked in the left side and one of the guns was hit by a cannon shell and knocked out of its mounting. The nose of the aircraft was on fire now and McGowan and the Canadian came back and began to drag me from the turret. McGowan put on my parachute and pushed me out the door. That is the last I ever saw of him.

As well as McGowan and Thornber, New Zealand wireless operator/air gunner Cyril Smith died in this aircraft.

Peryman and the rest of his crew perished when their plane, minus a wing, crashed. Baynton's Ventura plunged down on reclaimed land, the bodies not recovered from the wreckage until 1947. Coutts and Goodfellow died when their plane was shot into the sea. Terry Taylor was the only pilot that afternoon who managed to crash-land a damaged Ventura. He put it down, on fire, on marshy ground, saving himself and two of his crew.

Dutch aviation historian Han Hogendijk, 17 at the time, has vivid memories of the day.

> At about 5.30 p.m. the air raid warning sounded. As I was very much interested in the air war I climbed on the roof of our house in Haarlem. At first I did not see anything because the planes came from the west and so out of the sun. But I heard already the rattling of machine guns and 20-mm cannon shells above. When I saw the planes it was a big turmoil. Everywhere I saw planes coming down, one or two Venturas with thick black smoke from their tails.

Trent went through the bombing run-up unscathed and even nailed a German fighter that foolishly flew across his nose and the guns he controlled from his cockpit. But his luck didn't last and his aircraft was hit by enemy fire moments after the bombs, which fell short of the target, had been released. As the Ventura hurtled toward the ground it broke up and the New Zealander and his navigator were thrown clear. The other two crewmen died.

Trent, whom some New Zealanders on 487 found more British than the British and 'very RAF', became commanding officer in 1956 of 214 Squadron, at that time being equipped with Valiants as Britain's first V-Bomber squadron. Two years later he flew a Valiant to Ohakea to help celebrate the RNZAF's 21st birthday. That visit left a sour impression on Jack Sharp. He wrote to Trent care of Ohakea but got no acknowledgement. Sharp, who has lived in the Hutt Valley most of his life, drove to Ohakea just the same. He found Trent in the crowd and greeted him. Sharp says that when Trent professed not to know him and was told who he was, he turned to someone in his party and said, 'Jack was on our squadron but didn't take part in the raid.' Sharp hit back with, 'So who was in the cell next to you in Amsterdam jail?' But 'He gave me the cold shoulder, so I thought, "Bugger you."'

Trent retired to Perth in Western Australia but finally came home to New Zealand, where he died in 1986 at the age of 71.

'A fine captain'

New Zealand Defence Minister Fred Jones was at Newmarket, southeast England, on 24 May 1943 to talk to 75 Squadron crews the day after Bomber Command had dispatched 825 aircraft to bomb Dortmund. He was accompanied by Bill Jordan, a former Labour MP who served an unmatched 15 years as New Zealand High Commissioner in London, from 1936 to 1951. Jordan was popular with New Zealand airmen in Britain and frequently visited bases to check on the welfare of his 'boys', as he called them. He knew many personally and sent congratulations when decorations were announced. He was always available in his London office and helped in many personal emergencies.

Alan Mitchell, the New Zealand Press Association correspondent who filed hundreds of reports to Wellington for New Zealand newspapers throughout the war after his appointment in mid-1942, often accompanied him. It was from Mitchell's accounts that Mrs Smith in Te Kuiti or Mr Brown in Invercargill learned their sons had been on a big raid on Berlin or Cologne or some other target. And when their sons got their names in the newspapers, it was usually because they had distinguished themselves.

Censorship prevented Mitchell from filing any disaster stories. He couldn't write a piece starting, 'Seven New Zealand airmen are missing after a raid on Berlin last night.' There was nothing in the newspapers here about the loss of 33 New Zealand lives over Hamburg on 27–28 July 1942, nothing about the disastrous daylight attack that wiped out 487 Squadron, RNZAF, on 3 May 1943, and nothing about 75 Squadron's horrifying loss of seven Lancasters one night in July 1944.

New Zealand newspapers ran casualty lists but gave no squadron numbers, targets, dates or other details — just names, next of kin and hometowns.

The NZPA report of Jones' post-Dortmund visit to 75 Squadron featured an account of Jordan's meeting with pilot

Don Whitehead, which noted that the high commissioner was 'particularly interested to learn of the fine airmanship of Flight Sergeant W.D. Whitehead, of Papakura, who had a propeller shot away over the target. Others in the crew were Flight Sergeant M.E. Parker (Milford), and Sergeants P.G. Dobson (Blenheim) and V.R. Jamieson (Auckland).' Jamieson, who flew a second tour with 149 Squadron, was one of the best gunners of the war.

Mitchell reported Whitehead telling Jones:

> We were right over the target and had just bombed when flak hit the port outer engine. It caught fire and made us a sitter for a cone of searchlights which picked us up. We lost 5,000 feet, but the propeller flew off and the engine stopped, which put the fire out. We flew 500 miles home in three hours with the remaining three engines. It was our eleventh trip.

Whitehead, then a flight sergeant, was awarded the DFM in October 1943, the citation saying 'on more than one occasion his great skill has been largely responsible for the safe return of his aircraft . . . Whitehead is a fine captain.'

Whitehead's crew was a good one that survived the war with the exception of Dobson, the navigator. His tour almost complete, Dobson died at Mepal, 75's base, on 8 September 1943, when a Stirling trying to take off failed and careered to a halt between two houses in Sutton, a village bordering the airfield. The aircraft burst into flames and Dobson, who was near by, ran to help. But the airman, a WAAF and two civilians were killed when the Stirling's bombs exploded. The aircraft's New Zealand captain, Ian Menzies, 21 (Gisborne), and his bomb aimer were also killed.

One 75 Squadron Stirling had not come back from Dortmund, one of 41 aircraft lost that night, but Mitchell could not report its loss. Homebound over Holland, BK783 AA-Q (Queenie) was shot down by a night fighter, falling into a water-filled ditch a few miles from Utrecht with just one survivor. Three of the six dead were New Zealanders: pilot Stephen Tietjens, 26 (Auckland), navigator George Turnbull, 24 (Palmerston North), and bomb aimer Fred Joblin, 25, who left a wife in Gisborne. This crew was new to ops, a reminder, if one were needed, that so many 'sprog' crews were lost within their first five ops. Hard-bought experience counted for a lot in the survival stakes.

Les Munro and the Dambusters

Les Munro was determined to be a pilot: 'I'd never been up in a plane but I always wanted to fly.' So when war broke out he volunteered for the RNZAF, writing 'pilot' on the application form. He was 20 at the time, working on a farm in the Gisborne district, a self-described country bumpkin. But he had plenty of faith in himself, and when the air force told him he could start training immediately if he'd go in as an air gunner he responded, 'No, I want to be a pilot.'

He persevered and in due course fulfilled his ambition beyond his wildest dreams. The young farm lad without much formal education became a doubly decorated foundation pilot and eventually a flight commander with the rank of squadron leader on the best-known RAF squadron of all — 617, the Dambusters. And although he was forced to return to base without reaching the target, Munro participated in that most famous British air raid of World War II — the attack on the Ruhr dams on 16–17 May 1943.

The squadron was formed specifically for the dams raid, and Munro captained one of five Lancasters chosen to attack the Sorpe Dam, while other sections of the squadron raided the Mohne and Eder Dams. But his flight was cut short as he headed over the fringes of Holland just an hour or so into the mission. One light flak shell wrecked the aircraft's intercom and other communications. Critically, Munro could no longer talk to his bomb aimer and navigator, or indeed the rest of the crew, and would not be able to contact other aircraft over the target.

It was a bitter blow after weeks of precision training. But the Lancaster was a lame duck and Munro knew it. Reluctantly he turned for home and was back on the ground at Scampton, Lincolnshire, his bouncing bomb (really a 9250-pound cylindrical mine) intact when Guy Gibson flashed the news that the Mohne Dam had been breached.

There's a good chance the shell that hit Munro's Lancaster as he flew over the Dutch island of Vlieland saved the New Zealander's life. Eight of the 19-strong attacking force were lost on the dams raid, and of the five that set off for the Sorpe two crashed without a survivor. Munro lived to fly another 35 operations with 617 Squadron. His 15 months with the Dambusters ended on 6 July 1944, when 5 Group chief Ralph Cochrane grounded Leonard Cheshire, 617's then commanding officer, after four tours and 100 ops, and his three flight commanders — Munro, Australian David Shannon and American Joe McCarthy. Cochrane brooked no argument. The four men were not to go on operations again. They had done enough.

Munro spent the rest of the war flying Hurricanes, teaching bomber pilots how to avoid fighter attacks and training gunners in tactics. His service with the Dambusters earned him the DSO to go with the DFC he had been awarded earlier. He didn't intend to stop flying but all he managed after the war was five hours on Tiger Moths at the Gisborne Aero Club. 'I got married; I couldn't afford to fly,' he grins.

Munro soloed at Bell Block in the winter of 1941, flew twin-engined Cessna Cranes at Saskatoon under the Commonwealth training scheme, was commissioned and sailed to Britain. He flew his first operation from 29 OTU at North Luffenham, Leicestershire, to Dusseldorf on 10 September 1942, in the days when pilots under training were often used on raids. Three days later he was on the battle order again. This time his war-worn Wellington was to carry four 500-pound bombs to Bremen. The flight lasted all of three minutes and gave Munro the worst moments of his entire operational career. The Wimpy got off the ground but wouldn't go higher than about 40 feet. She clipped a belt of trees and crashed on the only flat open paddock for miles around. 'We got out and ran like hell. The five of us were almost in the next county before the bombs exploded.'

That escape seemed to mark Munro as a lucky man, for luck never deserted him. Throughout Munro's first tour and in all his time with 617 he never saw a fighter, was never attacked, and suffered only a few minor flak holes.

From OTU, Munro and his men were posted in December 1942 to 97, one of the original Lancaster squadrons, and on the second day of 1943 began flying operationally. First there were a couple of mining trips, then a long succession of raids on tough German targets — Essen, Berlin, Hamburg, Cologne, Nuremberg and all the others. By the time 5 Group came looking for personnel for the formation of a special squadron in March 1943, Munro and his men had completed 21 ops and 130 hours' flying, and were a senior crew. Munro himself was a flight lieutenant — rapid promotion.

What the new squadron was to do was not explained. 'I talked it over with the crew, although we didn't know what was involved. No one did. But they were happy to volunteer for whatever it was, and we did.' Munro's navigator, Scot Jock Rumbles, and wireless operator, Percy Pigeon, a Canadian, flew with Munro until he finished at 617. Two other captains from 97 joined the Dambusters: McCarthy, a New Yorker who had enlisted in the RCAF, and Englishman David Maltby.

Guy Gibson, whom Munro remembers as a typical pre-war RAF type and a disciplinarian but a man prepared to drink happily in the mess with his crews in off-duty hours, was named to command 617. In his celebrated 1951 book *The Dam Busters*, Paul Brickhill wrote of the first meeting between Gibson and Munro, in the Scampton airfield bar: 'Les Munro was a New Zealander, tall, blue-chinned and solemn, a little older than the others. He was standing by the bar looking into space when Gibson located him. "Glad to see you, Les," Gibson said. "I see you're setting a good example already, drinking a little and thinking a lot." Munro up-ended his pint and drained it. "No, sir," he said, "thinking a little and drinking a lot."'

Munro doesn't know where this story originated but doesn't really mind it and likes the book. But Brickhill never contacted him, and Gibson was long dead when Brickhill, an RAAF fighter pilot who'd been a POW for two years, began his research. Brickhill also says that Munro was known as 'Happy' because he was so solemn. Munro laughs about that too. He says he was a fairly typical New Zealander, though he admits he was perhaps a bit quieter than the average. But by all accounts the WAAFs at Scampton admired this tall, strong, silent man.

Munro and his crew had their first training flight with 617 on 31 March 1943 and then worked hard for six weeks, practising bombing and low-level flying all over Britain and out into the North Sea. 'Gibson kept the identity of the target to himself until just a week or so before the raid, when he told the flight commanders. But the rest of us weren't told until the briefing on 16 May, the day of the dams raid.'

Munro was second off that night, following Australian Bob Barlow down the runway at 9.29 p.m. Then followed the others of the Sorpe group: Englishman Geoff Rice, Canadian Vern Byers, and McCarthy. The New Zealander's Lancaster skimmed east across the North Sea, just 50 to 60 feet above the waves — the height from which they were to bomb. The aircraft was on course and on time as it reached Vlieland, one of the West Frisians, the chain of islands strung out like a protective barrier along the north coast of Holland. Behind the island lay the narrow Wadden Zee and then the Ijsselmeer.

'I could see the breakers ahead and the dunes of Vlieland behind and I lifted the aircraft a little to clear the dunes. But as I began losing height to go down to meet the Wadden Zee I saw the tracer of flak coming up on the port bow.' One 20-mm shell found the mark, its explosion rocking the big plane and tearing a hole two feet across in the thin metal skin by the roundel. The Lancaster flew on, its controls undamaged but all communication circuits destroyed. 'I asked the wireless operator to go and have a look. He came back and shouted in my ear that repairs were impossible. Without communications we had no choice but to abort the mission.'

The group of Lancasters led by Gibson found the Mohne and Eder Dams and blasted great breaches in them. Millions of tons of water foamed down the Ruhr valleys destroying everything in their paths and causing great damage.

Despite the heavy losses the raid was acclaimed a stunning success and its propaganda value was immense. The raid became a byword for bravery and achievement. Books and later a popular film fixed the raid for ever in the public's consciousness. A raft of decorations was awarded to the dams-raid airmen, including a Victoria Cross for Gibson and a DFC for Len Chambers, the only New Zealander on the mission apart from Munro.

West Coaster Chambers, wireless operator on Australian Mickey Martin's Lancaster, had flown 20 ops with 102 Squadron and another 37 with 75 Squadron before joining the Dambusters. He flew 10 more with 617 before being posted to Canada for pilot training. Chambers returned to New Zealand in 1944 with a Canadian wife and lived in Karamea until his death in 1985.

Gibson was taken off operations after the dams mission and replaced by George Holden. The new CO was killed on the disastrous Dortmund–Ems Canal raid in mid-September, when

617 lost five of the eight Lancasters it dispatched — an operation both Munro and McCarthy missed because they were ill. That brought Cheshire to 617 as its commander. Munro says: 'I had tremendous respect for Cheshire. He would never have asked anyone to do anything he wouldn't have done himself and he led by example in his quiet way.'

Munro's proudest 617 moment came on 14 June 1944 when he led the entire squadron, each aircraft carrying a 12,000-pound Tallboy bomb, to Le Havre in Bomber Command's first daylight mission since May 1943. While Cheshire and two other pilots in Mosquitoes marked concrete-covered E-boat pens from almost ground level, 617, headed by the New Zealander, came in to unload their great bombs. Another 200 Main Force Lancasters followed to attack the port facilities. 'Leading that raid gave me a great deal of satisfaction,' Munro says.

After the war, Munro was a farm appraiser for State Advances for 15 years, then farmed for the rest of his working life in the King Country, finding time to give more than 30 years' service to local authorities and community organisations in the region, including 17 years as chairman and mayor of Waitomo District Council. When he bought his first farm in the King Country he called it Scampton Downs.

When this book was completed in 2004, Munro, born in 1919, was the only one of the 19 Dambuster pilots still alive.

Te Kooti

Te Kooti flew for the last time on 26 May 1943. The 15 Squadron Stirling crash-landed in a Dutch field at 2.15 a.m., the quiet of the night shattered by the roar of engines then the awful rending of metal as the bomber hit the ground, bounced and broke into a thousand pieces.

The aircraft, flown by Australian John Wilson, came down about five miles from the Dutch town and German airfield of

Venlo, in southeast Holland, after being savaged by flak three-quarters of an hour earlier near Dusseldorf. Jonathan Falconer, who wrote about *Te Kooti*'s final flight in his book *Stirling Wings*, quotes rear gunner Joe Edgley as saying they were almost over Dusseldorf at about 12,300 feet when three or four shells burst close. 'Before we could take evasive action the next salvo hit our starboard engines. The aircraft shook violently and the pilot told us to prepare to bale out.' The propellers were knocked off both motors and flames flared from the outer. The mid-upper gunner parachuted in the confusion.

The two port engines were still running sweetly but the port wing was low and the rudder hard over to port as Wilson fought to counteract the plane's tendency to swing to starboard. The pilot did his best to keep the plane aloft but just after they'd crossed the border into Dutch airspace it was all over. 'Sorry lads, I can't keep her airborne any longer . . . bale out,' he told his crew. One of the two who jumped then was killed, and Wilson and his bomb aimer died in the cockpit trying bravely until the last moment to keep the Stirling level. Edgley and the wireless operator emerged alive from the wreck unscathed even though the plane, according to Edgley, 'turned over and over and sideways before finally coming to rest'.

No New Zealanders were on the Stirling that night but she had been a 'Kiwi' plane until three weeks earlier. She was almost new when skipper Irvine Renner's crew, four of them New Zealanders and all fresh to the squadron at Mildenhall, Suffolk, dubbed the plane *Te Kooti* in January 1943 and painted a large tiki on the fuselage under the cockpit. Renner — Bob to his wartime mates — wrote later they chose the name in memory of the 'famous Maori night marauder of my district in New Zealand, Poverty Bay'. The aircraft also carried elaborate artwork on the rear fuselage — a painting of a Stirling, falling bombs, names of targets and more. Officially she was BK611-U (Uncle), but whenever the bomber hauled its way back into the airfield circuit after long flights to Germany, the crew always called up control announcing the arrival of *Te Kooti*, not U (Uncle), and WAAFs on the RT knew instantly who was up above.

Renner grew up on a farm near Gisborne, as did his navigator and good friend Ron Nelson. The two men crewed up with wireless operator Norm Southern, son of a Taranaki dairy farmer, and bomb aimer Ian McColl, whose parents ran a beef and sheep property in the Taihape district. The rest of the crew were Londoners but it was not surprising the British press later tagged them the Flying Farmers, even though by then Nelson had gone to another unit, where he was killed during a raid on Hanover in September 1943.

The Renner team was still learning at OTU when they flew their maiden op, to Bremen, on 13–14 September 1942 — a maximum-effort night when many novice crews participated. They left with the comforting words of their deeply religious wing commander ringing in their ears: 'The Lord will never leave thee nor forsake thee.' Maybe the Lord *was* with them that night. They outfoxed a fighter, survived a frightening episode with a loose incendiary bomb, and shook off persistent searchlights by flying violent evasive manoeuvres that took them down to 2000 feet and used up a lot of petrol. Cloud cover over England posed more problems when they arrived over the country short of fuel, but they got a fix from Stradishall and made a beeline for Bassingbourn, 'landing not many minutes later, a wiser and more experienced crew'.

They made headlines when they dropped a special bomb on Berlin on 27 March 1943. The 500-pounder was one of three covered with savings stamps by Londoners in Trafalgar Square during a Wings for Victory Week. Wrote Renner: 'The bombs were literally plastered inches deep with stamps by the British public who were promised they would be duly delivered to the appropriate quarters. The day Victory Week closed, two of the bombs were hurried to our station and one of them found its way into *Te Kooti*.'

On a clear cold night over Berlin, McColl lined up his sight on the aiming point and released the bombs, the 500-pounder with its stamps among them. 'There was a deep feeling of satisfaction when finally the bombs had gone and I knew that I had kept faith with the thousands of ordinary folk who had stuck savings stamps on our bomb,' said Renner. The New Zealanders, feeling suitably patriotic, sang *Maori Battalion* — loudly.

'Flying Farmers Have Something to Write Home About,' trumpeted the *Daily Mail*, the newspaper going on to say that 'the three boys from New Zealand — all farmers — came to England so that they could write home to say "we have bombed Berlin". Last night they did it. Their plane is nicknamed after a Maori bandit who was never caught. And like the bandit, the Stirling has always returned to its base.'

The Flying Farmers flew to Berlin that night on their 22nd op, an experienced crew nearing the end of their tour. A few more sorties and they were safely finished and off on instructional duties. All three, all commissioned, survived the war to become farmers again, Renner in England, the other two back in New Zealand. *Te Kooti* took them to the target and brought them home 20 times. In all the aircraft did 29 ops, a solid total for a Stirling in 1943.

Twenty minutes after *Te Kooti* plunged onto Dutch soil on 26 May, two New Zealanders died when a 100 Squadron Lancaster, also winged by shells, crashed three miles away in open country. Only two of the seven crew survived. The dead included pilot Acel Moore, 29, whose parents lived in the Waitomo district, and rear gunner Les Maunsell, 24, who came from Masterton. They were among the countless aircrew who fell in their first five sorties, both on just their second. Like *Te Kooti* they were homebound from Dusseldorf.

Eleven months dying

The letter arrived at his parents' Dunedin home in mid-1946, two years after Leonard Townrow died in a hospital in Holland. It came from Hanover from a woman called Ruth Klose.

Dear Mrs Townrow, You will be very surprised to get mail from Germany, but I won't miss to tell you about your son who died on my station in the hospital. I have been a nurse there and I took great care of your son, because he was so badly wounded and nursed him until he died. He told me such a lot about his family and his wish was that I write to you and send you his last regards.

The woundings of your son were so serious that all the medical assistance was in vain. Only his willing kept him alive. Your son wasn't able to travel so it was impossible to bring him back to his home . . . I am sorry but I lost all my photos, if I had I would send them to you.

Len Townrow took a long time to die — almost 11 months. Captain of a 100 Squadron Lancaster flying out of Waltham, Lincolnshire, he was shot down by a night fighter while homebound from Essen, his bomber falling in northern Holland close to the sea early on 28 May 1943. The Germans took him to a hospital in Leeuwarden, today a city of 100,000, where he died on 24 April 1944, the day before Anzac Day and two years to the day since he had graduated with his wings at No. 3 Service Flying Training School in Calgary, Canada. He was 23.

Townrow succumbed to what are said to have been severe internal injuries. One source says he had a broken back, broken legs and died of kidney failure. Another indicates he lost his legs before dying. He was picked up out of a ditch on a farm near Witmarsum, just three miles from the coast and a short distance from the northern end of the great causeway built in the 1930s to enclose the Zuider Zee. An ambulance took him to St Boniface hospital, run by an order of German nuns, about 15 miles away. The Luftwaffe had taken over a wing for their own sick and wounded and for injured POWs such as Townrow, and it was there that Ruth Klose, a German nurse, looked after the New Zealander until his death. He lies today in a Leeuwarden cemetery.

Southland-born on 20 August 1920, Townrow enlisted in the RNZAF in September 1941, sailed for Canada in December and reached Britain in July 1942. Posted to 100 Squadron in March 1943, he had flown 484 hours and was halfway through his first tour by the time he was shot down.

The Germans stationed a night-fighter wing at Leeuwarden and Dutch researchers have established that Townrow's Lancaster was shot down by Rudolf Sigmund, flying from there. Sigmund, killed on 3 October 1943 with his tally of downed Allied aircraft at 28, was a skilful pilot and regarded as a chivalrous and humane airman. It's believed he drove to the crash site and directed the German troops who found Townrow, and stayed with him until the ambulance arrived.

The late Jan van der Veer investigated the Townrow crash extensively in 1980 after the New Zealander's only sister, Jean Flanagan, visited the area trying to find out exactly what had happened to her brother. In a remarkable series of coincidences she was put in touch with the family of a man who had found Townrow's watch while clearing the ditch three years after the crash. Apart from having lost its glass and hands, the watch was undamaged. It was given to Mrs Flanagan in an emotional meeting, and she took it home with her to Australia, where she lived. The back of the watch bore the engraving 'To Len from Sylvia 20.8.41'. Dunedin woman Sylvia Rodger had given the watch to Townrow when they had become engaged.

Howard Townrow, serving in New Zealand's Third Division

in the Pacific when his brother was reported missing, says the treasured keepsake was eventually returned to Holland and is now part of a permanent wartime display in a Leeuwarden museum.

Only Townrow and the English bomb aimer and wireless operator escaped alive as ED821 HW-A (Apple) came down in flames, riddled by fire from Sigmund's guns. Jan van der Veer figured that bomb aimer Eric Short, shot in the chest, was first out, followed by the wireless operator and then Townrow. He said that one of the bodies in the wreckage was one of the gunners, probably killed by the night fighter's fire. The other gunner was thrown clear, perhaps already dead. He believed the other two were either dead in the cockpit before Townrow took to his parachute, or that they had helped their skipper out and then didn't have time to jump themselves before the Lancaster exploded at low level, three-and-a-half miles from where Short landed. Grievously wounded and bleeding to death, Short crawled to a nearby farmhouse for help. The shocked Dutch phoned for a doctor but the Englishman died before help arrived.

The Lancaster crashed not long after midnight, according to the best evidence, and a Luftwaffe party was soon on the scene hunting for survivors. Thick, clammy fog hampered the operation and it wasn't until 4.30 a.m. that a farmer rounding up his cows found Townrow, shivering with shock and cold after lying badly injured in the open for four hours. The Germans fed the airman warm milk from the farmer's cows, wrapped him in gunny sacks and carried him gently to a warm barn to await the ambulance.

Hamburg firestorm

One day in the mid-1980s aviation historian Oliver Clutton-Brock was ambling round a car-boot sale at Newbury racecourse in England when he spotted a crayon caricature of a pilot, beer tankard in hand. The artist had written 'Kia Ora, Bob — 1943' on the framed drawing. Intrigued, the Englishman handed over a few pounds. As he was about to walk away he saw a similar frame, a set of signatures under the glass, and bought that too.

With a little information from the dealer and his own knowledge of how to check RAF records, Clutton-Brock soon discovered the drawing was of RNZAF flyer Bob Mosen, captain of a 115 Squadron Lancaster. The neatly done sheet of the seven signatures of Mosen and his crew is dated 30 July 1943 — four days before Mosen was lost over Hamburg in the last of the four RAF raids that ravaged Germany's second city and killed thousands of its citizens, most of them in the great firestorm that developed in the wake of the second attack.

Mosen and his crew flew their debut op on 24–25 July, the first of the great Hamburg raids. The very next night they bombed Essen, then went to Hamburg again on 29–30 July. Three successful missions and then their last. The drawing was perhaps done on the evening of the 30th in the mess bar at East Wretham, 115's Norfolk airfield, while Mosen was relaxing, not having to fly that night. Possibly he posed in the bar of a local pub. Maybe the artist finished it that day after an earlier "sitting". Whatever the case, it's a sad memorial.

Lightning exploded Mosen's aircraft, killing the entire crew as they flew to Hamburg through a severe storm — one of five aircraft known to have been lost that night because of appalling weather over northwest Germany. The thunderstorm generated such severe lightning, icing and turbulence that many planes aborted the mission or dropped their bombs elsewhere. According to *For Your Tomorrow*, Mosen's Lancaster crashed about 15 miles southwest of Hamburg. Clutton-Brock discussed the loss in a 1996 Bomber Command Association newsletter that reproduced the caricature.

Was this . . . the same aircraft seen by Walter Thompson DFC and Bar [who] wrote in his book *Lancaster to Berlin*, 'When approaching Hamburg a dazzling display of lightning lit up two clouds directly ahead of us and between them a Lancaster was flying. I saw a flash of what appeared to be lightning across the gap and then was shocked to see the Lancaster blow up in an orange and black ball of flame.'

Martin Middlebrook's *The Battle of Hamburg* records: 'A 115 Squadron Lancaster blew up, probably when struck by lightning, and scattered its dead crew members over three parishes.'

Mosen, 24, whose parents lived in Raetahi, and his New Zealand bomb aimer, Len Talbot, 32, were buried near where the main part of the bomber crashed but later reinterred in Hamburg War Cemetery. Talbot left a widow in Rotorua.

Trevor Dill, navigator on Hilton Williams' 75 Squadron crew, still remembers that night:

A great thunderstorm over the whole area. We got so iced up that we lost all our air speed and ice was smacking off the propellers into the fuselage . . . the sides were all dented . . . lightning everywhere . . . streaming off the guns, and the propellers were rings of light . . . lightning dancing off the windscreen . . . it was quite amazing . . . a violent storm . . . we had to get down out of the ice and came right down low into pouring rain before we got air speed up again . . . a bit dicey when you're flying around through searchlights and you get on the point of a stall and start shuddering and have to bang your nose down.

Sixteen New Zealanders were killed during Operation Gomorrah, designed to crush Hamburg, and several more were taken prisoner after parachuting. But losses were not severe in comparison with some raids; indeed, total battle casualties over Hamburg were relatively light, due largely to the introduction of *Window*, codename for narrow aluminium-backed paper strips designed to confuse the enemy's radar. They were carried in the bombers in bundles of 2200, and ejected in their millions, creating an immense cloud of baffling images on enemy radar screens. As German radar couldn't distinguish between bombers and *Window,* ground radar directing night fighters and controlling flak and searchlights, and airborne radar on night fighters, were all bamboozled. The Germans soon found ways to counter *Window* but they never totally succeeded in overcoming it and the British used it for the rest of the war, dropping thousands of tons.

Wireless operator Jim McQueen, shot down over Holland in 1942 and imprisoned in Poland, was astonished by the quantity of *Window* littering the countryside as he and fellow POWs were marched west in early 1945. Between Dresden and Leipzig 'the trees and soil . . . were sprinkled with tinsel — heaps of it. There was so much in places that some trees looked a bit like Christmas trees.'

Bomber Command aircrew who raided Hamburg will always remember *Window* and the monstrous electrical storm during the last attack, but above all they will remember the fires their bombs and incendiaries created on the night of 27–28 July. Dill wrote in his log after getting back from that trip: 'Smoke to 20,000 feet, fire visible from 200 miles away.' He and his fellow crewmen went right through the thick of this period, flying to Hamburg, Essen, Hamburg, Hamburg again ('getting sick of Hamburg; heavy attack, 800 aircraft engaged, defences greatly increased since last time, making it pretty hot; 75 okay but lost twenty-eight aircraft on the effort'), Remscheid and back to Hamburg again on 2–3 August. 'I know we were damned tired after that and we had a bit of a break,' he says.

Fires were still smouldering from the opening attack three nights earlier and the much smaller daylight raids by US 8th Army Air Force Fortresses on 25 and 26 July when the first pathfinders arrived over the target on the night of 27–28 July. Then Main Force began dropping hundreds of tons of bombs on built-up housing areas. Given high midsummer temperatures, low humidity and a tinder-dry city of many old and closely packed wooden buildings, fires quickly spread and met over a wide area to create a firestorm with hurricane-force winds that sucked all the oxygen out of the air.

The number killed that night has never been precisely determined but most estimates are about 40,000. The majority of the victims were simply asphyxiated, many in cellars and air-raid shelters. The storming fires raged unchecked until there was nothing left to burn. German fire-fighting units could do nothing in rubble-blocked streets, and thousands of people fled from the city, spreading fear throughout Germany. But German morale did not break, then or later in the war when most of the nation's cities lay in ruins.

New Zealander Nick Matich's Halifax from 35 Squadron, a pathfinder unit, was the first casualty of the entire sequence of raids, crashing on the first night takeoff at Graveley, Cambridgeshire. Matich, born in Te Kopuru, a settlement on the Northern Wairoa River in Northland, was to fly almost 50 ops and earn a DSO and DFM and acclaim for avoiding the clutches of the enemy after being shot down over Germany in the autumn of 1943. But he came to grief setting out for Hamburg.

One engine failed as the Halifax rolled down the runway but Matich was able to brake and halt the plane. The motor picked up as he taxied back and the crew agreed to try again. This time both outer engines failed on liftoff, starved of petrol. The Halifax smashed through the boundary fence and slammed down in a field. The crew left the plane in a twinkling, running for their lives. Middlebrook wrote their exit 'anticipated Roger Bannister's record by some years'. Amazingly no one was hurt and the plane did not burn or explode.

One exceptional achievement during the battle was Southland farmer Wilfred Elder's feat of beating off German night-fighter attacks, then bringing his battle-damaged 76 Squadron Halifax back to England. Elder, almost 31, had just won the DFM over the Ruhr, and on the morning of 27 July he learned he had been commissioned. With congratulations ringing in his ears he took off for Hamburg. His Halifax was among the early wave over the aiming point but already huge fires were burning. Flak was not as heavy as in the Ruhr but despite the confusion caused by *Window*, German night fighters were buzzing around.

As the Halifax wheeled away after bombing, the rear gunner shouted that a Ju 88 was closing quickly from behind. Dazzled by searchlight beams he told Elder to take evasive action. As Elder did so, tracer came at the plane from straight ahead. 'I didn't see it at all,' he said in a BBC broadcast to New Zealand, 'but heard a crash and sparks flying off the port inner engine and the bomb doors dropped open.'

The attacks snuffed out the intercom, smashed some of the controls and knocked out the port inner. The rear gunner suffered leg, arm and face wounds from fighter fire, his turret knocked out of action. Elder tried to ward off the fighters by corkscrewing the damaged plane but was handicapped by not knowing where they were. Shell splinters from more enemy fire now killed the mid-upper gunner as he stood at the flare chute. Flight engineer Bill Berry, an Ulsterman, climbed into the mid-upper turret and fired at a fighter that dived away in flames. But the attacks continued, shrapnel hitting Berry in the legs. Despite his injuries Berry quit the turret to fight a blaze in the empty bomb bay.

'I don't know whether the fighters attacked again but shortly afterwards they left us,' Elder said. The sustained 10-minute assault probably ended only because the attackers had exhausted their ammunition. Elder's wireless operator reported to base: 'Mid-upper killed, two injured. Request ambulance. Returning on three engines.' Luckily the three motors beat strongly as the Halifax ran home across the North Sea. The plane reached England with ample height and headed for Shipdham, an airfield west of Norwich.

'Our hydraulic system had been put out of action in the first attack and all our attempts to lower the undercarriage failed,' Elder said. 'Anyway, if we had got it down we had no pressure for the brakes. We were doubtful if the tyres were all right, so I knew we would have to do a belly landing.'

As the Halifax circled Shipdham, Elder ordered the second pilot, navigator, bomb aimer and wireless operator to bale out and prepared for a wheels-up crash-landing while the engineer, who refused to leave the bomber, strapped the wounded gunner on the rest bed and then went forward to help.

I brought the aircraft down on to the grass beside the runway but I did not quite manage to touch down as soon as I wanted to and we skidded along the grass to the end of the airfield. We jumped a ditch, went through a fence and finished up by tearing the port engines out on tree stumps and came to rest on fire.

Fire fighters doused the flames, an ambulance arrived for the injured and Elder raced to the control tower to check the others had parachuted safely. They had. Deeply religious, Elder said in his broadcast that he remembered uttering a prayer: 'Pay thy vows unto the Most High and call unto Me in the day of trouble. I will deliver thee.'

Elder's exploits earned him a mention in dispatches and then a DFC. Less than a month later he crashed in bad weather, on return from Berlin, at 76 Squadron's Yorkshire field at Holme-on-Spalding Moor. Bill Chorley quotes him in *To See the Dawn Breaking*: 'I decided to overshoot but left it too late and I felt something hit from underneath. Four propellers made a very good job of cutting a large hawthorn hedge, a better job than they would have made of a brick house which we just missed.' Elder was hurt and taken to hospital. When he was discharged his commanding officer decided he'd done enough and ended his tour.

Elder returned to the land after the war. He bought a property near Gore, married, and farmed for the rest of his working life. He was almost 89 when he died in 2001.

'The bumping stopped and I knew we were off the ground'

Navigator Jim Insull was another New Zealander whose first operation, like Mosen's, was the opening raid of the Hamburg firestorm series. Unlike Mosen, Insull survived Hamburg, a tour and the war. He was lucky, maybe because he always carried his talismans: a pair of dice and a bootie knitted for his infant daughter, Sue. He suffered only a minor back injury when his Wellington crashed at OTU, although later was twice in hospital when crews with whom he was flying were shot down on ops. He flew with seven different pilots and three different squadrons.

Insull wondered if he was ever going to make his operational debut. 'Three times we have been briefed and three times [the op] has been scrubbed,' he wrote in his diary in July 1943.

> Last night we were actually in the aircraft with the engines running ready to taxi on to the runway when the nav leader drew up in an Austin van and yelled, 'Scrubbed, chaps, scrubbed.' This afternoon it was called off just before tea. We all agree this 'on-off' business is a bigger strain than going and doing the job — we think!

Insull's 218 Squadron Stirling finally got away to Hamburg from Downham Market, Norfolk, on the night of 24–25 July. 'The bumping stopped and I knew we were off the ground. I made the first entry on my first operational log sheet: "2240 hours, airborne."' Keen to make a good impression with an experienced skipper, Insull worked carefully to guide the bomber to the target accurately and then, as the plane headed in to drop its load, handed over to the bomb aimer.

> Wanting to see where my navigation had brought us, I climbed into the seat alongside the skipper. All round us and reaching to all heights . . . were hundreds of search lights, most of them moving back and forth in ever changing criss-cross patterns of cones or apexes. Those close to us towered above like huge sword blades. Among them, the small flashes of hundreds of flak bursts appeared and disappeared, leaving only black splodges of smoke against the starlit sky. Dennie [the bomb aimer] was saying, 'Can see the greens [target markers], steady, left, left, that's it, steady.'

Insull was mesmerized.

> It was a shapeless mass of fire so far below that it all appeared like a badly focused technicoloured film of lights that seemed to move, twinkle and shimmer in a thousand shapes in colours of yellow, red and orange on a background of black velvet. I could soon distinguish bomb bursts and gun flashes among the blotches of light. I stared and stared. My heart was pounding and I felt I was not getting enough air. Dennie's 'bombs gone' brought me back to my senses and I slipped back to my desk to record, Time 0128. Bombs gone. Height 16,400 feet. Speed indicated 215mph. Course 194 true.

The Stirling skedaddled from the target area, the skipper weaving violently to confuse German gunners on the ground and lurking night fighters. The aircraft's motion made Insull feel nauseous and he was concerned for the flight engineer, who got airsick easily. 'I peeped into Boost's compartment. He had been ill and was crouched dejectedly over his instrument panel. [But] he raised his thumb when he caught my eye, and I returned the salute.'

Eight minutes after 'bombs gone' the Stirling's gun turrets burst into action as a fighter attacked, but the bomber dived away to safety in a wicked roll that almost threw Insull out of his seat. After that alarm they had a smooth run home to a touchdown six hours 35 minutes after liftoff. 'I felt tired but exhilarated with a feeling of having done something I had previously felt myself incapable of.' The briefing room was full of chattering men, and WAAFs moved among them with steaming coffee and sandwiches 'and a rum issue if you wished. I wished.'

Attacking Peenemunde

The RAF crews who bombed Peenemunde, Germany's rocket research and testing centre on the Baltic coast, on the night of 17–18 August 1943 were not told what went on at the site. However, it was impressed on them that destruction of the target was vital to Britain's security. If they did not succeed they would go back again and again. Most of them had never heard of Peenemunde. Neither had the Luftwaffe night-fighter pilots.

Rocket research began at Peenemunde in 1937 and it was there, over the next few years, that the V-2 rocket was designed and built. The area was ideal — a narrow neck of pine-clad land, easily closed off from the public, bounded on one side by the River Peene and on the other by the Baltic. The Germans erected workshops and assembly plants and, away from prying eyes, test-fired their rockets out to sea.

The V-2 was a liquid-fuelled rocket that reached supersonic speed and fell on its unsuspecting target without sound. It had a range of 200 miles, ample to reach the south of England from the Channel coast of occupied Europe, and carried a warhead of about a ton of explosive. A German army project, it was first fired successfully in October 1942. Among the men most responsible for its success was chief scientist Werner von Braun, snapped up by the Americans after the war to run their rocket programme.

It was also from Peenemunde that Germany tried out the V-1, or doodlebug as Londoners called it after the first of its kind fell on the British capital in 1944. The V-1 wasn't a rocket but a pilotless flying bomb with wings and a small but noisy pulsejet engine, and was launched from a ramp. Equipped with a crude guidance system, it was aimed at its target and fell when its fuel was exhausted. It flew at about 400 mph. A Luftwaffe weapon, the V-1 was developed and manufactured elsewhere in Germany and brought to Peenemunde for test-firing. Britain was not aware of its presence when the site was bombed in August 1943. The RAF was after the rocket establishment.

The British were slow to discover what was going on at Peenemunde but eventually intelligence authorities were alerted and photographic flights revealed the existence of the deadly weapons. In late June 1943 the War Cabinet ordered the RAF to bomb the facility. Less than two months later almost 600 Lancasters, Halifaxes and Stirlings were unleashed in a multi-wave precision night attack on three aiming points — the experimental works, the V-2 production works and the housing estate where scientists and other workers lived. The attack was the first to be directed in the target area by a master of ceremonies (known later in the war as a master bomber). Crews faced a 1300-mile round-trip across the North Sea and Denmark and home the same way.

The raid caused major damage and Bomber Command did not have to return. The V-2 programme was set back some months, and the first rockets didn't fall on England until September 1944. Although successful, however, the bombing didn't end rocket production because there were two other manufacturing plants, but the scientists and their equipment did have to be moved to underground caverns in the mountains of central Germany.

Bomber Command ordered a 'maximum effort' attack on Peenemunde. Every group and most squadrons, 75 among them, participated. The previous night 75 had taken part in the last raid against Italy before the Italian surrender, 12 Stirlings attacking Turin. Now 75 put up another dozen, flown by fresh crews. One aborted but 11 bombed and all got home. Indeed, casualties among the 3 Group Stirlings that night were remarkably light because the planes were in the first wave. Flak was light and few fighters had arrived by then.

75 pilot Allan Alexander, who now lives in Waikanae, remembers the bright moonlight that night. 'We could see planes everywhere.' The markers hadn't gone down when his Stirling arrived off Peenemunde, so he orbited, waiting for them. When he bombed at low level he could feel the explosions and see buildings below blowing up. 'It was like the old cowboy movies when buildings would lift up and then fall apart. Just like that. They disappeared.' Alexander and the rest of his crew had a quiet trip, but homebound over the Baltic they saw the end of a Lancaster or Halifax. The aircraft blew up close by. 'There was a big flash. I can still see it. It just went whoosh. One wing was hanging up and then the aircraft went straight down. He must have been hit by a night fighter in the petrol tanks. It was gone; a huge fireball, dark red and white.'

Another New Zealander flying in 3 Group that night was navigator Keith Evans, on an early trip with 214 Squadron.

We were in the front at Peenemunde and had absolutely no problems — no flak, no night fighters. We were still learners but we had learned to get the hell out of it as quickly as possible. I would say our bombs were among the first 10 loads to go down and they were close to the aiming point. We didn't hang around to see where the rest were going.

Bomber Command lost 39 aircraft on the Peenemunde raid, most in the second and third waves, and a 40th crashed in England. Among the dead aircrew were New Zealand pilots Bill Caldwell and Howard Spiers and rear gunner Lloyd English. Newly commissioned, Caldwell, from Wellington, had done about six ops when he flew a 158 Squadron Halifax that night. He was still only 19, three weeks short of his 20th birthday, when he was killed. Martin Middlebrook's 1982 book *The Peenemunde Raid* says his bomber was hit by flak over the target and crashed about 20 miles away. He quotes the English mid-upper gunner as saying they were hit almost at the same time as their bombs went.

> I heard the call, 'bombs gone' and at the same time swung my turret around and saw that flames were licking round the starboard inner engine . . . someone said 'okay' . . . it may have been the skipper . . . I heard him ordering the fire extinguisher to be pressed and the engine feathered. The fire didn't gain very fast but it was persistent and it eventually got a grip and the wing itself caught fire. I thought we may get away with it until I saw the wing burning. Things happened rapidly after that. I heard Caldwell saying, 'Prepare to abandon aircraft.' He seemed quite calm and the aircraft was still flying, apparently under control. There was no panic. I thought the others would follow and out I went.

He added that he was surprised to find the engineer the only other survivor. 'I can only assume the wing came off or the aircraft blew up.'

Spiers, born in Masterton in early 1916, was working as a teamster when he enlisted in September 1941. Like Caldwell he did his early flying at Harewood and went on to Canada. He was on his fourth op when he was lost with his entire crew. Their 100 Squadron Lancaster is believed to have been shot down over the Baltic north or east of the target. Only two bodies, neither of them Spiers', was subsequently washed ashore.

English, 26, a drapery buyer in Hamilton before the war, had come safely through 12 ops with 619 Squadron before being killed at Peenemunde. His Lancaster, flown by a Canadian, dived vertically into a boggy meadow right in the target area, killing everyone.

One New Zealander who survived by a whisker at Peenemunde was 61 Squadron pilot Tom Stewart. He was shot down on the last flight of his second tour, surviving when many in his squadron didn't. Arriving in the final wave, 61 lost four of its 10 Lancasters — a horrifying percentage. Of the 31 men aboard the four aircraft just two — Stewart and his navigator — reached the ground alive.

The New Zealander, founder of Stewart's Coffee Supplies in the South Island after the war, led a charmed life through some of the thickest action of the air war in 1942 and 1943. He did his opening half-dozen trips on the unreliable Manchester, including the first thousand-bomber raid on Cologne, then flew Lancasters exclusively, including once, unusually, over the Bay of Biscay to hunt submarines for Coastal Command. He was hit by flak, attacked by fighters, and one night over Dusseldorf was forced down to 1000 feet before he could get away from the searchlights and flak. His first tour of 34 ops yielded a DFM. After a spell instructing, he returned to 61 Squadron in May 1943 for a second tour of 20 ops, starting with the last two months of the Ruhr raids. A DFC was announced just after he was shot down.

Stewart, who died in Dunedin in 1995, still had vivid memories of Peenemunde years later. He recorded on tape what happened:

> As we approached, fires were burning and the target was quite visible. We were within seconds of letting the bombs go when I heard the MC saying the green target indicator had just gone

down slap bang on the target and to bomb on it. I couldn't turn quickly enough to get right over the green TI so I told the bomb aimer we were going around again. We ran up to the TI and let the bombs go. I held her steady to let the camera operate and then started a right-hand turn away.

The Lancaster had just left the target area when the rear gunner spotted a fighter approaching from behind. Stewart was waiting for the corkscrew order when his aircraft was hit from underneath by another fighter.

There didn't appear to be any great damage at first but a small fire started near the wireless operator's compartment. I asked the flight engineer to check and then went into a violent corkscrew as the fire was making us rather visible to the German fighters. Despite this we were hit a second time and the controls went. The aircraft didn't spin, the nose just dropped and we began to dive in. The intercom was completely out and so I reached over to the Canadian second pilot and screamed, 'Bale out! Bale out!' I couldn't do anything [for the rest of] the crew. I realised there was no hope of us getting out.

A split second later Stewart was out of the plane, flung clear. 'One moment I was in my seat, the next I found myself falling through space. The aircraft blew up. I have no recollection of any violent flash or the noise of an explosion. I can remember reaching for my ripcord [he was wearing a seat-type chute] but have no recollection at all of pulling it.'

Pull it he did though, for he landed safely and uninjured right in Peenemunde. Ridding himself of his chute, he bounded into a field of beet and threw himself down as the area was alive with shouting Germans. 'I crawled along the rows of beet, got to the end of them and took off.'

He was at large for four days before being captured. Then he was taken to a railway station where another 25 RAF airmen, fellow survivors from the raid, were awaiting a train. Among them was his navigator, Frank Barker. When the Lancaster had exploded, the Englishman had been standing behind Stewart, chute on as always at bombing time, and had been blown clear with his pilot. The flight engineer had also been blown clear. But he was dead. He hadn't been wearing his chute.

The Battle of Berlin

Vic Viggers, still blowing the trombone in that Hawke's Bay institution the Dixielanders, flew to the German capital 11 times during the Battle of Berlin. Norman Webb, a 90-year-old retired electrical engineer who lives at Paraparaumu Beach, did 10 trips. John Hegman, whose remains lie in the Berlin 1939–45 War Cemetery, was on his 14th when he was killed. Other New Zealand aircrew matched these totals but it's doubtful few did more, especially of the key 16 night raids during the late autumn and winter of 1943–44 that comprised the Battle of Berlin. Counting three strikes in August and September 1943, Bomber Command mounted 19 major attacks on the German capital with large forces of four-engined bombers during this period of the war. On many other nights it kept the sirens going and Berliners awake by sending small numbers of swift bomb-carrying Mosquitoes.

After the Ruhr raids, the Hamburg firestorm attacks and the special operation on Peenemunde, everyone, British and German alike, knew what was coming. Fleet Street trumpeted 'Berlin Next'. In early 1943 Bomber Command chief Arthur Harris had sent his squadrons to Berlin five times but he wasn't really ready for a major onslaught until August. Then, as the nights began to lengthen and it became possible to fly the long round trip in the dark, he ordered maximum-strength raids on the Big City, as it became known to aircrew.

Authorities differ on the starting date of the battle. Many reckon it began on 18–19 November and dismiss the three raids in late August and early September. Other specialists, among them Martin Middlebrook, who wrote *The Berlin Raids*, a fascinating account of the campaign, consider the earlier missions the opening phase of the battle.

August or November — it didn't make much difference to the men who manned the bombers. Harris hoped he could do to Berlin what he'd done to Hamburg, but the capital was a much bigger and more modern city, an enormous sprawling place with many open spaces, strongly built apartments and wide streets not easily blocked by rubble to prevent fire fighters from moving around.

Bomber Command also had to face an infinitely stronger defence system — bands of searchlights and flak batteries and swarming night fighters. The Germans built three enormous flak towers in Berlin on which they had mounted awesome 128-mm batteries. New tactics that allowed the fighters to roam around in the bomber stream and over the target took their toll. Bright-white flares dropped by high-flying German aircraft illuminated the bombers for the fighters.

The announcement that Berlin was the night's target always created a knot of anxiety in the stomachs of most crew because the city was the toughest target that autumn and winter, particularly as raid followed raid and casualties mounted. Bomber Command continued its attacks on other German cities throughout the battle, some of them costing more New Zealand casualties than those on the capital, but Berlin was the main focus. Viggers:

> Of course we never knew the target until briefing. The aircrew down to fly any particular night were listed on the battle order that came out at 10 o'clock in the morning, so you could see whether on not you were on, but you didn't know where you

were going until they'd say at briefing, 'The target tonight
is . . .' If it was Berlin a murmur would go around the briefing
room.

Even though there was uncertainty about the precise target,
experienced airmen like Viggers had a fair idea where they were
headed from the amount of fuel fed into their aircraft and the
weight of the bombs loaded. A heavy bomb load and relatively
light fuel injection meant a short-range target. The opposite meant
a long-haul trip — such as Berlin.

Viggers, a wireless operator on 101 Squadron, flew with a
crew headed by fellow countryman Doug Todd — 'Toddy' to
his men. Unusually, the two crewed up in Canada in 1942 as part
of a foursome to fly Venturas. In England they were posted to
98 Squadron to fly Mitchells in 2 Group, did one op and then
volunteered to fly heavies. They started operations in mid-
October 1943, going on to complete all their Berlin trips plus the
terrible raids whose losses loom so large in Bomber Command
history — Leipzig, Nuremberg and Mailly-le-Camp.

The only squadron in the command with *Airborne Cigar*, or
ABC, 101's Lancasters were equipped with special radio equipment
designed to jam German night-fighter communications. The gear
was operated by an extra German-speaking crew member, so the
101 Lancasters had crews of eight. Though they had a special role,
these aircraft still carried their regular bomb loads. The German
speaker in Todd's crew was a Scotland Yard detective constable
in civvy street. Viggers found him slumped over his microphone
one night on a Berlin trip, hit in the shoulder by flak. 'I dressed
his wound and put him down on the rest bed but the next time
I looked up he'd got up and gone back to his position. It was a
shaky do and we counted 220 flak holes the next morning but
he was the only one hit.'

Viggers did one more Berlin raid than the rest of his crew. On the morning of 23 December 1943, Todd was away at the funeral of a crew who had crashed at another drome after returning from an op a couple of nights earlier.

I knew we weren't due to fly and I'd had a night out. I got back to the base at 7.00 a.m., a bit scruffy with stubble on my chin, to hear the Tannoy calling me to the wing commander's office. I stepped into his office, saluted, said 'Sir' and told him with a bit of a grin I'd been out. He asked me if I'd fly that night to Berlin with another crew. I could have said no but you really don't say no to requests like that. He said, 'We're short and command has called for a maximum effort.' So I went.

Twice on this extra trip Viggers found the mid-upper gunner asleep. 'That filled me with horror, flying with a bastard who went to sleep, especially a gunner. Anyway, we got back and I told the captain, "Get rid of that man."' A few nights later the gunner was gone — a case of LMF.

Three times the Todd crew donned chutes and lined up to bale out, three times the 'Go' wasn't given and they got home. Viggers puts this down to the great cooperation between Todd and English flight engineer Stan Power.

Toddy would say in a crisis situation, 'Well Stan, we're not losing height now,' and Stan would reply in his broad accent, 'No, that's right. The engines are running pretty smoothly now and I've feathered the port inner.' He'd be talking away as though it were an everyday conversation. Once I switched on the intercom and heard Stan say, 'It's all right, Toddy. It's all right. I've put the bloody fire out.'

The Todd crew was unexpectedly screened and told they were finished after their 29th op. 'We knew we had to do at least 30 and if we'd been asked we'd have done more. But the day the wing commander said we'd done enough, well it was marvellous.' The entire crew was decorated at the end of the tour, both New Zealanders getting a DFC. Todd died in Palmerston North in 1969.

Norman Webb, former 61 Squadron pilot, doesn't remember much now about his 10 Berlin raids. Because they were so straightforward they pretty much fuse in his mind. The night he remembers best is 24–25 February 1944, when the RAF made its first raid on Schweinfurt, location of Germany's biggest ball-bearing factory. Webb ended up on the ground on the last op of his tour, shot down by an unseen fighter probably using Schrage Musik. He and his 'geriatric' crew lived a charmed life bombing Berlin — no flak holes, no fighter attacks, never coned by searchlights. Hundreds of planes were shot down trying to get to Berlin, over the target or homebound, and several thousand aircrew were killed. Others struggled back to England in crippled condition and with wounded aboard. Some crews, like Webb's, were either plain lucky or extra skilled — or both.

Webb turned 30 in December 1943, at the height of the Battle of Berlin. Two of his original crew, navigator Pat Walkins and wireless operator Bert Collingwood, were a couple of years older. 'They called us pensioners even then,' Webb laughs. The three met up again in England in 1995. 'They didn't say a word at first,' Webb's wife recalls. 'They just sat and smiled. They were so delighted to see each other speech wasn't necessary.'

The Webb crew began ops just as the Ruhr raids ended, flying their first serious mission to Gelsenkirchen on 9 July 1943. They did all four Hamburg raids, the Peenemunde raid and then the Berlin raids and other targets on 'off' nights. Webb enjoyed being a pilot but says modestly that it was only a job. 'I was just a bus driver. The gunners, they were supposed to look after us;

the wireless operator, the bomb aimer, the navigator, [the] flight engineer all had jobs to do, and I drove the thing along.' His DFC was announced two weeks before he was shot down.

Squadron Leader John Hegman, DSO, DFC, was four months short of his 40th birthday when he died attacking Berlin on 15–16 February 1944 on the second-to-last raid of the battle. The oldest RNZAF pilot killed in World War II, he was born in Auckland in June 1904 and was well beyond the acceptance age for pilots when he enlisted in March 1941. But he underdeclared his age by an astonishing 12 years to beat the rules, giving his birth date as 1916. He was twice the age of many volunteers and should have stuck out like a sore thumb. Perhaps he looked especially boyish or someone gave him a big wink. Whatever it was, he was accepted. When he joined the RNZAF he was working as a farm valuer.

Hegman was a first-generation New Zealander, the only son of an Auckland businessman born in Germany. It's ironic that he died bombing his father's homeland, and is buried there. After reaching England in October 1941 he was posted to the Middle East, flying Wellingtons. He returned to England in February 1943 with 53 ops to his credit and was awarded the DFC. After serving as an instructor he went to 7 Squadron. He arrived at the pathfinder unit as a flight lieutenant in early November 1943 but was promoted to squadron leader before Christmas, commanding one of 7's three flights. In January he won his DSO on one of the three Berlin raids that month and was fortunate to escape unscathed. Because of equipment problems he arrived over Berlin, a lone bomber, 10 minutes after the raid had finished. Although the flak batteries and remaining fighters had him to themselves, he dropped his bombs, somehow got away and flew home. 'He is a gallant and skilful leader whose sterling qualities have impressed all,' the citation said.

A month later he was dead. February 15–16 was a terrible

night for 7 Squadron, with four Lancasters, including Hegman's, lost with only three survivors. His mid-upper gunner, among the dead, was also 40, well past the average age for aircrew.

Another 'elderly' and experienced New Zealand airman was killed on one of 7 Squadron's aircraft. Bomb aimer Frank Jones' Lancaster crashed en route to its target. Jones, a 35-year-old Aucklander, had a distinguished and eventful war and was on his 36th op the night he died. He'd emerged safely from a tour with 149 Squadron on Wellingtons and Stirlings despite enduring 15 hours in a dinghy in the Channel in June 1942 after a raid on Essen. Homebound, his Stirling was hit by flak over Belgium before an Me 110 crashed into the tail, sheering off the rear turret and killing the gunner. The pilot tried to get the aircraft home but finally ditched at 3.00 a.m. The crew were picked up by an ASR launch out of Ramsgate. Jones' luck finally ran out on the way to Berlin. He had a DFC and two mentions in dispatches, one for bravery.

Eighty per cent of the 3583 Commonwealth graves in the Berlin 1939–45 War Cemetery are of airmen lost in raids over the capital and cities of eastern Germany such as Leipzig, Konigsberg, Dresden, Rostock, Magdeburg and Potsdam. Fifty-six New Zealand aircrew lie there. The site of the cemetery was selected by the British Occupation Authorities and Commonwealth War Graves Commission in 1945.

The RAF's sustained assault on Berlin cost 66 New Zealand lives, and only five of the 19 raids were without New Zealand deaths. Casualties were worst on the early raids, before Harris and Bomber Command decided in late November that Stirling losses were unacceptable and removed the planes from the roster for Berlin and all other operations to Germany. 75 Squadron, then still equipped with Stirlings, lost a total of nine aircraft on the three Berlin raids in which it participated — three on the opening night, four a week later on 31 August–1 September and another two on 22–23 November. Of the 64 aircrew aboard those nine Stirlings (one aircraft carried a second pilot) only 10 lived to become POWs. The Stirlings had become deathtraps and featured disproportionately in the battle statistics. 75 Squadron suffered the highest percentage loss of any squadron — an awful 19.6 per cent of aircraft dispatched.

All three aircraft 75 lost on the night of 23–24 August fell in the greater Berlin area, killing 21 men. An English mid-upper gunner was the only survivor. Three could so easily have been four. Bill White's Stirling, EF435-J (Johnny), was shot to pieces over the target but White got it home with only half its crew. The pilot wrote succinctly in his logbook: 'Badly shot up. Direct hit on rear turret. Rear gunner killed. Navigator, bomb aimer, W/Op baled out. Crash landed at base. Awarded CGM [Conspicuous Gallantry Medal].'

This air-force decoration, instituted in 1943 for conspicuous gallantry in air operations by airmen of non-commissioned rank, was awarded to just four New Zealanders in Bomber Command. The very first of the 111 World War II CGMs went to New Zealand wireless operator Bruce Wallace for his bravery in fighting and subduing a fire, despite being wounded in a night-fighter attack, on an 83 Squadron Lancaster flying to Munich in late December 1942. Wallace, who died in Invercargill in 2001, flew 46 ops with the pathfinder squadron. The other two New Zealanders to win the CGM were Ted de Joux and Dave Moriarty.

White grew up in Monck's Bay, Christchurch, 100 yards or so from where the Heathcote and Avon Rivers flow into the sea. As a boy he lived in the water, and by the time he was a young man he was a classy yachtsman who took his sport seriously and studied navigation. He could read the stars and it was this talent that helped him home on a dramatic night over Berlin.

White was on his 13th op when he got into trouble. Coned

by searchlights as it was nearing the target, his Stirling was peppered with flak, fragments of exploding shells smashing into the bomber and damaging the port wing. Then a Ju 88 attacked, mincing the rear turret and killing English gunner Jack Poole. The aircraft began to fall in an uncontrolled dive and White warned his crew to be ready to bale out. But in the horror of the moment and with the intercom fading, three crew, two of them New Zealanders, heard only the words 'bale out' and jumped — navigator Bill Rogerson (Palmerston North), bomb aimer John Murray (Invercargill), and the wireless operator. All survived to become POWs.

White calmly jettisoned his bombs over the target, somehow pulled the Stirling out of its apparent death dive at 6000 feet and then swung off to the northwest to get away. With only one functioning compass, no navigator and no wireless operator to give him a position fix, he used his knowledge of the heavens to set a course that one news report at the time said he had 'vaguely worked out in my head'. The same account says the Stirling was forced into a second steep dive by flak over another city but again got away. White made an English landfall off the Wash and followed canals and rivers to 75's base at Mepal. Without flaps or undercarriage he made a perfect crash-landing.

Fellow 75 pilot Allan Alexander, whose crew accounted for an Me 109 over Berlin on 23–24 August and then battled flak over Denmark on the way home, had to circle Mepal when he got back because of an obstruction on the airfield. Pleading petrol shortage he was finally permitted to land but was warned to be extra careful because the obstruction was an aircraft, very close to the runway, that might still have had bombs on board — White's.

A Canadian airman wrote years later that accounts of White's accomplishment didn't convey the magnitude of what he'd achieved — 'dodging fighters, going around towns to avoid flak, using stars in the Northern Hemisphere, upside down to the south, and on and on. Many would say he had a horse-shoe up his ass.'

White's flight engineer and mid-upper gunner, both Britons, were awarded DFMs for helping their skipper on the long hazardous flight home. White completed a tour of 25 ops, including several more over Germany but not Berlin, and then went to a conversion unit as an instructor. He wrote to his family on 2 December 1944 as Stirlings were being phased out of Main Force raids:

> I'm a bit sorry about finishing with the old Stirlings. I was very fond of the Queen of the Sky as we called them. I had [my] last flip in old P for Piwi the other day and gave her a sad farewell. She's still airworthy though she's had a couple of prangs since she's been on the conversion unit. The Lancs seem pretty small after the Stirling.

White died in Christchurch in 1982 at the age of 68.

Aucklander Doug Henley, killed on the 31 August–1 September 1943 Berlin raid, was another in the long line of pilots who died giving their crews a chance to survive. When the men who got out alive from 75 Squadron's Stirling EE878-P (Peter) returned to England from POW camp in 1945 and told their stories, Henley's actions were recognised by a mention in dispatches — 'For gallant service.'

Henley, 23, fought a long battle to keep his crippled bomber in the air after savage attacks by night fighters over the Big City, coaxing it back to just west of the Rhine south of Bonn. But it kept losing height and when he saw hills ahead that he knew he couldn't clear, he ordered his crew out. Four jumped, two of whom lived. The two who died were both New Zealanders. Henley had no show of escaping and went down with his bomber, the cockpit area taking the brunt of the impact. The two gunners, one of them New Zealander Jimmy Grant, were still in the plane when it hit the ground. Remarkably both survived.

English flight engineer Lew Parsons was by the rear escape hatch and plugged into the intercom when he heard Henley's urgent final command: 'Bale out, bale out. You must bale out.' 'Those were the last words I heard from a brave man and a good friend,' Parsons wrote almost 60 years later. The engineer urged wireless operator Bob Quelch out of the plane and followed immediately. Moments later the Stirling crashed, breaking in two.

Parsons says they were hit over Berlin by two Ju 88s attacking together and he heard Grant shout, 'Fighters, weave skipper, weave'.

> We dived away to the right and both gunners opened fire, the [Germans] used their cannons and we suffered several hits. When we pulled out of our dive about 10,000 feet we found we had lost the port inner engine, the tailplane and elevators were badly shot up, Jimmy was trapped in his turret and mid-upper Doug Box was concussed. I told the skipper to feather the engine and to lighten the aircraft jettisoned the fuel from the No. 2 main tank on the port side, now useless dead weight with the engine out.

Parsons and Quelch got Grant, wounded and splattered with flak fragments, and Box out of their turrets and sat them on the floor of the fuselage. 'We thought about going up to the North Sea and ditching but after conferring with the skipper we decided our best chance was to stick in the bomber stream [going home west across Germany] and get back if possible.' Navigator Cliff Watson, 34 (Christchurch), set a course and bomb aimer Ian Smith, 34 (Napier), helped Henley hold the aircraft steady. 'I opened the rear escape hatch in the floor and Bob and I started to throw out everything we could unbolt in an attempt to lighten the aircraft — armour plating, oxygen bottles, guns, ammunition. Doing that helped keep the aircraft in the air for more than an hour but we were losing height all the time.'

The aircraft continued to sink slowly because of structural and engine damage and may have been only a couple of thousand feet up when Henley ordered his crew out. Rising ground quickly cut the height even more and Parsons believes he leapt at 800 feet or less. He landed safely moments after his chute had opened, as did Quelch. Watson's and Smith's chutes failed to deploy in time and both men died. Parsons saw the plane burning in the distance after he'd landed.

Grant, who died in Central Otago in 1993, was quoted in the official history *New Zealanders with the RAF* as saying that he'd been wounded in the right arm and shoulder and hit again during a second attack. He said he'd opened fire on one fighter moving in for the kill 'and the enemy machine belched forth a cloud of smoke and flame and disappeared'. He watched the others bale out and sat waiting for the crash, which came on the top of high hills. 'I managed to scramble out of the burning machine, crawled away and went to sleep, only to be awakened some six hours later by a German search party.' All four survivors were quickly rounded up. Grant was left behind at Dulag Luft because of his injuries, Parsons says. 'We didn't see him again until we met post-war at Buckingham Palace for a garden party for 800 ex-POWs.'

It's always been on Parsons' conscience that he and Box baled out and left the gunners, 'but with the skipper's orders ringing in my ears there wasn't a lot of time to make a choice. The saving grace was of course that they both came out unscathed.' Parsons did the right thing jumping. He and Box would never have been able to get the gunners to the hatch in time. Probably all would have been killed.

Henley, Watson and Smith were among the 18 New Zealanders who died on the raid, one of the most unsatisfactory of the attacks on Berlin. More RAF aircrew were killed than were Germans on the ground.

Seventeen Stirlings failed to return, including four from 75 Squadron. Among the dead were four New Zealanders from EF501-K (King): pilot Keith McGregor, 21 (Waikouati), navigator James Lovelock, 26 (Christchurch), bomb aimer Bill Kilby, 40 (Wellington), and wireless operator James Baker, 27 (Pokaka, National Park). Lovelock was runner Jack Lovelock's brother and a good athlete himself. Ravaged by night fighters, his Stirling fell at Potsdam, a little southwest of Berlin, where his brother had scored his 1500-metres triumph in the Olympic Games of 1936, just seven years before. The loss card for this bomber contains a moving note, written from a POW camp by one of the two English survivors, the mid-upper gunner. It says:

> No news at all about any of my crew. The worst must have happened. If you see anything of Jimmy's wife, tell her I did all in my power until fate took a hand — for I was thrown out of the aircraft and didn't know anything until my chute opened. Afraid odds of three to one were too much for us.

The message was for Baker's wife, a Canadian the wireless operator had married while training in Canada. Lovelock was single. The comments suggest the aircraft was attacked by three fighters and that it exploded, throwing the gunner clear. As for Kilby, at 40 he was another man well over the age for aircrew. Born in 1903 he gave his year of birth as 1910 on enlistment.

The end of one of 75 Squadron's aircraft that night demonstrated the dangers the lower-flying Stirlings faced from above. George Helm and four of his experienced crew perished a short distance south of Berlin when their aircraft crashed after being hit by falling bombs. Helm, 23 (Invercargill), navigator Don Stewart, 29 (Tirau), and bomb aimer Joe Fisk, 28 (Wanganui), were among the dead. Earlier, in mid-June 1943, the three New Zealanders had endured a frightening time as a new crew over Dusseldorf. Coned as they were about to bomb, 'we could hear the shells crumping around us and lumps of iron flying through the Stirling,' Helm wrote home. 'Our weaving was so violent all four engines once stopped temporarily and we dropped 1000 feet before they picked up ... there was oil everywhere from leaking pipes.' They reached home that night but their lives ended over Berlin. And not even as a result of enemy fire.

New Zealander Claude Rowland and his 78 Squadron Halifax were among the early victims of *Schrage Musik* on the flight home 20 minutes after dropping bombs on Berlin on the night of 31 August–1 September. Rowland recounted what happened before he died in late 2001.

> We made it through the target area pretty well and got away and a while later watched the pathfinders dropping a track marker to make sure we were on course. We were dead on track — we had a bloody good navigator. But because I didn't want to be silhouetted against the bright marker we altered course 45 degrees to starboard for about five minutes. Just as we were coming back to our original course all hell broke loose.

Cannon shells burst through the floor of the fuselage, killing the flight engineer instantly, and more shells set the port inner alight. 'It was fairly obvious we were in serious trouble. The controls were sloppy and . . . I told the crew to prepare to abandon the aircraft.'

Rowland tried the fire extinguisher but it made no difference and he gave the order to quit the plane. He counted his crew out of the doomed Halifax and then tried to get out himself, but the moment he took his hands off the controls the plane began spinning, pinning him against the cockpit wall. 'I said to myself, "This is it." I don't know how I got out. All I can recall is a whoosh and I was in free-fall.'

Rowland was on his 15th op the night he was shot down, less than two months after arriving at 78's field at Breighton, Yorkshire. Six other New Zealand pilots flew with the squadron while he was there. By late September five of them were dead and Rowland was a POW. The survivor was Bob Neal, a flight commander who emerged with an end-of-tour DFC that many aircrew, not surprisingly, often referred to as a survival award. First to go was Ken Morrison (Christchurch), still only 19 and on just his second op when he was killed attacking Wuppertal on 25 June. Ken Toon, 21 (Christchurch), was next to die, shot down during a raid on Aachen on the night of 13–14 July. A close friend of Rowland's, George Bell, 21 (Huntly), was third, losing his life after the first August raid on Berlin. He reached England safely but was diverted to another airfield because of bad weather and collided with another 78 Halifax. No one in either bomber survived — 14 dead. Frank Poole, 22 (Lower Hutt), halfway through his tour, died when his bomber blew up over Mannheim on 23–24 September, and four nights later Bill Smith (Heddon Bush, Southland), only 21 but already on his 23rd op, was killed when his Halifax crashed near Hanover. Life was short on bomber squadrons in the second half of 1943.

South Islander Keith Evans, 21, a 218 Squadron navigator, got home from Berlin on 31 August–1 September in a Stirling minus one engine and another running roughly. The plane took a direct flak hit on the starboard inner as it flew out of the target area and although the shell didn't explode it knocked the engine right out of the wing.

I heard the pilot say to the flight engineer, 'I've lost power on the starboard inner,' and the flight engineer, even younger than I was, reply, 'You haven't got a starboard inner. It's gone.' According to him it just folded up and drifted back over the wing. It was a big enough shell and a big enough impact to break the bolts holding the engine and away it went.

Evans had doubts about their undercarriage that night too, but when they eventually struggled home it held up — until they'd got to dispersal, parked, disembarked and climbed into the truck to go to debriefing. Then it collapsed.

The last of the three late-summer/early-autumn Berlin raids was ordered for 3–4 September, and this time the Stirlings, badly hit in the opening two attacks, were rested and an all-Lancaster force of 316 bombers, carrying almost 1000 tons of high explosives and incendiaries, passed over the target in 16 minutes flat. Tighter and tighter bombing schedules meant aircraft spent less time over targets, saturating the aiming points and giving the defences less time to react. Twenty bombers were lost in this attack (which took place on the day the Allies invaded Italy). Among the dead were six New Zealanders from two 7 Squadron bombers.

Both of these pathfinder aircraft had New Zealand pilots. One was Dick French, 32 (Feilding), a full-tour 75 Squadron veteran with 46 ops and a DFC to his name. He was lost with all but one of his crew just south of Berlin and is commemorated at Runnymede. (His aircraft crashed in what, after the war, became the Soviet zone and the Russians wouldn't permit a search for graves.) The other crew had, unusually, five New Zealanders, all new to the job. Skipper Tom Hatchard, 31 (Wellington), was on just his fourth op, while the others — navigator Bernard Fdge, 21 (Onehunga), bomb aimer Bill Brosnahan, 25 (Wellington), wireless operator

George Dougherty, 21 (Hamilton), and rear gunner Lewis Squire, 21 (Kawakawa) — were just beginning operations. None of the Hatchard crew survived and the New Zealanders' names are on the Runnymede Memorial.

Australian Don Bennett, head of the pathfinders, had always wanted the pick of experienced crews for his unit but most other groups and squadron commanders resisted losing their best men so Bennett often had to make do with less-experienced and even, as in this case, new crews, especially at times of severe losses. It was asking a great deal of 'sprog' crews to act as pathfinders in front of the main force, particularly over targets like Berlin with night fighters trying especially hard to destroy them.

Anglican priest Michael Wadsworth, whose father was killed over Germany while serving with 156 Squadron, wrote an informal history of this pathfinder unit in 1992. In *They Led the Way* the Englishman says:

> The war the pathfinders fought demanded experience as well as courage. The night skies over Berlin [in this period] were no place for the neophyte, whether he was from pathfinders or main force. The fact that many crews made their debut [in 156 Squadron] at this time is an eloquent testimony to their courage [as well] as to the need of the group commander for constant replacements. Very few of the neophyte crews would survive this period.

What Wadsworth said about 156 applied to every pathfinder squadron. In one particularly bad period for 156, when 14 crews were lost in just four nights, a sardonic Australian on the squadron commented that it wasn't a case of 'Here today, gone tomorrow' but 'Here today, gone tonight.'

75 Squadron bombed Berlin for the last time on 22–23

November 1943, a night on which Harris ordered almost every Bomber Command unit into the air. An armada of 764 aircraft attacked the German capital. The raid was among the most successful of the long campaign. Marking was accurate and so was the bombing, 2500 tons raining down to cause widespread devastation. Hitler suffered personally even though he wasn't in the capital. His private luxury train, standing in a siding, was destroyed.

The 50 Stirlings in the force suffered heavy and disproportionate losses. 75 Squadron put up just four of the planes. One turned back but two of the other three were lost over Germany and six New Zealand lives were snuffed out, three on each aircraft, all the men concerned on just their fourth raid. Neither bomber was anywhere near Berlin. One fell near Osnabruck, the other on the eastern edge of the Ruhr. Nothing is known of what happened because none of the 14 crew survived to explain the circumstances. Stirling casualties were 14 per cent. 75's two out of three represented 66 per cent.

It was losses like these that meant the end for Stirlings over Germany. In *The Berlin Raids* Martin Middlebrook notes the heavy losses that afflicted the Stirling squadrons and their poor bomb loads compared with the other types of aircraft, and explains 'Harris decided that the Stirlings were a spent force and he was not prepared to force them to suffer further heavy casualties for slender results.' Middlebrook wrote that the conversion of 3 Group from Stirlings to Lancasters would be 'painfully slow because most of the Lancaster production would be needed to replace losses in existing Lancaster squadrons as the Battle of Berlin progressed'. So 75 Squadron was off the battle order for Germany, and until it completed re-equipping with Lancasters in the spring of 1944 was confined mainly to mining and bombing V-1 sites.

But the Battle of Berlin raged on, during periods of moonless nights. There were another 14 raids: two more in November, four in December, six in January 1944 and one each in February and March. When Bomber Command conducted its last major attack, on 24–25 March 1944 and lost a shocking 72 bombers, 57 of them downed on the way home, Berlin was a ravaged, rubble-strewn city. Like London in the Blitz, however, it was unbowed and undefeated. On the other hand the RAF had suffered heavily — 625 bombers lost, 5.8 per cent of the attacking force. Worse, 2690 aircrew had been killed and almost 1000 taken prisoner.

Although 75 Squadron was out of the action, hundreds of New Zealanders continued to fly to Berlin with other squadrons and their lives continued to bleed away. One of the dead on 16–17 December was Aucklander Ralph Crossgrove, 25, a wireless operator. He was a victim of atrocious weather conditions that claimed 40 aircraft returning from Berlin — more than were lost over Germany. Impenetrable cloud almost down to ground level blanketed England from the south coast to the Scottish border, and bombers, many of them short of fuel, crashed in record numbers. Some desperate captains, unable to find anywhere to land, ordered their crews to bale out rather than attempting a letdown through the murk. Crossgrove was in a 97 Squadron Lancaster that crashed and burned near its home base of Bourn, in Cambridgeshire. The rear gunner was the only survivor. Unbelievably, this pathfinder squadron lost eight aircraft on the raid, only one of them over Germany. Five crashed in England while the crews of the other two baled out.

Crossgrove had earlier flown a full tour with 57 Squadron and been decorated with the DFM. By the worst of luck he was killed on the first flight of his second tour. His death exemplifies the personal tragedy of war. He sailed from New Zealand three weeks before the birth of his only child, a son named after him. The little boy died short of his second birthday in January 1943, so his father, half a world away, mourned the death of a son he had never seen, unable to share the grief with his wife. Ten months later to the day he was dead himself.

New Zealand bomb aimer Bob Fenton, flying to Berlin for the seventh time, had a narrow squeak on the 30–31 January 1944 raid. Fenton, who lives in Christchurch, was the sole survivor when his 100 Squadron Lancaster spun down from four miles above the earth, right over the target. He was lying on his stomach in the nose, peering through his bombsight, calling instructions to his skipper, when a night fighter caught them. They were almost over the aiming point, bomb doors open.

> Although I didn't see the fighter I believe it attacked us from below and behind, sending cannon shells and incendiaries through the aircraft. Within seconds we were on fire and smoke filled the fuselage. I jettisoned everything. The engineer appeared at the entrance to my position yelling 'Out! Out!' I managed to unlock the escape hatch but had difficulty throwing it out due to the centrifugal force of the spin and [the] fire. The Perspex nose blister was damaged by cannon fire and I baled out through this.

Two greatly experienced New Zealand captains were killed on this last January raid. Harold Hicks, 28 (Wanganui), skipper of a 115 Squadron Lancaster, was flying his 29th op when his aircraft exploded in a sheet of flame over Berlin. There were no survivors and two of the dead were fellow New Zealanders — bomb aimer Alan Todd, 22 (Wellington), and wireless operator Charles Farquharson, 25 (Invercargill). All three were on their 10th Berlin attack when they died. The other New Zealand pilot who lost his life was Aucklander John Rule, whose 156 Squadron pathfinder aircraft fell in the eastern reaches of the Ijsselmeer, near where the village of Marknesse now stands on reclaimed land. Wreckage from the crash was found in March 1973.

In the mid-February strike on Berlin, when Hegman and Jones were killed, Bomber Command counted 47 aircraft lost. Harris had wanted to mount another attack on the capital immediately but weather conditions were unsuitable and when 823 aircraft took off on the night of 19–20 February they headed not for Berlin but Leipzig, another important city in eastern Germany. Many things went wrong and the raid turned into a rout as aircraft losses reached a staggering 82.

The Luftwaffe night fighters were now at their most powerful and well organised, and Harris decided to leave the capital for the time being. Instead he attacked cities in southern Germany, where casualties were less severe. However, in late March he decided to strike one final blow against Berlin before turning his force loose on preinvasion targets in France and Belgium. On the night of 24–25 March he dispatched more than 800 aircraft, but the raid was another disaster for Bomber Command, with 74 aircraft lost. This time the problem was wind, and the final Main Force attack on Berlin became known in RAF lore as the Night of the Big Winds. The enormous fleet of bombers was scattered by fierce northerlies exceeding 100 mph, a strength never before experienced by bomber crews. According to Middlebrook some crew, during debrief, heard the words 'jet stream' for the first time. Many Lancasters and Halifaxes, pushed along by the gale, arrived over Berlin before they knew they had reached it and some flew miles beyond the capital. Bombs fell over a wide area and damage was limited.

Many crews simply did not accept that the wind readings they were getting were correct or that they could be so far off course because of them. The attackers lost all semblance of a stream and many arrived over the target area before the pathfinders. Seeing no target indicators they kept flying, while some TIs went down well south of the target.

For New Zealand pilot John Sanderson, flying a 166 Squadron Lancaster, this raid was just his fourth op, a scant 10 days after his first, so he was new to the whole frightening business. The Christchurch man says: 'When we got to the target area we didn't seem to be in the right place. I know we were south of where we should have been and we had to turn around and go back again to bomb the markers.' Sanderson deserved full marks for doing this. Many other bombers, finding themselves south of the target, simply unloaded where they were and fled rather than turning back and facing the risk of colliding with oncoming planes.

Fighters and flak found plenty of targets in the scattered fleet as it made its way home, and the pyres of crashed bombers littered the German countryside. The planned route back to bases in England lay across Germany and then northern Holland, well north of the Ruhr, but the majority of the bombers flew far to the south of this. 'We were blown way to glory off course and finished over the middle of the Ruhr,' Sanderson says. 'We were coned by searchlights and it was pretty dodgy for a while but we got away with it.'

Sanderson resorted to violent action to shake off the lights, manoeuvres he describes as close to aerobatics. His evasion tactics put enormous stresses on the bomber's wings, and he was subsequently told by ground staff that he'd weakened the bolts holding on one of the wings. 'If we had had to do much more we would have lost a wing.' Flak burst close, made a few holes and damaged one engine. Sanderson feathered this and flew home on three — to the emergency field at Woodbridge on the East Anglian coast, just in case his undercarriage was damaged. It wasn't and he landed safely.

This final Berlin raid took the lives of almost 400 Commonwealth aircrew; another 131 became POWs. Eight New Zealanders were killed, including John Mee (page 504).

'At the beginning of the dangerous work'

Eileen Brosnahan and her mother were on their way home, walking up Hataitai Road in Wellington one afternoon in September 1943, when they saw an RNZAF car coming towards them. Nellie Brosnahan looked at her 12-year-old daughter and said, 'I wonder where it's been this time?' They knew neighbours Arthur and Louisa Murdoch had lost two sons in Bomber Command in six months in 1941 and 1942. Bernard Murdoch, 27, and a second pilot on 104 Squadron, was killed 7–8 December 1941 during a raid on Dunkirk; his brother Graham, 26, a pilot on 75 Squadron was killed 8–9 June 1942 during a raid on Essen.

The car had been to the Brosnahan home. Eileen Brosnahan, today a Sister of Mercy:

> When we got there, my father was sitting at the table with his head in his hands and he just showed us the letter from the air force and that was it. A letter saying, 'We regret to inform you that your son, Flying Officer Frederick Timothy Brosnahan, has been reported missing on air operations on the night of 3–4 September 1943. The Prime Minister desires me to . . .' I know the air force officer asked my father if he wanted him to stay until we got home but Dad said, 'No, just go.'

The family got a letter of regret from 7 Squadron's wing commander and, later, the formal word that Fred, known to the family as Bill, was presumed dead. Then a vast silence — until a letter arrived in the first mail delivery after the New Year holiday in 1945. 'Dear Madam,' it began, going on to tell Nellie Brosnahan that her son's personal effects had arrived in New Zealand and would be delivered 'on Wednesday morning next 7th instant'. It then suggested she might like to return his uniform so it could be used by someone else in England.

By that stage my father was dead and my mother was terribly upset by that letter; she was absolutely fuming; it was all very traumatic. I've still got the big suitcase, with [Bill's] name and service number on the side. I can remember it being opened on the floor in our living room and mother saying, 'What am I going to do with it all? What am I going to do with all this stuff?' One or two things were taken out, the rest were packed back in and my mother put it away. She couldn't handle it. Eventually she asked her brother to take the uniform and get rid of it for her.

Finally, not long before she died in the mid-1970s, aged 80, Nellie Brosnahan threw away her son's letters. Only two escaped destruction, one to Eileen, the other the last he wrote.

The Brosnahan family, like hundreds of others in New Zealand, were left to their own devices to deal with the shock and grief and the final dashing of hope that their son and brother might somehow have survived. The air force offered no help; counselling was a half-century away. Families coped as best they could. The day after they had received the news that their brother was missing, elder sister Kathleen went to work and Eileen, a late addition to the family, went to school. Nellie Brosnahan later suffered what today would be called depression, and the death of his only son finished off Timothy Brosnahan, already a sick man. Sister Eileen:

He and Bill were great cobbers, and after Bill went missing Dad used to sit over the fire at night time, just sit until it died. He just faded away, pined away. He was only 60 when he died in July 1944. That left Mum carrying the burden and she wouldn't talk about it.

Brosnahan's last letter home was full of gossip about station life ('We live in the Mess itself and have a room for three') and members of his crew ('George Dougherty from Hamilton has the largest appetite I've ever seen'). He went on: 'The news seems to be looking much better these days and although the end is not yet in sight it cannot be too far off. I reckon I should be home for Xmas 1944, if not sooner.'

He was about to start ops: 'Right now I am at the beginning of the dangerous work and I hope I see it through O.K. A lot of lads have fallen on this hard road of aerial warfare. You know a few and I know a lot . . . they will be remembered as the grandest bunch of fellows.' He was clearly thinking about what lay ahead but was optimistic:

> I am fully confident that I will be O.K., the bullet that will get me hasn't been made and now we've plastered so many of his armament factories I doubt very much if it will ever be made. I must go and eat now so cheerio to you all and I hope it won't be long before I can throw my parachute away and need it no more. Once again many, many thanks for your lovely parcels, letters and above all your prayers. Love Bill.

He was dead before the letter arrived.

The four pilots

Although Bomber Command concentrated on Berlin for seven months from the autumn of 1943, RAF fleets bombed other cities all over Germany at the same time. None was a soft target and each raid cost the RAF dearly in men and machines. And, usually, New Zealand casualties. Among eight New Zealanders killed in an attack on Mannheim on 5–6 September 1943 were pilots from 75, 76, 77 and 623 Squadrons.

The 75 skipper was Tom Wilkinson, 25. He'd told his crew he would never bale out and he didn't on this night, going down with his Stirling a little to the north of Mannheim. The three survivors included the other two New Zealanders aboard — navigator Gordon Simes and bomb aimer Neil Treacher. Simes says he'd argued with Wilkinson about baling out.

> They called 75 the death squadron and we knew we were going to get hit sooner or later. All the crews that reached the squadron about the same time as us had gone. We didn't stand a chance of surviving. We'd had so many narrow escapes. Tom always maintained he'd never jump. I told him he had to for his mother's sake. But no, he said he'd never bale out.

Wilkinson, Simes and Treacher were living in Nelson when they enlisted although they didn't know each other until they crewed up. Now in his late 80s, Simes recalls Wilkinson as a skilled flyer. 'He was a damned good pilot for landing and taking off and that's what interested me. He'd run a trucking business in Brightwater and had a nice touch that had come from his driving.'

Wilkinson's crew were on their 18th trip the night they were clobbered. Simes doesn't know what happened or how he got out of the plane. 'I remember our earlier trips but nothing about the night we were shot down. I woke up 19 days afterwards in a German hospital.' There he found the back of his head had been bashed in, probably from hitting something as he jumped. When he got back to England at the end of the war he met Treacher, now dead, who told him flak had blown the two port motors clean out of the wing just after they had dropped their bombs.

When Simes regained consciousness he was woozy and ravenous. 'I can remember them helping me downstairs to breakfast. I was starving by then. I finished my plate, whatever it was, held it up and asked for more like Oliver. They said they didn't have any more.' He was quickly shipped off to Obermassfeld, a hospital for injured Allied POW airmen. He has no trouble remembering the two-day horror trip without food in a railway cattle truck accompanied by a British officer who'd had an arm torn off, a badly burned Hurricane pilot and an American with both legs broken.

Simes still couldn't remember his own name but he could see a bit better than when he'd come to. English POW doctors told him his memory would come back. It did — prompted one morning when compatriot Alister Boulton walked past his bed, stopped in stunned surprise and said, 'Christ, Gordon, what the hell are you doing here?' The two men had trained together, and Boulton, who had been shot down over Holland, was at Obermassfeld to have a smashed arm reset.

Peggy Gibbons never met pilot Stan Schmidt but she was engaged to Ted Dean, the English wireless operator on the New Zealander's 76 Squadron Halifax. She spent a few hours in York with her fiance the day after he'd come back from a sticky trip to Berlin and just before he flew to Mannheim. Now living in Upper Hutt, she has never forgotten that snatched afternoon when the airman came from his base at Holme-on-Spalding Moor, Yorkshire, to meet her. It was the last time she saw him. 'They were all at their wits' end I think. They'd had a terrible time over Berlin with the flak and fighters and Ted was very pessimistic about their chances. He said they wouldn't survive. Maybe he had a premonition.' Peggy remembers Dean saying he had complete faith in Schmidt's ability as a pilot and that the New Zealander cared a great deal about the welfare of his crew and often said to them, 'We have to do what has to be done to stop the Nazis.'

Schmidt's crew were on their 17th trip when they flew to Mannheim. According to a report from the sole survivor, the bomb aimer, the starboard inner inexplicably caught fire after the plane had dropped its bombs and left the target area. A minute later a night fighter attacked and Schmidt appeared to be hit. The

Halifax nosed into a dive from 18,000 feet and then exploded, the wreckage falling near Saarbrucken. The six dead were buried locally but after the war were reinterred at Choloy, in France. Schmidt, 23, came from Turua on the Hauraki Plains.

Peggy married after the war and she and her husband moved to New Zealand. Sixty years later, a widow, she still mourns the loss of Dean and the rest of the crew, including the New Zealand pilot she never knew.

The death of 77 Squadron pilot Douglas Hamblyn, 24 (Auckland), was uncannily similar to Schmidt's. 77, like 76 a 4 Group unit, was based at Elvington, also close to York. Hamblyn was on his 15th op when he was killed. His aircraft was hit twice by a night fighter over Mannheim and he was apparently killed then. According to a survivor, Hamblyn had dived steeply to avoid a collision with another bomber, and his plane was attacked after levelling out at 11,000 feet. A burst of fire raked the fuselage, killing the rear gunner. The bomb aimer later wrote: 'In a second attack a few seconds later the captain must have been mortally wounded as he fell over the controls. The machine went into a vicious dive.' Just three crewmen got out.

The fourth New Zealand pilot killed that night was Noel Humphreys, 20, of Wellington, one of a group of New Zealanders who had endured four or five days in a lifeboat after the *Waiwera* had been torpedoed in the Atlantic in mid-1942. There is some debate about exactly where his 623 Squadron Stirling crashed in Germany but *Bomber Command Losses* says it was a victim of night-fighter pilot Hans-Heinz Augenstein, falling to the ace's guns five hours after takeoff from Downham Market, Norfolk.

The book says that Augenstein also shot down New Zealander Keith Shaw's Stirling a month later over Kassel. Humphreys and Shaw would have known each other well because they served on the same squadron at the same time and Shaw was also on the *Waiwera* when she was torpedoed. Twelve minutes after Shaw's plane went down, Augenstein is thought to have accounted for another 623 bomber on the same Kassel raid, an aircraft with a largely Canadian crew. Three months earlier, Augenstein had claimed New Zealanders Stan Brown and Charlie Chambers in the space of just a few minutes.

'Basil, look after Dick please'

Rear gunner Basil Williams escaped with his life twice on ops. On 3–4 April 1943 his 51 Squadron Halifax crashed trying to land at Snaith, Yorkshire, on return from Essen. Three of the seven crew lost their lives, including pilot Charles Pheloung, 25 (Oamaru). Another had a leg amputated. New Zealand navigator Vern McKenzie, who suffered a broken leg, survived the war only to drown in the Whanganui River in 1946. Williams, pulled out of the broken-off turret, got away with shock and a severe shaking. After recovering he served with 431 Squadron and was then posted to 432 in August 1943.

Williams, an Aucklander, cast a serviceman's vote in New Zealand's 1943 general election on the afternoon of 22 September and then, just before 7.00 p.m., climbed into a Wellington bound for Hanover. Coned by searchlights over the target, Canadian pilot Les Tierney put the bomber into a steep, fast dive to escape them, then pulled out so abruptly that Williams says the whiplash almost took his head off. 'I thought the turret was going to come away and my eardrums seemed ready to burst.'

Tierney regained some height, circled and dropped his bombs. Then they discovered fuel was disastrously low, the tanks holed by flak. They voted unanimously to make for the North Sea, ditch and hope they were rescued by their own side. No such luck. Tierney made a superb landing off the German Frisian Islands on a pitch-black night with a decent sea running. Williams squeezed out of his turret, climbed on to the tailplane and then, with a sharp pocketknife, hacked his way along the fuselage, stabbing the fabric for grips. He joined two of the crew on the starboard wing, wondering if this was the end. 'I thought, what a way to go. No one will ever know what happened. A known grave seemed lovely.' Then, miraculously, Tierney appeared from nowhere in the Wellington's dinghy. Williams, the nearest, joined him and then helped rescue the others, now in the water. As he hauled in navigator Dick Sewell, sodden and heavy, he remembered the visit he'd made to the man's Norfolk home and the plea his widowed mother had made to him when she'd seen them off at Great Yarmouth railway station: 'Basil, look after Dick please.' Soaked and cold, their limbs stiff with cramp, the five airmen endured five hungry days before a German aircraft spotted them and dropped marker dye. An enemy air-sea rescue launch picked them up.

Two weeks later, another 432 Squadron aircraft was the last Main Force Wellington lost on a bombing raid in World War II.

On the run in Germany

The 27–28 September 1943 raid on Hanover spawned an epic getaway by a downed New Zealand pilot and a valiant try by another, both Northlanders. Nick Matich reached England from Germany, making an acclaimed 'home run', while Ralph Martin was on the loose for five days before he was nabbed. Both men were shot down during the raid, which fellow Northlander Trevor Dill described in his log as a 'Dirty little target, plenty of fighters up. Thirty-eight lost.'

Thirteen New Zealand families received chilling 'missing' telegrams after the Hanover attack although five eventually learned their sons were alive — Martin and three of his crew, in German hands, and Matich, safe in England.

Matich, who came from the Dargaville area, evaded capture in a striking feat of endurance, courage and determination. He walked 100 miles across heavily populated northwest Germany to the Dutch border, hiding by day, walking by night. Once in

Holland he was passed into an escape line and got back to England four months after takeoff. His brilliant dash to freedom won him a DSO to go with an earlier DFM.

Matich began operations in November 1942, flying 14 ops on Halifaxes with 102 (Ceylon) Squadron before a posting to 35 Squadron, one of the original pathfinder units. He flew his first trip with 35 in late March 1943 and by the time he was shot down he had 46 ops to his credit. A story about his exploits appeared in the *North Auckland Times* in August 1944, after he'd returned to New Zealand.

Matich's Halifax was attacked by fighters soon after he had swung the plane for home. Three of the engines were shot out and flames spread menacingly along one wing. Enemy fire killed the rear gunner outright, and badly wounded the Australian mid-upper gunner. His mates got the wounded man out of the aircraft on a chute but he died on the ground. Matich counted out the rest of his crew and then jumped himself, landing 20 miles west of Hanover with 100 miles of hostile territory between him and Holland.

'I walked at night and hid up during the day in whatever cover I could find. After my escape rations of chocolate and Horlicks tablets gave out, I lived on carrots and turnips and anything else I could find.'

His scariest moments involved the Dortmund–Ems Canal, which barred his way. It was too wide to swim so he scouted the waterway in both directions until he found a bridge guarded by a single German. Accosting the sentry, he smashed him over the head, tossed him in the canal and sprinted off into the darkness. 'I managed after nine nights to make my way over the border into Holland,' he said.

Exhausted, cold and hungry he found himself in the small Dutch town of Ootmarsum, where, by an astonishing coincidence, he received immediate help. He walked into a church, slumped into a back pew and was discovered by a priest. He followed the churchman into the presbytery, where he was questioned closely. The Dutch needed to be careful. They risked their lives helping aircrew on the run so had to know they were not being set up by sham escapers. The New Zealander learned the priest was a member of a Dutch Catholic order of fathers, one of whom had served in the Dargaville area in the 1930s and been chauffeured around the parish by the young Matich. The airman quoted the man's name, and his Dutch questioner actually knew the priest and knew he had been in New Zealand. When the priest was satisfied Matich was genuine, the New Zealander was fed, checked by a doctor, given a hot bath and put to bed.

For the next two months Matich hid in a forest dugout in nearby Hengelo while the Dutch 'repaired' escape lines infiltrated by the Gestapo. Then he was moved through Belgium and France, over the Pyrenees into Spain and thence to Gibraltar, from where he was flown back to England in January 1944, now a member of the Caterpillar and Late Arrivals Clubs.

After leave, Matich lectured at RAF stations about trying to stay free on the continent and was then posted home. His DSO citation lauded his 'skill and courage of the highest order', and his station commander, recommending the honour, wrote that the pilot's 'determination and calm on his last operational flight were instrumental in saving the lives of the remainder of his crew'. Matich, who ran a men's clothing store in Dargaville after the war, died in Auckland in 1992.

Martin, a 75 Squadron pilot, also aimed for Holland but didn't quite make it. Like Matich, he walked at night and slept in forests or under bridges during the day. 'I was eventually picked up at a farmhouse about four o'clock in the morning. I was just about buggered by then,' he says. 'I'd been walking all night and I was nosing around in a cattle barn, looking for somewhere to hide. Suddenly this young dog comes rushing out of the house — yap,

yap, yap.' The farmer followed and it was all over.

Martin was locked up in a cell in the old castle at Hamelin, the town famous for the Pied Piper. He doesn't remember much about the town or its castle because he was driven there in a closed van, but he does remember his interrogation and the Luftwaffe man who pinched his prized New Zealand-made flying boots. 'The bastard told me, "We can't let you keep those."'

Martin, who still lives on the farm at Ruatangata, outside Whangarei, where he spent his teenage years, was shot down on his fifth op.

> We were a bit late getting there, that was probably half the trouble. It was a brand-new plane but it just wouldn't go. Like a new car sometimes. Anyway, we had just dropped our bombs and were on the way out when the *Boozer* light, indicating a fighter on our tail, came on in the cockpit. I yelled out, 'Boozer! Boozer!' and was just going into a corkscrew when we got a burst right across the top of the aircraft that cut out all controls — elevator, rudder, everything.

The aircraft stalled and starting spinning but Martin levelled her out with power on the inner motors, giving everyone time to parachute. 'I'd just got out when I saw the plane crash, about a mile away over a little rise.' The only casualty was the mid-upper gunner, an Englishman, killed by the fighter's first blast.

Rear gunner Ron Summerhays, 34 (Auckland), who smashed a leg when he landed, was repatriated from Germany in early 1945 with an Irish New Zealander from Martin's crew whose mind had been affected by the bale-out and life as a POW. Martin and his navigator, Harold Dwight, 35 (Waipawa), had to wait until the end of the war to get back to England.

Pilot 'Speedy' Williams, Trevor Dill and the rest of their crew brought 75 Squadron's EF135-W (William) safely back to Mepal from that September raid on Hanover — and then crashed in a rainstorm. Dill:

> Visibility was almost nil. We circled that bloody drome for about an hour and were almost out of gas when it was our turn. We were off the end of the runway when we were told, 'OK, Willie, you can land now.' Speedy wasn't going to lose sight of that runway so he pulled back all the throttles, put the nose down and went in very steep. We must have hit the ground very hard because they estimated she bounced 100 feet. Then she floated — and floated. We went 1500 yards down that runway before she hit again. She went in on the port wing, smashed off half that wing and one motor, and the undercarriage, and slid across the runway with lumps of concrete and stuff flying up. We finally stopped on the perimeter track, the props on the other wing all bent back from hitting the concrete — bump, bump, bump. Speedy calls up control and says, 'OK, Willie landed and clear of the runway.' The next moment Wing Commander Roy Max [the squadron CO] is out there with cars and fire engines rushing around and he's saying, 'Bloody good show, chaps, bloody good show,' and here's this new and very expensive aircraft lying there broken in bits.

Everyone got out unhurt but Willie never flew again.

'It's my duty to go'

Their names appeared in an air-force casualty list in the *Southland Times* on Monday, 15 November 1943 under the heading 'Missing on Air Operations': Ralph James Buckham (mother, Mrs HC Buckham, Queenstown), Frank Ian Calvert (wife, Mrs AJ Calvert, Invercargill), Keith Fred Shaw (wife, Mrs HD Shaw, Invercargill). Three young local men, all pilot officers, two of them married.

Nothing else. Nothing. There never was. Only the families were likely to know, from letters, that they were flying in the same crew. The next of kin had received individual telegrams a couple of days after the men's aircraft failed to return to England after a 3–4 October raid and had been told not to give up hope because there was a chance their men could be POWs. But two of the three were dead. Only Buckham had got down alive. Mrs Calvert and Mrs Shaw, each the mother of an infant, were widows before the telegrams had arrived.

The Southlanders were among the foundation crews of 3 Group's 623 Squadron, a new unit formed on 10 August 1943 at Downham Market, Norfolk, from one of the flights comprising 218 Squadron, which was based at the same airfield. But 623 was short-lived, disbanded for some reason in early December 1943. During its brief life it lost 10 Stirlings in action, one of them EF158-S (Sugar), captained by Shaw with Calvert as his navigator and Buckham in the rear turret, on a raid on Kassel, a city 70 miles due south of Hanover. Only Buckham and the mid-upper gunner got out. The crew had done 10 trips with 218 before they were switched to 623 and had completed another 12 with their new unit. Another seven and they would have finished their tour but this was as bad a time of the war as any to be in a bomber crew. *For Your Tomorrow* says the Stirling exploded over the target area, the wreckage falling in woods four miles from Kassel.

Buckham, married after the war, told his wife they had just dropped their bombs and were turning away when they were attacked by a fighter no one saw. The right wing flared into flames and the order to abandon the aircraft was given. Buckham had had trouble with his turret that morning — it wouldn't rotate properly. In this moment of crisis it played up again and he had a struggle getting it open far enough for him to squeeze out. The city was on fire as he drifted down towards it but an updraught caught his chute and wafted him away to an area with trees. He was on the loose for five days until a thick fog that had been hiding him as he walked along an autobahn one morning suddenly lifted. Farmers working in a nearby field spotted him, and when they threatened him with pitchforks he put up his hands.

Keith Shaw, only son of Fred and Helen Shaw of Invercargill, was educated at Southland Technical College and worked as a stereotyper for *The Times* before the war. He was a crack swimmer, taking part in the national championships. Ailsa Galilee, his one sister, says he was called up for the army in 1940 but was turned down because he had flat feet. He then volunteered for the RNZAF. She remembers the air force wanted Shaw to stay in New Zealand as an instructor after he qualified as a pilot but he declined, saying, 'It's my duty to go.'

Ailsa was a high-school student when Keith was in Invercargill on final leave before sailing for Britain on the *Waiwera* in late May 1942. 'I had a feeling that I wouldn't see him again.' The day he was reported missing, she got home from school to find her mother sitting at the kitchen table.

> She just pointed to the telegram she was holding. She couldn't speak she was so stunned. She hadn't even called my father, who was away working in a garage out in the country. She was just so dazed and shaken by it. Keith's death changed her personality. She was never the same after that and she acted as if it was only her that had suffered this loss and she seemed to forget my father had lost his only son and I had lost my only brother. Keith's death really destroyed her.

Hazel Shaw was pregnant when she bid her husband farewell. Their son, Robin, was born in Invercargill on 4 September 1942, just three days after Shaw had arrived in England. He grew up to be a marine engineer and now lives in Canada. Hazel remarried in 1947 and had five more children.

Frank Calvert didn't need to go to war because he was a farmer, a 'reserved' occupation. But he wanted to fly and, after talking it over with his wife of two years, he enlisted in March 1942. 'I just knew he was going to join up,' she says. Jean Calvert is another New Zealand woman who has been an air-force widow for 60 years.

Calvert, born in January 1916, was the son of Joan and Flora Calvert, who had a farm at Roslyn Bush, near Invercargill. When he went into the air force he was working the farm on lease from his parents. Jean Caldwell lived in the same district and they'd known each other all their lives. They married in March 1940, and their daughter, Frances Jean, was born two months before he sailed for Canada to train. Calvert was at Rotorua in the Initial Training Wing when the baby arrived, but he saw her on his final leave in Invercargill. Then he was gone.

Mrs Calvert never remarried: 'I guess I was a one-man band.' She joined the work force in Invercargill and didn't retire until she was 72. She raised her daughter without a husband, and watched her grow up, marry and have three children of her own. 'She's been the joy of my life.' Mrs Calvert now has eight great-grandchildren.

An unfortunate night

Ted Anderson's Anzac Day is 4 November — the anniversary of the night in 1943 when Wally Hurdle, a young New Zealander on his plane, died in a hail of German fire over the northern tip of Denmark. Other friends were killed that night too, and Anderson came perilously close to losing his own life.

Four New Zealanders were aboard 75 Squadron's Stirling EJ108 when it took off from Mepal, Cambridgeshire, on the stroke of 4.00 p.m. that late autumn day: pilot Eric Witting (Invercargill), navigator Anderson (Christchurch), wireless operator Glen Marshall (Wairoa), and Hurdle (Feilding), in the coldest, loneliest part of the bomber, the rear turret, nearly eighty feet behind the cockpit. The other three crew members were English: bomb aimer Jack Thomas, flight engineer Reg Gunn and mid-upper Ron Morfett.

The big bomber gathered height slowly and slanted east, across Norfolk and out to sea for the long run over the North Sea to drop mines. Four of the 36 aircraft on the mine-laying operation were from 75 Squadron, all four charged with leaving their deadly cargoes in the Kattegat, the narrow 140-mile long strait between Denmark and Sweden.

Witting's crew, flying their seventh op together, were bedding down nicely. The New Zealanders and Thomas had come together at 11 OTU, Westcott. They hadn't known each other before then. Anderson, born in 1918, had spent five years at Christchurch Boys' High School and one full-time year at university before starting work as a chemist in Woolston Tanneries' lab and continuing his studies part-time. He enlisted in late 1941 and was trained and commissioned in Canada.

Hurdle had been happy to join the crew. At 28 he was older than many gunners — some were so young they didn't even shave. He was working as a New Zealand Post and Telegraph linesman when he enlisted. He had tried earlier for an RAF short-service commission but his education level wasn't of the standard required. Anderson remembers him as quiet and somewhat reserved, although not shy and ready for a laugh. The five picked up Gunn and Morfett when they converted to Stirlings at Stradishall before their posting to 75 Squadron. Their tour began in mid-September, and by 4 November they'd learned a lot.

On mining trips at this stage of the war navigators had to find a specific spot on a coast and then do a precise time-and-distance run on the correct bearing to reach the target point. 'When we got over Denmark that night it was covered by a complete sheet of cloud,' Anderson remembers.

We just couldn't see anything of the eastern coastline so the
trip was wasted. We couldn't lay the mines and our instructions
were to bring them back in such a case. Our route for home
was straight up the Kattegat to the northern tip of Denmark,
down the Skagerrak and out into the North Sea again at 9000
feet. Just before we were due to turn into the Skagerrak I gave
Eric the course to bring us back to East Anglia.

At that moment the fighter struck. No one on the Stirling saw it
as it streaked in, pouring fire into the rear turret and fuselage.
Hurdle, probably dead before he realised what was happening,
never had a chance. Amazingly, no one else was hit. Anderson
was between the astrodome and his chart table when the attack
occurred. Unplugged from the intercom he didn't know what was
going on but was thumped in the shoulder by a piece of shattered
Perspex as the plane went into a steep dive.

Witting reacted instinctively, falling off into a dive to try to
escape. The German didn't attack again, perhaps believing the
Stirling doomed as it plunged toward the sea. Anderson says
Witting told him later he didn't think he was going to get the
bomber out of its breakneck dive. 'I think we were down to under
1000 feet when we levelled out. I could see the unwelcoming sea
very clearly.'

As he recovered and jettisoned the mines, Witting called up
the crew. One by one everyone but Hurdle replied. The skipper
sent Thomas and Gunn aft to check what had happened. They
found the turret torn to pieces and Hurdle dead.

The Stirling was groggy, severely damaged, while the compass
master unit in the back of the aircraft had been shot out and the
magnetic compass was faulty. Anderson's astronavigation and *Gee*,
when they reached its range, got them back to base. Fearful the
plane's tyres might have been damaged, Witting sent the crew
to crash stations as he muscled the difficult-to-control Stirling

into Mepal, seven hours 20 minutes after takeoff and more than three hours after they'd been attacked — the longest three hours of their lives. The tyres were OK and the undercarriage held up. Anderson: 'He made a bloody marvellous landing.'

Gee, the first major British navigation advance of the war, was introduced to the bomber squadrons in early 1942. A *Gee* 'box' with a cathode-ray tube to receive radio pulses from ground stations in Britain, the intersecting points of which could then be read off a grid chart, enabled a navigator to determine his position simply and quickly. The signals were effective over 350–400 miles.

The fighter's onslaught and Hurdle's death shattered everyone on EJ108 but the shocks weren't over. None of the other three Stirlings came home. Eight New Zealanders besides Hurdle were dead. No wonder the squadron's operations record book called 4–5 November 1943 'an unfortunate night'. The Witting crew mourned. 'We had lost friends in those other planes, but, more than that, one from our own crew,' Anderson says. 'That is why my personal remembrance day is not 25 April but 4 November.'

Anderson and the rest of the crew were sent on leave for 48 hours and then returned to act as pallbearers and bury their comrade in Cambridge. The day after that they woke up to find they had a new plane and a new rear gunner. They were at war again.

Two of the lost Stirlings went down without survivors, four New Zealanders on each plane. One disappeared without trace, almost certainly shot into the sea. On board was Ted Anderson's navigator friend Tom Lodge, 35 (Rotorua), a married man. Also lost were pilot Norman Wilson, 23 (Auckland), bomb aimer Alfred Dance, 25 (Blenheim), and rear gunner Arnold Fawcett, 31 (Stratford).

The other, flown by Bill Masters, 21 (Waiuku), was shot down by a night fighter over Denmark and crashed near Thisted, in the northwest. No one survived. Killed with Masters were navigator George Imrie, 22 (Auckland), bomb aimer Charles James, 34 (Balclutha), and Lewis Crawford-Watson, 21 (Devonport). They are buried at Frederikshavn.

The third Stirling also fell near Thisted but six of the seven crew parachuted safely. Pilot Gordon Williams, 22 (Hamilton), and bomb aimer Francis McGregor, 28 (Christchurch), were captured, but the third New Zealander on the aircraft eluded the Germans in a remarkable effort. Gisborne-born navigator Walter Morice, just three months past his 21st birthday, landed heavily, spraining both ankles severely. Despite the pain he began walking. He was sheltered and fed at a farmhouse later in the morning when he could go no further, but the Danish police were called and he was taken to hospital in Thisted for treatment. Unguarded briefly after being told the Germans would have to be informed, Morice bolted and struggled east in bitterly cold weather. With luck and more help from the Danes, the airman was put in touch with the underground and eventually spirited to Sweden, reaching England on 29 December. He then served with Transport Command, and after the war flew with BOAC. He died in England in 1996.

'Your son was directly behind me'

While a Lancasters-only fleet bombed Berlin on 18–19 November 1943, a mixed Halifax–Stirling force of almost 400 aircraft attacked the Rhine city of Mannheim, a raid that cost five New Zealand lives in four crashed Stirlings. Two died on a 90 Squadron aircraft that exploded and crashed near the target — wireless operator Stuart Simpson, 23, on his ninth op, and John Fleming, 28, making his debut raid as second pilot to the Australian skipper.

English flight engineer Edward Northard, the only survivor,

wrote to the Simpson family in Christchurch the moment he reached England from POW camp in 1945 to tell them what had happened to their son and brother. Northard's gesture was all the more appreciated because he hadn't known Simpson. His unexpected letter explained that he had only met the crew on the morning of the flight. Northard's own crew had all been killed the week before and he had been a stand-in flight engineer on the trip to Mannheim.

> Everything went smoothly from takeoff until reaching the target. As we were going in to bomb we were hit in the starboard inner engine by an anti-aircraft shell and the engine immediately caught fire. The pilot put the aircraft into a dive in an attempt to put the flames out [but] fire then broke out inside the aircraft. After he pulled out of the dive the pilot realised it was useless to stay in the aircraft and gave the order to bale out. I immediately put on my parachute and made my way to the front escape hatch which had just been opened by the bomb aimer. Your son was directly behind me. The bomb aimer was kneeling at one side of the hatch, I was at the other side waiting for him to bale out. Your son would have followed me. That was the last thing I remember. When I came to, I was lying in a field with my parachute open beside me, my face and hands badly cut. My assumption was I had been blown through the hatch. I must have been slightly conscious to have pulled the rip cord of my chute but I don't remember doing so.

Northard said he was afraid that was all he knew, and it seemed the rest of the crew had died when the aircraft had blown up. 'You have my deepest sympathies on your loss. I only wish I could have given you more satisfying news. However, I hope that your minds will be eased after my account of this unfortunate occurrence.'

Such letters were rare and deeply valued by families in New

Zealand. Most received only the telegram telling them loved ones were missing, followed by a letter from the squadron commander which almost never had any information about the circumstances of the loss, and finally notification of presumed death. Few had any inkling of what precisely had happened. For many there wasn't even a grave to visit on an overseas pilgrimage. For the Simpsons there was. Stuart Simpson and John Fleming are buried in Rheinberg War Cemetery, where 102 other New Zealand airmen lie.

Born in Invercargill in May 1920, Simpson was an electrician and second-oldest of four children. His parents were living in Christchurch when they got word he was missing. Mabel Stone, 16 at the time her big brother was lost, was working for a lawyer in Christchurch.

> I arrived at work the following day to find on my typewriter a caustic note berating me for having left the machine uncovered and telling me to type out 50 times 'I must cover my machine before going home each day.' I dissolved in tears and walked out. Mother rang my employer to explain. V-E Day was another event when tears rendered me useless. Everyone but us seemed so happy. It was not possible that Stuart would not be returning. Not until Edward Northard's letter arrived could we accept that he was dead.

Some unit commanders mailed the names and addresses of next-of-kin of everyone on the aircraft to families of missing aircrew. Simpson's grieving mother got such a list and wrote to all the mothers of her son's crew. One reply came from pilot John Fleming's father, whose wife had just died in Palmerston North. He had now also lost two sons in action with the RNZAF. Andrew Fleming, flying a biplane Albacore torpedo bomber, was shot down and killed on 26 January 1942 while attacking a Japanese invasion convoy from his Singapore base. Thirty at the time, he had married two weeks before leaving New Zealand.

Braving fire to rescue mates

Tony Lindsay, a quiet young man from the Whangarei-area township of Portland, won the British Empire Medal on 16–17 December 1943 — Black Thursday in Bomber Command memory. That night 40 returning bombers crashed in England, defeated in their attempts to land by thick fog. The tally was the worst of its kind of the war. Some pilots ordered their crews to bale out but many airmen were killed in failed landings.

Lindsay's 83 Squadron Lancaster crashed and burned at Wyton, its Cambridgeshire field, at 12.20 a.m. on 17 December, eight hours and 1500 miles after takeoff. It was a disastrous end to the pathfinder aircraft's mission, during which it had experienced intense flak over Berlin and beaten off a fighter attack. Lindsay, the navigator, on just his third op, wrote succinctly in his log after the crash, 'Visibility zero. Fog.'

Lindsay found himself on the ground moments after the impact, 50 feet clear of the burning wreck. He regained his senses to discover he had burns on his face and a broken right arm and ankle. Despite these injuries, he hobbled back to the blaze to pull out trapped and badly burned bomb aimer Greg Tankard and flight engineer Greg Day. Even when the ambulance arrived to pick everyone up, he insisted the others be treated first. 'He displayed high courage and unselfish devotion to duty,' the citation said. Tankard died of his injuries that day but Day lived.

Lindsay's fractures were patched up at the RAF hospital at nearby Ely, and he later became a patient of New Zealand plastic surgeon Archie McIndoe. He was lucky because the burns on his face didn't leave lasting scars, though he did have some light scarring on his upper body. The burns and broken limbs kept him off ops for many months.

When he resumed flying it was with a commission and another pathfinder squadron — 635, based at Downham Market, Norfolk, where he was navigator/bomb aimer, the man who worked the H_2S radar set and was known as Nav 2. When the war ended he had done 30 raids with 635. His logbook discloses that he was in the master bomber flown by Squadron Leader Peter de Wesselow as it orbited Dresden on 13–14 February 1945, the night of the controversial firestorm raid that killed thousands and destroyed the inner city. Bomber Command laid on two attacks that night, three hours apart, de Wesselow directing the second. Lindsay's log shows that the bomber was over the target area for 21 minutes. Never one for many words, he wrote simply, 'Enormous fires.'

A few days after V-E Day, Lindsay caught a train to London to receive his BEM from the hand of King George. Officials closeted him and others awarded the same decoration in a room as they waited their turn. He wrote to his parents: 'The halls had thick red carpets . . . the room I was in was half as big as the public hall at home with big French windows, three fireplaces and big marble pillars.'

> Five paces forward and a left turn brought me in front of His Majesty. A bow and one forward pace, and His Majesty with the medal in his hand leant forward and pinned the medal on [my] left breast. Then, whilst shaking my hand, he asked me what I had performed to win the award and also was I still flying. He then wished me luck and dismissed me — a bow and right turn and a walk through the spectators and it was all over.

Lindsay's family moved from Portland into Whangarei after the war, and he worked for the Department of Social Security, gradually climbing the rungs to become number two in the Whangarei office. He would have had to shift elsewhere to advance his career but he had a comfortable home and no desire to move. A bachelor, he enjoyed playing bowls at the RSA, liked fishing and spent summer holidays at the family beach place up the coast a bit. He was content.

As the years passed hardly anyone remembered he had won a BEM for braving fire while injured to rescue mates in a horrific crash. In war ordinary men do extraordinary things. Flying Officer Raymond Anthony Lindsay, BEM, of the Pathfinder Force, died in Whangarei in 1991 in his 71st year.

Another New Zealander decorated for similar bravery did not survive the war. Charlie Eddy, 29 (Wellington), was made an MBE for rescuing one crew member from his burning bomber and making desperate but unsuccessful efforts to save a second. Skipper of a damaged 75 Squadron Stirling, Eddy crash-landed at Oakington on return from a raid on Aachen on 13–14 July 1943. A flat tyre triggered an undercarriage collapse and the big bomber flipped on to its back before grinding to a halt and bursting into flames. Despite being hurt, Eddy got the bomb aimer out of the second pilot's seat and dragged him from the plane. When he learned the mid-upper gunner was trapped in his turret he went back into the fuselage with a medical officer, the two of them braving the flames to try to rescue the man. The fierce fire drove them back, scorching Eddy's face. They were unable to reach the gunner, who lost his life.

Eddy collapsed and was taken to hospital. He didn't fly again for months and when he did resume operations it was with 115 Squadron. He had flown four ops with his new unit when he was killed in the early hours of 19 April 1944 on return from a raid on railway yards at Rouen, France, a victim of a prowling German night fighter.

The intruder poured fire into Eddy's Lancaster as he was preparing to land at Witchford, 115's station. The aircraft crashed without survivors at 3.48 a.m. on a farm near the base.

Eddy and his Canadian rear gunner were buried side by side in Cambridge. Their Lancaster was the second of two 115 bombers shot down by intruders that night. The entire crew of the other plane also died.

Eddy's MBE was announced five weeks after his death.

'It fills me with awe and gratitude'

Six hundred and fifty Lancasters and Halifaxes bombed Frankfurt on the night of 20–21 December 1943. Forty were lost and many aircrew made the ultimate sacrifice, among them seven New Zealanders, the 'missing' telegrams delivered to their homes right on Christmas. One of the seven was navigator John Lamb, at 34 the 'old man' of a 76 Squadron crew on its ninth op. His Halifax was homebound when it went into the sea off the Dutch coast. No one survived. Lamb's body washed up on 6 January near Castricum aan Zee, south of Petten, where pilot Charles Matthews' remains were found. Theirs were the only bodies the sea delivered. Lamb lies today in the churchyard of Castricum Protestant Church, his grave shaded by a line of stately trees.

The pilot, a flight sergeant like Lamb, was a 20-year-old Londoner. Despite their difference in age, the two men became firm friends and Lamb was a welcome visitor at his captain's home. Matthews' sister, now Jean Muir, was just 13 when they were killed. She wrote of Lamb in 2003: 'I remember him as quiet and gentle. It still fills me with awe and gratitude that this young married man came across the world to fight.'

She says Lamb's widow, Lorna, a Palmerston North nurse, eventually remarried and lived the rest of her life in Queensland, where she died in 1997. 'She was touched that local schoolchildren care for John's grave and was pleased my husband and I were able to visit Castricum and lay flowers.'

She adds:

Please don't think that the exploits of these young men have been forgotten. There is a most beautiful memorial garden for 76 Squadron on the old airfield at Holme-on-Spalding Moor, Yorkshire. Services of remembrance are held there with due dignity and respect; the local school is involved; the local pub is packed with memorabilia, and the local church has a book of remembrance and a stained-glass window carrying the squadron motto, 'To See the Dawn Breaking'.

Baling out

Gunner Mo Drummond was so close to the ground when he pulled his ripcord that the parachute had barely opened to halt his free fall before he smashed to earth in a patch of brambles in France. Another second or two's delay and he would have been dead. As it was his right leg was shattered in four places and his body left a deep imprint in the ground.

Drummond, a Taranaki farmer until his death in the late 1980s, was mid-upper gunner on a 75 Squadron Lancaster the night he parachuted. Flown by New Zealander Noel Stokes, 25 (Christchurch), on his 28th op, the aircraft was shot up by a fighter between the cathedral city of Chartres and Orleans while bound for Stuttgart on 28–29 July 1944. The rear gunner was killed instantly and the flying controls badly damaged.

Bombs jettisoned, Stokes wrestled the plane but had barely turned it for home before he could hold it up no longer. Drummond's son, Roger, says he remembers his father telling him the plane skewed all over the sky, flames sprouting in the fuselage, as Stokes shouted, 'Get to hell out!' Drummond hit something as he jumped and was knocked out. He came to his senses only a few hundred feet above the ground, pulling the ripcord in the nick of time.

Black and blue from his landing and in excruciating pain from splintered bones, Drummond lay all day in the sun, desperate for water. He could see and hear French farm workers in the field near him, but they seemed to ignore his calls for help. They came for him as soon as night arrived, explaining the Germans were hunting survivors and to have aided him during the day would have been fatal. In the dark the New Zealander was spirited away, given medical treatment and hidden. Eventually, as the Allied land forces drew near, the underground contacted the Americans, who rescued him.

Four other New Zealanders on Stokes' Lancaster got out safely but Stokes himself died keeping the plane airborne for them to jump. Several years ago the French dedicated a stained-glass window to him in a church near where the Lancaster crashed, believing Stokes also steered the aircraft away from their village.

Drummond and the other New Zealanders — second pilot John Morris, 21 (Cambridge), navigator George Sanders, 20 (Christchurch), bomb aimer Newton Sampson, 23 (New Plymouth), and wireless operator Bill Raynel, 29 (Matamata) — owed their lives to their chutes and Stokes. They were among several hundred New Zealanders who floated to earth safely from crippled bombers during World War II, all entitled to join the exclusive Caterpillar Club. The club awarded a small gold pin shaped like a caterpillar to airmen whose lives had been saved by a parachute. It was symbolic of the silkworm whose threads created the silk from which parachutes were made until late in the war, when nylon began to be used.

By the end of the war, a few New Zealand aircrew were members twice over, having made two life-saving parachute jumps. Morris was one. He made his second leap over Germany six months after his first. The night he escaped from Stokes' Lancaster he was only a few hundred feet from the ground. 'I dived headfirst straight through the hatch and pulled the ripcord immediately. As it opened the aeroplane crashed and blew up on the ground right beneath me. Initially I went upwards, the pressure and heat from the blast blowing the chute skywards.'

Morris was on ops that night for the first time, flying with Stokes to gain experience before operating with his own crew, with whom he'd been training for months. He eluded the Germans after landing in France and was back in England in three weeks. On survivors' leave in London he bumped into Wellingtonian Jim Wilkinson, his navigator, and was astonished to find that he too had parachuted over France and also evaded capture. Although he had been shot down 10 days later, he made it back to England before Morris. When Morris was posted missing his 'headless' crew were allotted another pilot but were brought down almost immediately, on 7 August.

The two New Zealanders agreed to fly with each other again and eventually found their way to 15 Squadron at Mildenhall, three other New Zealanders with them — bomb aimer Alan Taylor (Auckland), rear gunner Toby Temperton (Gisborne) and mid-upper gunner John Creevey (Christchurch). They flew together until a night fighter got them on 3–4 February 1945 over Dortmund. 'We dived down steeply, twisting and turning to shake off lights that had coned us, but when we pulled up and levelled off this fighter gave us everything. He'd obviously followed us right through our dive. He killed both gunners and knocked out the port inner, which burst into flames.' Morris and Wilkinson made their second successful jumps but this time they were captured. The other three not killed by the fighter got out too. Creevey hadn't flown that night because he was ill — mumps almost certainly saved his life. He now lives in Whangarei.

Leaping from a doomed bomber into the great unknown blackness was a scary business. Just the same, when it came to the point few hesitated. Jim McQueen, shot down in August 1942, remembers: 'I sat on the edge of the escape hatch with my legs dangling for a moment or two while I thought about my first and only jump. Sparks or burning oil were coming back from the starboard engine. I put my head between my knees and just dropped out.'

The vast majority didn't wait on their going. Anything was better than staying in a blazing aircraft headed for the earth and a fiery end. Flames roaring through an aircraft's fuselage or licking along a wing gnawing at petrol tanks were a mighty incentive to jump.

Chutes sometimes spilled out of their packs inside the aircraft, often when the cord was pulled mistakenly in an emergency or snagged on something. Jumping with an opened chute lessened the chances of survival because at the moment of baling out it could billow and catch the tail wheel or tailplane. The trick was to wrap one's arms tightly around the opened canopy until well clear of the aircraft. Easier said than done.

Pathfinder pilot Nick Matich found his chute partially opened the night his Halifax was crippled over Hanover in 1943 . He gathered it up, struggled with it to the escape hatch, shouted 'Hail, Mary' and jumped. And lived.

Some men who jumped fought a life-and-death struggle to get their parachutes open. Wireless operator Phil Donovan did the night he leapt from a Wellington over Northamptonshire. Donovan, who grew up at Raumati, north of Wellington, flew a tour with 90 Squadron on Stirlings late in 1943 and was then posted to an OTU as an instructor.

Just before 1.00 a.m. on 5 September 1944, during a training flight, his Wimpy's port motor cut out and the skipper ordered the crew to jump at 10,000 feet. Something went badly wrong as Donovan pulled the ripcord. Suddenly he was thrashing about in tangled billowing silk that wouldn't unfold properly from its pack and deploy. 'I thought I was finished. I had no chance of coming out of this. I said goodbye to Mum — "See you up there" sort of thing.'

He ripped desperately at the silk, trying to get it out of its pack. 'I didn't think there was any show of it coming free but all the time I was pulling it with both hands and shoving it away.' He knows he was close to the ground when the chute suddenly burst open with a violent jolt that made him feel as if his harness had cut him in two. He thumped onto the ground in a field and lay there dazed, hardly daring to believe he wasn't dead.

He staggered to his feet and made for a village whose lights he could see — carting his chute with him. 'I'd been told if you didn't bring your chute back the RAF would charge you. I didn't want to lose my pay.' He found a phone box, talked to the operator and waited for an ambulance. Eight days later he was back flying.

Bomb aimer Doug Hill had an astonishing descent when he jumped from a blazing 75 Squadron Stirling at 15,000 feet after dropping mines in Kiel Bay on the night of 18–19 April 1944. Two night fighters caught the bomber as it headed home over the southeast coast of Denmark's Jutland peninsula. The attackers killed both gunners and then flew under the Stirling, raking it with fire. A powerful flare was set alight and ignited the ammunition belts.

'A wall of flames erupted back in the fuselage and the skipper ordered us out,' says Hill, now 87 and living in Leigh, north of Auckland. He was hit by bullets ricocheting around the front compartment, and though he didn't know it one of them cut one of the shoulder straps on his harness. As he jumped and pulled the ripcord, the chute jerked open, snapping the damaged strap. Free of restraint, Hill tumbled sideways and then upside down, falling out of his harness — almost. At the last moment, when he was apparently doomed to die, the toe of his left flying boot snagged on the harness and held.

For thousands of feet, Hill hung like a pendulum, twisting and turning under the chute, attached by the merest toehold. 'It just happened to catch. I didn't think it would stay there but I couldn't do anything about it. I couldn't reach up to it. Had I tried it would have come off.' He was also terrified his foot would slide out of his boot. Somehow it didn't, the calm night proving crucial. Strong winds would have jumped the chute about and spelled the end of the dangling airman.

A second miracle saved Hill's life. He landed on his head and shoulders in a soft ploughed field. He damaged his back and left thigh and still suffers (he's had three new left hips), but 'if I'd come down on hard ground, I'd have been killed'. Two other men baled out successfully — RNZAF wireless operator Gordon Irwin, a Northlander, and the RAF navigator. Pilot Jim Murray, 26 (Oamaru), halfway through his tour, held the Stirling up as long as he could while his men jumped but he was still aboard, and died, when the bomber crashed. 'He was a brave man,' says Hill.

Aircrew stowed their chutes close to their flight stations so they were within arm's reach. But even in 1943 nearby stowage wasn't automatic. Jack Hardie wrote in his wartime memoir *From Timaru to Stalag VIIIB* that as he entered his Halifax for a raid on Dusseldorf on 27–28 January that year 'both the pilot and I put our parachutes in the chute rack just inside the door . . . way down by the tail'. Hardie flew second pilot that night with a crew that got badly off course. A night fighter hit their aircraft over Holland, a burst of fire setting everything alight and shooting away the controls.

As the Canadian pilot shouted 'Get those chutes,' Hardie opened the armour-plated doors at the rear of the cockpit to find the fuselage a mass of flames.

> From each of the inboard motors was a pipe of about six inches diameter which normally delivered warm air into the plane. Now these were like two giant flame-throwers, sending out jets of flame the length of the fuselage. I had to run down between them [and] climb over the two wing-roots . . . I reached the two parachutes [and] clipped one on.

Hardie started back with the pilot's but two other crew appeared from between the wing-roots and one grabbed the chute and pushed him back to the rear.

> At that moment the plane must have gone into a spin and the three of us were pinned to the floor by the G forces. After a few seconds we were thrown to the ceiling and pinned there. Later in the war [watching from POW camp] I was to see the same thing happen to planes being shot down. They would spin belly down a few times, then

flip over and do a few turns in an inverted position. This happened to us several times and I think I was knocked unconscious.

Hardie got out of the aircraft somehow and so did the two who'd come haring back from the nose because they hadn't been able to get the escape hatch there open. They were the only survivors. Hardie says he isn't sure what happened. 'The wreckage was in five different places spread over about three miles so it must have disintegrated or blown up.'

Hardie, who now lives in Motueka, remains astonished that the pilots' chutes were stowed by the rear door. 'Incredible — it must have killed a lot of pilots. Later, pilots wore seat chutes — they sat on them — but when I was shot down there were two little containers just inside the Halifax door. That's where the pilot had to get his chute from.'

For many reasons aircrew did not do practice jumps but they were drilled in preparation for ditching, crash-landing and parachuting, and good skippers ordered regular practices. Christchurch-born Trevor Teague, later a widely known court registrar in Nelson, was grateful for those drills just a week before the D-Day invasion, when his 622 Squadron Lancaster was knocked down by flak over France. 'We had an instructor in a dummy fuselage at OTU and he drilled us hard. If any member of the crew slipped up we had to do it again and again if necessary. So when I said "Out" over France they knew what they had to do and everyone got out in a few seconds.'

Teague's bomber was lost attacking the railway junction and yards at Angers, between Nantes and Le Mans, on 28–29 May 1944. Flak took out both port motors at 8500 feet and then a third engine stopped. Teague, flying the flight commander's new aircraft that night, remembered his squadron leader's last words to him: 'Right, Trev, I want that kite back in one piece.'

Teague counted his crew out and as they went watched, fascinated, as the flames from the port wing trailed back 30 feet behind the aircraft.

'Why the fuel tanks didn't explode I can't explain. Once all the boys had gone, well, I was quite anxious to get out myself. I put George [the automatic pilot] in, went to the escape hatch, dangled my legs over the side, threw off my helmet and oxygen, and rolled forward and out into space.' Remembering to discard helmets with their oxygen tubes and intercom leads was important. Men jumping with them still attached were sometimes strangled when unfolding parachute lines twisted tubes and leads around their throats.

Before pilots began wearing seat chutes a designated crewman in the front of the aircraft was responsible for finding and clipping the skipper's chute to his chest when the bale-out order threatened or was given. It didn't always work that way though. Artie Ashworth, a noted early-days 75 Squadron pilot who finished two tours with a DSO and DFC, received a mention in dispatches in the 1943 New Year's honours for bringing a Wellington home from Germany without a crew — because he didn't have a parachute.

Flak set off a flare in the aircraft over Saarbrucken, deep inside Germany, and choking fumes and bright-yellow light filled the fuselage. 'The glare was worse than trying to look at the sun. It was like being at the centre of a continuous photographic flash,' Ashworth said later. He thought the Wellington would break up and ordered the crew out. When they'd all gone it was his turn but he couldn't find a parachute. 'Alone, I searched everywhere.'

Ashworth had dropped the Wimpy down to 1000 feet intending to try a crash-landing when suddenly everything became normal again. The flare had either burnt out or dropped out of the bomb bay. 'It seemed a long chance but I set a course for Dieppe because I knew the countryside around there. I had to leave my seat several times to make adjustments. Flak came up occasionally but nothing very near.' Eventually, he spotted the French coast, skirted Dieppe and flew out over the Channel. At 4500 feet both engines stopped, out of fuel, but he got them going again by dashing back into the fuselage and changing to the emergency supply. 'Then the Wellington flew on and made a good landing.'

The peace of the night outside stunned many aircrew escaping the maelstrom of burning and shattered bombers. When Alister Boulton found himself in space over the Ruhr in June 1943, 'there wasn't a sound and I thought to myself, "I'm dead. I'm in paradise."' But then he touched the ripcord on his parachute and knew he wasn't.

Bill Hickson remembers the silence after leaving the hatch of his roaring, flaming Halifax as it began to break up. Shot down over Holland on the shortest night of 1943, he jumped and, head back, watched the chute open above him. 'The canopy didn't look big enough.' But it was and it carried him down safely into a field of rye, well away from the power lines, pine trees and church spires that he imagined waiting for him.

Some airmen have clear memories of jumping and of their descent. Others do not. Some don't remember even getting out of the plane. Many aircrew saved by parachutes have no recollection of pulling the ripcord, especially if they were knocked about and dazed. Others only remember waking up on the ground, opened parachute beside them. Subconsciously or not, they *all* pulled their ripcords. Those who didn't were killed.

Some remember nothing about floating down, don't even know what happened to their chutes. Chunks of memory are gone. Phil Langsford has no recollection of his parachute descent when he was shot down homebound from Czechoslovakia in April 1943. 'I was suddenly walking about on the ground, no sign of my parachute or Mae West.'

Jack Hardie scribbled a few words in fellow New Zealander Ron Marquet's notebook at Dulag Luft: 'Halifax hit by NF at 20,000 feet over Holland and started spinning . . . landed in a monastery garden at feet of a bunch of priests.'

It wasn't until 1991 that Hardie learned what had really happened. A neighbour, originally from Holland, visited the place where Hardie had landed and discovered the truth. The locals had seen three parachutes against the glow of the burning bomber and had gone looking for the airmen. They found Hardie crumpled unconscious in a field and carried him 300 yards to a parsonage, where he recovered his senses to find a group of people, churchmen among them, looking down at him. Injured, he was helped inside and greeted warmly. Eventually, though, the Germans arrived, seven of them, one with a Tommy gun, the others with rifles and fixed bayonets: 'Fer you der vorr is oafer. If you at empt to es cape, I vill shoot you det.'

Sixty years later to the day, in January 2003, Hardie celebrated his life-saving jump by leaping in tandem from a small plane over Motueka airfield.

Boulton has only the haziest recollections of parachuting. His 218 Squadron Stirling, inbound to Gelsenkirchen on the night of 25–26 June 1943, was attacked by a night fighter over the Dutch–German border. He was working on his navigation papers when the rear gunner alerted the crew: 'There's a Mosquito on our starboard bow.'

> Of course it was no Mosquito. The next moment the plane was full of smoke and fire. I don't remember much else, and how I got out of the aircraft I have no bloody idea at all. There was an escape hatch in the floor. I couldn't have found that . . . maybe I went out through a hole in the plane. I don't know.

Boulton hit the ground with a sickening thud just inside Holland near the town of Lichtenvoorde, east of Arnhem. As he drifted in and out of consciousness he heard a man saying in fractured English, 'You must be prepared to die.' 'I thought, "You bastard, you're a German and you're going to kill me." Then I heard other people talking and I was taken to hospital.' He had a broken wrist, a smashed knee and deep cuts on the back of his head. But he was alive, sole survivor of his crew.

Moved to a hospital in Germany, Boulton was nursed by a woman he thinks was Dutch. Surreptitiously she brought him gifts of extra food, once even a small bottle of beer. And one day she gave him a scrap of paper, an envelope and the stub of a pencil. He wrote a brief note to his wife assuring her he was alive and OK. Somehow it reached her in Christchurch.

Years later Boulton discovered that the Dutchman who'd said 'You must be prepared to die' had immigrated to New Zealand after the war and was working in Nelson. 'I was so intrigued I went over to meet him and asked him why he'd said that. I found out he was 16 at the time. He told me, "You were so badly knocked about that I was sure you must have had internal injuries and I was only trying to prepare you religiously for death."' The two men exchange greetings every year on 26 June.

Men baling out at 18–20,000 feet were shocked by the cold, especially in winter. Some who jumped at high altitude dropped thousands of feet before they opened their chutes so they would get down more quickly into warmer and thicker air, where breathing was easier. Others did the same for different reasons. Bob Fenton, sole survivor of a Lancaster shot down over the centre of Berlin in January 1944, was four miles up when he escaped, and knew it. Far below him fires glowed red, searchlights crisscrossed the sky and hundreds of guns belched flak, coloured balls of tracer showing the path of shells as they sought the attackers. Fenton free-fell for a long time. 'I didn't fancy floating all the way with all that stuff in the air.' When he opened his chute a mobile gun fired at him without success, and at lower levels firewatchers took pot shots from the tops of warehouses. They also missed.

Most New Zealanders who parachuted over Germany were picked up quickly but some avoided capture for days, sometimes weeks. Nick Matich got back to England but his success was rare. Ian Herbert was among those who made courageous attempts to remain free. He was on the brink of finishing his tour when his 227 Squadron Lancaster was shot down on the night of 4–5 December 1944 after a fighter struck near Heilbronn in southern Germany, about 50 miles east of the Rhine.

German researchers believe Herbert, a retired Taranaki farmer, was one of ace Peter Spoden's three victims that night. Herbert isn't convinced, but he has come to know Spoden in recent years through emails and letters, and granddaughters of the two men have met in Germany, much to their families' delight.

Herbert remembers the fighter's tracer and shells lacing over and through the top of the bomber, killing the mid-upper gunner and starting two engine fires, one of which caused a runaway prop. Herbert was anxious about the prop. 'That was the most frightening thing of all. They could go so fast they could screw off and then they were liable to make a big hole in the fuselage.' He got one fire out and mastered the prop, but the other fire persisted. When the flames started to melt the fairings around the motor with the petrol tanks just behind, he told the crew, including bomb aimer Doug Cleary, an Aucklander, to go, and followed. 'Two jumps [down the stairs] and I was out.'

Herbert leapt at 7–8000 feet and was hit by the intense early-winter cold. Floating down he could see the loops of a river that reminded him of the Waitara.

> I thought, 'I'm going into that and if I do I'll last about one minute.' But I landed in a field bounded by a big loop. Just before I touched down I could hear people walking along a road and chattering away. Church bells ringing too — did that mean the raid was over? And the boys were going home and I was thinking of bacon and eggs.

Herbert hid for a day or two among hay stooks before starting to walk west. He was on the loose for 23 days, frozen stiff and famished for much of the time. He weighed 14 stone when he jumped, nine-and-a-half when captured. One night he got his feet wet crossing a stream and suffered frostbite. Scared he'd never get his boots back on, he didn't remove them. He was found in a hay barn one afternoon by forced labourers. To have helped him escape would have cost them their lives but they did give him some life-saving hot milk before taking him to the farmhouse and captivity.

Evading capture in occupied Europe was easier than in Germany but was always difficult. Knocking on doors to seek help was a chancy business. The right dwelling and aid was forthcoming. The wrong house and an airman might be turned over to the Germans. Even if a flyer on the run was put in contact with the underground and passed into one of the escape networks organised by patriots, there was no guarantee of ultimate success. Security police and Gestapo infiltrated numerous networks, often assisted by traitors.

Bill Hickson approached a woman outside a Dutch farmhouse and was extraordinarily lucky. She and her family sheltered him at vast risk and then took him to a hiding place in a wood. He was at large for about six weeks, moving along an escape line and confident of getting home until he and a number of other RAF flyers were betrayed.

The family who helped Hickson had not been involved with downed airmen until they'd met him, but by the end of the war had helped many other aircrew and never been apprehended. Hickson was so grateful to them that later he sponsored Cornelius van Staveren, the young man who had been his prime carer on the farm, and his wife and children as migrants. Other members of the family settled in New Zealand later.

Men who survived crash-landings faced the same problems finding help as parachutists did. Some were lucky, some weren't. A year after his 101 Squadron Wellington came down in France southeast of Paris, halfway to the Swiss border, rear gunner Pat Hickton finally got back to Britain. The six men in the Wimpy survived a rough crash-landing on the night of 10–11 September 1941 after a propeller wrenched off a flak-damaged engine while they were flying home from Turin. They quickly contacted the Resistance and were spirited first to Paris, then south to Marseilles. But Hickton and a crewmate were arrested on a train heading for Spain, picked up by gendarmes hunting two rapists who'd escaped from jail, and imprisoned for several months in Fort de la Revere, near Nice. Hickton escaped in the confusion leading up to the German occupation of Vichy France, made his way to a beach near Perpignan and was taken out to a Royal Navy ship to begin his voyage to safety, which ended when he reached Britain in October 1942. Hickton, who lives in Palmerston North, says the entire crew of six evaded capture by the Germans — the first of the war to do so.

Wellingtonian Eddie Worsdale also got back to England from France after a crash-landing, but he took 20 months to complete his 'home run'. He was the wireless operator on a 75 Squadron Wellington caught by an Me 110 the night of 24–25 October 1942 during a raid on Milan. Pilot Howard Hugill, 21, who came from Huapai, near Auckland, couldn't get the Wimpy to go above 12,000 feet, so had insufficient altitude to clear the Alps in the thick cloud concealing the peaks. After he'd turned back, the cloud broke and Z1652-D (Donald) was attacked northeast of Reims in bright moonlight at low level. Recalls Worsdale:

> The first I knew . . . was the sound of crackling machine-gun and cannon fire, blueish sparks all around and being thrown violently on to the stretcher bed . . . We had a large gaping hole in the starboard wing, the fuselage was torn to ribbons, the tailplane the same.

He figured Hugill would try to crash-land, as they were too low to jump. Then fire broke out.

> Things happened fast. I remember yelling to Howard to release the bomb load, as I didn't relish the thought of landing on top of them. He did so. I then took my [crash] position on the bed and waited for the impact. It seemed ages coming. I saw Johnny [the navigator] standing alongside Howard as we went down. This was the last I saw of them. I was violently shaken as we slid along on our belly. My helmet was torn off and . . . my flying suit ripped the whole length of the leg.

Flames and smoke made it impossible for Worsdale to reach the cockpit and he and English rear gunner Len Newbold just managed to get out through the gunner's turret before the wing tanks exploded.

'Howard made a superb belly landing and by some miracle we had survived.' Hugill and the navigator were killed in the landing and fire — 'they never had a chance' — but Worsdale didn't learn until later that the third New Zealander in the crew had survived. At the time he assumed bomb aimer/front gunner Jim Barnes had perished too. In fact, Barnes parachuted, landed in a pine forest, broke an ankle and was taken prisoner. Although 'elderly' for an airman at 34, he had an indomitable spirit and was made an MBE in December 1945 for his work in improving the lot of POWs in various camps. Following the war he was National MP for St Kilda from 1951 to 1957, Dunedin mayor from 1968 to 1977 and knighted in 1976. He died in 1995. Longtime friend Worsdale: 'A real sport in every way and just one of the best.'

Eighteen days after the crash Worsdale and Newbold crossed the French–Swiss border into Switzerland after an epic 250-mile walk. They covered an astonishing 28 miles on the second-to-last day, quickening their pace as they neared the border. They walked by day through largely rural areas, given food and shelter by French farmers. Luck was with them the whole way, even in their worst moment on the 13th day. While trudging along a clay road they spotted a car coming towards them. It stopped 100 yards away and two six-foot-tall SS toughs, both armed, emerged from the vehicle — for a roadside pee. The airmen, still wearing RAF-issue heavy white jerseys and battle-dress tops, albeit scruffy by now and sans insignia, breathed deeply and continued walking. The Germans glared as they came abreast but said nothing, got back into their car and drove off.

Worsdale and Newbold were a novelty in Switzerland, just the eighth and ninth Allied evaders or escapers to seek sanctuary. When Worsdale left 18 months later the number had been swollen by hordes of Allied troops escaping from Italy. Halfway through his stay in Switzerland, he got sick of doing nothing and volunteered to become a cipher clerk at the British consulate in Geneva. He worked for nine months before crossing back into France the day before D-Day — with false papers, a companion in Lieutenant-Commander Billie Stephens, RNVR, and a Resistance guide. Newbold remained in Switzerland. Worsdale and the navy man, one of the celebrated escapers from Colditz Castle in Germany, rode trains packed with German troops to Toulouse, in the south of France, walked some more and crossed the Pyrenees into Spain. They were handed over to British authorities and were back in England, via Gibraltar, on 11 July 1944. Worsdale's exploits gained him a mention in dispatches in the 1945 New Year's honours.

All aircrew carried compasses and simple escape maps covering their bombing routes, but after parachuting it was often difficult to pinpoint an exact location. Down safely after a Ruhr raid in June 1943, Stan Brown was sure he was in Holland when daylight came because he could see windmills. He didn't know windmills were common in the German border area too and that he was in fact just inside Germany. Desperate for water later in the day, he approached a woman working in her vegetable garden. She turned, saw the bedraggled airman and screamed. German soldiers billeted in her home tumbled out. Brown put up his hands.

Aircrew underwent a variety of unnerving experiences after parachuting. Gunner Geoff Gane, from Blenheim, shot down during the Cologne thousand-bomber raid, landed on a cart track in the middle of a forest two hours after takeoff and was captured next morning. He was taken to a village lockup and picked up later in the day by a truck carrying coffins. He and two guards sat on the coffins for the drive to a nearby cemetery. 'I wondered whether I was about to be shot and thought perhaps one of the coffins was for me.' The guards and cemetery caretaker talked, then signalled Gane to join them to look in a coffin. 'Fearing treachery, I stepped slowly forward. The lid of the coffin was lifted and there was the body of my skipper. His chin carried a two-inch cut from a piece of shrapnel which must have hit him and gone through his head during his descent. Otherwise he was unmarked.'

Halfway through his second tour, pilot Jock Stanford baled out over Duisberg on 21–22 July 1942. Flak set fire to the load of flares his

115 Squadron Wellington was carrying to light up marshalling yards for the following bombers, and flames were soon roaring through the aircraft. Stanford dived out of the Wellington right over his target and landed in the yards. Bombs began to fall around him, close to where he was crouching in the lee of a railway wagon. 'It was very unpleasant,' he recalls. 'They made a big whoosh and an enormous noise as they hit, and the ground shook as they exploded.' One blast toppled the wagon protecting him away from him. 'I wondered if I'd get out alive but suddenly, after 20 minutes, it was over and quiet.' And then he was captured.

Pilot Claude Rowland parachuted on his way home from Berlin in the autumn of 1943, his Halifax knocked down by a night fighter. He landed on the roof of a two-storey concrete building, his chute billowing over the side. A moment later he was under shotgun fire, peppered by Germans in a building opposite. He threw up his hands, shouting 'Achtung', the only German word he knew. The firing stopped and the Germans brought a ladder so he could climb down. Until the day he died in Wellington in late 2001, pellets from the shooting made little bumps under the skin of his scalp.

Many airmen floating down worried about what they would land on — as Bill Hickson did when he imagined power lines and church spires. He was lucky and had a soft touchdown. Others had a more uncomfortable arrival, crashing onto roads or through trees. Broken ankles and legs often resulted — sometimes death.

Some airmen made bizarre landfalls. Wireless operator Mike Mora, from Christchurch, smashed through the roof of a greenhouse in a market garden when he jumped from his blazing 15 Squadron Stirling over Holland at 2.00 a.m. on 27 April 1943. He was unhurt but made a mess of the greenhouse. After hiding in the garden for an hour he skedaddled. He was given coffee and shelter in a house 300 yards away but before going to bed wisely returned to the glasshouse with a young Dutchman to retrieve his incriminating parachute. He was put into an escape line the next day and was back in England amazingly quickly on 6 May, the only one of his crew to evade capture.

Wellingtonian Bruce Cunningham thumped down on the steeply pitched roof of a Belgian cafe or pub at Rixensart, Waterloo, on the night of 11–12 May 1944. He didn't slide off because his parachute caught and held him there. Eventually rescuers got to him through a trapdoor in the roof. *Bomber Command Losses* describes the building as a cafe but Cunningham thinks it was a pub. 'I'm not sure but there were plenty of bottles in the place.' He wasn't greatly interested, however, because he was a teetotaller. Anyway, there was no time for drinking of any sort — the Germans were waiting for him.

Cunningham was halfway through a tour when he was shot down piloting a 514 Squadron Lancaster raiding the railway yards at Leuven. The bomber is recorded as being hit by a FW 190 but Cunningham says his rear gunner swears a Lancaster behind got them. The entire crew leapt as the starboard wing was engulfed in flames, and two made it home.

Owen Pratt, a navigator with 462 Squadron, an Australian Halifax unit, jumped at 17,000 feet over Belgium in October 1944. *New Zealanders with the RAF* quotes him: 'There was a terrific gale at that height and I thought I should never get down as I was being blown along almost horizontally.' But the Southlander did get down, crashing through the roof of a village granary. Suspended by his chute in the darkness he unclipped his harness and knocked himself out falling to the floor. People sleeping below thought a delayed-action bomb had fallen through the roof and fled. Pratt was rescued by locals at daybreak.

Parachuting over England was preferable to doing so over the continent but that also had its hazards. Wellingtonian Jim Robinson jumped at 1000 feet above Devon on his first op after the 75 Squadron Wellington he was flying in was hit by flak over Brest on 27 December 1941. The port motor failed soon after the strike and the Wimpy barely reached England. Robinson sprained an ankle when he landed heavily in a hillside paddock but he did better than his mates. One crashed into a deep quarry and another brought down telephone lines, while a third crunched down on a churchyard tombstone. A local farmer and his wife gave Robinson a big feed of bacon and eggs and a tumbler of whisky before putting him to bed for the night. A navigator/bomb aimer, he survived the war and now lives in Sydney.

Generally, aircrew were reasonably well treated when first captured, but later in the war some Allied airmen were murdered by mobs of German citizens enraged by the destruction of their cities and homes, or done to death when they fell into the hands of the Gestapo or groups like the Hitler Youth. High-level edicts went out to Nazi organisations that captured airmen — called *Terrorfliegers* (literally, terror flyers) by the Germans — were to be summarily executed. At least two New Zealand airmen were murdered, both gunned down by Nazi thugs in October 1944: wireless operator Bruce Hosie, after his aircraft landed in the Rhine near Switzerland, and pilot Brian Hynes, taken after his bomber was shot down near Cologne the same month.

Most regular German soldiers, police and Home Guard units, however, were decent and behaved well towards captured airmen. Indeed, some New Zealanders owe their lives to a soldier or an elderly member of the Home Guard, often a World War I veteran armed only with a rifle or revolver, who defied crowds of German citizens baying for blood.

When Bob Fenton came down in Berlin he landed in a tree in a small park, his feet dangling just off the ground. Almost immediately he was surrounded by a group of armed and angry Hitler Youths. An army sergeant sprinted to the rescue. 'He straightened them out; told them to keep back and took me prisoner.' The same sergeant protected him again when he was taken to a civilian shelter where Berliners were anxious to have a go at him. Fenton only felt safe when he was shifted to a Luftwaffe shelter holding other aircrew who'd been rounded up. The next day the airmen were put on the back of a truck and shown bomb damage in the city. 'I think we were supposed to feel ashamed but it cheered us up a bit.'

Ron Noice, a bomb aimer on 405 Squadron, a Canadian pathfinder unit flying out of Gransden Lodge, Cambridgeshire, has an old Home Guard serviceman to thank for his life. Noice, who now lives outside Cambridge in the Waikato, was shot down raiding Dortmund on 20–21 February 1945. He was free for a couple of days until he got to the River Ruhr. 'I was pondering how to get across when this old guy, who must have been about 75, appeared. His gun was shaking so much when he arrested me I thought it might go off.' The same man guarded Noice on the train to Dulag Luft. While they were waiting on a platform in Dortmund, Mosquitoes began dropping bombs and the New Zealander was taken downstairs to shelter. 'Hitler Youth guys were down there and they would have had me but my guard put me in a corner, fixed a bayonet on his rifle and told them, "Stop right there!" Oh, they were bad those young guys. And the girls. The girls were worse, with their knives.'

Arthur Robson, now living in Motueka, floated down from his 75 Squadron Lancaster on a beautiful spring day in March 1945. He landed in a field next to a village outside Munster where a German farmer was ploughing.

I was very light and the breeze pulled me along on my stomach. Earth clogged the chute release and I couldn't get it undone. About 20 Home Guard types came out and circled me but another gust of wind would take me off again. In the finish one of the Germans held me while they got the chute off. Then they marched me to the village, showing me off; very proud of me they were, like Dad's Army.

Hands tied behind his back, Robson was surprised by a woman who came out of a dilapidated dwelling, shouted *'Terrorflieger!'* and splintered her washing board over his head. 'The German guards laughed like hell. I didn't at the time but I've often thought about it since and chuckled.'

Bomb aimer Bill Wilson had completed 29 ops with 158 Squadron when he was shot down. His pilot on a daylight op to Essen on 25 October 1944 led the squadron on a straight, steady line into a carpet of flak bursting dead ahead. Despite Wilson's entreaties to deviate or weave to avoid it, the pilot wouldn't. 'So I switched off my intercom, got my parachute out of the rack and put it on. Immediately, we were hit.'

The pilot turned the plane for Allied lines but couldn't control it and one by one the crew jumped at 18,000 feet. 'I was last out, above the clouds. The pilot was still sitting there . . . he was killed. The plane came down spinning past me about 100 yards away. I thanked God when my chute opened. A lovely feeling. I felt I was floating on a feather bed.'

Wilson broke his right ankle landing in a field and was picked up almost instantly by two older Germans, Home Guarders armed with rifles. Their tattered uniforms surprised the New Zealander, who believed all German forces had smart dress. He thought he might just be in Holland and said, 'Dutch?' The reply? 'Ja, Deutsch.' 'I should have said "Hollander." They thought I said "Deutsch." Anyway, there were big smiles and the three of us sat down and had a cigarette.' The Germans carried their captive out to the road and flagged down a car, swastika flag waving on its bonnet and a high-ranking officer inside. 'He refused to take me, but these old guys insisted and eventually they put me in the front seat alongside the chauffeur and off we went. That was the last I saw of those two but I would have liked to have thanked them; they were so considerate.'

Some airmen actually had trouble giving themselves up. Pilot Leicester Kingsbury jumped from his Lancaster over Germany on 2 January 1944 and almost immediately hit the ground — hard. 'Came to some time later lying on my back in snow and mud,' he wrote in POW camp. 'Felt pretty good so sat up and smoked a cigarette to review the situation . . . decided to start walking home but found right leg broken and collapsed when I stood up.' He made himself a crutch from a tree branch and limped off in search of someone to whom he could surrender. In a small village after daylight he tried to give himself up to a policeman.

> Went up to him and tried to tell him I was a British flyer but he broke into a torrent of German and started to move off. Called him back and showed him the wings on my tunic but he continued talking volubly in German so I cursed him roundly and hobbled off . . . continued on down the road and passed a number of people but they made no attempt to stop me.

After resting under a hedge, leg swollen and painful, Kingsbury pushed on through snow and slush to a small railway station and approached a man in uniform. 'I went up to him and raised both hands above my head. He instinctively raised one hand and said "Heil Hitler"! But then he grasped the situation and took me into custody.'

Parachuting often interrupted carefully laid plans. Ron Noice's sudden arrival on German soil in February 1945 scuppered his 21st birthday party, and Bruce Lethbridge, downed by 'friendly' bombs a month later on a daylight op to Hanover, should have been picnicking in the English countryside at the time his chute was blossoming. Noice was three days from celebrating his big day when he was shot down; his Canadian skipper, Howie Marcou, turned 21 that very day.

> We'd got a case of whisky organised and were going to have a big party the night of my 21st. Instead I was in a cell in Gestapo headquarters in Dortmund with slice of black bread and a drink of water. And you know, back home they still had a do that night and drank our whisky. When we got back to base after the war one of the guys we knew who was still there told us, 'Christ, we had a good party for you buggers!'

Bomb aimer Lethbridge, whose father had served right through World War I in the Auckland Mounted Rifles, came to grief attacking Hanover's railway yards. His 166 Squadron Lancaster was hit and destroyed by a bomb falling from above at 9.45 a.m. on 25 March 1945. Lethbridge and navigator Charlie Bott, later chairman of the Hokianga County Council, had been on the scoot the night before.

> We got home about 2.00 a.m. in our little car and one of our ground crew, on guard at the gate, said, 'God, you guys had better hurry up, the briefing's at half past four.' We told him we weren't on but he replied, 'Oh yes you are, you're on the battle order.' He was right. We went to bed for an hour or so, got up and had a 6.30 a.m. takeoff.

Their bomber was at 18,000 feet five miles south of Hanover, sailing along serenely just in behind the leaders of their wave, when disaster struck. Lethbridge was lying in the nose, poised over the sight, 40 seconds from pressing the release switch, when a bomb from a straggler in a previous wave smashed into the starboard wing.

> There was an enormous bang, the outer engine caught fire, the wing folded up and we went into a dive. Then the spin in the dive wound up so tightly that the plane came out and went the other way. Either that or the skipper straightened it up. I don't know but there was a piece of flat calm and four of us got out. We'd been pinned until then; couldn't move. Up front where I was the chute was just behind me on the bulkhead and I was able to turn around, clip it on, open the forward hatch and go. Charlie and the engineer went out the little square hatch in the roof. They hauled themselves out a bit, pulled their chutes up after them, clipped on and went. The rear gunner opened his chute in the turret and let it rip him out through the clear vision panel gap between the guns. When it opened the chute had the whole weight of the plane on it and tore right across. It held him up but he went down much faster than us. He passed us; thought we were going up.

Lethbridge and Bott had arranged a picnic with a couple of WAAFs that morning. 'We were going to drive out somewhere and have a nice day. Instead we were down in Germany and captured. The WAAFs phoned the station to see where we were. They thought they'd been stood up. The CO had to tell them we were missing.'

Men down safely owed a debt of gratitude to their chutes, and Noice for one felt positively guilty dealing with his chute before scarpering. 'Though it had saved my life I knew I had to get rid of it but I felt badly about chucking it into the mud in a big drain.'

Parachute survivors also owed thanks to the WAAFs who packed their chutes so carefully. When Bill Hickson got back to Graveley almost two years after being shot down, the first thing he did was to go to the parachute section 'and give all the girls who packed the chutes a big hug'.

The post-war return of POWs to bases from which they'd taken off on their final flights was often emotional. When Hickson was in the mess before his last op that June night in 1943, he was offered bacon and eggs by a WAAF. 'I said, "No, thanks. Save them and I'll have them in the morning when I get back." When I walked into the mess after the war, the same WAAF was on duty. Without saying anything she went away and brought me bacon and eggs. I burst into tears.'

The Moon Squadrons

They were called the Moon Squadrons because that's when they mostly flew — on fine nights at full moon and on several days on either side. They flew then for the simple reason that they needed moonlight to see where they were going. Officially called Special Duties Squadrons, they dropped and picked up agents in occupied Europe and delivered weapons, ammunition and other equipment to Resistance forces. 138, formed in August 1941, and 161, established in February 1942, operated from Tempsford, Bedfordshire. They flew a variety of aircraft, including Lysanders and Hudsons, which landed on occupied territory to drop off and pick up agents. Agents were often parachuted, too. The aircraft operated at low level on nights when the moon was big and bright, using it to navigate to, say, a field in central France where members of the Resistance would be waiting with flashlights to signal to the crew. The flights were organised by the Special Operations Executive and the Secret Intelligence Service (MI6), British cloak-and-dagger groups that played an important role supporting the Resistance. At various times, especially in the lead-up to the Allied invasion of Europe, 138 and 161 were backed up by 3 Group Stirling Squadrons, which had been ordered off German targets late the previous year because of unacceptable losses.

Ernie Clow richly deserved the Netherlands Flying Cross he was awarded for his work for the Dutch Resistance with 138 Squadron. The citation noted his 'assignments of the utmost importance for the Netherlands' and his 'courage, perseverance and ability'. He needed all three qualities on the night of 24–25 March 1943 when his Halifax was shot down into the Ijsselmeer. But there was more to it than that. The crash began a sequence of events that led to the eventual death of a brave Dutchman in a German concentration camp.

New Plymouth-born and educated, Clow joined the RNZAF in late 1940 and left New Zealand in June 1941 with 49 other pilots. After further training in England he was posted in mid-October to 51 Squadron to fly Whitleys at Dishforth, one of the chain of 4 Group airfields in Yorkshire.

What with training and serving as second pilot to more experienced flyers, Clow didn't get to captain his own Whitley until 27–28 December 1941, on a raid on the French port of Boulogne. His second pilot that night was fellow New Zealander Noel Cresswell, who was to end the war a squadron leader with two tours to his credit, one with 51, the other with 161, the special-duties sister squadron to Clow's 138.

Clow flew one of the 51 Squadron Whitleys that dropped paratroopers in a daring operation to capture equipment from a German radar station at Bruneval, on the French coast near Le Havre, in February 1942, and the following month took part in the bombing raid on St Nazaire supporting the commando attack on the French port's dry-dock gates. Thick, uninterrupted cloud covered the target on the night of the second of these missions, and Clow turned for home, bombs still aboard because the crews had been told not to unload unless they could see the target. The Whitley crashed in the English countryside as Clow was searching for Dishforth in thick murk. The bombs didn't go off and the pilot wrote laconically in his logbook: 'Returned with bombs. Crashed in hills. No one hurt. Minor cuts — Mac [MacKay, the Scottish wireless operator] the worst — but ok.'

After 10 ops with 51, Clow instructed, then converted to Halifaxes and joined 138 at Tempsford in January 1943. He soon learned that dropping agents and supplies could be frustrating and easily defeated by cloud-obscured drop zones. His logbook entries during his time at 138 are peppered with 'DNCO' — Duty Not Carried Out. Clow's first four operations fell into this category, one of them a marathon flight of 12 hours 45 minutes to Poland and back. On another long flight, deep into Czechoslovakia, a bird crashed through the aircraft's Perspex nose on the way home — remarkable at night when the aircraft was thousands of feet high.

English Navigator Frank Ross flew 12 times with Clow and was with him on the night of his final operation, when their Halifax was downed while carrying two Dutch agents. In 1985 he wrote: 'Ernie was a very good pilot . . . his main asset was his coolness. He never "flapped" and it was this that undoubtedly saved our lives over the Zuider Zee [Ijsselmeer].' Ross noted the crew had been briefed to make three drops in Holland on their 24–25 March 1943 flight.

Looking back I know now that we were simply asking for trouble. Our plane was probably the only one over Holland that night. We were either too conscientious or too confident because we flew around as though we were over the UK. All the fighter bases in that area must have been alerted to our presence and an Me 110 picked us up as we turned for home. It had been touch and go as to whether we dropped the agents but we decided against it after we had made several approaches to the target which was obscured by cloud on every run . . . within a few minutes we were attacked and the plane was set on fire by a heavy burst of fire. The flames were streaming back beyond the tailplane and Ernie asked quite coolly, "What shall we do?" I was looking out through the front windows and saw that we were nearly on the water and I can remember saying, "You'd better make your mind up, we're nearly in the drink." He told me afterwards that he could hardly see through the front and pulled the side window open, saw the sea and picked up the nose. He gave the order to ditch but within two seconds we were in. All the crew got out but one of the agents died.

According to various accounts the agent, a man called Aernoud Bergman, was badly injured by fire from the German fighter and died in the Halifax's dinghy just as the crew and the second agent were about to be rescued by a passing freighter. *Stanfries IV* skipper Gerben Bootsma, heading for the western Ijsselmeer port of Enkhuizen, spotted the dinghy bobbing about in the water and stopped his small ship to pick up the men. The dead agent was left behind in the dinghy. Unfortunately the pick-up was seen and Germans were waiting when the *Stanfries* nosed into dock. Bootsma skilfully nudged the bow of his freighter to touch the quay at the spot where the Germans were standing. They and Dutch police leapt aboard but as they did so Bootsma threw the engines into reverse and swung the wheel. The bow pulled away and the stern hit the quay. As it touched, the second agent, Piet Gerbrands, bounded ashore from the quarterdeck and was soon lost in the maze of portside alleyways. He survived the war. Clow and his crew were taken into captivity.

Bootsma paid with his life. When the Germans found Bergman's body in the dinghy and examined it they found papers and, so it has been said, microfilm in the heels of his shoes. The Germans twigged that it was an agent who had fled the ship, not a seaman as they'd been told. They suspected Bootsma of harbouring the man at his nearby home and the skipper was arrested the following month. Sent to a German concentration camp, he died on 2 April 1945, broken by forced labour and starvation, three days after the camp was liberated. A Dutch traitor involved in his arrest was executed in 1950.

Clow suffered ill health in POW camp and was repatriated to Britain in late 1944. He spent months there recuperating and when he was well enough, soon after the war ended, flew to Holland to have the Flying Cross pinned on his chest by Queen Wilhelmina. He died in 1973.

RNZAF pilot Kevin O'Connor and his crew fought off one German night fighter as they searched the ground for the French Resistance party waiting for the supplies they were to deliver on the night of 3–4 March 1944 but succumbed to a second. The 199 Squadron Stirling began spewing fire from a wing tank and O'Connor couldn't extinguish the flames despite diving as near to the ground as he dared in an attempt to blow them out. So he took the aircraft up again, clawing back height as it burned to give his men the chance to bale out. By the time it was his turn it was too late.

Four survived, two of them New Zealanders — both called Chisholm, both from Invercargill. Rear gunner Adam Chisholm and wireless operator Dick Chisholm, who died some years ago, were not related although they'd known each other vaguely before enlisting.

O'Connor, 27, was working in Wellington when he joined up. He was on his 18th op the night he died. Adam Chisholm, born in Owaka, South Otago, in September 1920, the son of a Presbyterian minister who then moved to Invercargill, was working on a mixed farm near Winton when he finally overcame his 'working in an essential industry' classification and got into the RNZAF in mid-1942. He didn't want to be anything other than a gunner and was added to the O'Connor crew when he reached his OTU in England. 'I'd met Dick again in Canada and they were keeping a place in the crew for me. They wanted someone they knew.'

Chisholm remembers those moonlit low-level SOE flights to France:

> We'd go over the Channel at 500 feet, climb to cross the French coast to avoid the flak and then drop down again to 500 feet. We 'map read' our way, bomb aimer Eddie Brown in the nose looking for particular roads and other features and referring them back to the navigator to make sure we were on the right course. Eddie was very interested in cathedrals and he always liked to get a good look at them if we were near any on the way home. One night we diverted a bit to look at one and nearly got shot down. We ran into light anti-aircraft fire but were low enough to fire back and got away with it. But from then on cathedrals were out of bounds!

When the Stirling throttled back and flew low over its drop point south of Dijon in eastern France, the night they were shot down, there was no activity on the ground — no lights, nothing.

> So we went around again, really low. Still nothing, and skip said there might be Germans about and if so the French wouldn't flash their torches. As we climbed away we were attacked. An Me 110 came in slightly to port of dead astern. It was almost as light as day and we expected him to open up with cannon out of range of our .303s so we held our fire. Maybe he thought we were asleep or wanted to make sure of putting the rear turret out first burst. When he seemed almost on top of us, I opened up and at the same instant he did likewise. He broke away to port and though he didn't seem damaged he didn't return.

Despite the attack O'Connor decided to go down again. Still no lights from the ground. As the Stirling climbed away once more it was attacked a second time. Chisholm identified their adversary as a Dornier 217, a rarely met type of night fighter. Chisholm watched it come in from the rear.

> Its fire seemed to part at the rear turret and go up both sides of the aircraft. He made several passes and some shots went into a starboard wing tank and started a fire. Kev took the plane up and dived unsuccessfully to try to put the flames out. I can remember him asking the mid-upper [Englishman Laurie Crick], 'What's the fire like, Laurie?' and Laurie, only a lad not started shaving, replying in a cool clear voice, 'I am afraid it's getting fairly extensive, skipper.' Kev came back saying it was too hilly to try a crash-landing. 'We can't put it down, so I'll take it up as high as I can and we'll bale out.' At that stage I climbed out of my turret to get my chute off the escape-hatch door. I disconnected the intercom and plugged in again at the escape hatch. In that brief time he must have given the bale-out order but I'd missed it. Looking out I could see the Dornier flying alongside, so I just reached back into the turret and fired a burst at him. Then Kev shouted back through the intercom, 'Who's that firing?' When I told him it was me he yelled back, 'I told you to get out . . . get out, we're going down!'

Chisholm went feet first, flames from the wing swirling back at him. He pulled his ripcord and landed almost immediately, crashing through a tree that broke his fall and almost certainly saved his life. Five escaped from the Stirling but Brown was killed somehow and Crick didn't get out. The two Chisholms and the flight engineer were captured, but navigator Bob Charters, a Canadian, evaded capture. Resistance people who helped him in Dijon were later executed by the Germans.

Chisholm, still a bit dazed from a blow he'd taken as he quit the Stirling, was picked up next morning by several elderly Germans. He'd left easily followed footprints in the snow. The soldiers who caught him laughed because they were armed with Sten guns — British weapons the SOE was dropping.

Chisholm remembers the actions of his skipper with respect and deep gratitude. 'If it hadn't been for the fact he stayed with the plane, we wouldn't have got out. We owe our lives to him. All he got for fighting to keep Queenie up until we left was a headstone in the parish cemetery alongside Laurie in Is-sur-Tille.'

On a country roadside west of the city of Clermont-Ferrand in south-central France, there's a stone cairn about two metres high. It's a simple structure, a flat surface carrying a few words and a large V (for Victory) surrounded by rough-cut blocks of stone. Without reading the inscription it's obvious the memorial has got something to do with airmen because a battered propeller blade is attached to the back. The blade is from Stirling EF215-M (Mike), which crashed on the grassy hill above the cairn on the night of 4–5 March 1944 — 24 hours after O'Connor's plane had been lost. Six men perished, four of them New Zealanders. The sole survivor — an Englishman — escaped with a few cuts.

The 75 (NZ) Squadron Stirling was on a supply drop to the French Resistance in filthy weather when it struck Puy Mandon (4100 feet), one of a chain of more than 100 cone-shaped extinct volcanoes in the Massif Central. One moment the aircraft was aloft, searching for a break in the thick cloud while trying to locate the target area and the men on the ground who would signal with torches, the next it was a wreck with a dead or dying crew.

The captain was Ray Watson, 27 (Dunedin), a pilot with more than 40 ops to his credit. He'd flown a tour in the Middle East and after instructing joined 75 in December 1943. He was well into his second tour when he was killed. The other New Zealanders were navigator Hugh Henderson, 24 (Dunedin), wireless operator Stan Jones, 28 (Wanganui), and rear gunner Bob Melville, 26 (Auckland). The rest of the crew were English.

Watson was a law clerk when he joined the RNZAF in December 1940. Henderson, a brilliant academic, was *proxime accessit* to the dux at Otago Boys' High School in 1936, then majored in chemistry at Otago University and gained a senior scholarship. A highly promising scientific career was cut short by his death, a fellow classmate wrote years later. Welsh-born Jones, a farm worker, married nine days before he left New Zealand to go to war in late April 1942. Melville also left a widow, an English woman he married while overseas.

Survivor Colin Armstrong, the mid-upper gunner, remembers the awful weather in the dropping zone the night of the crash. 'To make sure our supplies were dropped in the right place, our skipper decided to do another circuit, as we could not detect any signal from the ground. All I can remember next is this terrible noise as we hit the ground.'

Armstrong, 19 at the time, probably lived because he was perched in his turret on the top of the fuselage while the body of the plane below him absorbed the impact as the Stirling hit the mountain slope on a relatively level piece of ground. But the crash still knocked him out cold.

I woke up in the turret and managed to smash my way out. It was bitterly cold and there was a blinding snowstorm. I tried to see if any of my crew were still alive but the conditions were atrocious. I staggered for what seemed an eternity and reached a farmhouse. I tried to explain but knowing no French it was very awkward. I eventually managed to reach a village to try to get help for my crew. By now I was absolutely shattered. They doctored my cuts and gave me a warm drink.

Soon a Vichy policeman arrived, called in by local farmers. He locked up Armstrong and refused to understand his requests for rescuers to check the wreck for survivors on that bleak hillside. Claude Grimaud, a French schoolteacher who has researched this crash, says the policeman was executed by the Resistance after the war. Many French people took enormous risks to help downed Allied airmen but it isn't surprising that some didn't. Every day French rural newspapers carried a small front-page box, etched in black, with the words: 'Advice for Everyone — Anyone who accommodates or hides an enemy airman will be shot without trial.'

Next day the crashed Stirling was covered with a thick layer of snow, and snow continued to fall for several days. Germans recovered the bodies of the dead crewmen and buried them in Clermont-Ferrand. Soldiers also salvaged what they could of the cargo that had been destined for the Resistance, but weapons and ammunition were strewn everywhere, hidden by the snow. Locals helped themselves. Some even cut sheets of metal from the wreck to make rabbit hutches.

The roadside memorial, erected by the French Resistance, reads: 'To the Memory of six Allied airmen killed in an accident on 4 March 1944 in the course of a flight of parachuting to the Maquis.' A small tablet at the foot of the cairn adds: 'Homage from FFI [French Forces of the Interior] of Zone III to the valour of English aviators killed on the mission.'

75 Squadron sent Stirlings on supply-drop missions over France on seven nights during the war, all in March 1944. Of the 77 aircraft dispatched on such SOE flights EF215 was the only one that didn't come home.

Frank Evans couldn't believe what was happening. Three nights earlier, 8 August 1944, his Halifax had taken off from Tempsford for what should have been another routine drop of arms and ammunition to the Resistance in Belgium. Now he was sitting in the front pew of the church in the little French village of Lusigny-sur-Barse near Troyes, southeast of Paris, taking part in a full Catholic mass for the other six members of his crew. They were all there, what was left of them, in a single flower-covered coffin. The village mayor sat on one side of Evans, the local Resistance leader on the other. The priest conducting the service was also in the Resistance.

'A German officer came into the church during the service,' Evans remembers.

I heard a vehicle stop outside and thought, 'Hello, here we go.' But the soldier just strode down the aisle, had a good look around and then went out again. When we followed the coffin outside at the finish, the officer was still there with five or six men. They all stood to attention and saluted as the coffin was taken away. The Allied salute too, not the German stiff-arm salute. It was all very moving.

The Germans clearly knew the villagers were paying their respects to an RAF crew but did not interfere. The officer may have been on the lookout for the one missing crew member, but Evans didn't stand out. He was wearing similar clothes to everyone else and didn't look anyone in the eye. He had been warned not to by a local gendarme who had visited him the day before and said to him in good English, 'We are having a funeral for your crew. Will you come?'

So Evans paid tribute to his dead friends, two of them fellow New Zealanders — pilot Graham Paterson, 22 (Invercargill), and bomb aimer Paul Searell, 20 (Wellington). After the service he followed the coffin to the cemetery and took his turn to sprinkle holy water at the graveside. Close by were other fresh graves, the last resting places of an entire crew of a 166 Squadron Lancaster that had fallen a mile from the village three weeks earlier, shot down on its way home after raiding the railway junction of Revigny. Among that crew had been one New Zealander, Alan Rodgers, 21 (Palmerston North), killed on his very first op as a second pilot. When the graveyard ceremony was over, the Resistance took Evans back to the dwelling where he was being sheltered. 'About then, I burst into tears and they led me into a bedroom. I slept for hours.'

Evans, who now lives in a retirement home in Hastings, was rear gunner on the 138 Squadron Halifax flown by Paterson with Searell hunched up most of the time in the nose watching for roads, canals and other ground features for the navigator and pilot. The rest of the crew were English. They'd all trained together but when they'd finished at OTU their names hadn't appeared on the postings list. Paterson found the squadron adjutant and asked why. He was told: 'You're volunteers for special-duty flying. I suggest you go back to your hut and discuss it.' Evans says Paterson wasn't told what they were to do but the crew took a secret vote and all seven said 'Yes' to whatever it was they had volunteered for. When the adjutant heard their decision he said he was pleased. 'You really had no choice. Come back at three o'clock and I'll tell you all about it.' So the crew were sent to 138.

By the time their big aircraft went down at 3.00 a.m. on 9 August, less than three weeks before the liberation of Paris, they'd become an experienced crew, all with more than 20 operations to their credit. 'We'd had a beautiful run up to the time we were shot down,' Evans says. 'Even that night was straightforward at the start.' The Halifax made a huge swing south of Paris before flying north to the drop target in Belgium, found the Resistance waiting and delivered its load. It was at 7000 feet on the way home on the same route when Evans spotted a fighter, glinting in the pale moonlight on the port beam.

> I told the crew, 'Something's out there . . . he's level with us about 500 yards away.' I couldn't get the guns around to bear on him [and this Halifax had no mid-upper turret]. Then briefly I couldn't see him but he came up again on the starboard side, up level, same as before, and I said to myself, 'This bastard's going to make trouble.'

Suddenly the fighter disappeared and Evans shouted into the intercom. 'I've lost him, I've lost him. I think he's gone underneath. Can anyone see him?' The next moment gunfire pelted the Halifax. One port engine, then the other, erupted in flames and the bomber began a shallow dive. 'I remember a tremendous explosion in the front of the aircraft. Graham yelled out, "Bale out, bale out!" and I responded, "What about you skipper?"'

Paterson cried back urgently, 'Don't worry about me . . . go, go!' With that, Evans shed his helmet and intercom, grabbed his chute and clipped it on. He swung the turret and, hanging half out, pulled the ripcord as the bomber plunged earthwards. The canopy snapped open, jerking the gunner free. Minutes later a dazed and bruised Evans woke on the ground behind a hedge, the Halifax burning 300 yards away in a huge bonfire of petrol and exploding ammunition. He didn't know then that he was the sole survivor. When the Maquis later took him to see the wreckage there was almost nothing left.

Evans had landed near a big farmhouse and during the day chanced his liberty by making contact with people moving around outside. He was lucky. Taken in, he was given a big shot of whisky, fed and put to bed. He woke to find a bunch of men surrounding his bed. Once he'd convinced them he was RAF, they smiled and put their Sten guns down.

He was taken to the provincial town of Troyes to get false papers identifying him as a Belgian worker, attended his crew's funeral and then worked briefly for 'Maurice' in a small motor garage, sometimes repairing German vehicles. But the front line was now close and one day he cycled away and after evading a German column identified himself to some Americans in a Jeep. He was handed over to a British army unit working with an SAS regiment and liaising with the Resistance. The unit was headed by Captain John Astor, Nancy and Waldorf Astor's youngest son, who told Evans when he learned he was from New Zealand: 'Not many sheep around here.' A month after he had been shot down, Evans was back in England.

1944

THE END IN SIGHT

1944

By the spring of 1944 Germany had clearly lost the war. In the East the Russians were exerting relentless pressure, in the West invasion was coming, and inexorably British and American bombers were destroying Germany. Hitler declared new wonder-weapons would turn the tide of war but he was dreaming. The V-1 flying bomb and the V-2 supersonic rocket would pummel London and southeast England from mid-year, causing widespread damage and killing many civilians, but they were too little and too late.

German night fighters scored a series of stunning successes in the first three months of the year, inflicting devastating losses on Bomber Command over Berlin, Leipzig and Nuremberg. But the Nuremberg raid, in late March — an attack in which Bomber Command lost more than 100 aircraft — marked the high point of the night fighters' war. There would be other victories for the Luftwaffe but nothing approaching the same scale. And when British disasters did occur, such as Mailly-le-Camp in May 1944, the attackers themselves sometimes carried much of the responsibility.

German airmen fought bravely in a lost cause but little by little, and then faster as 1944 wore on, the Luftwaffe crumbled. Under the genius of armaments minister Albert Speer fighter output soared, reaching record levels in September 1944, but other factors intervened to offset production highs. Long-range Allied fighters, particularly the Americans' brilliant Merlin-engined Mustangs, took an increasingly heavy toll on German day fighters in the air and infrastructure on the ground. Gradually the Luftwaffe was destroyed.

Although German aviation produced some exceptional and advanced fighter aircraft late in the war and was ahead in jet-aircraft design, in general it had not kept pace with the Allies, and the Me 109s and FW 190s, still the mainstays of the Luftwaffe's day-fighter ranks, were outperformed by many Allied fighters in the last 18 months of the war.

German day-fighter aircraft losses grew to catastrophic proportions in combat with Mustangs now protecting American bombers, and in one-on-one battles; even worse was the loss of combat-hardened pilots Germany simply could not replace. Night-fighter crews also began to decline in number and quality. Luftwaffe aircrew flew until they were maimed or killed. They had leave and short rests but there was no finite term to their service. As the British and Americans, backed by hugely greater technological and production capabilities, put ever-increasing pressure on the Luftwaffe. German aircrew who survived became evermore twitchy, less effective and ruined in body and mind.

In April 1944 Germany's production of aviation fuel reached a peak but plummeted thereafter as British and American bombers began smashing oil refineries and synthetic-fuel plants. The Germans quickly ate into their reserve stocks and shortages became desperate, compounding the already major problems the Luftwaffe faced. Fuel became severely rationed, restricting both day and night operations, and quotas for training were cut and cut again. Training schedules for Luftwaffe pilots became shorter and shorter, and were soon less than half the length of Allied pilots'. Ill-trained airmen proved easy game for superior British and American flyers in superior aircraft. Ever-increasing numbers of Allied fighters overwhelmed German aircraft and crews. Caught in a vicious cycle, the power and effectiveness of the Luftwaffe collapsed.

The German day fighters were much more severely mauled than the night fighters but the night squadrons also suffered. Their ranks dribbled away, gradually thinned as single-engined fighters were redeployed to bolster the day squadrons in a vain attempt to stem Allied daylight bombing. Sharply increased numbers of British intruders and night fighters, equipped with the latest electronic gear, made life difficult and dangerous for Me 110s and Ju 88s — and their airfields. Night-fighter stations came under heavier and heavier attack by day and night, aircraft were pounded on the ground, and runways and ground facilities were strafed and bombed. The effectiveness of the night-fighter fleets declined precipitately.

The Normandy landings in June, by which time the Allies had complete superiority in the air by day, followed by the Allies' autumn break-outs into France, Belgium and Holland, tore great holes in the Germans' early-warning radar chains. As a result, Bomber Command had much greater freedom of action, and German night fighters less time to react and find the bombers.

The Luftwaffe placed great hopes on their new jet and rocket-powered fighters but in the event these made little impact. Had the Me 262 jet flown in large numbers earlier, and had it been more reliable, it might have turned the air war. But, introduced before it was ready, it was bedevilled by engine problems that were never properly overcome. The fuel shortage meant training restrictions, and underdone pilots had trouble handling the new jet — a lethal catch-22.

A deep breath and a header out

The first of thousands of names in the thick 1944 volume of Bill Chorley's *Bomber Command Losses* is 'Flight Lieutenant L.C. Kingsbury, RNZAF, pow'. The book then lists the rest of his 7 Squadron crew, all survivors, all taken prisoner on a raid on Berlin on the night of 1–2 January 1944.

Born in Christchurch in 1916, Leicester Kingsbury was chosen for a short-service commission in the RAF and sailed to Britain in late 1938. After the outbreak of war he served briefly on 90 and 101 Squadrons and then became a flying and navigation instructor in Southern Rhodesia for two years. On his return to Britain he flew with 218 Squadron, winning the DFC in September 1943, the citation specifically mentioning his feats over Peenemunde, where he and his crew beat off four fighter attacks. Kingsbury transferred to the RNZAF on 1 January 1944, the day he took off for Berlin, his five-year SSC with the RAF completed.

He wrote about his final flight while in prison camp. It was one of those ops on which everything had gone wrong.

> The aircraft swung violently to port on takeoff due to the outer engine not giving full revs. Throttled back and taxied back on to the runway. Managed to get airborne on second attempt but the climbing performance of the aircraft was poor with two engines overheating badly. [They] continued to overheat in spite of reducing revs and boost, and found it impossible to maintain 16,000 feet.

Kingsbury said he should have turned back but at the time had decided to carry on and 'hope hard'.

> The flight over enemy coast and into Germany was uneventful so far as opposition was concerned with very little flak and no fighters seen. Weather conditions, however, steadily deteriorated and [we] found it difficult to keep above the cloud at 14,000 feet. Ice started forming in spite of flogging the engines and [we] could not maintain either height or air speed. Approximately sixty miles from the target we were already far too late to carry out the operation as pff markers but intended to get in on the tail end of the raid and drop [the bombs]. At this point heavy flak engaged us, bursting ahead and slightly above the aircraft [which] appeared to sustain damage from shell splinters in the port wing, the inner engine being put out of action. No 2 petrol tank [was] holed and the port aileron must also have been damaged as [we] experienced great difficulty in keeping that wing up in spite of trimming. Commenced losing height down

to 8000 feet. Weaved over Berlin and got rid of bombs — every gun in the place appeared to be banging away at us.

Continued weaving and praying hard — managed to climb to 12,000 feet after bombs had gone and high hopes of getting home again but could not clear cloud. Ice commenced forming again on wings, turrets and windscreen. Continued on for about twenty minutes when the aircraft went into a steep nose-down dive and swung to port. May have been due to flak damage or icing. Ordered crew to bale out as had no control. After crew had gone it seemed strange being alone in a Lanc with the wind howling in the open hatch.

Kingsbury regained control temporarily at 4000 feet and hoped for a few more minutes to make the French frontier. 'However, the Lanc had other ideas and fell out of the sky again. Decided it was high time we parted company so clipped on chute and scrambled for the hatch. Took a deep breath and a header out.'

And the king said to me . . .

Many New Zealand airmen met King George and Queen Elizabeth during World War II — at bomber stations when the royal couple visited, at receptions, or at Buckingham Palace, where they went to receive decorations. But few matched Keith Evans' tete-a-tete with Their Majesties.

Temuka-born Evans, a navigator, flew a tour on 214 Squadron Stirlings in the second half of 1943 and then another after the squadron had converted to Fortresses and joined 100 Group as a radio-countermeasures unit in early 1944. As part of that operation Evans visited Alconbury air base, in Cambridgeshire, where US forces were flying Fortresses.

One day while I was there the king and queen visited to meet the Americans. I wasn't involved in all of that and made myself

scarce. The thing to do was keep away from the big parade they
put on, so I went over to the bar in the officers' club and had
a drink. Just the barman and me. We were having a quiet one
when I heard a hubbub of voices outside. As far as I knew no
one was coming back to the mess and bar but suddenly the
door opens and the king walks in. No one was with him and
the door closed behind him.

I didn't know what to say but the barman said the obvious:
'Would you like a drink, sir?' and he said, 'Yes, I'll have a
Scotch, thanks.' Then he turned to me, saw my shoulder flashes
and said, 'You're from New Zealand. What are you doing here?'
I told him, 'I'm here because I was trying to dodge you, sir.' He
replied, 'Well, that was unsuccessful.' We carried on drinking
and talking until there were raised voices outside. The king
said, 'They've just missed me.'

They had. 'The door opened again and the queen walked in,
saying just like any wife, "I might have known I'd find you here."
The king told her who I was.'

The queen, soon with a glass in her hand too, was accompanied
by Princess Elizabeth, then 17, the American CO and a few other
top brass. The small group, a young New Zealand officer among
them, stood around talking and drinking for another 15 minutes
before it was time for the royals to go. After they'd left, a stunned
Evans called for another drink, not quite believing what had
happened.

The Great Escape

New Zealander Johnny Pohe, murdered by the Gestapo after the
mass break-out from prisoner-of-war camp Stalag Luft III, Sagan,
in March 1944, performed his greatest feat of flying the night
six months earlier when he failed to return from his last raid.
He saved the lives of two of his crew and himself by a masterly

ditching during a raid that, but for navigation errors, could easily have ended with a triumphant return to England.

It's always been said that Pohe was shot down by a fighter over Germany but what happened was much different. Research for this book has established that Pohe's 51 Squadron Halifax was not brought down over Hanover, the target on 22–23 September 1943, or even over Germany. In fact, Pohe landed the bomber in the western reaches of the English Channel somewhere near Brest, France.

The source for the ditching story is impeccable — one of the crew. Tom Thomson, who lives in Medicine Hat, Alberta, was rear gunner on the Halifax, barely 20 at the time, and he and Pohe had become firm friends as the only 'colonials' on the crew. The Canadian believes they were hit by flak over the target and says the tail area was struck and the port inner caught fire. 'I'm assuming it was flak and that we just got the outside of the burst.' The rear turret doors jammed and he couldn't get to his parachute.

Thomson says panic followed, and the navigator, flight engineer, wireless operator and mid-upper jumped. 'Johnny didn't tell them to go. He put the plane in a dive to try to blow the fire out and succeeded, but we were left with only three engines and the three of us as we turned away from Hanover.' The intercom had failed but Thomson signalled to Pohe with his system of lights that he was OK and bomb aimer Dave Wells came down the fuselage to free him.

When they got back to the cockpit they discussed the situation, and Wells and Thomson organised the fuel supply, switching the flow from different tanks. 'Dave and I had paid some attention to what the engineer did and we were able to do it. I don't think we had lost any fuel but anyway we had enough to keep going.'

The real problem was navigation. Compasses and radio were out and Pohe tried to get home using the stars. 'Johnny was looking at the North Star but I think he was confused with the sky he'd look at down in New Zealand. It was a clear night so we were able to see the stars but misinterpreted something I guess.'

Eventually they realised they were lost. 'We'd flown long enough to be over England but weren't and we knew if we kept going we'd be out into the Atlantic. So we decided to put it down. The sea was pretty calm and fortunately there was enough of a ripple for Johnny to see the water and he dropped the tail in first.'

Pohe made a perfect landing and all three got out and into the dinghy safely. The plane broke in two aft of the wings but the front section floated for about 15 minutes before it disappeared.

Pohe, Wells and Thomson bobbed around in the sea for a couple of days, seeing land at times. 'We hoped it was Cornwall but it wasn't. A German plane spotted us and sent a boat out to get us. We were taken into Brest so we couldn't have been far away from there.'

After interrogation at Dulag Luft, Pohe, an officer, was sent to Sagan, while Thomson and Wells, both sergeants, went to a different camp. Thomson never saw Pohe again. 'A sad end to a very nice guy.'

The 28-year-old Pohe and two compatriots were among the 50 RAF officers callously executed after escaping by tunnel from Sagan, in Silesia, 100 miles southeast of Berlin, in March 1944 — a break-out that became famous as the Great Escape. After their recapture, the men were murdered on Hitler's personal order.

The other slain New Zealanders were fighter pilots Arnold Christensen, 21 (Hastings), and John Williams, 23, who had lived in Sydney before the war but was originally from Wellington. Christensen was shot down in August 1942 flying reconnaissance during the Dieppe raid, while Williams, an RAF officer, was captured in Egypt in October 1942 four days after taking command of an RAAF squadron.

Seventy-six airmen fled into the countryside surrounding Sagan on the night of 24–25 March, emerging outside the wire from the mouth of an elaborate 360-foot tunnel that was as much as 30 feet below the surface. Called Harry, the tunnel had taken months to excavate, the soil being hoisted to the surface inside one of the prison huts.

The men who carried the sandy soil out to the compound in bags inside their trousers to disperse and tramp into the ground were known as 'penguins', as Halifax pilot Bill Hickson remembers. Captured in mid-1943, Hickson arrived in the Sagan compound looking for his future brother-in-law. 'I inquired about him as soon as I was marched in and someone said, "Bill Harden? He's just over there." He was, shuffling along like a bloody old man, and I thought, "God, is that what prison camp does to you?" But he was dropping sand out of his pants. He was on penguin duty'. Harden, a physicist and mathematician heading for Britain to join a radar research unit, had been captured following the sinking of the *Rangitane* in November 1940.

Just three of the Sagan escapers made it back to England, the rest rounded up quickly in the great hue and cry that followed the mass escape. Hitler, incandescent with rage after learning of the huge break-out — on the night of Bomber Command's last Main Force raid on Berlin — screamed that every recaptured Allied flyer would be shot. Only after the intervention of Luftwaffe boss Herman Goering and armed forces chief Wilhelm Keitel was the number reduced to fifty.

New Zealanders Mick Shand and Len Trent, later Trent VC, were on the point of escaping when a guard patrolling outside the wire stumbled on them. The German loosed off a shot as Shand dashed into the trees and away but Trent was captured on the spot and was soon back inside the camp. When Shand, a Battle of Britain pilot, was arrested, he and others picked up locally were lodged in a jail at nearby Gorlitz camp for interrogation.

Englishman Johnny Marshall, a member of the escape committee and first out that night, wrote in a 1947 account that he could remember seeing or talking to 35 of the recaptured POWs when he was at Gorlitz, Pohe and Shand among them.

Gradually, the prisoners were moved out, Marshall being told they were going for further interrogation before return to Sagan. In fact they were being taken away and murdered. Pohe went on 31 March. Mostly they were driven by car into forested areas, told to get out and then shot. The same thing happened to other prisoners nabbed further away. Williams was arrested in Czechoslovakia and murdered there, while Christensen was recaptured at Flensburg, not far from the German–Danish border, and killed in a field near Kiel. Shand was lucky. He and Marshall were among the last eight left and all were taken back to Sagan and survived.

Gestapo district chiefs and their goons paid a heavy price for involvement in the Sagan slaughter. British Foreign Secretary Anthony Eden promised 'these foul criminals shall be tracked down', and they were. Frank McKenna, a former policeman and 15 Squadron flight engineer with 30 ops to his credit, began the hunt in Germany in September 1945. A brilliant investigator, he and his team arrested the Gestapo killers all over Germany, many of whom were executed. Only a few escaped vengeance.

Johnny Pohe — Porokoru Patapu Pohe to give him his full name — was the first Maori pilot of World War II and the first to be commissioned. Born 10 December 1914, he was educated at Te Aute College and was working for his father on the family farm near Taihape when the war started. He enlisted in September 1940, trained in New Zealand and sailed for Britain in April 1941. Posted to 51 Squadron at Dishforth, Yorkshire, in August that year, he flew Whitleys for the next eight months on 22 ops to Germany, France and Italy.

In February 1942 he was one of the dozen 51 Squadron pilots, five of them New Zealanders (the others were Pat Towsey, Reg Coates, Ernie Clow and Ron Cook), chosen to pilot the Whitleys which dropped paratroops in the celebrated raid on Bruneval, on the French coast north of Le Havre, to seize vital parts of a German cliff-top radar station. On his 'rest' tour he instructed for more than a year, then converted to Halifaxes, flew one op with 102 Squadron and was then posted back to 51, now at Snaith, Yorkshire, for his second tour. He was lost the night after he arrived there.

Thomson paid Pohe a nice tribute in a letter he wrote in 1988 to aviation researcher Harry Widdup, a former 100 Squadron flight engineer living in Matamata:

> Johnny was obviously a brave person and rather fearless, witness his staying with the aircraft after being hit and saving my life, and his immediate involvement in The Great Escape upon reaching Luft 3. It is hard to imagine what hope there was for a black man to be seen in Germany and not attract a lot of attention. Johnny went out with little hope of getting very far but with the purpose of making the Jerries search and involve troops.

Disaster at Nuremberg

Bomber Command's worst night of the war, the attack on Nuremberg in southern Germany, occurred on 30–31 March 1944. Just on 800 Lancasters and Halifaxes were dispatched and one in eight was lost. Ninety-four aircraft were scythed down by the German defences and 11 crashed on return to England — a tally of 105. The raid, a disaster for the RAF, was a triumph for the Luftwaffe.

Many things went wrong: a controversial route to the target putting the bombers over too many fighter bases; forecast cloud over Germany clearing away; and strong winds that made navigation difficult. Some target indicators fell on Schweinfurt, well to the north, and bombing was scattered, inaccurate and ineffective. Little damage was done to Nuremberg. Bomber Command's human casualties were appalling — 545 aircrew dead and more than 150 taken prisoner. Ten New Zealanders were killed and two captured after landing by parachute.

Much has been written about this awful night, including Martin Middlebrook's masterful account *The Nuremberg Raid,* published in 1973. The route — over Belgium, then a long straight leg right across Germany to a point north-northeast of Schweinfurt, followed by a southerly run of about 75 miles to the target — turned out to be a horror for the bombers, a turkey shoot for the enemy. German defence controllers ignored diversionary raids, and night fighters began attacking the bombers before they entered Belgium.

New Zealand pilot Phil Lamason was critical of the route to Nuremberg the moment he learned about it at the preraid briefing. A squadron leader and flight commander with 15 Squadron, with a DFC and two mentions in dispatches to his name, he tackled fellow New Zealander Andrew 'Square' McKee, then an air commodore and Base Commander, Mildenhall. He protested about the outward route, forecasting heavy losses, and said the force should fly more or less the homebound route, thus avoiding the worst belts of searchlights, flak and night-fighter bases. The homeward run, via southern Germany and France, crossing the French coast near Dieppe, did indeed prove less perilous.

Lamason says McKee phoned Bomber Command chief Arthur Harris there and then and was told that the command was aware the route to Nuremberg had shortcomings but that the pathfinders wanted it because there were more features on it that they could pick up on their *H2S* radar sets. It would therefore stand.

Lamason took no joy from being vindicated. He was in the first wave and watched dismayed as bombers went down all along the route to the target. Fighter bases along the bombers' path put up flocks of planes to intercept and harry the attackers.

Nine of the participating RAF squadrons lost three aircraft apiece, another five counted four aircraft missing the following morning. 51 and 514 Squadrons each lost six bombers and 101 Squadron no fewer than seven.

Napier octogenarian Vic Viggers, wireless operator on a 101 Squadron Lancaster that did make it back, calls the night a 'proper cockup, a shambles' and says:

> The winds given to us were wrong and we must have got off track. It was cloudy over the target and then we saw the sky lit up and we actually bombed Schweinfurt. We got hell from the wing commander after the bombing photo was developed but a couple of weeks later when the photo had been studied again he congratulated us. It seemed we had dropped a couple on a ball-bearing factory in Schweinfurt.

The 7 Squadron Lancaster in which New Zealander Trevor Dill was navigating acted as a primary blind marker, flying over Nuremberg at zero minus two minutes to mark the target.

> That was our job that night with other pathfinders. Because of a wind change many of the crews went wrong and started marking Schweinfurt, but I'm absolutely certain we marked Nuremberg. We marked blind on our H_2S, marked exactly from it. Coming out south of Nuremberg we could see all the combats going on among the Main Force aircraft coming in, a terrific number. A lot of the crews reckoned the Germans knew where we were going and knew our route. The fighters were right there and right in among them, shooting them down with *Schrage Musik*. It was a great German victory.

The two New Zealanders who parachuted from stricken bombers to become prisoners were in Lancasters from units that suffered severely. Both aircraft were far short of the target when they were shot down by fighters. Albert Lander, 31, was the pilot of a 101 aircraft and on just his second op when his bomber fell at Dillenburg, about 70 miles southeast of Dusseldorf. Bomb aimer Don Hall was the only airman to escape safely from a 514 plane which plunged to earth at a small village near Sinzig, on the west bank of the Rhine southeast of Cologne.

Lander wrote to Middlebrook about his experience on the Nuremberg trip, and what happened to him is quoted here with Middlebrook's permission. His Lanc was attacked and set afire at 18,000 feet.

> After I told the crew to abandon the aircraft, I tried to keep the plane straight and level as long as I could until the flames entered the cockpit. Covered my face with my left arm but lost control of the aircraft which went into a spin throwing me out of my seat into a position with my back against the cockpit window. Many thoughts flashed through my mind as I lay there. Anyway things were getting bloody hot and my clothes were starting to burn, so I put my feet against the pilot's seat and, by straightening my legs, I managed to push myself out through the window and flipped out over the wing. How quiet and cool everything was then. I realised I still had a chance and felt for the ripcord.

Lander got out at low level, his chute opening only seconds before he landed in a small river.

> One o'clock in the morning in a river fed by melting snows. Boy was it cold after the fire! The water was slightly over my head and I was able to push myself up to the surface every time I

sank. Eventually, I drifted into shallower water where I met the radio op who helped me out of the river. He was minus an ear and an eyelid. I had very few clothes left, a badly burnt wrist and my face felt it didn't belong to me because of the burns.

Lander died in Auckland in 1975.

Three of the five who didn't get out of Lander's plane were New Zealanders: navigator Mervyn Hutchinson, 28 (Christchurch), bomb aimer Ray Cato, 20 (Takapuna), and rear gunner Cyril Parkinson, 25 (Te Awamutu).

Hall, 22, and fellow New Zealander, navigator Llew Smith, 26, were both on their 18th op when their aircraft was shot down. Hall became a noted DSIR plant scientist in later civilian life, breeding maize in Canterbury. His widow says he never talked about his traumatic survival and didn't write anything about it. Three bombers crashed in Sinzig parish and it's possible Hall's Lancaster was the one described by a Westum resident as drenching the village with burning fragments and petrol which set three barns on fire. Middlebrook says the wreckage of this Lancaster burned for two weeks.

Phil Lamason reckons he saw between 40 and 50 bombers shot down on the way in to Nuremberg.

I felt I was the only one left. When I landed back at base that night, first home, I caused myself much embarrassment. McKee was in the interrogation room, waiting, and as soon as I walked in he said, 'Was it as bad as you thought?' I said, 'Yes, maybe worse; we've taken one hell of a hiding.' I also said, 'Christ, in the first wave I seemed to be the only one left. It was just me and the German bloody air force. But it was a pretty fair fight.'

The room rocked with laughter but unfortunately someone repeated the statement to a reporter, who promptly splashed the comments under a headline saying, more or less, 'New Zealander versus the German air force — a fair fight.' Lamason laughs about it now but he got hell from his mates at the time, accused of the biggest line ever shot. 'It cost me a beer or two I can tell you.'

Schweinfurt

In mid-April 1944 Bomber Command began attacking preinvasion targets in northwest Europe — coastal defences, troop positions, railway yards, road and rail junctions and bridges. The crews welcomed the shorter trips to Belgium and France, but the bombers still flew a number of raids to Germany which proved costly. Two hundred and fifteen Lancasters attacked industrial plants in Schweinfurt, 70 miles northwest of Nuremberg, on the night of 26–27 April, while almost 500 aircraft bombed Essen and another 200 attacked the railway yards at Villeneuve-St Georges, in France. Twenty-one Lancasters were lost on the Schweinfurt raid — almost 10 per cent — and three of the captains were New Zealanders: George Mee (page 504), Bill Kewley and Anthony Murdoch.

Kewley, 25, whose family lived in Eketahuna, joined 44 Squadron at Dunholme Lodge, Lincolnshire, a month before the Schweinfurt operation. His crew was nicely mixed: Kewley and fellow countryman and navigator Len Mitchell, 21, three Britons and two Canadian gunners. Their Lancaster was just southwest of Stuttgart preparing to swing north for the target when it was hit by a wicked burst of *Schrage Musik* fire. The plane shuddered violently, smoke and flames instantly filling the fuselage. The wireless operator is thought to have been shot in the stomach and the two gunners killed instantly. Before he died in 2000, Mitchell said he shouted to Kewley that the flames couldn't be put out. The captain was still struggling to control the plane when Mitchell and English bomb aimer John Reseigh jumped, the only two to survive. They were captured next morning — the day before the New Zealander's 22nd birthday. Kewley and the other four are buried in Durnbach War Cemetery near Munich, five of 3000 Commonwealth servicemen, most of them airmen, who lie there.

Murdoch's Lancaster crashed with just one survivor southeast of Reims, although whether on the way to the target or homebound isn't known. Murdoch, 28, joined the RAF before the war in Christchurch and had accumulated more than 2300 hours' flying time, including 11 ops during the 1941 Syrian campaign on Gloster Gladiators, the last biplane fighter built for the RAF. Murdoch and the other five dead from his plane still lie where they were first buried — in a churchyard in the village of Laneuville-a-Bayard.

Perhaps the luckiest New Zealander on the Schweinfurt raid was John Young, flying second dicky on a 619 Squadron Lancaster. He was the sole survivor of the eight crew. Born in Bulls in 1916, he enlisted in May 1942 and did all his training in New Zealand. He'd had one leaflet-dropping trip before flying with the 619 crew to experience ops over Germany. He died in 1991 but his widow says he told her at least four men got out of the plane. 'He landed in a tree in the Black Forest and could hear shots,' Elsie Young says, 'so he hung there quietly until daylight. Then he got down, buried his parachute [and] started walking toward Switzerland but was picked up by Home Guard types.' None of the others survived and all are buried in Durnbach.

The Schweinfurt raid was notable for the award of a Victoria Cross to Englishman Norman Jackson for an act a la Jimmy Ward. Many New Zealanders are familiar with Ward's brave 1941 foray out onto the wing of a Wellington to try to put out a fire. Few know about Jackson's feat, virtually a mirror image of Ward's except that he ventured onto the wing of a 106 Squadron Lancaster flying faster and higher than a Wellington and had to find grips on a metal surface. Burned by the fire he was trying to extinguish, Jackson was blown off the aircraft, his chute partially burned too. He landed heavily, broke an ankle and was in a German hospital for 10 months. Four of his crewmates parachuted to safety as the fire spread beyond control but his captain and the rear gunner perished.

In a flying bonfire

Eight hundred bombers left England on the night of 1–2 May 1944 on 14 separate operations. Most targets were in France, as Harris ratcheted up preinvasion bombing. The attackers hit railway yards, stores, repair depots, motor works, and aircraft and explosives factories. One of the most important was the raid carried out by 120 Lancasters, Stirlings and Mosquitoes on the railway depot at Chambly, a key point on the rail system in northern France.

Two New Zealanders died in one of the three Lancasters lost on this operation but their skipper had an extraordinary escape. Alan Speirs, 19 the day he sailed from New Zealand in April 1942, flew 15 ops with 75 Squadron from August 1943 and then volunteered for 7 Squadron pathfinders with his crew, among them navigator Jack Wain, 33, and rear gunner Johnny Clift, 21 (Auckland). Speirs and Wain were from Christchurch.

Flying Stirlings with 75 they'd been lucky, not receiving so much as a scratch. Says Speirs: 'I remember the RAF seeking advice one day from pilots and crews about enemy tactics and so on and our team saying, "Sorry, we haven't experienced any opposition so we're unable to answer those questions." We'd had a very easy time of it up to then.'

Speirs' crew also had it fairly easy on their opening raids with 7 Squadron on tough targets in early 1944 — Berlin (twice) and Leipzig — but were shot about by a night fighter in March while raiding Stuttgart, and again on 24–25 April while flying to Karlsruhe. They were hit so badly on the second occasion that they had to land at Woodbridge, an emergency field. Chambly was an awful end. And awful luck. The crew were dressed up and on their way off the base on leave that day when they were called back, their week off abruptly cancelled because the squadron was short of crews.

Their Lancaster lifted off from Oakington, Cambridgeshire, at 10.45 p.m. and took part in a successful raid that knocked the Chambly depot out of action for 10 days. 'We'd marked and bombed and just turned away when all hell broke loose,' Speirs remembers. 'There was no warning, no indication of anything untoward. Suddenly we were in a flying bonfire.' Speirs has no idea what hit them.

> I just told the crew to get out and get out fast. I had an attached seat-type chute, the others had to grab their chutes and clip them on. There was nothing I could do, there was nothing anyone could do. I don't even know how many engines were on fire. We were in a steep dive and I was trying to pull the aircraft out, to stabilise it, to give the crew a chance to get out. I don't know what happened then. My next recollection is hanging by my seat harness and from the waist up I was outside the aircraft. The Lancaster was upside down and I was hanging there. At that stage there was nothing whatsoever I personally could do except release my seat harness. I just fell out and that was it. I'd actually crashed through the Perspex and I fell out with a bit of help from my legs.

No one else got out of the flaming aircraft. It went into the ground just a mile or two from Chambly, at Nointel, where the crew are buried in a collective grave.

Like other sole survivors, especially captains, Speirs has been haunted ever since by the loss of his six men and by their fiery deaths. But the air war is full of countless heartbreaking stories like his, and it was only by a quirk of fate that he survived.

Speirs floated down unharmed, made contact with the Resistance next morning and, amazingly, was holed up in a flat in Paris with three American airmen that afternoon. He had enough adventures to fill a book before he reached London safely in late August. His worst moment followed his rescue by American trucks from a forest camp hiding many escaped airmen, when a drunken driver overturned Speirs' vehicle and the New Zealander broke a collarbone. A telegram he sent his mother when he reached England four months after his plane went down was the first word she'd had that he was alive.

Speirs converted to Mosquitoes after his return to duty and flew 20 ops with 128 Squadron, of the Light Night Striking Force, on Mossies adapted to carry 4000-pound cookies. On 10 of them he went to Berlin. He was awarded the DFC in October 1944. Wain was also honoured with the same decoration at the end of the war, dated from 30 April 1944.

Mailly-le-Camp: a cockup

New Zealander Alan Gibson's 166 Squadron Lancaster reached England from France on three engines after the disastrous raid on Mailly-le-Camp on 3–4 May 1944, the fourth motor knocked out by a fighter. By the time it was over the south coast its petrol tanks were empty and one by one the remaining three motors coughed, spluttered and died. The usual engine roar was replaced by an eerie quiet.

At that moment, Gibson spotted a searchlight beam, a *Sandra* that told him there was an airfield there. Making a snap decision, he put the Lancaster's nose down and headed straight for it, with just enough speed to keep him airborne until his wheels hit the grass runway. 'So I've got one confirmed glide landing at night in a Lanc,' he says rather matter-of-factly when he talks about that touchdown, a rarely performed feat. He had landed at Tangmere, a famous Battle of Britain field in West Sussex, just in from the coast between Southampton and Brighton.

The RAF awarded Gibson, then a flight sergeant, an immediate DFM, lauding his skill and courage. His English rear gunner got the same decoration for shooting down the Me 110 that had damaged them. The fighter had flashed across their bow as they were making for home after bombing, seen them and made a tight turn to whirl in from behind, opening fire at 300 yards with cannon and machine-gun.

'Dive port, dive port, go,' rear gunner Alf Bowden directed Gibson calmly as he returned fire. He saw his tracer hit the nose of the fighter, which broke away to starboard. But the German fire had also hit home, damaging control surfaces, the petrol-supply system, the leading edge of the starboard wing, the coolant tank and the magneto system, and severing the hydraulic lines to the mid-upper turret, putting it out of action.

The Me 110 steadied below, 600 yards from the bomber, and followed for about 10 minutes, taking pot shots from time to time, a couple of which went into the wings. Gibson finally forced the issue.

> I dropped down on top of him and he began firing again. This time Alf fired straight at him, no deflection, nothing. There was a bloody great explosion; he just exploded and crashed down on the ground. We were down to 2000 feet by now and saw the fighter go in. We had one confirmed, and there was a hell of a lot of joy and shouting.

Gibson climbed back to 14,000 feet, but the starboard engine, damaged by the fighter, began running so roughly it had to be feathered. More seriously, the combat had used up an enormous amount of fuel, and petrol was being lost from a cut line somewhere. 'As we came out from France the navigator was giving the minutes to the English coast and the flight engineer the number of gallons left. It was remarkable how they matched.'

Gibson finished his tour and came home, but went back to England in 1947 and flew with the peacetime RAF for 25 years before returning to New Zealand for good with the rank of squadron leader. He lives near Motueka.

Forty-two of the attacking force of 346 Lancasters — more than 12 per cent — were shot down on the Mailly raid. After this and a couple of other raids with serious losses, Bomber Command's unpopular early-spring edict that a mission to the near continent would count as only one-third of a 'full' operation in a crew's logbook was quietly abandoned. Preinvasion raids to France and Belgium could be just as deadly as raids into Germany even if flight times were much shorter.

The 3–4 May operation aimed to smash German armour massing and training at the former French army base just outside the village of Mailly, about 80 miles east-southeast of Paris. Among the units at Mailly-le-Camp was 21 Panzer Division, a key element of Rommel's Afrika Korps during the North African campaign. It had faced and fought New Zealanders in many bloody battles. The division had reformed in Normandy in 1943 and, though weakened, it and other German armour at Mailly would pose a threat in the coming battles in France. Ten thousand German troops were in the camp. Bomber Command ordered an attack.

Aucklander Les Porteous, a 9 Squadron bomb aimer about to do his ninth op, cheered silently when he heard panzers were at Mailly-le-Camp. Forty-eight years later he wrote to the niece of his Yorkshire skipper, killed when their plane went down: 'I was quite elated when I heard the target as several of my older friends at the tennis club at which I played pre-war had been killed by panzers in the desert.'

The Mailly-le-Camp raid should have been straightforward,

with minimal casualties. Instead it turned into a horror affair, bombers burning on the ground on all sides of the target. Many of the participants had a simple description: 'cockup'. On a bright moonlit night, ideal for bombing accurately from a medium height — 7000 to 8000 feet — to avoid causing French civilian casualties, nothing went right.

Pathfinder aircraft bathed the target in flares and Wing Commander Leonard Cheshire, CO of 617 Squadron, dived low in his Mosquito to drop red markers to indicate the first aiming point. Dissatisfied with where they fell, Cheshire forbade bombing and sent in dams-raid veteran Dave Shannon, whose markers were spot on. The Main Force controller now called in the first wave of bombers, orbiting 15 miles from the target, but his transmission was drowned out by an American forces radio programme and only a few Lancasters heard the order to bomb. The desperate controller tried sending signals by Morse code. His set didn't work. The deputy controller was heard by pilots to say, 'Don't bomb, wait!' Some pilots ignored this order and bore in on the target. The second wave of Lancasters had now joined the first that continued to orbit and some frustrated pilots — uniquely — broke radio silence to ask what the hell was going on. The air was thick with shouts and curses.

Cheshire called his other two Mosquitos, one flown by veteran New Zealand duo Terry Kearns and navigator John Barclay, to mark the second aiming point. They did so in the face of flak and falling bombs. One pilot has been quoted as saying that when the bombing order was finally given and heard, 'the rush was like the starting gate at the Derby'. From 5000 feet a hail of bombs fell on Mailly, and awed airmen watched the camp become a writhing inferno as barracks, tanks and equipment burned and ammunition dumps exploded.

Amid the delays and confusion, German night fighters began arriving in large numbers, attracted by the armada of Lancasters flying in bright moonlight. The raid took far longer than it should have and enemy controllers had ample time to direct their fighters to Mailly. German guns exacted a mounting toll.

Porteous had been busy pushing out *Window* as his Lancaster ran in to the orbiting marker. 'We got to the marker, turned on our VHF receiver to the bombing leader's channel but instead of hearing him it was some goddam Yank giving what sounded like an election address. Shortly, planes were getting shot down.'

The Lancaster finally got a signal to start bombing, but as it lined up for its run-in the stop-bombing signal was fired. 'So we turned off and started doing orbits again and I started *windowing* again.' Suddenly they were attacked. 'There was a popping noise like an old two-stroke outboard marine engine starting. A trail of white lights [ran] through the step which separated my "office" from the bomb bay, just missing my back and continuing down the aircraft past the main spar.' Soon the plane was on fire.

Told to bale out by skipper and friend Jimmy Ineson, Porteous clipped on his chute, lifted the cushions, pulled the trap up, turned it round sideways, threw it out and rolled out of the plane into the cold night air. 'I pulled the rip cord handle, there was a whoosh and a bang and there I was hanging from a canopy of white nylon'. Porteous and the mid-upper gunner were the only two to escape.

John Sanderson, born in Christchurch and still living there, was at the precise midpoint of his tour when a fighter got his Lancaster over Mailly. Like Gibson, he was serving with 166 Squadron.

> As we came up to the target we could see planes going down in all directions. We released our bombs and turned west for home. It was then a fighter came up from under us, and of course we were silhouetted against the moon. He just strafed us from front to rear and in the process killed the rear gunner.

A fire started near the front escape hatch but the aircraft was still flying straight and level, the engines delivering full power, and Sanderson began to think he might get home. An instant later he knew the end was close. 'I waggled the control stick and discovered I had no controls at all. The fighter's attack must have severed everything because the stick couldn't do a thing.'

The bomber was still flying smoothly, even climbing slightly, so the crew had time to get out. Sanderson, last to go, suffered burns on the face and hands but in a perverse way his injuries, not bad enough to leave lasting scars, proved helpful. He was free for about 10 days after contacting the Resistance and was helped by two families, one in Troyes, another in the village of Laine-aux-Bois, where he was captured.

> We were all asleep after midnight when Germans hammered on the door. The house was surrounded and there was no chance of escape. When the Gestapo caught up with me my face looked an awful mess and so they put me in hospital immediately and I came under Army control rather than the Gestapo, so that was fortunate.

He thus missed what might have been a sticky interrogation following his arrest at the home of the French who had sheltered him.

Some airmen on the run in France were betrayed by people either sympathetic to the German cause or simply scared stiff of the possible consequences of harbouring members of the RAF. It didn't happen either way with Sanderson: it was much sadder. Emil and Yvette Patris, the couple who sheltered him in Laine, had a young son just old enough to attend school. 'The story I've been told is that he was so excited about having an airman in his home he couldn't keep quiet, talked at school about me and of course it got back to the Gestapo.' Both families who gave him sanctuary paid dearly: each husband died in a concentration camp. Yvette Patris' pregnancy at the time saved her from immediate deportation to a German work camp, and by the time her daughter was born her village had been liberated. From Troyes, Georgette Duquesne survived appalling conditions in a work camp in Berlin. She made her way home in 1945 and later remarried.

Sanderson completed his accountancy studies after the war, married and raised a family. In 1975 he and his wife visited France and met the women who had paid so dearly for aiding him. 'I was very apprehensive about how I'd be received. I didn't know whether they would blame me for what had happened.' He need not have worried. The Sandersons were given a wonderful reception, stayed with Georgette for a week and visited Yvette in her village too. The ex-pilot remembers the sacrifice made by people in the occupied countries to get airmen like him back to Britain. 'Our generation lived through it and I think it's good for younger people to know what happened — the price that was paid.'

Two New Zealanders died on the Mailly-le-Camp raid, both new to operations. Bomb aimer Eric Blake, 24 (Huntly), flying with 44 Squadron, was on just his second trip when he was killed. None of the Lancaster crew survived. The bomber, captained by an Australian, is recorded as being shot down homebound and slightly off track near Dreux, in the department of Eure-et-Loir, where all seven men are buried. According to *Bomber Command Losses* the plane may have been one of the several victims claimed that night by German ace Martin Drewes.

Pilot Leslie Lissette, 26, the other New Zealander killed, was on his fourth op with 207 Squadron. Known to his friends as Lizzy, he grew up in a big family in Hastings. He was working as a teamster with the Hawke's Bay River Board when he enlisted at Ohakea in October 1939. He worked on ground duties for two-and-a-half long years before starting pilot training. He reached England in April 1943 and was posted to his squadron a year later.

A good deal is known about Lissette's death. He was another young pilot who died holding a crippled and burning bomber aloft long enough for his crew to bale out. Perhaps he tried to crash-land the flaming plane because the gunner was still in his turret, maybe alive.

The Lancaster was well on the way home when chasing night fighters caught it. Bomb aimer Phil King wrote to Lissette's mother after the war from his home in Northern Ireland. Such heartbreaking letters were the way some women learned how their sons had died. King disclosed that two fighters found them 40 minutes after they'd left the target area.

> We fought them off successfully for about ten minutes but during one of our evasive manoeuvres one of our engines was set on fire. We managed to put the fire out but on three engines our speed was cut down and the aircraft could not be manoeuvred as much as before. Our rear gun turret was next put out of action, then another fighter came in and hit us with incendiary cannon shells.
>
> The aircraft caught fire in the bomb bay and [the fire] spread very rapidly to the rest of the kite. There was nothing we could do about it so Les gave us the order to bale out. Four of the crew got out easily but the rear gunner Ron Ellis was sprawled out across his guns. I told Les this as I went forward. Les ordered me to jump and the last thing I saw of him [he] was fighting the controls to keep the aircraft on an even keel. No, Mrs Lissette, Les was not frightened. He was in my estimation cool and courageous and I'm proud that I flew with such a grand skipper and pal . . . we all owe our lives to your son and you can perhaps find comfort in the thought that he did his duty for his king and country and for you. I speak for all

of us when I say he will always be honoured in our memories as a brave man.

After the Lancaster crashed, not far from the town of Chaintreaux, southeast of Nemours, gendarmes recovered the two bodies, identifying Lissette from the tags around his neck. The remains, sealed in a single coffin, were buried at Chaintreaux. The grave was covered with flowers, and red, white and blue ribbons in the shape of a V laid on it.

New Zealand wireless operator Vic Viggers, over Mailly that night with 101 Squadron, got home to find four of the squadron's Lancasters missing. Of the 32 men aboard two survived. Viggers and his New Zealand skipper, Doug Todd, flew that night with a passenger, an unpopular new group captain, the station commander, a disciplinarian who'd done no operational flying.

He wanted to do an op and thought he'd picked an easy one. We were chosen to take him so Toddy got us together and said: 'The boss is coming tonight and you know what a stickler he is for bullshit. So don't call me Toddy on the intercom. It's skipper or sir.' Right, so we get over there and there's all this combat and planes going down everywhere and I'm up in the astrodome giving Toddy directions about evading the night fighters. Cannon shells above us, cannon shells below us, and the rear gunner calls up: 'Toddy, Toddy, the bastards are everywhere!' On comes the groupie: 'Never fear, never fear, rear gunner, the Lord is with us.' The rear gunner comes straight back: 'He might be up your fucking end but there's no sign of him down here.' There's a deathly silence. The groupie had nothing more to say. Anyway, we got through it all and when we got back he was a changed man. That night made all the difference. Before that flight he had no bloody idea of what went on. He had a good idea after it.

Attacking the V-1 launch ramps

Laurie Johnston still has one of the small pieces of shrapnel that hit him in the back over Belgium on 24 June 1944 while his Lancaster was attacking V-1 flying-bomb launch ramps. Fragments of a bursting shell smashed through the nose of the 635 Squadron bomber, catching Johnston as he lay on his stomach peering through the bombsight on the run-in to the V-1 site at Les Hayons.

More than 320 aircraft attacked three targets on the Channel coast that afternoon as part of *Operation Crossbow*, Bomber Command's campaign to knock out the fixed launch sites of the V-1s, or doodlebugs, that were killing people and causing much damage in southeast England, particularly London. The noisy, slow-flying V-1s began falling on Britain on 13 June 1944, and between then and early September, when most of the ramps had been destroyed or overrun by advancing Allied armies, more than 6700 approached England. Half were destroyed by anti-aircraft fire, balloons or fighters, but of those that got through the defences 2300 fell on London, killing almost 5500 people. In all the Germans launched about 10,500 V-1s at Britain in 1944–45, 82 per cent from the ground, the rest — about 1600 — from the air. The land-launched V-1s fell in the south of England because they had a limited range, the reason they were launched from sites near the Channel coast.

(More than 1050 V-2s, the supersonic rockets carrying a one-ton warhead, landed on British soil, about half of them in London — the first on 8 September 1944, the last on 27 March 1945. The V-2, which also had a limited range but against which there was no defence, was the object of Bomber Command's raid on Peenemunde in August 1943. Flying bombs and rockets destroyed 30,000 homes in London and damaged another 1.35 million.)

Operation Crossbow almost cost Johnston, then 30, his life. As his Lancaster closed on the target in the squadron's second wave he could see a tremendous barrage of flak exploding among the first planes. He remains critical of the fact that the follow-up aircraft were expected to go in two minutes after the first group, at the same height, heading and speed, and without any chance of taking evasive action because they were in formation. 'We were going straight into the muck coming up ahead of us and the German gunners would have time to rectify any errors by the time we got there. We were sitting ducks.'

Wary of the black puffs of flak spraying up, Johnston reached for his chute and clipped it on his chest. He thought that it would give him some front protection as he lay over the bombsight. As it was that decision almost killed him. If he hadn't raised his back by the thickness of the chute the flak would have passed over him.

A shell-burst nearby sent slivers of hot metal flying into the plane's nose and into Johnston's back. The fragments missed the vital artery and his spine but hit and punctured a lung, and soon blood was pumping out of a hole in his back. Johnston had the bombsight lined up but the front gunner had to drop the bombs. The New Zealander was the only man wounded but the plane was badly knocked about — one wing tip gone, one engine and the hydraulics out of action and the radio disabled. Crew slapped a dressing on Johnston's wound and gave him morphine but it was more than an hour before the Lancaster landed at an American field in England.

Johnston was forever grateful to the Americans who treated him. Still gushing blood, he was whipped off to a US general hospital by ambulance with motorcycle escort, sirens blaring. He was losing blood so fast the surgeons risked resupplying him at three times the safety level, and they worked on him for more than 11 hours to get his blood pumping properly and the shrapnel out. Johnston's war was over but he was alive.

Losing an eye and winning a CGM

A flak-burst in front of his Lancaster cockpit over the Normandy battle front in July 1944 cost pilot Dave Moriarty his left eye and has caused him pain ever since. But the morning he was hit he ignored the terrible hurt and loss of sight to fly his plane and crew back to a safe landing in England. That act of bravery earned Moriarty the Conspicuous Gallantry Medal, the fourth and last awarded to a New Zealander in Bomber Command.

Moriarty was on his 11th op when injured, the only casualty in the plane. He and his crew, New Zealanders Tom Monaghan (navigator, Mataura), Ian Ward (bomb aimer, Hastings) and Dave Fox (rear gunner, Oamaru) among them, had joined 75 Squadron the previous month from an HCU and an LFS and had had an active few weeks, flying in quick succession to the invasion beachhead area in support of Allied troops, and attacking marshalling yards in France and Belgium and V-1 sites on the coast.

75 put a record 28 Lancasters into the air at dawn on 18 July, one more than the squadron had ever had airborne before. The aircraft wheeled away from Mepal heading for Cagny, near Caen, as part of an almost 1000-strong force attacking five German positions in support of the 2nd Army. Spitfires flew escort but by now German day fighters were rare and the real concern was the ever-present flak.

Moriarty, born in Wanganui in August 1921 and resident there ever since he was repatriated, his war over, at the end of 1944, remembers bombing at 7500 feet — 'a bit low in daylight' — and then the flak burst.

> Everything was fine and we'd just closed the bomb doors when a big puff of black smoke erupted in front of the cockpit, perhaps 100 yards away. It's often been written that the shell burst in the cockpit [and says so in the CGM citation]; it didn't.

But it burst right in front of me and punched a hole about the size of a cabbage in the Perspex.

To this day Moriarty is not certain what smashed into his face, a piece of Perspex or a sliver of shell. Whatever it was it drove through his left eye, terminally damaging it, and exited behind his left ear. Momentarily knocked out, he recovered to find his clothing soaked in blood and more blood pouring from the wound. He put his hand across his uninjured eye and couldn't see. Crew members put a field dressing over the wound but he wouldn't have a morphine shot: 'I wanted my wits about me.'

Despite the pain, Moriarty deliberately called for a course for Mepal.

People have asked me why I didn't go to Woodbridge [the emergency field on the Suffolk coast], but I felt familiar with our circuit. I knew it was going to be a difficult landing. The others couldn't really fly the plane. They told me later they had talked about putting me out on a static line if I'd passed out and following me.

(Severely wounded or unconscious aircrew incapable of pulling their ripcord were dropped from an escape hatch attached to a static line connected to the aircraft, which automatically opened their parachute once they were clear. Static lines were used to deploy the parachutes of agents dropped from low-flying aircraft, and also of paratroopers jumping into action.)

Moriarty agrees the flight home to Mepal was the worst 90 minutes of his life because of pain from the wound, nausea, and heavy watering in his right eye caused by the stream of cold air screaming in through the shattered windscreen. Mepal, alerted to the emergency by radio, took the Lancaster on a straight-in approach. The crew helped, the bomb aimer calling off key instrument readings and the engineer working the flaps.

'It wasn't a great landing,' Moriarty admits.

> I mistook the height, which was fair enough, and landed fairly
> heavily. But I did no damage and didn't run very far. I got her
> to dispersal and then the medics took over. They climbed in
> over the spar and lifted me out. I didn't smoke but I asked for
> a cigarette. I must have seen too many Westerns.

Moriarty was in hospital for three months as surgeons did their
best to save his eye. In the end they couldn't. 'For a while I could
see the difference between light and day but that's as far as it
went and I had to have an artificial eye.'

After the war Moriarty went back to the company with whom
he had started before enlisting and eventually became manager.
He worked until the early 1980s and for all those years suffered
from his war wound — shocking headaches that laid him flat on
his back, and other problems related to the injury. His right eye
has gradually failed too; his longer-distance sight is all right but
he can't read a newspaper any more.

'What a shambles'

The Lancasters began taking off from Mepal at about 11.20 p.m.
on the night of 20 July 1944 and less than half an hour later
they were all gone — 26 of them. Another maximum effort by
75 Squadron. It should have been an easy enough raid, a doddle
really. A short run to the western edge of the Ruhr Valley near
Duisberg to bomb the Homberg synthetic-fuel plant, then home.
Flak? Sure. Fighters? Certainly. But nothing out of the ordinary.
Just another op. Instead it turned into a horror night for 75, the
word 'missing' chalked against seven Lancasters on the big board
in the squadron operations room. Perhaps some of them had got
back damaged and put down at other fields. But there were no

morning phone calls to say 'We're here, we're safe.' Seven aircraft and their crews — 49 men — gone.

It was 75's worst night of the war for crew and aircraft losses. Only eight of the men aboard the bombers that went down survived. Seven became POWs, and one evaded capture and got back to England. Sixteen of the dead were New Zealanders, and another four New Zealanders were killed when the entire crew of a 514 Squadron Lancaster perished over Homberg.

The loss of seven aircraft and their crews left a gaping hole in the squadron. Nothing like this had happened before, and wouldn't again. Homberg was a name that would stick in everybody's memory for years. It became a bit of a hoodoo target for 75. The squadron went back there three times after the July 1944 raid, each time in daylight. Twice they got home without loss, but on the middle raid, precisely four months after the disastrous July night, another three Lancasters were shot down. This time, though, and unusually, the three crews included just one New Zealander, who survived with the rest of his mates to be taken prisoner. Thirteen of the 14 crew on the other two Lancasters died. In an amazing coincidence another 514 Squadron Lanc was lost on the same raid with all its crew, one of them a New Zealander. 75 Squadron flew 85 raids after the middle Homburg daylight one, and only once more did they lose as many as three Lancasters.

Homberg is imprinted in the memory of navigator David Mercier, who flew the raid with fellow New Zealanders skipper Arnel Meyer and bomb aimer Simon Snowden, plus an Australian and three Poms. The Meyer crew had started ops in mid-June and by the time they went to Homberg had completed 11 trips and rated as experienced. But what with the invasion, raids on front-line enemy troops and positions in France, hitting flying-bomb supply bases and sites, and attacks on French and Belgian railway yards to disrupt German transport, they had not been to Germany.

That night was a rude awakening. Mercier, two weeks short of his 21st birthday, wrote in his log:

> So this is the Reich! What a shambles. Don't know whether they knew we were coming but the fighters were waiting for us as we crossed the coast [into Holland]. Kites were going down all the way in . . . to the Ruhr and back out again. Happy Valley? . . . it was some of the heaviest and most accurate flak I've seen. 3 Group [of which 75 Squadron was a member] really took a beating.

Mercier added that the three fields making up the base of RAF Waterbeach had lost 13 Lancasters — seven from 75 at Mepal, two from 115 at Witchford and four from 514 at Waterbeach itself. He jotted down the stark 75 Squadron figures: 'Seven crews out of twenty-six, three out of ten on B flight, our flight; by noon next day we were among the senior crews. Crews on their 26th and 27th trips bought it. Rather a shaky do.' Under the heading 'Duration' he put '3hr 3min' and 'Only that? The bombing run seemed to last that long.'

Mercier says today, 'It really shook us that such senior crews so near the end of their tour could buy it like that.' He remembers walking back to his quarters with Snowden after breakfast and seeing the *Sandra* light still shining in the first glimmer of the new day over sister field Waterbeach and hearing his friend say, 'There's not much point in having it on now; no one's coming back now.' Mercier: 'It sounds so matter of fact but it was pure pathos, coupled with a sense of relief that at least we were back.' *Sandra* was a single searchlight that shone vertically, a navigation aid that was moved each night among the three fields comprising the station.

Among 75 Squadron veterans it seems there was a belief the Germans knew their route that night and where they were going to be crossing the coast into Holland. A security leak perhaps? Possibly. More likely a combination of circumstances and bad luck. The timing of diversion raids aimed at drawing up enemy fighters and having them refuelling on the ground when the bombers were flying over Holland was apparently poor. At all events, the Luftwaffe were in the area waiting for the bombers and full of fight. Twenty of the 147 Lancasters sent to blast Homberg crashed — almost 14 per cent. 75 Squadron's seven from 26 amounted to almost 30 per cent. With the exception of Lancaster ND800-J (Johnny), lost without trace, all the 75 Squadron Lancasters destroyed fell in Holland, probably claimed by fighters. The six crashed in the space of 40 minutes, the first at 1.00 a.m., the last at 1.40 a.m., most in the southeast quadrant of Holland.

Dutch aviation historians have provided graphic accounts of what happened to two of the aircraft: ME752-Z (Zebra) and HK569-Q (Queenie). They fell within a few miles of each other, one on the outskirts of Heythuysen, a small town of about 3000 people, the other on the west bank of the River Maas at Kessel.

ME752 plunged to its doom at 1.15 a.m., its bomb load still aboard. In its last moments the Lancaster, blazing fiercely after being set on fire by a night fighter, skimmed over Heythuysen's rooftops and slammed down in a field, scattering wreckage far and wide. One of its 4000-pound bombs went off, causing extensive blast damage.

No one was asleep in the vicinity at the time because the night was alive with the sound of bombers flying to Germany, and the villagers could hear the clatter of aerial combat as night fighters from the nearby Luftwaffe base at Venlo attacked the Lancaster force. Certainly no one slept after ME752 came down. Ria Schmieder, who has researched and written about the crash, remembers her father, Daniel Brouns, telling her that the blazing Lancaster passed so close over their home that he could almost have touched it. The bomber thundered overhead, just clearing the dwelling a second before it hit the ground 80 yards away. Brouns' sister and father were already sheltering in their basement but he and his mother hadn't quite got there when the blast from the bomb blew off the roof and the old brick building collapsed. The family escaped uninjured. Another house alongside was totally destroyed, two others were uninhabitable and another 34 damaged. An unexploded bomb lay in front of the Brouns' house and one of the Lancaster's engines was found in a neighbour's garden. Amazingly, no one in the area was injured but five of the crew were dead. 'My father ran to the plane to see if he could help the crew, but he only saw bodies,' Schmieder says.

Three of the dead and the two survivors were New Zealanders. Killed were pilot Gerald Roche, 21 (Feilding), navigator Horace Callow, 27 (Wellington), and rear gunner Keith Smith, 21 (Auckland). The two who parachuted were mid-upper gunner Bill McGee, 34 (Whakapara, Northland), and bomb aimer John Burgess, 30 (Wellington). McGee escaped the German security net to become the sole evader among those who parachuted during the Homberg raid. McGee and Burgess didn't know each other for Burgess was a last-minute replacement for a sick crewman, and they never met again.

Like many aircrew, Burgess didn't talk much to his family about the war but a son remembers he did say he'd had great difficulty getting the escape hatch open. He also kept a diary, which said of that night: 'Shot down . . . while flying at 18,500 feet. Descent in terror. Heavenly feeling on reaching deck in spud field. Walked five miles to lock-keepers house (6am), cop station at 2pm, then to Luft jail at Weert for night.' The next day: 'Taken to Venlo in bus and kept in cell for five days and answered two interrogations.' His family say Burgess was given civilian clothes by sympathetic

Dutch but felt too many people were aware of his presence, that he was putting the Dutch at risk, so surrendered.

McGee, a transport driver, was back in England less than two months after the crash. He said in his debriefing that he'd parachuted after the Lancaster had been attacked by a fighter and set afire, landed, buried his chute and then slept in nearby woods. The next morning he walked into the centre of Heythuysen, 'where I was picked up by someone in contact with an organisation' (shorthand for the underground movement). McGee was sheltered in various places, taken across the border into Belgium, where he narrowly escaped capture in a church in Liege, then hidden in a village and liberated by the Allies as they advanced into Belgium.

Roche, Callow, Smith and the other two RAF crew killed in the ME752 crash were buried in the local cemetery but after the war were reinterred in Jonkerbos, in Nijmegen, where a total of 22 New Zealanders lie.

Schmieder says Germans based near Heythuysen quickly cordoned off the crash site, but her father spotted a briefcase lying on the ground, picked it up and eventually got it to a safe hiding place. The briefcase was in fact Callow's bag, holding his navigation papers, maps and books, plus a sheet stamped 'secret' giving details of how to use *Gee*, the onboard navigation aid, on the approach to Mepal. 'My father did not know a word of English but understood this was something special. One night he visited an English pilot hiding in the village and showed him everything. He was told to burn it immediately because if the Germans found the material they would shoot him.' He was frightened but never destroyed the papers and kept them hidden. 'I am very proud of my father.'

Sometime after her father's death in 1996, Schmieder donated the material to the local war museum, and today Callow's bag and papers are on display with wreckage from ME752. The museum director told Schmieder the crew had been made up largely of New Zealanders. 'At that time a little "fire" was lit into my heart and since then I've been trying to obtain as much information as possible about this plane and its crew.'

Many Dutch like Schmieder have uncovered huge amounts of information about wartime crashes in their enthusiastic and unrelenting research to record details of local combat history and to honour RAF men who died in the battle to defeat Germany.

The bomb load on New Zealander Neil Davidson's Lancaster, HK569 also exploded when the flaming aircraft crashed in shallow, muddy water on the west bank of the River Maas at Kessel at 1.25 a.m. A narrow ribbon of marshy land not much more than 100 yards wide bordered the river at the point of impact, and then the land rose sharply to a low plateau. Kessel, a compact village of about 1000 people, sat atop the rise looking out over the river and the countryside beyond. The rectangular marketplace, surrounded by buildings, including the town hall and municipal offices, was closest to the crash site.

The blast from the Lancaster's bombs all but destroyed the town hall, levelled an attached pub and house and flattened half a dozen other nearby dwellings. It also blew off thousands of roof tiles and shattered almost every window in Kessel, even some in Beesel, across the river. The deafening explosion was heard for miles around. Twenty-two people were left homeless. Surprisingly no one was killed but a number of people were badly injured. The five men still aboard the Lancaster when it crashed would have died instantly — if they weren't already dead from combat with the German fighter that shot them down. This was not a crash from which survivors emerged. Killed with Davidson, the only New Zealander in the crew, were his flight engineer, navigator, wireless operator and mid-upper gunner. The bomb aimer, an Englishman called Little, and rear gunner John Hiscox,

35, reached the ground alive but Hiscox died some hours after the crash.

Little successfully parachuted from the blazing bomber but Dutch aviation historian Ed Muijsers, who has researched the crash, says Hiscox came down in part of the tail section, including the rear turret, which separated from the Lancaster just before it crashed and landed in a cornfield next to Beesel. Hiscox may have been thrown free or he may have crawled away, for when his body was finally found it was 30 yards from the turret.

Muijsers says the bomber was attacked by a night fighter some distance west of the Maas, was hit in the forward section and began burning furiously. Losing height, it continued east until it was above Beesel. Out of control and burning like a torch, it twisted back and fell on the bank of the Maas. The crash and explosion destroyed what was left of the aircraft but the river filled in the deep crater, covering the shattered remains. Small pieces of the aircraft were scattered about but no bodies or even parts of bodies were ever found. The five airmen who died are remembered on the Runnymede Memorial.

Little came down in the back garden of a house near Kessel, injuring his back as he crashed through a clothesline into a bean patch. He lay there, unable to move, using the whistle attached to his battledress to try to summon aid. The house owner, coming home from air-raid duty a couple of hours after the crash, eventually found him, gave him cigarettes and coffee, then had him taken to hospital. Little is said to have heard Hiscox's whistle blowing faintly from time to time for about two hours, then the sound stopped. Although the turret was found next day, the body of the rear gunner was not discovered in the tall corn for two weeks.

When Hiscox's grave was being dug in Beesel, the Dutch brought flowers for it but the Germans threatened the sexton with death if he put them on the grave after the burial. Just the same, the grave was covered in flowers the next day.

Davidson, 21, was one of eight children of Hawke's Bay couple James and Margaret Davidson, who had a sheep and cattle farm 12 miles from Porangahau. James Davidson had also fought for his country, wounded in Palestine in World War I while serving with the Wellington Mounted Rifles. His son went first to the one-teacher Mangaorapa country school and later Hastings Boys' High School. When he finished his education he got a job with Hawke's Bay Farmers Co-op at Waipukurau and while there did the correspondence course to get into the air force and pilot training.

Phyllis Mullinder, one of his sisters, says: 'When I look at 21-year-olds now, I just marvel when I think of him in that Lancaster. We always hoped that he might turn up and we kept on hoping until the end of the war. Then we gave up hope. We've always missed him.'

NOTE: The squadron code and serial number AA-O and ND752, painted on one side of the fuselage of the Lancaster at Auckland's Museum of Transport, Technology and Social History (MOTAT), commemorate one of the seven 75 Squadron aircraft lost on the Homberg raid. Piloted by Henry Burtt, 31 (Wanganui), who had almost finished his tour, ND752 crashed near Tilburg. Burtt and wireless operator Gottfred Gillan, 31 (Auckland), were among the dead. A Canadian and an Australian survived.

The MOTAT Lancaster, built in 1945, was gifted to New Zealand by France in 1964. In a key RAF Bomber Command Association (NZ) project led by Bill Simpson, a Mosquito pathfinder squadron pilot, she has been superbly restored by volunteers, mainly former aircrew, to what she would have looked like in 1944 battle trim. ND752, a magnificent example of the finest bomber of World War II, is a fitting memorial to New Zealanders who flew and died in the service of Bomber Command.

Greater love hath no man than this

Scottish flight engineer Tommy Young tried to help his New Zealand pilot as their Lancaster continued its inexorable path to the ground. He strove to clip John Lawrie's parachute to his harness while there was time. Lawrie shook his head and waved him away. Young said years later the pilot had the control yoke pulled right back into his chest as he fought desperately to keep the nose up. The hydraulics had gone, and undercart, flaps and bomb doors were hanging down. Had Lawrie eased off, the Lancaster would have lost height even faster and no one would have got out.

A fighter's fire had hit them in both wings, knocking out the starboard inner. The plane flew on but then both port engines quit and Lawrie ordered his crew out. The one remaining engine roared at full boost as the young man from Taranaki tried to gain a little height. For Young it was now or never. He took a last look at his skipper, patted him on the knee, leapt down the steps to the escape hatch and jumped. Three crewmen went from the front, the others from the back. Young was last to go at less than 900 feet. Lawrie, left behind, died at the controls as 514 Squadron Lancaster LM180-G (George) crashed and exploded southeast of Ghent, Belgium, at about 1.30 a.m. on 13 August 1944.

Lawrie gave his crew their lives and lost his. Like so many others, he watched his men jump, knowing he himself had little or no chance. But he was doing his duty — what captains did. They died alone, bravely, their young lives cut short. 'Greater love hath no man than this . . .' One or two airmen were awarded posthumous Victoria Crosses for doing precisely what Lawrie did. But most, like him, went to their deaths unrecognised, mourned only by survivors and families. A headstone in a foreign graveyard is all they have. And in Lawrie's case his name on several memorials in Taranaki, among them the gates of the little country primary school he attended.

Lawrie, just 21, had always wanted to join the RNZAF, and pestered his parents on their farm off the coast road at Otakeho, west of Manaia, to sign the papers. Just like his good friend Rex Furey, another Taranaki farm boy from Okaiawa. Both young men joined up as soon as they were eligible and the air force would take them. Furey didn't come home either. A wireless operator, he was one of five youthful New Zealand flight sergeants killed when their Stirling slammed into a peak in the Pennines and burned on a training flight in October 1944. He lies today in a cemetery in Harrogate, Yorkshire.

Three Australians, two Englishmen, Young and Lawrie made up the crew of LM180 as she lifted off from Waterbeach, Cambridgeshire, at 9.44 p.m. on 12 August 1944. The seven men had come together at 1657 HCU, learning to flying Stirlings, before spending a week or two at No. 3 LFS at Feltwell prior to joining 514 Squadron. They had done 12 operations, becoming welded together as an experienced team. Now they were on their way to Russelsheim, near Frankfurt, to bomb the Opel motor factory, a plant that also manufactured parts for the flying bombs that were hitting England.

Some of the crew were uneasy about G (George). They normally flew U (Uncle) but it was under repair. Planes named George had a bad reputation on 514, the last having been downed two weeks earlier over Caen. And LM181, lost over Homberg on 20–21 July with all its crew, including four New Zealanders, pilot among them, had come from the same batch as LM180. George carried H_2S but no one on the aircraft knew how to operate it, nor *Fishpond*, which on George took the place of *Monica*, a little radar gadget that could detect enemy fighters closing from the rear.

George carried Lawrie's team safely to their target, where they unloaded their cookie and incendiaries at 12.15 a.m. on the 13th before turning for home. Forty-five minutes later they were attacked crossing the River Meuse in Belgium, the fire from a Ju

88 astern missing the rear turret but smashing into the wings. Australian gunner Sam Burford, in his turret atop the fuselage, called the cockpit to say the starboard inner was afire. Young said it wasn't, his instruments showed it was fine. 'Well, come up here and have a look,' Burford said. 'I can see bloody great flames coming out of it.'

Lawrie feathered the prop and punched the button setting off the engine's inbuilt fire extinguisher. The flames went out. The crew knew they could make England easily enough on three engines and flew on for another 40 or 50 miles, Lawrie asking the navigator to plot a course for Manston, an emergency field on the Kent coast. But they were losing height, and then someone reported petrol or engine coolant streaming from the plane. Moments later the port engines failed and LM180 was on her way down. Six parachutes blossomed, six men survived.

The Lancaster plunged to earth in a field near the church in the village of Bavegem, 10 miles from Ghent. The deafening explosion shook shoemaker Nestor van der Heyden's dwelling and he stumbled outside to find his fruit trees ablaze and still whipping about from the concussion. Windows all over the village were shattered and roofs damaged. The crater gouged by the fallen bomber was a mass of flame. Hot metal debris lay everywhere.

Then the Belgian found parts of a body and quietly buried them in his yard. He said nothing to anyone, especially not to the Germans who came asking questions. But after the war he contacted Allied authorities, and John Lawrie's body was exhumed and reinterred with honour in Schoonselhof Cemetery, in Antwerp. He lies there with 1500 other casualties from the 1939–45 war.

The riddle of Ted Brunton's death

Ted Brunton, another young pilot from Taranaki, died bravely flying his Lancaster home from a raid on Nuremberg on the night of 19–20 October 1944. He was alone in the big bomber when he was killed, pitched against hopeless odds, but quite what happened and why is a mystery that is unlikely to be solved now, 60 years later. Letters to his parents from crew who parachuted to safety have long since disappeared. Research has not turned up any surviving crew.

What is known is that Brunton's bomber was attacked and shot down on to Echterdingen airfield, Stuttgart, by Me 110s — four of them. Loss records disclose that at some stage on the journey — perhaps over Nuremberg, perhaps after turning for home, maybe even before that — the aircraft was badly damaged by flak. Brunton ordered his crew to jump and they did so, leaving him by himself. Free of responsibility for his crew, did he then decide the plane was still flying well enough for him to try to reach France and Allied lines? If not, why didn't he parachute? Did he think he was too low to get to the escape hatch and jump? Was his parachute damaged? Was he injured? Were there other unknown factors?

For Your Tomorrow says that at 11.30 p.m. (six-and-a-half hours after takeoff) the four night fighters, approaching Echterdingen after a patrol, spotted the Lancaster flying at 1000 feet. 'It appeared to be heading to the airfield for a forced landing.' The fighters attacked. 'Without means of returning fire, the captain is said to have put up such a remarkable display of airmanship that it took at least four attacks over the next twelve minutes before [the Lancaster] was shot down in flames from 700 feet on to the airfield below.'

Two of the German pilots who survived the war were full of praise for Brunton's flying skills and said he proved a very difficult target to hit.

Puzzling questions persist. If Brunton planned a forced landing, why did he not so indicate to the Germans by waggling his wings in surrender? It's unlikely they would have attacked in such circumstances. He must have known he had no chance of emerging alive from any attempt to escape the fighters. Is it possible his crew had jumped so much earlier that Brunton did not know where he was and thought perhaps he was approaching a field in France, one in Allied hands? No one will ever know.

Brunton, born in Cardiff, Taranaki, on 19 April 1920, was educated at Stratford Technical High School and then worked on his father's farm. He enlisted in May 1942, trained in New Zealand and sailed for Britain in July 1943. He flew six ops with 106 Squadron from late August 1944, then joined 57 Squadron at East Kirkby, Lincolnshire. He was on his ninth op with 57 when he was killed. He was buried in Echterdingen but later reinterred in Durnbach War Cemetery.

Sinking the *Tirpitz*

A small piece of dark wood inside a glass frame hangs on a wall in Arthur Joplin's Auckland home, a constant reminder of the day almost 60 years ago when he flew a 617 Squadron Lancaster in the raid that finally sank the *Tirpitz*. The segment of teak, 150 mm by 50 mm, salvaged from the deck of the great German battleship when she was cut up for scrap after the war, was sent to Joplin some years ago in recognition of his part in the attack.

When the *Tirpitz* capsized at her moorings in Tromso Fjord, Norway, on 12 November 1944, British defence chiefs heaved a sigh of relief. Her destruction, by 12,000-pound Tallboys dropped by 617 and 9 Squadrons, signalled the end of a long and costly campaign and finally freed the Royal Navy from maintaining a strong force in northern waters to counter her threat.

The ship, sister of the mighty *Bismarck*, spent most of her life lurking in the fjords on the northern and western coasts of Norway. She arrived in Norwegian waters in January 1942, never returned to Germany and ventured from her lairs into the North Atlantic only on occasional short missions before scuttling back to the protection of the steep-sided fjords. She was never engaged by British warships and fired her 15-inch guns at sea only once — to wreck an isolated and defenceless Anglo-Norwegian weather station at Spitzbergen.

Hitler and his naval commanders, mindful of the 1941 loss of the *Bismarck*, acted overcautiously with the *Tirpitz*, never allowing her to do much more than poke her nose out to sea. Just the same, this immensely powerful ship always posed an enormous menace to the Allies' northern convoys and to Allied shipping in the Atlantic.

The Royal Navy watched her construction in the late 1930s with apprehension, and the air force began unrelenting efforts to destroy her even before she had been commissioned in February 1941, attacking her at Wilhelmshaven, the North Sea port where she had been built, and at Kiel on the Baltic. During her three years in Norwegian waters, Bomber Command aircraft and carrier-borne planes of the Fleet Air Arm launched many flights against her. They inflicted little more than superficial damage while the battleship's guns and the shore-mounted flak batteries protecting her exacted a mounting toll on RAF and FAA crews, New Zealanders among them. Brave midget-submariners — two of them awarded the Victoria Cross — placed charges on her hull in September 1943, causing serious damage, but it wasn't until 617, the Dambusters squadron, and No. 9 got to work with Tallboys in late 1944 that the *Tirpitz* was destroyed.

One early RAF attack on the battleship won Wanganui-born Alexander Gould a DFC. Gould took his flimsy Hampden in at mast height in Wilhelmshaven on 20–21 July 1940. A wicked flak barrage riddled his aircraft and he crashed, to be taken prisoner. According to his graphic account:

> The first hits we received came from destroyers anchored in the harbour when we were about a mile from the shore. From

then on the Hampden was hit continually all the way to the target — both engines, parts of the wing and fuselage were on fire before we passed over the first wharves. My navigator released our bombs as we approached the battleship. Flames lit up buildings and assisted me to clear masts and gantries. As soon as level ground appeared I pulled everything back to come down on what appeared to be a beach. It turned out to be mudflats exposed by the low tide. Our rear gunner was killed and the navigator thrown through the nose of the aircraft. We three survivors were challenged a few minutes later and captured.

Raids like this were mere pinpricks. The RAF did not have powerful-enough bombs to seriously damage a ship such as the *Tirpitz* in the early stages of the war.

The first New Zealand deaths on raids aimed at the *Tirpitz* occurred on 20–21 June 1941, when 115 bombers were sent to bomb Kiel and to try to identify and hit the ship. None succeeded and two Wellingtons were gunned down with the loss of 12 airmen. Both aircraft, from 218 Squadron, were captained by experienced RNZAF airmen: Gordon Jillett, 23 (New Plymouth), and Mason Fraser, 23 (Napier). The navigator on Fraser's aircraft was also a New Zealander, Des Dacre, 26 (Auckland).

After the *Tirpitz* sneaked north to Norway in January 1942, Bomber Command mounted three attacks on her in the spring from bases in Scotland. Some hits were reported but they weren't verified, and the big ship, berthed near Trondheim in Faettenfjord, an arm of Asenfjord, was undamaged. 4 Group Halifaxes from 10, 35 and 76 Squadrons raided on 30–31 March but the *Tirpitz* was obscured by thick fog and cloud. Six bombers were lost, including a 10 Squadron aircraft captained by New Zealander Neil Blunden, 26, which crashed without survivors just offshore in Hemnefjord, about 55 miles in a straight line from the battleship. Blunden had flown 11 ops on Whitleys before converting to Halifaxes. Four days before the operation he and the other crews flew from their Yorkshire bases to Lossiemouth, in northeast Scotland, where they waited for decent weather. Blunden finally took off just before 7.00 p.m. on 30 March, carrying four 1000-pound mines in his bomb bay. The weapons were designed to sink alongside their target, then pop up and explode.

Scot Linzee Druce, whose grandfather, a 35 Squadron pilot, was killed on the same raid, has researched the events of that night exhaustively. In the northern summer of 2002 she flew to Norway and interviewed people living in the Hemnefjord area who remembered what happened to Blunden's W1044 ZA-D. She established it had been heard flying low, 'engines coughing and spluttering', just before it crashed and exploded in the fjord. The following morning fishermen retrieved the bodies of three crewmen from the water but Blunden's was never found. Druce couldn't pinpoint whether the aircraft was damaged flying in to the target or while homebound.

Blunden, promoted to flying officer a week before his last op, filled in his diary the night before he died. His final entry: 'Sunday, 29th March 1942. Warmer day and some sunshine. Met [forecast] no joy for this evening — decided on at briefing 1530hrs. Quiet evening in mess and went to bed at 2130hrs. After briefing cancelled I got crew together and showed and explained to them the target and my plan of action.'

Mixed forces of Halifaxes and Lancasters raided the *Tirpitz* on successive nights at the end of April — 10, 35 and 76 Squadron Halifaxes again plus Lancasters from 44 and 97 Squadrons, the pioneer Lancaster units. One Lancaster got its 4000-pound blast bomb away — and missed — before the *Tirpitz* and smoke ships poured out an enormous cloud of black smoke to screen the target. Shoreline batteries poured fire up at the bombers, claiming one Lancaster and four Halifaxes.

Among the victims was a 10 Squadron Halifax skippered by an Australian with New Zealander Keith Gregory on board, a skipper in his own right but second pilot on this trip because the regular man was ill. The plane was hammered by the ship's defences, was hit again by fire from the cruiser *Prinz Eugen* in the next fjord, and ditched, flames gushing from the starboard wing, in nearby Asen Fjord.

The impact of hitting the water threw Gregory down the steps into the navigator's compartment. His brother Harvey, who flew Wellingtons with Coastal Command from 1942 to 1945, says that Gregory, who died in Auckland in 1992, got a couple of nasty thumps as he tumbled. 'Keith told me he came to in time to see the skipper's soles going through the escape hatch in the cockpit.' Gregory followed and plopped into the water, the rubber dinghy having been torn to shreds by enemy gunfire. The five survivors must have been picked up quickly because they wouldn't have survived more than a few minutes in the freezing Arctic sea. Gregory's children say their father told them he had no feeling left in his extremities when he was rescued and taken into captivity.

Halifaxes and Lancasters returned to Trondheim the next night but were no more successful, and another two Halifaxes were lost, one of them carrying RNZAF wireless operator Arthur Evans, last of three close friends of Norm Bidwell to be killed. Evans' mine-carrying aircraft was hit by an intense barrage of fire, which set the port wing aflame. The pilot ditched safely in Asen Fjord but Evans and the navigator were lost. The tail gunner bravely went back into the fuselage to look for his mates but as the plane began to go under was forced to retreat without finding them. The surviving airmen sat silently in their dinghy, watching their burning Halifax sink in the cold grey darkness.

The *Tirpitz* now moved to Norway's far north, beyond the range of bombers from Scotland, and went unmolested by Bomber

Command for more than two years. The Royal Navy, however, launched midget submarines against her, and the Fleet Air Arm attacked in April, July and August 1944. On 24 August New Zealand FAA pilot Lt Cdr (A) Archibald Ronald Richardson, 27, commanding officer of 1840 Squadron, was recommended for a posthumous Victoria Cross. Flying from the fleet carrier HMS *Indefatigable,* the Aucklander was killed dive-bombing the *Tirpitz*, his Grumman Hellcat blown to pieces by ferocious flak. The VC recommendation by the carrier's captain, turned down by higher authority, said Richardson was 'utterly fearless'.

The *Tirpitz* was finally done to death by 617 and 9 Squadron Lancs, which made three attacks in late 1944, the first by way of a Russian staging base near Archangel, the bombers flying in to attack from the east. They'd hoped for surprise but German radar spotted them and a heavy smoke screen obscured the target. Only Wing Commander Willie Tait saw the ship and just one Tallboy struck. It was enough. The bomb tore through the *Tirpitz*'s bow and exploded under it, tearing an enormous hole.

The damage was not apparent to reconnaissance aircraft but the battleship was now doomed. Repairs couldn't be done in Norway and the ship couldn't be taken to Germany. Patched up and barely seaworthy, she limped south in mid-October to Tromso Fjord, where she was to be turned into a fortress aimed at repelling any invasion by the Allies in the area.

But the ship got no rest. Now she was again within range of British bombers flying from Scotland. Bomber Command installed more powerful Merlin engines and extra fuel tanks on the Lancasters and removed all extraneous weight, and at 1.00 a.m. on 29 October the attacking force struggled into the air. Moments before they reached the target heavy cloud rolled in to hide it. The crews bombed but no hits were reported.

The bombers tried again on 12 November as the long dark nights of the Norwegian winter closed in. This time they succeeded. The Luftwaffe had served the *Tirpitz* poorly over the years, never providing aerial cover despite promises to do so. With the RAF clearly determined to sink the ship, the Germans moved a couple of fighter squadrons to a field near Tromso. Amazingly, these failed to show on 12 November despite desperate pleas for help from the ship.

Four of the 30 Lancasters that flew this final mission from Lossiemouth were skippered by New Zealanders: Arthur Joplin and Barnie Gumbley of 617 Squadron, and Dave Coster and Merv Harper of 9 Squadron. Four other New Zealanders took part: Loftus Hebbard (Joplin's bomb aimer), Frank Cardwell (navigator on another 617 Lanc), and Cliff Black and Jim Boag (navigator and bomb aimer on Coster's bomber). Remarkably, Joplin, Coster and Harper had got their wings together at Wigram, sailed on the same ship to England and there completed their training together.

Fifty years later Hebbard wrote an account of the attack for an anniversary dinner in Queenstown:

> We flew due north at 2000 feet until we were over the Shetlands and then due east, climbing to 5000 feet to cross the Norwegian coast and [on] into Sweden where we flew due north for the full length of the country up the valleys in the mountains so as to be undetected by German radar. About 100 miles south of Tromso we rendezvoused and climbed in formation to our bombing height of 12,000 to 15,000 feet. We came over the mountains about thirty miles south of the ship at 220mph. There were no fighters or smoke screen so for the seven minutes bombing run we flew straight and level and all bombed on the first run.

Although the *Tirpitz* and shore batteries threw up intense flak, this was the end. The attacking crews saw their enormous bombs strike and watched great gouts of flame, smoke and steam erupt into the air. The ship began listing and capsized soon after the aircraft had gone, her hull left poking out of shallow water. One thousand Germans perished, most trapped inside the vessel.

Joplin remembers the sense of satisfaction on the way home when his wireless operator picked up a message that the ship had turned turtle. 'But we missed all the fun at Lossiemouth because we were short of fuel and had to put down at a drome in the Orkneys. We had a bit of a party there that night ourselves and flew back the next morning.'

One Lancaster did not get home. Flak reached up and hit Coster's aircraft. Cliff Black, a retired farmer who has lived almost all his life at the mouth of the Mokau River in Taranaki and is now the only one of the three New Zealand crew still alive, remembers the moment.

> One motor sort of started smoking and another lost oil pressure. The one smoking came right but we had to shut the other one down. Getting home on three was risky and we would have had no hope if the second had gone. Sweden was really the only choice for us . . . we all agreed. We headed away southeast over the mountain spine, losing height, and finally broke cloud to see the ground and pick out somewhere to land.

With the crew at crash stations, Coster made a perfect wheels-up landing in a snowy Swedish field, the Lanc skidding along the ground to a halt near a small village. Friendly Swedes fed the crew herrings and sausages for lunch, and then the airmen were taken to Stockholm and put up in a hotel for 10 days before being flown back to England. After leave the Coster crew went back on ops, finishing the war by bombing Hitler's Berchtesgaden chalet on Anzac Day 1945.

Home from Politz

Less than six months before the war ended, pilots sometimes still had huge problems getting their planes down on returning from a raid. Trying to land in bad weather one night just before Christmas 1944 ended well for one New Zealand pilot, in disaster for another. Merv Croker touched down safely on the far north coast of Scotland; Arthur 'Joppy' Joplin crashed in Lincolnshire. Croker and his crew escaped without a scratch; Joplin suffered appallingly, both legs smashed, and two of his men died. The pilots had been on the same raid.

Croker, born in Wanganui in 1918, enlisted in May 1942, trained in Canada and reached 44 Squadron in September 1944, his Lancaster crew including fellow New Zealander and wireless operator Wyn Henshaw. The two had met on a train going to an OTU to crew up.

Croker did a second-dicky trip with a pilot on his 29th op on 10–11 September, valuable experience with a skipper almost at the end of his tour. The next night he took his own crew on his debut trip as skipper, to Darmstadt. This raid — an attack on a medium-sized city without much industry — became one of the most controversial of the war. A firestorm developed and 8500 Germans lost their lives. Two aircraft from 44 Squadron were brought down, including the team with whom Croker had flown the previous night. There were no survivors.

Croker had done seven ops with 44 when 227 Squadron was re-formed with Lancasters in October 1944. 5 Group squadrons were ordered to provide two aircraft each for the new unit, and Croker and his men, and their flight commander's crew, were selected. Another pilot posted to the new unit with his crew was compatriot Ian Herbert.

Joplin, born in Auckland in 1923, began flying training in New Zealand in January 1943 and was commissioned here. When he got to England in 1943 he did the usual — flew Oxfords,

Wellingtons and Stirlings. But then something happened that was highly unusual. He was posted straight to 617 Squadron, a move that surprised him and a lot of other people. But the Dambusters' then commander, Willie Tait, had been taking all the top squadron crews, and 5 Group headquarters decided it was time 617 had some sprog crews.

617 Squadron historian Robert Owen says that 5 Group chief Ralph Cochrane decided that a few new crews who had shown promise and ability would be what is now termed 'fast-tracked' into 617. Documentation covering official reasoning hasn't survived, 'but it can be surmised the intention was that the new crews should quickly learn battle-proven operational technique from the experts. In general the experiment does appear to have worked. The inexperienced teams did not let Cochrane down.'

Joplin's crew was one of perhaps half a dozen chosen for the elite squadron over the middle and second half of 1944, and their selection was well merited. They and another crew posted to 617 had finished top of their conversion course. But it was still a tough call, thrown into battle without operational experience among many who had flown two or three tours. 'We were trying to learn our way,' Joplin says today. 'The first few times we didn't know much about it. We were up alongside one guy who had done 71 trips. We just had to try to work our way up the ladder.'

Joplin was doing nicely by the time he came to grief. He started about the same time as Croker, also doing a familiarisation trip. Then he went to Brest on 27 August with his own crew, among them South Islander Loftus Hebbard as bomb aimer, and then in succession Holland's Walcheren Island, the Kembs Barrage (a dam in Germany where he dropped a 12,000-pound Tallboy for the first time), the battleship *Tirpitz* (twice), the Urft Dam in Germany (twice) and Ijmuiden, in Holland, to attack E-boat pens.

The raid on Politz was his tenth. In the middle of all this activity he had his 21st birthday — in the air on a long cross-country exercise. 'Tait wouldn't hear of a birthday party that night. We were training. Full stop.'

The 21–22 December 5 Group attack on a synthetic-oil refinery at Politz, northeast of Stettin (now Szczecin, in Poland) by 207 Lancasters entailed a long and difficult flight and turned into a messy operation. Some damage was inflicted but results were minimal considering the effort and the casualty list. One aircraft was lost without trace, two crashed in Norway and five crashed in England, one of them Joplin's. Forty-four men lost their lives. Croker found himself in some trouble but made a masterful landing.

The 227 Squadron bomber had been hit by flak over the target, sustaining substantial damage, including a gash in a petrol tank from which fuel was lost — a severe problem in view of the long trip home. But Croker husbanded the remaining petrol carefully as he flew over the North Sea. When the Lancaster had taken off from Balderton, Nottinghamshire, in the gathering dark that winter's afternoon, thick fog had been forecast for the return and crews had been told to make for airfields around Moray Firth, in the far northeast of Scotland, where it would be clearer.

Croker's crew talked it over after leaving the target. They thought they had enough fuel to reach British soil and so took the risk because they wanted to be home for Christmas. 'Nearly back, we came down to see if we could find Scotland in the murk for starters,' Croker remembers 60 years on.

We were just coming up with some dark coastline about half three in the morning. Ditching wasn't a proposition — it was too cold. The next thing to do was to get above any high ground that might be there because it wasn't as though we could fly around looking for somewhere to land. But we got up and then of course we didn't know whether we were over sea or land, so jumping out wasn't really a sensible proposition either. The obvious thing was to call up on Mayday, and we did. And this lovely Scottish voice came back giving us a course to steer, the whole bit.

Wick, on the coast north of Moray Firth, was a smaller field than Croker was used to and there were no welcoming runway lights. He put on his landing lights and touched down on the grass strip, feeling his way carefully. Even then the Lanc's port undercarriage ran up a steep bank in the dark, coming to a halt almost at the top of it with the port outer prop blades twisted and the wing hanging over a torpedo dump. The crew had been in the air more than 10-and-a-half hours.

Joplin's Lancaster, undamaged over Politz, set a course for Scotland, but his woes began when 617's planes were ordered home direct and had to turn south-southeast for Woodhall Spa, in Lincolnshire. The plane had sufficient fuel, but as it neared its home station the fog was still thick and another change of order was received: planes were to get down at the first available field.

Joplin's crew spotted a weak glow from a field equipped with *FIDO*, runway fire pots fed by pipelines to burn off fog. Ludford Magna had been ordered to switch its system on even though officers there knew it wouldn't function properly given the way fog in the area settled. Officialdom insisted. The Lancaster began circling but couldn't get landing instructions and now had insufficient fuel to fly to Scotland.

What caused the crash is still a mystery, but at low level a thump reverberated through the plane. Perhaps one of the wings brushed something. The aircraft shuddered and began to sink. Joplin calmly ordered the crew to crash stations and tried to hold the big plane level. She hit, slewing along the ground, bouncing, roaring, metal tearing apart. Then fire. Stunned crew began tumbling out, and someone found Joplin still strapped in his seat, legs shattered, in the torn-off front section. They pulled him clear. But it was too late for two of the men trapped in the fiercely burning wreckage.

One of the less injured crew stumbled away into the cold, fog-covered, dripping-wet countryside to seek help. He eventually reached a farmhouse but by the time rescue teams arrived and found the survivors almost three hours had elapsed. One of the dead was Arthur Walker, one of the best bomb aimers in the squadron. He had taken Loftus Hebbard's place that night because Hebbard had been ill.

Walker had wanted to do his 45th and last op.

Mosquito: the wooden wonder

Pilot Steve Watts deserved to survive the war. He had done more than his fair share but by the worst of luck was lost in mid-1944 just when he was due to return to New Zealand. His fiancee in Morrinsville was so sure he was coming home she had bought her wedding dress. He had written to say they would be married the moment he got back. It was not to be. Wing Commander Stephen Delancy Watts, DSO, DFC, mid, commanding officer of 692 Squadron, a Light Night Striking Force (LNSF) Mosquito unit, was killed flying to Berlin the night of 10–11 July.

He was on his 70th op, his war virtually over. It was the 17th time he had been to the German capital in a Mosquito to drop bombs, to cause havoc, to allow the defences no peace, to make the air-raid sirens wail to deny the population sleep. The LNSF did that night after night.

What happened to Watts and his navigator, fellow countryman Arch

Matheson, that night will remain forever a mystery. Destroyed by flak, shot down by night fighters or brought down by engine failure, perhaps falling into the North Sea? No one knows. Their Mosquito is simply recorded as lost without trace.

English navigator Cyril Hassall teamed up with Watts before the two of them went to 692 Squadron at Graveley, Cambridgeshire, and flew countless times with the New Zealander. He remembered Watts as 'cool, unflappable and highly efficient', and called his death a tragedy. 'I so admired the man that when our son was born on 10 March 1946 we named him Stephen as a tribute to a wonderful airman and hoped he would grow up to exhibit as fine a character as Stephen Watts.' Hassall's elder grandson also carries the name.

Bill Holland, another Englishman who flew with Watts in 77 Squadron and served under him at 24 OTU, took the trouble to write to the RNZAF after the war when he learnt Watts had been killed. He said the people at the OTU remembered Watts as 'the finest fellow whoever came to this station . . . with his death you have lost a superb New Zealander'.

Steve Watts, only son of John and Edith Watts, followed two girls. He was born in Morrinsville on 3 March 1916. His father was a builder responsible for some fine buildings in the town, including the Nottingham Castle Hotel, still standing today. After his son was born, John Watts enlisted in the army, even though he was approaching the age of 40. He didn't really want to go to war — he was happily married with a young family and a new son and enjoyed his work — but his mother was very much a king-and-empire type and she wanted her three boys to serve. John Watts was standing alongside his brother Ross in the 2nd Battalion, Auckland Regiment, when he was shot dead in France on 30 March 1918. He lies in Euston Road Cemetery in the village of Colincamps.

Like so many New Zealand World War I widows, Edith Watts brought up her family alone. Steve Watts went to school in Morrinsville and then in Auckland at Mount Albert Grammar where he matriculated in 1932.

He was working in Morrinsville for the family building firm, Watts and Brayshaw, when war broke out, volunteered immediately and enlisted in October 1940.

He was posted to 77 Squadron in England, piloting slow, cold Whitleys. Hassall, who flew on an OTU Whitley on one of the thousand-bomber raids, recalled climbing aboard with flasks of coffee and sandwiches. 'It seemed like we were going on a polar expedition. We flew for seven hours at 110 knots at about 6000 feet in full moonlight. Not my idea of a pleasant night out.' Watts made his mark as a lowly pilot officer at 77, bringing back two shot-up Whitleys, crash-landing one and setting another down on a Norfolk beach. In the second incident, in September 1941, his bomber plunged from 10,000 feet to 600 feet after a fighter attack over the Dutch Frisians before he got it back under control. With one motor out he manhandled it home over the North Sea at 200 feet, once dipping so low the tail wheel cut the water. Barely airborne over the English coast, he saw barbed wire and trees so flew on until he found a clear stretch of beach, where he put the Whitley down on her belly. Then he realised the land above the waterline was mined and had to wait until troops arrived to guide the crew through the minefield.

Watts was awarded a DFC, spent a year instructing, and met Hassall. Together they were posted to 139 Squadron to fly Mosquitoes in November 1943, and on to 692 two months later. Watts was promoted to squadron leader in January 1944 and wing commander to lead 692 two months after that.

Before he took over the squadron he wrote his name in Mosquito history as the pilot of the first Mosquito to drop a 4000-pound cookie on Germany. He and Hassall roared down the runway at Graveley fractionally after 7.00 p.m. on 23 February 1944, the huge blast weapon tucked in the aircraft's enlarged bomb bay. Two other Mossies, similarly armed, accompanied them, and the race to Dusseldorf was on. One of the others was piloted by fellow New Zealander Val Moore, a dashing pilot who was to finish the war with the DSO, DFC and DFM. The contest was so close Hassall timed his bomb drop on 105 Squadron target indicators at 2045.30, logging the half-minute because it might have made all the difference. Moore lost precious time avoiding flak and loosed his bomb precisely one minute later. The third Mossie wasn't in the hunt, third by 90 seconds.

On 13 May 1944 Watts led 13 Mosquitoes of 692 Squadron on a daring and dangerous flight to plant mines in the Kiel Canal to block it and prevent the Germans using it at a vital time just before the invasion of France. Pathfinders commander Don Bennett attended the briefing, a mark of the operation's importance, and according to Hassall told Watts: 'Well, good luck Steve. I fear you may lose three-quarters of your force but if you pull it off you should be in line for a VC.'

In fact only one aircraft was lost. Hassall compared the operation to the Dambusters' raid of 1943. As with the Lancasters of 617 Squadron, pinpoint accuracy was required of 692 to place mines at low level along a three-mile stretch of the canal with balloons at one end and heavy guns at the other. It was the first time Mosquitoes had been used to drop mines at night.

Watts' Mosquito lifted off from Graveley just after 2.00 a.m. and swept down on the canal just as dawn began to colour the sky. 'It seemed we were in the backyards of houses backing on to the canal,' Hassall said. 'We released our mine in the centre, turned sharply away and climbed steeply. All hell started to break loose behind us.'

The mission succeeded brilliantly. The canal was blocked for days as the Germans tried to deal with the new type of mine, partly acoustic, partly magnetic, and set with delayed fuses of varying times. One photograph showed more than 60 German ships carrying an estimated one million tons of cargo backed up behind the mined area.

A special honours list was published in the *London Gazette* on 13 June to cover the triumphs of the raid — immediate DSOs for Watts and his deputy, a DFC bar for Hassall and DFCs for nine other participants, among them Phil Farrow, back on operations after his tour with 408, a Canadian squadron, and a spell as an instructor. Farrow was third off from Graveley that night with his navigator and fellow New Zealander Clem Strang. Arch Matheson, who was to lose his life with Watts, flew with another pilot.

When his prediction of dire losses proved mistaken, Bennett apparently forgot about his Victoria Cross comment, which in any case didn't sit well with his oft-repeated statement that there would be no live VC holders in 8 Group while he was in charge of it. Bennett had a worse memory lapse when he wrote a glowing account of the operation in his book *Pathfinder* in 1958 and said: 'It is an interesting reflection on the appreciation of the efforts of various people during the war that this little episode was not even mentioned to the British public, and no honours or awards were given in relation to it.' He was quite wrong about the decorations and publicity. The British press lavished front-page praise on the canal mining when news about it was released.

Hassall completed his 50th Mosquito trip with Watts on 22–23 June 1944, the last of his tour, and was posted away. He went on to compile a record of 102 ops, 26 of them to Berlin, and was awarded a DSO at the end of the war. He said that when he left Graveley Watts had basically finished too but, as CO, continued to attend briefings and debriefings, watch takeoffs and meet his men on return while waiting for a ship to New Zealand. 'Unfortunately, this was not enough for as keen a flyer as Steve and in early July he decided to go on another operation with Matheson as navigator. They failed to return. The news came as a great shock to me.' Watts was 28, Matheson 29. The navigator, who held a DFM from his time at 218 Squadron, had done 42 ops with 692 when he was killed. He left a wife in Featherston.

Phil Farrow had a good run over the Kiel Canal on 13 May but his luck ran out the following month. A night of anguish ended with him a POW and Strang dead. Strang's death has troubled Farrow for 60 years. He still grieves. Their Mosquito, one of 35 sent to attack railway workshops south of Hanover, was hit by flak near Aachen.

It was a lousy night, the main force raid had been scrubbed; we were the only aircraft operating and ours was the only one missing. We were flying in very high cloud at 25,000 feet. There were some flashes around and I thought it was just lightning. I didn't smell any cordite so didn't take much notice. Without warning there was one God almighty crash. They'd blown the tail off the Mosquito. It was very good shooting at that height and at our speed of 250–260 mph. I assume it was an 88 [mm] that got us.

The Mosquito immediately went down in a screaming dive and Farrow thought it was the end.

There was no possibility of getting out of this but suddenly the aircraft came up again on its back. Terrifying. Why it did so I don't know but I was hanging upside down from my straps. My poor navigator was down in the nose. He'd been sitting alongside me when all this happened and [slid] straight down there. He may have unbuckled himself when we were hit.

Farrow tried to turn the plane over, to get some control to release the 4000-pound cookie. He couldn't, and then the main spar behind him shattered. The wings folded up and his seat was shoved forward under the instrument panel. As he struggled to free his legs and escape through the cockpit roof, now below him, he could do nothing for Strang. Suddenly Farrow broke free as the plane disintegrated and he was looking for the ripcord on his seat-type chute. It opened, whether at 20,000 feet or 2000 feet Farrow has no idea. He hit the ground heavily not far from Aachen, hurt his legs, couldn't walk and was picked up next morning.

Because only two men flew a Mosquito they often became a close team, totally dependent on each other — closer than the members of a heavy-bomber crew of six or seven. Strang's death shattered Farrow. It's unfair that men should have to carry such burdens but Farrow felt that somehow he'd let his navigator down. 'I couldn't do anything to save him and I regret that very much.'

Clement Russell Strang, 22 when he was killed, was on his 65th op that night. The Germans found his body and buried him at Ederen, just inside Germany, where the bulk of the Mosquito fell. *For Your Tomorrow* says it appears an American graves-registration unit removed his remains after the war to Holland, where they were later reinterred in a British cemetery as those of an unknown airman. Positive identification was not possible by then and Strang's name is thus commemorated at Runnymede.

There is more. Strang's father was also a war casualty. He survived service with the Rifle Brigade on the Western Front in World War I but came home wounded and died on 11 July 1921. His son was born in Riverton ten weeks later.

Three of the last four New Zealanders killed on World War II air operations in Europe died flying Mosquitoes. Ron Dawson, 24 (Rahotu, Opunake), and his navigator, Phil Childs, 32 (Wellington), were lost when their 141 Squadron Mosquito was hit by light flak over a Munich airfield on 18–19 April 1945, while John McGreal, 32, was killed on Anzac Day trying to land his 109 Squadron aircraft at a Belgian airfield. Both Childs and McGreal were married, the former with a son and McGreal with a daughter he never saw.

The loss of both these men so close to the German surrender was poignant, but that of Childs was particularly so. He was three-and-a-half when his father, Arthur James Childs, a major in the Rifle Brigade, was killed during the capture of Flers-Courcelette, France, by New Zealanders on 15 September 1916. Phil Childs' son, Barry, who died in 1990, was also a toddler when his father sailed away.

Dawson and Childs were the victims of airfield-defence guns manned by a quick-thinking German pilot who had finished flying for the night. The New Zealanders had taken off from their base at West Raynham, Suffolk, on a spring afternoon at 4.40 p.m. and refuelled at Melsbroek, near Brussels. They were among Mosquitoes striking at airfields around Munich, deep in southeast Germany, an area not yet fallen to the Allied armies.

The Luftwaffe was beaten but flew on in the face of hopeless odds. Just before 9.00 p.m. on 18 April Wolfhard Galinsky piloted his plane from Neubiberg field near Munich to attack American ground forces in eastern France. He returned three hours later and remained at the field command talking with duty personnel.

At 1.30 a.m. a couple of Mosquitoes, cannon blazing, roared over Neubiberg. They set a hangar afire as Galinsky and others sprinted to a vehicle to race to the gun pits. The German pilot-turned-gunner and those with him wrenched the covers off the light-flak weapons and poured shells up at one of the British aircraft making another pass over the field. It was flown by Dawson and Childs. Suddenly, one of the attacker's wings was flaming.

Years later Galinsky wrote: 'We shouted out our victory and were very glad to have put up such a good defence . . . the Mosquito pilot lifted his plane immediately . . . [but] soon after, we heard a big bang as the aircraft hit the ground.'

It took an hour for Galinsky to locate the crash site. He'd hoped to find survivors but both Mosquito crew were dead. The aircraft had come down in the garden of a housing estate and exploded in flames. Firemen already had Dawson, killed instantly when the Mosquito crashed, out of the wreck. Childs had jumped from the plane but had been far too low despite Dawson's brave effort to gain some height. His chute hadn't opened and he'd smashed through the roof of a building, also dying instantly.

Galinsky: 'Now our minds were quite different to immediately after the aircraft had been shot down . . . None of us could see any sense in such action any more, so shortly before the expected end of this terrible war. We felt the senselessness of the loss of these victims.'

Galinsky, who rose to be a major general in the German defence forces after the war, found the graves of the two New Zealanders in

Durnbach War Cemetery in 1993, took photographs and set about locating relatives. The RNZAF found Childs' widow (she had remarried) and the Dawson family, and the story of the New Zealanders' final mission was told on its 50th anniversary in *RNZAF News* in 1995. Childs' widow (now dead) and Galinsky began corresponding in 1994, and she said in a follow-up letter to the *News* article that the German had been overwhelmed 'by the friendliness of those who have written to him. He has found peace at last . . . Mr Galinsky is a very fine human being and I am pleased to call him a friend.'

John McGreal was the final New Zealand operational casualty in Bomber Command. An Aucklander who left his own panel-beating business to serve, he had instructed in England for more than a year before joining 109 Squadron. He began flying operationally towards the end of 1944, and on the night he was killed was on his 52nd op.

McGreal, like Dawson and Childs, had also been attacking an airfield near Munich, flying from Little Staughton, Bedfordshire. At some stage he must have lost an engine and was given permission to land at Melsbroek. *For Your Tomorrow* says that he approached fast and high with one engine closed down. Halfway along the runway, without having touched down, the Mosquito opened up and attempted to go round again. But as it began turning to port it dived straight into the ground and burst into flames. McGreal and his navigator are buried in Brussels.

Prisoners of war

Aircrew captured after parachuting endured dreary prisoner-of-war camps scattered across Germany, Poland and Lithuania. They didn't quite starve but there was never enough food; it was subsistence living. They shivered in Spartan quarters during the fierce European winters.

Red Cross parcels and food and clothing packages from home often made the difference between hunger and starvation, especially in the later stages of the war.

As the Russian armies destroyed the Nazi empire from the east in late 1944 and early 1945, the Germans ordered thousands of Allied prisoners out of the relative safety of their camps and moved them west. A lucky few were moved from camp to camp in railway cattle trucks; the rest were marched off in the depths of winter. Long lines of unkempt, malnourished men snaked across Germany's frozen countryside in the first four months of 1945.

They slept in barns, barracks, brickworks, tents — anything; occasionally in the open, in the snow. Sometimes they were fed, the rest of the time they scrounged to supplement the meagre rations that kept them alive. Some columns occasionally received food parcels even as Germany disintegrated; others did not. Some men became desperately ill, most suffered awful dysentery, some died.

They all experienced a barbaric time that was etched into their memories for the rest of their lives.

Jack Hardie was moved out of a camp at Lamsdorf, near the Czech border, with hundreds of others in late January 1945 carrying two blankets, one of them hand-knitted, 200 French cigarettes, toilet gear, several pairs of socks and six cakes of Red Cross soap. 'I wore everything else I owned.' He needed every stitch of clothing he had. The prisoners marched in heavy falling snow and howling winds, in piercing subzero cold, and, when the thaw came, in drenching rain. 'The details all merge into a painful, cold, hungry and sometimes cruel memory,' Hardie wrote in 1991.

He walked for 11 weeks, stopping in a different place for 53 consecutive nights. Patton's Third Army overtook his column on 10 April and he was one of the first New Zealand airmen to get back to England. X-rays in New Zealand five months later disclosed he had pleurisy and tuberculosis.

Maurice Robison made it back even earlier. He was freed by the

Americans in central Germany on 30 March and flown to England and hospital on 8 April. Enduring dysentery for much of his long march, Robison still managed to keep a brief diary. On the 50th day of the trek, 12 March, he wrote, 'we have covered 700 km on foot, in very difficult wintry conditions . . . very ill and weak, big loss of weight'. After a week in a camp 'hospital' he was released, though he admitted 'still got dysentery, with blood, but can control it'. On 28 March the camp was evacuated. 'Unless they come with bayonet, I'm not leaving.' The guards were now not interested in sick POWs and vanished. Two days later the Americans arrived. 'Hard to believe we are free at last.' In England he was put into an RAF hospital and gained five stone in a few weeks.

Jim McQueen trudged across Germany in another Lamsdorf column to Ziegenhain, south of Kassel, the same camp where Robison ended up. He started out in 'a woollen singlet and woollen long johns (which I had got in clothing parcels from home), RAF shirt, woollen jersey, battledress trousers, a jacket made from RAF overcoat material and an RAF greatcoat. I wore a woollen hat with side flaps . . . that I had crocheted from wool unravelled from the tops of old socks.'

Two entries from an account McQueen wrote give a glimpse of what it was like on these horror marches in appalling weather:

28 January 1945 — One of the worst [days]. About 22 km to Peterswitz. Open country with no fences, hedges or shelter of any kind, and blowing a blizzard all day. Eyebrows iced up. At one stage the Jerries seemed to change direction as if lost. In the whiteout conditions it was impossible to tell which direction was which. No rations. Another barn [at night].

29 January — About 21 km to Goldberg through weather almost as bad as the day before. One fifth of a loaf and small piece of margarine. This was a collective farm . . . manned by Polish forced labour. The Polish people were sympathetic to our plight and allowed us to light fires to make a brew. Another barn.

One day McQueen's column encountered Jewish women in farm wagons being hauled by horses and bullocks. They were guarded by SS troops with dogs and fixed bayonets. 'As we passed, one of them sang in a clear voice in beautiful English, *It's a Long Way to Tipperary*. We had some hope of surviving the war [but] these poor half starved women in rags? Did she sing to raise our spirits or to announce that her spirit remained unbroken? Both I think. Her singing still haunts me.'

As prisoners, some aircrew saw cruelty no man ever should. Owen Foster, shot down raiding Amsterdam in May 1943, was marched out of Belaria, a Sagan-area camp, on 28 January 1945. But he and 1100 others had been on the road only four or five days when they were packed into railway cattle trucks for an all-day ride to Luckenwalde, a decaying prison camp near Berlin.

Russian tanks arrived at Luckenwalde on 22 April, and Foster and others witnessed killing and raping beyond comprehension. They dared not refuse Russian invitations to ride tanks into the nearby town. German officers and guards from the camp hung from every light pole outside the railway station. The newly freed prisoners watched Mongolian Russians drag women from houses, raping and killing, thrusting bayonets between their legs.

> A Russian soldier came for the officer I was with to see this woman because it was thought she knew where German soldiers where hiding. She was stripped naked, blood pouring down between her legs. Obviously she had been raped. She wouldn't talk so they sat her on an electric stove, turned the element on and held her there. To this day I still feel ill when I think of the smell of her burning flesh. She ended up being killed.

The officer didn't interfere. He told Foster his wife and two daughters had been raped and killed by Germans in Russia.

As well as the terrible marches, POW columns faced a frightening threat of a different kind in the spring of 1945 — attack from the air by Allied fighters. With the Luftwaffe virtually swept from the skies, thousands of British and American fighters cruised unchecked over a collapsing Germany, hitting anything that moved. Aircrew POW accounts are laced with tales of bullets and shells hitting trains and barns and other buildings where they were camped as fighters zeroed in on accompanying Germans who dared fire at them, or on nearby targets. Columns of prisoners were often mistaken for German troops on the move, sometimes with tragic results.

On 19 April, less than three weeks before V-E Day, RAF Typhoons attacked a column at Gresse, near Hamburg, leaving 30 dead and dozens maimed. Among those killed were New Zealanders Bill Watson, 30 (Auckland), and Lawrie Hope, 29 (French Pass, Marlborough Sounds). Watson had been a POW for five years. A wireless operator, he'd been captured in April 1940 when his Hampden was downed in Danish waters. Hope, rear gunner on a 75 Squadron Wellington, was rounded up after his bomber had been shot down by flak in Holland in November 1941. He was the sole survivor of his crew.

New Zealand Halifax pilot Charlie Chambers, a POW since June 1943, had a close shave when his column was attacked. Hiding behind a tree, he watched a rocket blast a deep hole in the ground nearby. As the fighters turned for another run, he leapt into the smoking hole. 'I figured rockets wouldn't hit the same place twice.' When the strafing was over he clambered out to find the nearby tree split to the base, its top blown away. Bodies were strewn everywhere.

More than 20 New Zealanders were victims of one of the most unsavoury episodes involving aircrew POWs — the infamous mistreatment of prisoners that came to be known as the Run up the Road. In July 1944, the New Zealanders were among about 700 airmen evacuated from Stalag Luft VI at Heydekrug, Lithuania, in the face of advancing Soviet armies. The men were marched a few miles to the port of Memel on the Baltic coast and packed into the holds of the ancient collier *Insterburg* without food, water or toilet facilities for a two-and-a-half-day trip at eight knots to the German port of Swinemunde, at the mouth of the Oder. A torpedo, bomb or mine would have sent the old tub to the bottom with grievous loss of life, and the terrified prisoners sweated out every hour of the journey.

On the dockside at Swinemunde the men were shackled in pairs and chained to bars in railway boxcars while a warship moored nearby fired at a stray bomber unleashing its load. Then they were taken east into Poland and offloaded at a station four or five miles from Stalag Luft IV at Gross Tychow, about halfway between Stettin and Danzig. Under a blazing sun and given no water, the men were closed up in tight ranks, still shackled. Then an insane Nazi officer, frothing at the mouth, labelled the men Terrorfliegers and urged his guards to deal harshly with them. The move to the new camp began at a fast march but the men were soon ordered to run. Snarling dogs on leashes were allowed to bite the POWs, and guards swung rifle butts and began using their bayonets. Men who fell often dragged down the mate to whom they were shackled and both were then clubbed. No prisoners were killed but later an English newspaper's outraged account said 160 prisoners had been wounded by bayonets and 90 bitten by dogs.

Handcuffs bound Christchurch bomb aimer Bob Fenton to fellow South Islander Jack Hyde. Recalls Fenton: 'Jack had a bad limp before the run, but got rid of it pretty fast that day and it's never troubled him since.' Aucklander Basil Williams suffered the indignity of a German bayonet thrust into his bum. 'It only went in half an inch but . . . cold steel was unusual for aircrew. When we arrived in a clearing I thought they were going to shoot us. All they wanted to do was to intimidate us and let us know they were the master race. They failed.'

On 6 February 1945 Fenton, Hyde, Williams and hundreds of others were moved out of the camp. During the next 86 days, before liberation by British troops, they walked to a camp at Fallingbostel, southwest of Hamburg, and then further north — 600 miles in total. John Nichol and Tony Rennell, authors of the recent book *The Last Escape*, about Allied prisoners in Germany in 1944–45, call this epic march 'one of the great — yet unrecognised — acts of heroism of the Second World War'.

At least three New Zealand bomber aircrew were made MBEs after the war for escape attempts in Germany. Warrant Officers Thor Larson, Charles Croall and Galbraith Hyde all gave their captors a huge amount of trouble and were fortunate to survive.

Larson, a navigator, was taken prisoner in June 1942 when his 150 Squadron Wellington crashed during a raid on Bremen. In September 1942, he tried, and failed, to escape from Lamsdorf, but he succeeded in June 1944 when he fled from a working party in a munitions factory after severely damaging machinery. Recaptured five days later, he was condemned to death for sabotage. However, the sentence was commuted to 10 years' penal servitude with hard labour. From September 1944 to February 1945, Larson was put to work by the Germans on deadly bomb-disposal work, some of the time in Dresden, where he was one of 11 survivors of a bombed prison. He survived another bombing and developed pneumonia before release in May 1945.

Croall, who lives in Hamilton, was captain of one of the 75 Squadron Wellingtons lost on the July 1942 Hamburg raids. He earned a reputation as an inveterate escaper. Though often unwell, he squeezed through holes cut in prison-camp fences, absconded from working parties and once emerged for a brief spell of freedom from a tunnel he helped dig. He tried to steal an aeroplane from a German airfield. Seven times he got away from the clutches of his jailers. Seven times he was recaptured. Late in the war when he was nabbed yet again, near Prague after being on the loose for a week, he ended up in the sinister concentration camp Theresienstadt, touted as a 'model Jewish town' but in reality little more than a transit point from which thousands of Jews were transferred to extermination camps. By 1945 Theresienstadt was crammed with thousands of other prisoners and conditions were extreme. Croall and other POWs, marched west by their captors in the final weeks of the war, were finally liberated by the

Americans. Croall's exploits were recognised with a glowing citation and his MBE in 1947.

Hyde's 218 Squadron Stirling, bound for the mouth of the Gironde in France, to drop mines in November 1942, crashed on the coast of the Brest peninsula near St Malo. The New Zealander was on the loose until the last day of the year, when he was betrayed and nabbed by the Germans. Thrown into Amiens prison, a Gestapo centre later blown open by pinpoint Mosquito attacks, he was interrogated for a month and threatened with death. Lodged eventually at Lamsdorf, he got into a work party near an airfield with three others and tried to steal an aircraft to fly to Sweden. The four men actually got into a Junkers 34 but were collared while trying to work out how to fly it. In January 1944 a German court martial gave them two years in a civil jail on a charge of sabotage. One of the party escaped to Switzerland, where he complained loudly, and after the Red Cross had intervened the sentence was cut to six months. Hyde served his term in a jail in a town in the Polish Corridor, and when he was finally released joined one of the marches across Germany. He died in 1994.

Gordon Woodroofe was the only New Zealand airman POW of the war to escape back to Britain from Germany. He walked off a ship to freedom in Sweden in late August 1944 and a week or so later was flown to a Scottish airfield, just three days short of the third anniversary of his capture. The magnitude of his triumph is underlined by the fact that only 33 other RAF airmen held in German POW camps matched his achievement. His feat earned him a Military Medal.

Woodroofe was the second pilot of a 104 Squadron Wellington that went down, out of fuel, in the sea after bombing Turin on the night of 11–12 September 1941. A terrifying electrical storm over France on the way home wrecked the aircraft's radio and disabled the compass. When the plane ditched the crew had no idea where they were. Astonishingly they had come down alongside two Danish fishing boats — tiny specks in the vastness of the North Sea — halfway between Denmark and England. They were taken into Esbjerg and captivity the next day.

In mid-1943 Woodroofe escaped from a working-party billet near Germany's border with Czechoslovakia and cycled all the way to southern Austria before being recaptured. Returned to Germany, he got away from another work party in August 1944. This time he rode German trains north through Breslau, Halle, Magdeburg, Hanover and Hamburg to the Baltic port of Wismar, phoney papers and his ability to speak some German getting him through. He strode aboard a Swedish coal vessel in Wismar and was hidden by seamen and carried to Sweden. He published an account of his exploits in *GeTaWay*, a title with a nice play on his initials, two years before he died in Orewa in 2000.

Phil Lamason and Buchenwald

Phil Lamason's path to Germany's infamous Buchenwald concentration camp, where his life hung by a thread, began the night after D-Day, when he was shot down over France. The last thing on his mind that night was jumping from a blazing plane. He'd been in England since 1941, flown a tour on Stirlings with 218 Squadron, won an immediate DFC for beating off fighters with some skilled flying after a trip to Pilsen, been twice mentioned in dispatches for 'bravery' and 'distinguished service' with 1657 HCU, and flown to the tough targets early in 1944 — Berlin, Leipzig, Nuremberg — as A-Flight commander with 15 Squadron. Two weeks after he was shot down he was awarded a second DFC for 'gallantry, leadership and enthusiasm' with 15.

On his last flight Lamason's Lancaster was hit while attacking a major road bridge on the outskirts of Paris, trying to bring it down onto a railway used by the Germans to bring reinforcements to the front. 'We thought it would be an easy stooge, a simple trip,' he says. He was 10 minutes from the target when a night fighter struck.

Tommy Dunk, the Rhodesian rear gunner, said suddenly, 'There's an aircraft behind us. I think it's another Lanc.' I wasn't so sure so I started to take evasive action immediately. But the fighter opened fire at the same time. I thought I'd beaten him but when I rolled over and pulled out of my dive and looked out there was a little fire burning in the middle of the starboard wing. It spread rapidly and the next minute the whole wing was on fire.

'Out, out, bale out!' Lamason yelled, holding the aircraft steady for perhaps as much as a minute as bomb aimer, wireless operator and flight engineer jumped. Before he went, the engineer nonchalantly undid Lamason's seat straps, got his chute and clipped it onto the pilot's chest. (The New Zealander found seat-type chutes uncomfortable and always swapped with one of his crew.) 'If he hadn't done that, I wouldn't have got out.'

The next moment Lamason was flung from the cockpit down the steps and into the nose as the starboard wing fell off and the plane started to spin, going down in a ball of fire, bombs still aboard. 'Chappie [Ken Chapman, the navigator] was down there, stuck, so I had to get him up and push him out — it's a funny thing the strength you have sometimes.' They got out at low altitude — 1000 feet, perhaps 2000. Lamason remembers saying to his navigator, 'My God, Chappie, you're making it short for me.' He jumped a second after Chapman and the two men floated down together. Both gunners were killed, Dunk hit in the throat by a shell, the mid-upper jumping too late.

Lamason and Chapman were sheltered by French patriots until they were captured by the Gestapo in Paris seven weeks later, when their escape line was betrayed. They were held and interrogated in the grim Fresnes prison near Paris, the same awful place where political prisoners, members of the Resistance and captured British agents were imprisoned and tortured. The Germans refused to acknowledge that Lamason, Chapman and many others like them were members of the RAF and therefore POWs, using the excuse that they were wearing civilian clothes when arrested to treat them as agents.

On 15 August 1944, five days before American forces liberated Paris, 168 Allied airmen in Fresnes, Lamason and Chapman among them, were herded aboard buses and transferred to boxcars at a Paris station. They were packed in with hundreds of other prisoners, grossly overcrowded, and when Lamason protested he was punched in the face. The men were told they were being taken to a labour camp. A hideous five-day rail journey across France and Germany delivered them to Buchenwald, at Weimar, southwest of Leipzig.

Precise figures are hard to determine but various sources suggest that more than 55,000 people died in Buchenwald, one of Germany's most notorious concentration camps. Established in 1937, it was opened as a camp for political opponents of Hitler's regime but by the end of the war held few Germans. It wasn't an extermination camp but thousands of prisoners slaving in nearby munitions plants died from disease and malnutrition. Hundreds more were killed by random acts of brutality and their bodies thrown in the camp crematorium.

Into this hellhole, on 20 August 1944, the Germans marched the shocked Allied flyers — two New Zealanders, nine Australians, 29 Canadians, 47 Britons and 81 Americans. The second New Zealander was Malcolm Cullen, who came from Maungaturoto, north of Auckland. A Typhoon pilot with 257 Squadron, a fighter-bomber unit, he'd been hit by flak while attacking a petrol dump near Amiens, France, on 24 May 1944. He'd crash-landed successfully and been on the loose until captured in Paris on 3 August.

The airmen prisoners' hair was shorn when they arrived at the camp, and the group slept in the open on cobblestones to begin with and existed on a starvation diet. Most suffered from sores and dysentery. Lamason battled these problems plus a bout of diphtheria but he was young and fit and withstood the appalling conditions well, although his weight quickly dwindled.

A squadron leader and the senior officer, Lamason emerged from Buchenwald with a giant reputation. Despite the obvious dangers he stood up to the Germans and his work as spokesman for the group, his personality, spirit and leadership skills are acknowledged in several books. In his bestselling 1952 work *The White Rabbit*, the story of celebrated British agent Wing Commander Forest Yeo-Thomas, Bruce Marshall said the Briton, also confined in Buchenwald at the time, hit it off with Lamason and helped him meet the leaders of the camp factions. One RAF man wrote later that Lamason 'epitomised all that is good in a leader and there is no doubt in my mind that his commendable, sustained effort as the front man for our group . . . was a major contributing factor in us ... getting transferred in October 1944 to a recognised POW camp'.

SS guards manned the camp but much of the prison administration was run by inmates, and Lamason quickly began to make contacts in an effort to get word to the Luftwaffe that Allied airmen were in the camp against all rules of the Geneva Convention. He had particular help from a Dutchman whom he asked to get a message out. 'I told him just to say we were here and to get us out. He achieved it but I don't know how. I never inquired and didn't want to know. I'd seen how the Germans handled people. If you didn't know something they couldn't get it out of you.'

In the latter stages of the airmen's incarceration, Lamason was told by camp sources that an order had arrived from Berlin that the entire group was to be exterminated. As he worked frantically to alert the Luftwaffe to the airmen's presence in Buchenwald, he laboured under the knowledge that he was the only airman who knew the fate planned for them.

Eventually, a message for help was smuggled to a nearby Luftwaffe airfield and the German air force came to the aid of the British and Americans. The Luftwaffe had no love for the SS, and at a high level the airmen's release was ordered. They were moved out of the camp on 19 October 1944 and taken to Sagan, where their shaven-headed, emaciated forms shocked the POWs. Two of the group never reached Sagan: an Englishman and an American died from illness in Buchenwald.

After he returned to England, Lamason was picked to command one of the 12 RAF squadrons chosen for service in the Far East against Japan — Tiger Force. But before he reached New Zealand on furlough prior to taking up this command the atomic bombs were dropped. The war was over. He was offered work by Shorts, the makers of the Stirling, and BOAC, but in the end stayed in New Zealand and went farming just outside Dannevirke. In mid-2004, at the age of 85, he was still running his farm. Cullen, also a farmer, died in September 2003.

Lamason doesn't talk much about his role in Buchenwald but has never forgotten or forgiven the conduct of the Germans there.

> It amazed me that people could be so inhuman, people from a nation that was supposed to be Christian. They hung prisoners and bet on how long the victims would continue to kick. I saw their museum while I was there — skins and heads and other bits of bodies on the walls with descriptions of what had happened to them. The inhumanity of it all amazed me.

United Kingdom airmen held in the vile camp were awarded token compensation in the mid-1960s after the British government came to an agreement with West Germany. But there was nothing for New Zealanders until May 1987, when the cabinet in Wellington approved a $250,000 fund to compensate servicemen held in German concentration camps, stating: 'This . . . will recognise the wrong suffered by imprisonment in concentration camps in breach of the Geneva Convention.' Twenty-six claimants were found eligible. Lamason was awarded $13,000, Cullen $12,000. Charles Croall also received $13,000. Lamason, however, has never been honoured by his homeland for his leading role in saving the lives of the airmen in Buchenwald — and didn't even rate a mention in Wynn Mason's official history of New Zealand POWs.

The New Zealanders who were murdered

The toss of a coin cost Bruce Hosie his life on 7 October 1944, the day 617 Squadron attacked the Kembs Barrage, a dam on the Rhine eight miles from the Swiss frontier. Because the regular wireless operator in Drew Wyness' crew had an ear infection and couldn't fly, the New Zealander took his place — after flipping with another airman to see who'd go instead. It was a fatal outcome. The Wyness Lancaster, boring in at low level in daylight to drop its 12,000-pound Tallboy against the dam gates, was hit by flak and crashed on the western side of the river. Hosie and several others who survived the crash floated away on the current in their dinghy. But two-and-a-half miles downstream four were captured — and doomed when they were handed over to a Nazi official. The airmen were machine-gunned, their bodies tossed back into the Rhine. Allied investigators arrested the perpetrator after the war but somehow he escaped from captivity and was never seen again.

Tall and handsome, Hosie was only 21 when he was murdered but was vastly experienced, having completed a tour of 25 ops with 75 Squadron, then another of 47 with the Dambusters squadron — more than any of the other 20 or so New Zealanders who served with the famous unit. The young man, born and raised in Taranaki, worked on his parents' Inaha farm after leaving Hawera High School and was barely 18 when he left to train in Canada. He was posted to 75 Squadron in September 1942 with a crew of five skippered by New Zealander Jack Bailey. Fray Ormerod, who ended the war as station navigation and operations officer at Mepal, 75's base, was the navigator. Before his death in Waikanae in 2003, Ormerod wrote that he was surprised Hosie had never been decorated despite an equivalent of three tours. 'There is no doubt whatever in my mind that Bruce should have been given a decoration. Seventy-two operations is a very large number and many people were given awards for less.'

After serving with 75, Hosie was commissioned, spent a period instructing and was then posted to 617 in January 1944, three months before his 21st birthday. He joined the crew of Jim Cooper, also newly arrived, and flew with Cooper for three months before falling sick. That began a sequence of events that was to lead to his death. While he was ill Cooper's Lancaster was shot down over Munich. Save the bomb aimer, all the crew became POWs. Had Hosie been with them he would probably have survived the war.

When he returned to operations Hosie was a spare, but Bobby Knights needed a wireless operator and Hosie linked up with him, flying with his crew throughout the summer. His last raid with Knights was in mid-September 1944, when 617 made its famous first attack on the battleship *Tirpitz* in Norway from a Russian airfield. Because of the coin toss the following month, Hosie flew the Kembs op with Wyness, a newcomer to 617 but an experienced pilot, commissioned as far back as 1941.

The Kembs raid was ordered as American troops swept towards the Rhine from France. The Allies feared that if left intact the huge sluice gates in the dam controlling the flow of water down the Rhine might be dynamited by the Germans. A great surge of water in the river at the wrong time could have a catastrophic effect on troops trying to force a crossing. The plan was for seven Lancasters — one captained by New Zealander Arthur Joplin with Loftus Hebberd, also in the RNZAF, as bomb aimer — to bomb from 8000 feet in an attempt to draw fire from the flak batteries. Six more aircraft in pairs were to sweep in from the east at 600 feet, turn up the river and plant their Tallboys, armed with 30-minute delay fuses, at the base of the dam.

Mustangs attacking the defences had little effect, and 20-mm and 37-mm flak streamed up at the low-level Lancasters, shooting two of them down. One crashed in flames, its entire crew perishing.

Official 617 Squadron historian Robert Owen says that as far as can be determined from the evidence, Wyness' aircraft was hit several times during the run-in and one engine, possibly two, set on fire. But Wyness dropped his Tallboy and managed to put the Lancaster down safely in shallow water on the western bank of the Rhine near Petit-Landau, just north of Kembs.

'Two crew ran along the wing and on to the French bank, heading off into woodland,' Owen says. 'The remaining five inflated the dinghy and began paddling down the river. A boat was sent out by the Germans to intercept them, and seeing this another crewman dived overboard and swam to the bank.'

The three who escaped into German-held French countryside were never seen again, nor were their bodies found, and it's believed they were captured by the Germans, killed and buried in unmarked graves. Hosie, Wyness, Bert Honig and Ron Williams were taken by their captors to nearby Rheinweiler, where they fell into the hands of Hugo Gruener, the local Nazi boss.

In pairs, the four men were driven downstream for some distance and then, at the water's edge, gunned down by Gruener and thrown into the Rhine. The bodies of the slain flyers were eventually recovered from the river miles from the spot where they had been summarily executed, and buried in different places. After the war investigators found all four graves and reinterred the bodies in war cemeteries, those of Hosie and Wyness in Choloy, France.

Gruener was captured by the Allies after the war but escaped from American custody in early 1947 and was never recaptured. He was convicted of murder *in absentia* in 1948 and sentenced to death. He had confessed: 'I murdered them by firing a machine-gun salvo at each of them in the back, after which each airman was dragged by the feet and thrown into the Rhine.'

The brutal killing of the Lancaster crew was a terrible end to what turned out to be a successful raid. Half an hour after the surviving bombers had turned for home the delayed-action bombs exploded, rupturing the dam gates. Water foamed out into the river and surged downstream, emptying the dam and robbing the Germans of what could have been an offensive weapon for use against a southern Rhine crossing.

Three weeks after Hosie's death a second New Zealand airman was murdered in Germany. Brian Hynes, 26, was cold-bloodedly shot to death in a wood near Cologne by SS personnel and youths from an army camp. After the war British authorities hunted down the killers and at least two of them were tried, convicted and executed.

A flight lieutenant at the time of his death, Hynes was captain of a 115 Squadron Lancaster knocked down by flak as it was approaching Cologne on a daylight raid on 28 October 1944. His was one of a force of 733 bombers, just seven of which were lost, an indication of just how weak the German day fighters had become by late 1944 under the Allied air forces' onslaught.

Hynes' bomber was hit over Leverkusen and came down in a farmyard about 12 miles northeast of the city. Hynes jumped with his bomb aimer, navigator and flight engineer, all stationed in the front of the aircraft, as the aircraft began its plunge to earth. For some reason, the wireless operator and two gunners didn't get out. When the Lancaster hit the ground its bomb load exploded, killing the farm's owner and a Polish girl working on the property. The huge explosion dug an astonishing crater 50 yards wide and 20 yards deep.

The navigator's chute didn't open and he died, but the engineer and the Australian bomb aimer landed safely. They were taken prisoner and survived the war. Hynes came down some distance away. Investigations begun soon after the war's end revealed a number of people watched his descent, and that civilians and two paratroopers living in a house near his touch-down place had raced to the spot. Toolmaker Paul Brosseder said in a statement in July 1946 that the airman drifted across his dwelling and landed in a little wood. 'When we reached [him] the soldiers took out their pistols but the airman lifted his hands immediately [and] said: "Ich nichts Amerikaner, ich nichts Englander" and showed a piece of uniform inscribed "New Zealand" which he was wearing under his flying jacket.'

Brosseder said the soldiers hadn't found any arms when they had searched Hynes, who had given his escape package to the soldiers, who in turn had handed it on to watching children. Hynes was then directed to roll up his parachute and started walking through the wood with the paratroopers towards the nearest police station.

'In this moment several SS soldiers and a few youths from [an] SS camp came, and they guided the New Zealander up the hill,' Brosseder said.

> The paratroopers then did not worry any more about the airman. When they reached the top of the hill, no one of the civilians was allowed to follow. The SS soldiers had already said that they were going to shoot him when we were still present. From the hill they went down again into the wood, passing a little wood of fir trees. We were still waiting above. Suddenly we heard a shot. Half a minute later a second one. Afterwards we went down to the spot where they had shot the airman. The SS soldiers had left the place immediately, only the youths from the camp were still present. They started immediately searching and stripping the airman. He was lying on his face and had been shot in the chest and the head. They took his boots and his flying jacket off . . . On the same day the boys of the camp buried him in the ground.

Brosseder added that Hynes' body was exhumed later by police and buried in a cemetery. His remains lie today in Reichswald Forest Cemetery.

It seems clear that many people in the area knew of Hynes' murder and talked to officials from Cologne and to police who went to the crash scene looking for bodies or survivors. An investigating officer from an RAF Missing Research and Enquiry Unit reported in March 1947 that Hynes' fate had been established beyond doubt. In June 1948 Reuters reported the execution in Germany of Peter Kloss and Georg Griesel, both 'convicted of killing Flight Lieutenant B.M. Hynes, of the Royal New Zealand Air Force when he was a prisoner of war in October 1944'.

Hynes was born on 6 June 1918 in Hong Kong, where his father worked for the colonial postal service. Hynes senior, a New Zealander, fought in the Boer War before going to Hong Kong, where he spent the rest of his working life. He was in London with his wife when World War II broke out and was killed on 11 May 1941 while serving as an air-raid warden.

The young Hynes was educated in New Zealand and was here when he joined up. He did his early flying training at Taieri and then in Canada. He was commissioned before he arrived in England in November 1942. Posted to 115 Squadron in September 1944, he was murdered three years to the day after he had enlisted.

1945

LAST MONTHS OF A LONG WAR

1945

One hundred New Zealanders serving with Bomber Command lost their lives between 1 January 1945 and the end of the war in Europe in early May, three-quarters of them killed on operations. Most of the deaths in combat occurred just as in the previous five long years — in aircraft lost without trace, in bombers hacked down by flak or enemy fighters, or as victims of midair collisions, crashes on landing, bombs from other aircraft, friendly fire or attacks by enemy intruders over English airfields. The men died in Lancasters and Halifaxes, in Mosquitoes and Boeing Fortresses of 100 Group, the bomber-support unit. They died attacking German cities and ports, railway yards, oil refineries, synthetic-petroleum plants, bridges, canals, shipyards and U-boat pens.

Compared with losses a year earlier, Bomber Command's casualties in the last few months of the war were minute — just one or two planes and a handful of men on some big raids. Germany's night-fighter forces had collapsed by the start of 1945 but Luftwaffe crews still did their best with limited means to stem the tide of bombers wrecking their country, and occasionally they managed to take a significant toll. Over Chemnitz in eastern Germany, on the night of 5–6 March, Bomber Command lost 20 of 760 attacking aircraft.

Bombing the canals

Bomber Command frequently attacked key points in the maze of canals linking Germany's rivers with her great cities, because the barge traffic on them carried millions of tons of cargo vital to the country's war effort and survival. After each raid forced labour was drafted in to repair the damage and the bombers had to return time and again. One crucial segment was that part of the Dortmund–Ems Canal, near the town of Ladbergen, where it was borne over the River Glane on two aqueducts — the Glane Bypass. It had been bombed as early as 12–13 August 1940 when

49 Squadron pilot Rod Learoyd, flying a Hampden, had earned Bomber Command's first Victoria Cross of the war.

Protection of the bypass was vital for Germany and it was heavily defended by flak. Bomber losses were often severe. On 15–16 September 1943 the Dambusters squadron lost five of eight Lancasters bombing Ladbergen at low level. Attacks intensified from September 1944, when the bypass was breached, draining water from 18 miles of the canal and stranding more than 100 barges.

On 1 January 1945, 102 Lancasters of 5 Group struck at Ladbergen while another 152 attacked the Mittelland Canal, running east–west to join the Dortmund–Ems Canal near Gravenhorst.

One of the bombers bound for Ladbergen was piloted by a young South Island farmer. Harry Denton, flying with 9 Squadron, was on just his fifth op when he took off from Bardney, Lincolnshire, at 7.44 a.m. on the daylight raid. He had no idea what was in store — or that one of his crew would win the Victoria Cross. His Lanc had an easy run to the target but what followed was nightmarish. As the last of 12 1000-pound bombs tumbled from the plane, the aircraft shook violently from two close 105-mm flak bursts.

One exploding shell blasted a hole in the bottom of the fuselage in line with the mid-upper turret, the other knocked out the port inner engine, smashed open the nose and took off the top of the cockpit, leaving only the windshield. Oil in ruptured hydraulic lines in the midsection began burning fiercely, enveloping the mid-upper turret, while flames streaming back under the fuselage from the gaping hole engulfed the rear gunner as he opened his doors and tried to bale out.

A frigid gale roaring through the cockpit revived Denton, who had been knocked out briefly, but before he regained his senses the plane plunged 2000 feet to 8000 feet. He heard the

Welsh mid-upper Ernie Potts shout 'We're on fire, skip' before the intercom went dead. Because the flak hits had damaged the cables controlling the trim tabs — small aerofoils on the trailing edges of the rudders and elevators — Denton had a huge physical struggle to manage the aircraft. 'It was a sheer battle to keep it flying straight and level — about the limit of my strength.'

The shocked bomb aimer staggered up from the nose with a partly opened chute in his arms and as he reached the cockpit floor the wind sucked the canopy from his grasp and out of the plane. But it snagged as it went and flapped along the fuselage for the rest of the trip, adding to the drag of the open bomb-bay doors.

Denton had been flying without gloves but now he needed some badly. He pulled a leather pair from the inside of his tunic but the roaring wind whipped them away from his rapidly numbing fingers and they sailed off into space. With the failure of the intercom Denton had no further contact with his crew, whom he thought were all now sheltered behind the wing spar, and was unaware of the drama going on down in the cramped fuselage. Burly wireless operator George Thompson, a Scot, braved fierce flames to get the now unconscious and badly burned Potts out of his turret. He needed all his immense strength to wrestle the man free and get him to safety past the yawning gap in the floor of the fuselage. He beat out the fire burning Potts' clothes, then went down to the rear turret to get Haydn Price, also Welsh, who had taken off his helmet before trying to bale out. Flames had surged over him, burning off his ears.

Ladbergen was only 30 miles in a direct line from the Dutch border, but the Germans still held that sector and Denton had to turn southwest and fly a long leg to get over the Rhine into Allied-held Holland. Shortly after crossing the river, the plane's handling improved when the starboard inner suddenly failed, leaving it flying on the two outer engines. But it continued to lose height and was soon down to 1000 feet.

Now a Spitfire ranged alongside, formed up protectively on the wounded bomber, and turned. Denton remembers:

It was trying to lead us back to his landing field. I followed but we were down to about 500 feet. We flew over a big plantation of trees and then I could see a huge paddock with what looked like a hedge across it and a mile before any trees, so I decided to go straight in and land. I took the diagonal to get the longest possible distance and I just forced the plane on to the ground.

Wheels up, bomb doors hanging open, the Lancaster crunched down on the snow-sprinkled Dutch field. 'We hit at about 100 mph, then slithered three-quarters of a mile. What I thought was the hedge was a line of 10-foot saplings. They didn't do much to stop the plane but trees on a culvert beyond the saplings tore the port inner right off the wing.'

When he scrambled clear of the broken plane Denton was shocked to see the badly burned Thompson, his clothes hanging in blackened tatters. The Scot managed to say 'Good landing, skipper' before collapsing. The crew were taken to a hospital near Eindhoven, where Potts died 15 hours later. Price recovered but spent two years in and out of hospital in England having his ears rebuilt. Thompson seemed likely to live but his burns proved too extensive and he died of pneumonia three weeks after the crash-landing. His posthumous Victoria Cross was hugely merited.

Denton was awarded an immediate DFC for his 'skill, courage and determination' in 'most perilous circumstances'. Briefly he had a DSO, too. 'It was gazetted in New Zealand that I had won the DSO and DFC, and the *Weekly News* so published it with my photograph.' Denton had quite a job convincing the authorities in England they had it wrong, and a squadron leader at New

Zealand air headquarters in London reprimanded him for not having his DSO ribbon up. 'I explained it all to him and he went away to check. He came back looking a bit sheepish and said, "You're right."' The mistake had occurred while recommendations for an award had been doing the rounds. Someone had urged a DSO, someone else the DFC. Both had slipped through. 'I knew from the start a mistake had been made but it took some time to sort out.'

Hugh Skilling, another South Islander, captained one of the bombers that attacked the Mittelland Canal on New Year's Day, and like Denton he put his flak-damaged Lancaster down in Allied-held territory, this time in France. None of his crew was injured but he landed with only six aboard. The seventh, a fellow New Zealander, jumped before a bale-out order was countermanded. Skilling's rear gunner, Yorkshireman Allan McDonald, remembers the night of 1 January 1945 as if it were yesterday and is still full of praise for his skipper. 'He was a marvellous pilot and it was due to him that we survived.'

The 50 Squadron Lancaster took off from Skellingthorpe, Lincolnshire, just before 5.00 p.m., when the sun had already gone down. 'We had been briefed that the Germans were moving Tiger tanks by barge and we were to try to burst the canal banks,' says McDonald. 'It was extremely dark over the target and we bombed on flares put down on the clouds by the pathfinders.'

Fighters were active and nearly got Skilling's plane. While McDonald was keeping a wary eye on the blur of a fighter behind, an unseen FW 190 suddenly attacked. 'The mid-upper screamed, "Corkscrew port, go, go!" and Hugh put it over in a split second. The 190 came from the port quarter up between us and a following Lanc and fired a rocket, which missed but exploded very close to the tail.'

The Lancaster escaped the ambush and got away without

damage, but on the way home, somewhere near Maastricht in southern Holland, it was coned by five lights, peppered by flak and took a hit which peeled away the starboard-side skin from the nose back to the engineer's seat, holed petrol tanks and punctured the starboard engines' coolant system. Both motors had to be shut down.

The intercom was knocked out but as the emergency system kicked in McDonald heard someone say 'Dougie's gone.' He shuddered, believing New Zealander Doug Cruickshank, his bomb-aimer buddy, had been killed by the flak strike. 'It wasn't until after we landed that I discovered they meant he had jumped. He'd gone before the bale-out order was reversed when Hugh got the plane out of a steep dive.'

The navigator consulted his list of emergency airfields and chose Juvincourt, near Reims, as the closest. The badly damaged Lancaster was almost out of fuel when it reached the American-held base and put down on the steel-mat runway at 9.15 p.m. McDonald: 'Hugh warned us as we went in, "I can't tell you whether the tyres are burst or not but we're not in very good shape so just expect anything. I'll do the best I can." He made a perfect landing.'

The crew were ferried home the next day, to be joined joyously and fortunately six days later by Cruickshank. He'd landed in German-held territory but got through to United States lines. Not understanding his accent, the Americans accused him of being a German spy masquerading as an RAF airman and threatened to shoot him. He was close to facing a firing squad by the time he convinced the Americans he was genuine, McDonald says.

An awful start for 75 Squadron

1945 began disastrously for 75 Squadron. Commanding officer Ray Newton, a New Zealander, was killed on New Year's Day, three weeks after arriving to take over from compatriot Jack Leslie. He died during a raid on the Ruhr, his Lancaster crashing with great violence in a farm orchard near Valkenburg in the far south of Holland. No one parachuted from the doomed bomber before it crashed and gouged a hole 15 feet deep. The blast destroyed all vestiges of the men inside, save for some remains of the English mid-upper gunner, which were identifiable. Newton and the rest, fellow New Zealander Dick Aitchison among them, are named on the Runnymede Memorial.

Newton had completed a tour on Wellingtons with 75 early in 1942 as a flight commander and had won a DFC. After later service in India and New Zealand he returned to England in July 1944, groomed for 75. He flew an op in his new job on 28 December and then on the first day of 1945 chose to go with Aitchison and his men, a newly arrived crew.

The New Zealanders presented a clear contrast — Newton, a battle-hardened veteran of almost 50 ops, second pilot Aitchison making his operational debut after 10 months' training. They had been born within three weeks of each other in 1916, Aitchison in Onehunga, Newton in Christchurch. Newton, a commercial traveller before the war, enlisted in April 1940 while Aitchison, married for more than three years when war broke out, joined up in July 1942. A storeman working for Dominion Breweries in Otahuhu when he enlisted, Aitchison was on ground duties until posted for pilot training at Harewood in March 1943. He was commissioned before leaving New Zealand the following October, farewelled by his wife, Olga, and two small daughters — Heather, six, and Patricia, five. They never saw him again.

The Newton–Aitchison Lancaster took off from Mepal just before 4.00 p.m. to attack railway yards at Vohwinkel, near Wuppertal. The force of the explosion when it crashed suggests its bomb load was still aboard but it isn't known whether the plane was the victim of a fighter, flak or something else, perhaps even friendly fire. It is certain that American anti-aircraft fire

from Namur, southeast of Brussels, Belgium, hit and destroyed
two homebound Lancasters also on the Vohwinkel raid. One,
a 115 Squadron aircraft, crashed and exploded in a field near
Namur, killing its eight crew including second pilot Joe Sterling,
23 (Matakohe, Northland), who was flying his seventh op. It was
bad enough losing your life as the war entered its final stages,
but it was a cruel fate to die at the hands of your allies. Trigger-
happy Americans manning anti-aircraft batteries claimed not
inconsiderable numbers of RAF bombers in the last months of
the conflict, although it wasn't only the Americans at fault. Royal
Navy and British land-based anti-aircraft guns accounted for a
good number of own bombers during the war, and Bill Chorley
records, for example, that a coastal battery in Essex shot down
an RCAF Halifax on the night of 5–6 March 1945, killing all eight
crewmen.

One New Zealander definitely blown out of the sky by
American fire in the final months of the war lived to tell the
tale. The 199 Squadron Stirling carrying wireless operator Alan
Twaddle was clawed down while flying radio-countermeasures
duties in France just south of Luxembourg near the front lines
on the night of 5–6 March. The Americans hit LJ617-E (Easy)
with a heavy-calibre shell armed with a proximity fuse. Twaddle,
who lives in Tauranga today, didn't know then that American fire
had claimed them. Otherwise he might have given the American
medical staff who cared for him next day more of his tongue
than he did.

We were stooging along at 15,000 feet and I was waiting for my
7.30 p.m. half-hourly broadcast from group headquarters when
there was one almighty great crash. I heard the rear gunner
yelling on the intercom that the starboard outer and part of the
wing were on fire and that flames were trailing back beyond
his turret. At the same time petrol began to spray over me from

fractured fuel lines running across the interior of the fuselage. The flight engineer, the walls and floor were doused too.

When the engineer told Canadian pilot 'Tiny' Thurlow (six feet four inches and 18-plus stone) he couldn't isolate the break and stop the fuel spewing out, the skipper ordered his men to jump. Twaddle, chute on, was crouched at an escape hatch ready to go when the plane exploded. The next moment he was in cold air, 100 yards from the Stirling, flying horizontally, still crouching and watching the plane burning fiercely as it went down.

Soaked in petrol, Twaddle was flash-burned as the aircraft blew up before the blast snuffed out the flames. He was badly burned on the face and hands and was swaddled in bandages next day, but not enough to leave scars. Everyone but Thurlow survived. E (Easy), the last Stirling lost by Bomber Command, crashed near Thionville, France.

Twaddle remembers landing with a bone-jarring crunch in a frozen ploughed paddock but nothing more until daylight, when he found himself in a roadside ditch. An American patrol picked him up and took him to a tented hospital for treatment. Suffering from pain, exhaustion and shock, he wasn't in great shape for questions.

'Name?'

'Twaddle.'

'Spell it, please.'

'T-W-A-D-D-L-E.'

'OK, Twiddle.'

'No, Twaddle.'

'Yes, that's what we've got — Twiddle.'

The conversation went downhill from there.

I was starting to go into secondary shock, my fuse got shorter and I started to yell. I was told all about it later. It appears I

shouted 'A for Apple' over and over, with, I am sorry to say, a
number of descriptive phrases concerning the medical staff's
breeding and personal habits.

Plasma calmed him down, stopping the shaking, shivering
and teeth-chattering, and he was treated royally. The mummy-
dressings stayed on for a week and then he was flown back to
England to an RAF hospital for seven weeks.

On leave a couple of months later, Twaddle visited a Cotswolds
pub one day with the English woman who was to become his wife.
They met an American and talked over a drink. The American
told them he'd met only one other New Zealander — an airman
in a hospital in France who had ranted on about apples.

Bombs gone and then . . .

Pilot Keith Beattie had an amazing war — a little bit of almost
everything. He enlisted early, in 1940, trained in New Zealand and
Canada, did eight ops on Wellingtons with 115 Squadron, then
flew to the Middle East expecting to go to India, got no further
than Cairo, bombed Rommel's troops as he flew a tour, returned to
England, instructed for 18 months, and then, in November 1944,
was posted to pathfinders on 635 Squadron at Downham Market,
Norfolk. To cap it all, when the war was almost over he was shot
down, a sole survivor and fortunate not to be murdered.

Beattie was on his 17th op with 635, marking Chemnitz,
40 miles southwest of Dresden, on the night of 5–6 March 1945,
when his Lancaster was smashed out of the sky. The bomber,
among the van of an armada of 760 aircraft, was called in by the
master bomber to drop sky markers over the target. 'We went in
right on time, dropped the markers, and I remember the bomb
aimer saying "Bombs gone." I leant down to close the bomb-bay
doors with the lever to my left and that's all I remember.'

Beattie is certain they were hit by another aircraft. He isn't sure what type or whose but thinks a night fighter slammed head-on into the starboard wing, ripping it off — the force was much too great for anything else. Although restrained by his seat belt, Beattie was thrown against the instrument panel and knocked out. When he came to he was pinned, the plane spinning down. The intercom was dead and he didn't see any of his crew again.

'I just couldn't move, couldn't do a thing. Then the aircraft started to break up. The starboard wing had obviously gone and once the port wing came off the spinning stopped.' In a desperate last bid to escape, Beattie heaved himself out of his seat, opened the window and pushed himself out. There was no chance of getting down to open the nose escape hatch. 'I seemed to hear a voice saying, "Get out the window, get out the window."' Normally that would have been a suicidal leap into the propellers, but they were gone. 'It took a bit of manoeuvring to get out but I don't remember actually leaving or pulling the rip cord.' But he did and floated down right into the middle of the target at the start of a major, 15-minute Main Force raid. 'I was fairly shocked but the noise of the bombs was indescribable.'

Beattie had a soft landing in falling snow, his chute settling over a splintered tree in a square, and threw himself into a bomb crater. He didn't want to be caught by angry civilians, so five minutes before the bombing was due to end he floundered through the snow to a block of nearby flats, scuttled inside and climbed several flights of stairs into an attic, the end of which had been blown off. Looking out into the square he could see heavy snow had covered his footprints and felt reasonably safe in what turned out to be a deserted building. Rummaging around, he found curtains and wrapped himself up to try to keep warm. He stayed there all next day while fires raged unchecked in the neighbourhood because the water mains had been ploughed up by bombs. At dusk he left the building and joined a file of people leaving town, inconspicuous enough in the stained flying overalls he always wore, zipped up high over his battledress.

Beattie had been on the go for about 10 minutes, trudging up a rise, when he saw something that shocked him to his core. There, in the remains of a block of dwellings, was the wreck of his Lancaster. 'She had ploughed in nose first. I knew it was mine. I could read the squadron code and the numbers — PB921. She was buried well up the fuselage. The tail and rear turret were still attached. She hadn't burned because the wing tanks had gone.'

Beattie walked on, stunned. The longer he walked the fewer people there were, and in falling snow he became sodden and desperately cold. In such conditions he had no chance of getting 80 miles east to the Russian lines and little hope of survival in the open. By now he could hardly see the road.

Trying to find someone to whom he could surrender safely, he trudged back to a small village.

> It was a tricky situation. I didn't want to give myself up to hostile civilians. I was pondering what to do when a door opened and in the light I saw a soldier. He picked up a push-bike and came out through the gate. I went up to him, spoke, and he soon cottoned on. The armed soldier called out and a woman came out of the house. He motioned to me to walk along in front of them. She talked to him very loudly and angrily and I could tell what she was saying quite easily. She wanted him to shoot me. He could have done so and said I was trying to escape.

Luck was on Beattie's side. The soldier ignored the woman's entreaties and marched his captive back to town to his barracks. Several days later Beattie was collected up with other prisoners and taken off to a POW camp.

Flying the Fortresses

214 (Federated Malay States) Squadron was a prominent 3 Group squadron for much of the war but in January 1944 it was transferred to 100 [Bomber Support] Group as a radio-countermeasures (RCM) squadron, carrying electronic equipment for broadcasting signals to confuse the enemy. When it moved it converted to American Fortresses — B17s — the mainstays of the US 8th Army Air Force in England. The term 'Flying Fortress' was coined by a headline writer on a Seattle newspaper when Boeing rolled out the big bomber in July 1935, and the plane was registered as such, but the Allies used the single word 'Fortress'.

A small batch of early-model Fortresses — B-17Cs — was delivered to the RAF in the first six months of 1941 and tried operationally with 90 Squadron. They proved a failure and Fortresses disappeared from Bomber Command until January 1944, when 214 Squadron began equipping itself with the later B-17Gs for their RCM mission. The Fortress could carry only half the bomb load of a Lancaster but its layout and space were ideal for the bulky radio gear, as well as a 10th crew member — the specialist equipment operator. The Fortress had a higher ceiling than the Lancaster and Halifax — a useful feature for some RCM ops.

During the war 33 New Zealanders died while attached to 214 Squadron, 10 of them in Fortresses — four in 1944, the rest in 1945. 214 flew 1225 Fortress sorties in 1944–45, from Sculthorpe, Norfolk, and nearby Oulton, losing a total of 13 aircraft. One of the lost bombers meant captivity and the end of the war for three South Islanders. Russell 'Doug' Douglas, Bill Lovell-Smith and Joe Cuttance leapt from their blazing plane over the Black Forest, just short of the French frontier, on 14–15 March 1945.

The three New Zealanders lived in Christchurch before the war, Douglas and Cuttance serving together in the Air Training

Corps before enlisting. These two began training as pilots but remustered as gunners in Canada. Cuttance remembers Douglas suggesting that if they became gunners they'd be on ops in six months, and that's what happened. They reached England in February 1944, met up with bomb aimer Lovell-Smith, who'd been a bit ahead of Douglas at Christchurch Boys' High School, and crewed up. Cuttance says their team was to have gone to India to fly Mitchells, but skipper Norman Rix, an Englishman, was apparently too short to fly a Mitchell easily so the crew was posted to 214.

They did their first operation in mid-August, and by the time they jumped seven months later they had completed 38 trips, roaming all over the continent transmitting phoney radio signals, blasting out walls of sound and radar signals, dropping reams of *Window* to deceive the Germans — generally trying to make life difficult for the enemy radar and night-fighter controllers. Sometimes they succeeded brilliantly, as an HQ message copied into Douglas' logbook after a *Window* spoof raid near Saarbrucken on 9 November 1944 shows: 'Our aim was amply achieved in that the enemy was induced to react in a very big way indeed, first in the threatened area until he eventually became aware he was being spoofed after the *Windowers* had returned, and then in the Ruhr area when he believed a real raid was to follow the spoof.' Complex electronic mind games were being played with high stakes.

During their months together, Douglas at the rear and Cuttance in the big turret atop the fuselage at the back of the cockpit fired a few rounds from their .5-inch machine-guns but their plane didn't run into much trouble. However, they watched other bombers on fire or blowing up. One night Douglas saw three or four go down and thought, 'Christ, a guy could get killed doing this.' But the Rix crew sailed through a first tour of 33 ops, finishing on 3 February 1945, then volunteered for a second. Another five trips and — *finis*. Their Fortress was destroyed after playing its role in an attack on a synthetic-oil plant at Lutzkendorf, 100 miles southwest of Berlin. Heading home on a great south and west circle that would have brought them to the French border near Strasbourg, the aircraft was hit.

Douglas thinks flak got them. Looking back up the fuselage he could see through a whopping gash in the fuselage that one of the port engines was burning. Lovell-Smith wrote years later that the aircraft had been hit by flak and five minutes later by a fighter. 'The kite gave three or four shudders that were obviously hits from a fighter, and Norm corkscrewed away immediately.'

Perched in his high turret, Cuttance had the best view of the spreading flames, an engine on fire on each wing.

> I called the captain and said, 'I tell you what, there are tongues of fire coming up through the wings, through the rivet holes over the main fuel tanks; we're liable to blow at any stage.' Norm called the navigator and asked how long to Strasbourg on the Rhine [to parachute into Allied-held territory]. Eight minutes. We couldn't have kept going that long.

One by one the crew baled out, Douglas thankful he'd had his harness tightened before takeoff. Under his chute, Lovell-Smith watched the Fortress plunge earthward and saw the colours of the day burst skyward, the flames firing the cartridges in the Very pistol positioned in the roof of the fuselage.

75 Squadron's last losses

21 March 1945 was a bad day for 75 Squadron. Three of its Lancasters were brought down over Munster, just north of the Ruhr, on a daylight raid, 12 of the 21 crewmen losing their lives. Six of the dead were New Zealanders. At this late stage in the war 75 didn't expect to lose three bombers on a single op. In fact

these were the last aircraft losses suffered by the squadron in its five years of operations. Particularly distressing was the news that popular skipper Jack Plummer, a decorated veteran on his 30th and probably final op, was among the missing. A ripple of genuine sadness spread through the squadron.

What made everything worse was the knowledge that the operation had been an utter cockup. One hundred and sixty 3 Group Lancasters, 21 of them from 75 Squadron, had been detailed to bomb the railway yards and a viaduct at Munster. According to navigator and Southlander 'Tiny' Humphries, the leaders from 75 overshot the target, flew on and then turned back to bomb — on the wrong course. The New Zealand bombers met a hail of heavy flak and bombs falling from planes overhead. Flak claimed Plummer's Lancaster but bombs hit and destroyed the aircraft in which wireless operator Arthur 'Shorty' Robson was flying and probably shattered the third Lanc, which exploded. The three 75 Squadron bombers were the only losses on the raid.

Plummer's death devastated Humphries, who'd flown with the Wellington man throughout their tour. They'd shared a lot of close shaves and tough trips, none more so than the moment over Duisberg on a daylight sortie on 14 October 1944 when flak smashed into the Lancaster's nose at 21,500 feet. The windows in the cockpit blew out, and as the plane went into a steep dive Humphries shook hands with the wireless operator, convinced the end was close. But Plummer pulled the bomber out at 1500 feet and flew home at that altitude. Plummer, dressed only in light battledress, suffered dreadfully from the cold and his hands were frostbitten. Rescuers rushed to the Lancaster as it landed and the story goes that the stick had to be sawn off to release the pilot's hands because they were frozen to it. Humphries smiles about that but lauds Plummer as a great pilot — 'the best'.

Plummer didn't lose any fingers but was off flying for three months. The rest of the crew threatened mutiny when it was suggested they get another skipper. Says Humphries: 'We knew Jack was going to come back sooner or later and we were going to wait on him. We made that clear.' Apart from a trip or two with the CO they didn't go on ops while Plummer was mending. Plummer was awarded the DFC for getting them home and Humphries the DFM for navigating them sans papers, blown away in the freezing gale that whistled through the homebound plane.

On the Munster raid that cost Plummer his life the Lancaster took a direct flak hit on the starboard outer. 'The engine fell off the wing, because I saw it fall off,' Humphries declares. The port outer was on fire too, and the plane had clearly been fatally hit.

> One of the rules we had was that on the run-in to the target everyone who could put on a chute. I'd left my position and was standing alongside the flight engineer, chute on, when we got the order to go out. Jock [Holloway, the bomb aimer, from Christchurch] was trying to get the jammed hatch open. Then we went into a spin. I remember my feet leaving the floor, then nothing more until I was in the air and falling free.

Humphries thinks that as the starboard wing came off it tore a great hole in the fuselage through which he, the flight engineer and the wireless operator were tossed alive. The only other survivor was New Zealand rear gunner 'Mac' MacDonald, 23 (Lauder, Central Otago), who parachuted out of the back. Crews on other aircraft saw the wing come off and parachutes appear. The Germans saw them too and were waiting when Humphries and the others landed. Plummer, 29, Holloway, 29, and mid-upper gunner Russell 'Scotty' Scott, 23 (Dunedin), went down with the Lancaster.

Shorty Robson, from Dunedin — all five feet four inches of him — could hardly have had a briefer time with 75 Squadron. He arrived at Mepal with his crewmates on 19 March, flew a daylight op to Hamm the next day and was knocked down by own bombs on the 21st. 'There's not a hell of a lot of red ink in my log [noting my ops],' he chuckles. Five of the crew, including Robson and New Zealand navigator Arthur 'Bake' Baker, survived. New Zealand pilot Alf Brown, 25 (Dunedin), and bomb aimer Jimmy Wood, 29 (Christchurch), perished.

A bomb or bombs hit the front of the aircraft. One knocked the nose right off taking Wood with it as he huddled over his bombsight. 'There was a massive explosion and the *Window* the flight engineer was throwing out was whirling through the aircraft.' Robson had already seen what he thinks was the third 75 Lancaster going down — 'the one in which they were all killed [including navigator Arthur Oakey, 33, a married man with two young sons, who had been living in Dannevirke when he enlisted]. It was all buckled up, hit right in the bloody middle.' Now the same thing was happening to his own bomber. He could see one engine poking up, another hanging down. Ordered out, he recalls telling his skipper 'I'm ready to go, Alf' and Brown replying 'OK'.

> I think he was holding it up for us. Bake was right behind me and gave me a boot in the arse and said, 'Get out there, you little bugger!' I looked around as I was jumping from the rear door to see Bake going back up the fuselage. When we were put together in the same German cell a day or two later I asked him why and he told me that he realised he didn't have his harness on. He had his chute with him but had forgotten he'd removed his harness earlier to tighten it up and hadn't put it back on.

Robson, who lives in Motueka, and Baker, a school principal in Auckland, kept in touch until the latter died in 1992. 'We'd get together every now and then and we'd always get into trouble when we did.' Not surprising.

A New Zealand pilot in 617 Squadron dies

Barnie Gumbley, 29, killed the same day as Plummer, was the pilot of one of 20 Lancasters from 617 Squadron attacking the Arbergen railway bridge just outside Bremen. His was the only bomber lost on a successful mission that blew out two piers.

Gumbley, raised at Fernhill, Hastings, was working as a movie projectionist when he enlisted in August 1941. His family travelled Hawke's Bay–East Coast showing films in small town halls. Trained in New Zealand, he was posted to 49 Squadron, a 5 Group Lancaster unit, in late October 1942 and flew 33 ops to targets all over Germany and Italy. Awarded an end-of-tour DFM and then commissioned, he instructed until he was posted to 617 in September 1944. He flew 18 times with the Dambusters.

Gumbley's body was never found, and neither were those of the other men aboard the Lancaster, which was carrying a 12,000-pound Tallboy. However, quite a lot is known about the final moments of the aircraft's flight. PD117-L (Love) took off from Woodhall Spa at 7.45 a.m. on 21 March and was over the target area at 10.00 a.m. Flying low at 2000 feet the Lancaster took direct flak hits and, streaming flames, crashed in a field about seven miles from the bridge.

A Missing Research and Enquiry Unit (MREU) conducted an intense investigation after the war trying to establish what had happened to the bodies. RAF officers interviewed more than 60 witnesses, some of them twice, in an effort to establish the truth. They were told that PD117, flying unusually slowly, was hit in an engine and in the fuselage by local flak batteries, strikes that began a fire. The aircraft turned sharply, lost all its height in the next 30 seconds and then crashed.

Villagers living in Okel raced for the site but before they could reach the burning wreckage a violent explosion shook the countryside as the Tallboy exploded. The blast reduced the plane to fragments and dug a crater 60 feet deep and 100 feet in diameter. According to some witnesses Luftwaffe salvage teams removed bodies or parts of bodies for burial. The MREU scoured the country for miles around but was never able to identify any burial site, although the investigation went on intermittently for several years. In 1949 Gumbley's family was notified that nothing more could be achieved. His name and those of his crewmen are recorded on Runnymede's panels.

The final raid

Bomber Command's final act of war took place on the night of 2–3 May 1945, when 8 Group Mosquitoes swooped on long-suffering Kiel — a last attack following reports that the Germans might be assembling ships there to take troops to Norway for a defiant stand.

New Zealanders had been in action from day one of the long air war, and they were still in action on this final strike. One of them was pilot Allan George, who had volunteered in September 1939, enlisting a year later at age 22 from his parents' Taranaki farm. Trained at Bell Block and Ohakea, George was in England by May 1941 and on 115 Squadron a few weeks later. He survived the early era of Wellington ICs that couldn't get much above 12,000 feet carrying bombs, and won the DFC and DFM during a fine tour of 33 ops.

His worst moment was over Essen in October 1941, when flak fractured the main fuel line. Petrol flooded into the fuselage, poured down the catwalk and sprayed out of the aircraft. Both engines stopped. Quick-thinking wireless operator Viv Broad, a Londoner, grabbed bandages from the medical kit and bound up the hole. By the time the motors picked up the bomber was in searchlights and down to 4000 feet, but it got away and reached home to crash-land near Norwich.

Tour over in May 1942, George instructed, attended a staff-college course, and was then posted back to New Zealand to command a training unit near Blenheim. But he succeeded in getting back to England in September 1944, volunteered for pathfinders and went to 139 Squadron to fly Mosquitoes. He dropped flares and target indicators for Main Force raids and when he wasn't doing that flew to Berlin with 4000-pounders. Over the German capital one night he narrowly escaped death from the cannon shells of an Me 262. His onboard radar detected the jet at the last moment, the winking yellow light on his panel just giving him time to ram the stick forward and drop. 'The Messerschmitt shot over the top of me, guns firing. He missed.'

George flew 40 ops with 139 on a punishing two-nights-on, one-night-off routine, every one with Broad, who had trained as a navigator while George was in New Zealand.

> On our night off we went down to the pub, had a few beers, wrote letters, went to bed early. Then back on ops. Sometimes you'd sit and look around at your cobbers and think, 'We aren't all going to be here tomorrow. I wonder who it'll be.' We might not have any casualties for a while and then, suddenly, one or two. They'd just disappear . . . but we didn't dwell on it. We lived for the moment, for the day; lived to the fullest. We never thought of tomorrow.

As George's Mosquito, cookie tucked up in the bomb bay, roared down the runway at Upwood, Huntingdonshire, late in the evening of 2 May 1945, the CO's words at briefing rang in his ears: 'Well, boys, this is the last time you'll fly. Get home tonight and you're through the war.' The emotion surrounding that last flight still floods back 60 years on. 'Jesus,' George says. 'All the bloody war and to be told that. One more. Will I make it?' They were all scared stiff that night, those 139 Squadron airmen. But they dropped their bombs, the last, and all came home safely to Upwood. For them the war *was* over and they were still alive. They had survived.

Flying accidents

Two hundred and fifty New Zealanders lost their lives in flying accidents while serving in Bomber Command. It was bad enough being lost in combat, killed in the air by enemy shot or shell, but to come from the far side of the world to get to grips with the Germans and die in an accident seemed so unfair, so pointless.

Flying by its nature is hazardous. In World War II, an age away now in terms of aviation development and air-traffic control, flying was just plain dangerous. Under the exigencies of the time, flying-accident deaths were to be endured, sad but inevitable. Accidents caused by bad weather, the huge numbers of aircraft flying, inexperience, mistakes, aircraft defects and other factors took 8000 lives in Bomber Command during the war years.

Skies are always blue in Battle of Britain movies. In reality the weather was often just plain awful and caused countless crashes. But poor flying conditions were only part of a lethal mix. Wartime Britain had hundreds of operational airfields and the air was usually thick with planes. Many were flown by inexperienced crews or crews under instruction. Mistakes were made, even by instructors. The wrong switches were pushed or pulled, fuel lines were closed off in error at critical times. Pilots made fatal errors or got too low, navigators lost their way, and planes slammed into hillsides or flew out to sea and simply disappeared.

Because frontline squadrons needed the best aircraft available, OTUs often flew combat-scarred hand-me-downs. Many New Zealanders in Bomber Command, especially in the early years of the war, learned to fly on clapped-out Wellingtons. Stirlings, Halifaxes and Lancasters used for training were sometimes battered, worn out and hard to operate.

OTU maintenance could be sloppy. Engines faltered at critical moments, caught fire or shed propellers. Controls failed, wings fell off. Burning aircraft came down from great heights or crashed when they flamed at low level. Some planes belly-landed, others crunched in nose first. Some hit the ground with their wings before cartwheeling in balls of fire. Planes crash-landed on airfields, on farmland, in forested areas. They demolished airfield buildings, fell on houses, pubs and factories in town and countryside, ploughed through crops, killed stock, smashed through stone walls, had wings and engines wrenched off and came to rest in ditches, against trees, on roads, or even, in one famous case, in a railway cutting with a passenger express bearing down.

Sometimes aircrew emerged from wrecks with a few scratches and a shaking; others were pulled out with shattered limbs and internal injuries that ranged from minor to life-threatening. Many were killed outright or burned to cinders.

Inexperienced crews were most at risk — on early flights after crewing up, doing 'circuits and bumps' (takeoffs and landings) at night, or winging away into the blackness on long cross-country training exercises in less-than-ideal weather. The toll was frightening and many crews never made it to operational squadrons. The saddest cases involved veterans who had survived many ops only to lose their lives in training crashes while instructing.

Bomb aimer Adrian 'Shorty' Carson perished teaching someone else just as his war was about to finish. Carson, 32, from the little farming community of Brunswick, north of Wanganui, was a key member of a close-knit crew with three other New Zealanders — Hilton Williams, Trevor Dill and Ivon Kaye. They did a tough tour with 75 Squadron and then volunteered for pathfinders with 7 Squadron at Oakington, Cambridgeshire. In early May 1944 they were on the verge of finishing at 7.

On the morning of 5 May Carson went up with a new crew in a Lancaster skippered as it happened by another New Zealander, Ian Bennington, 34 (Masterton), with Cecil Todd, 22 (Palmerston North), in the rear turret. 'He just went up to show them how to work the H_2S radar equipment in the aircraft,' Dill remembers. 'I'd been up the day before and Shorty said, "Oh, I'll go up today." And damn me, they got caught in a big thunderstorm and iced up.' At 10.40 the Lancaster emerged from cloud in a high-speed dive and plunged to earth near

Rugby, Warwickshire. Eight dead, no survivors. 'Shorty hadn't even taken a parachute.' Carson, Bennington and Todd lie side by side in Botley Cemetery, Oxford.

Carson's loss devastated his friends, but just the same they flew to Nantes, France, two nights later to bomb an aircraft-repair works — the first time they'd flown without their mate. Says Dill: 'But we'd had enough and I think they [senior officers] knew, and after that op, our 20th on 7, they said we had finished and sent us on leave.'

Luck rode with some men, deserted others. Consider Rae Simpson and Ivan Styles. Simpson, brought up on a farm near Ruawai, south of Dargaville, enlisted in May 1942, trained in Canada and joined 77 Squadron in Yorkshire as a bomb aimer. On 9 December 1943 he and his crew went up in a brand-new Halifax on a training flight. Simpson told his younger brother after the war that the rudders jammed. The bomber crashed from 8500 feet near York at 11.05 that morning, Simpson and wireless operator Jimmy Clark, a Scot, the only survivors.

Just before his death in 2004, Simpson wrote about the terrifying few moments as the Halifax went down in an ever-quickening, almost vertical spiral dive. At 3000 feet the pilot wrestled the plane into a flat spin, breaking the pressure pinning the crew. In the one chance he had Simpson heaved himself six feet to the escape hatch and followed Clark out at about 1500 feet. Seconds later he was down and not badly hurt, but for the rest of his life he was haunted by the last words of his Canadian pilot, Ken Forrest: 'We are out of control, am crashing, am crash . . .'

Fate was on Simpson's side once more seven weeks later when he baled out again, this time over Germany during a raid on Magdeburg, this time the only survivor. A night fighter's cannon fire ripped through the Halifax. 'Baled out at 10,000 feet,' Simpson wrote afterwards. 'The terrible whistling noises and swooshing of falling bombs around me as I floated down were quite unnerving.' He landed at 12.20 a.m. on 21 January 1944 and was captured two days later.

Gunner Ivan Styles survived both a crash-landing and a takeoff crash and was then killed in a third crash — before he even reached a squadron. Born in Dunedin in 1915, Styles was working as a salesman and display artist in Wellington when he enlisted in mid-1941. Posted to 11 OTU at Westcott, Buckinghamshire, he did one op — to Bremen, while training, on 13–14 September 1942. His Wellington crash-landed on return but he walked away uninjured. He did so again the next day when another Wellington crashed on takeoff. Exactly a month later, however, Styles was killed when his Wellington, on a night cross-country exercise, dived into the ground in Nottinghamshire and burst into flames. The rest of the crew, all New Zealanders, died too.

Crashes often occurred with frightening suddenness. Rear gunner Hec Frew and the rest of his crew — five other New Zealanders and an English flight engineer — were at 1657 HCU, Stradishall, Suffolk, when their Stirling crashed on the airfield shortly after 3.00 a.m. on 20 April 1944. Frew, who came off a farm in Doubtless Bay in the Far North, and mid-upper Frank Hudson (Kaipara Flats) were the only survivors. Killed were pilot Jock Gold, 23 (Dunedin), navigator Murray Aitken, 21 (Wellington), bomb aimer Goff Weston, 22 (Nelson), and wireless operator Doug De Laney, 20 (Hikurangi). They had been posted to 75 Squadron and were due to go to Mepal the next day.

'It all happened in a few seconds, but they were a long few seconds,' Frew says. He likens their fatal plunge to the shooting of a pheasant or duck. 'We were flying along under control and suddenly we weren't. We were falling like a stone.' For some reason a couple of motors failed as they came down for a landing, the plane stopped flying, went in at an angle of about 45 degrees, and crashed on the runway right in front of the control tower. Gold had time only to shout 'Crashing!' before impact. That was his last word. The aft portion of the aircraft, carrying Frew and Hudson, went up and forward as the bomber hit, and then whipped back, crashing down onto the ground. The force flicked the rear turret right off the fuselage. With Frew inside, it flew through the air and then rolled along the ground. The crash was followed instantly by clouds of smoke, explosions, and then a huge fire as the wing tanks went up. Hudson staggered clear, somehow unscathed but those in the front section never had a chance. Frew found himself out of his turret with a damaged spine and part of his scalp hanging over his eyes.

Now living in Rotorua, Frew remembers that Hudson got to him first but that of all the witnesses to the crash the only one who rushed to offer aid was a WAAF, who flung herself over him to protect him from flames and exploding ammunition. Then an ambulance arrived. Frew spent several months in hospital, then saw out the war on non-flying ground duties at Stradishall.

He seems to have expected some disaster. He wrote in a family memoir years later that it had dawned on them at OTU that their chances of surviving training and bombing operations were 'very slim'. He'd only met one gunner who'd done as many as two tours and he was well aware of Bomber Command's heavy operational losses. While he was at his HCU awaiting posting, an aircraft failed to return from a training flight over the North Sea one night. His crew took part in the fruitless search. Two nights later a crew they knew flew into a barrage-balloon cable and lost a wing. The men parachuted. 'Now the dreaded crashes-happen-in-threes superstition took hold,' he wrote. Two nights later his Stirling crashed.

But Frew also recalls the good times and the joy of flying on fine sunny days. 'The startling brightness of the sun shining on banks of white clouds. Above, the blue of the sky extended for ever. The whole crew relaxed in the safety of daylight and the warmth of the sun. A world exclusive to airmen.'

Bomber Command and its men suffered a thousand crashes like Frew's. The frightening impact, the flames — and death. The sad and awful aftermath. The clearance of wreckage. The recovery of broken and charred bodies. The sad, slow march of airmen accompanying coffins on gun carriages to local cemeteries for the burial of Commonwealth aircrew. The dispatch of coffins by rail to all parts of the United Kingdom for the committal of bodies, or what was left of bodies, in hometown cemeteries. Words by chaplains, volleys of shots, more fresh graves.

The RAF investigated all loss-of-life crashes but because there were so many inquiries they had to be done quickly. The results of some are still disputed. One involves New Zealand Lancaster pilot Bill Shirley, 22, who died with all his crew when their bomber ploughed into an Essex wheat field and exploded on 23 September 1944. Shirley, nine ops behind him, two of them for his then current squadron, 582 (a pathfinder unit operating from Little Staughton, Bedfordshire), was killed on a fighter-affiliation flight — a work-out between fighter and bomber.

An Englishman who saw the crash as an eight-year-old and who later joined the RAF himself has spent years researching it. He and Shirley's relatives in New Zealand believe the finding of 'pilot error' was wrong. They are satisfied PB512 had been damaged earlier and that something failed under the stress of the exercise. Research is also said to have uncovered other factors that tend to clear the pilot.

The Shirley family has been told the court of inquiry was perfunctory in the execution of its duties with no examination of the wreckage, no eyewitnesses and no mention in its report of input from 582 Squadron maintenance. One of the most extraordinary aspects of what happened is that the regular rear gunner did not fly that day. His place was taken by an unqualified ground-crew mechanic, astonishing in view of the fact that the flight was a training exercise for the benefit of the Lancaster's gunners and pilot. The researcher has never been able to find out why the ground-crew man was aboard.

As a millennium project, a village near the crash site organised a service in September 1999 to mark the 55th anniversary of the accident. A memorial plaque was unveiled in the village church, and the Battle of Britain Flight Lancaster overflew in tribute.

A disproportionate share of suffering

The telegrams and letters of regret from the authorities came twice in the late summer of 1944 to the farm homestead near Becks, in Central Otago's Manuherikia Valley. First for John Milward Mee, 25; a month later for his brother, George James Mee, 26.

Invercargill barrister and solicitor James Mee, a nephew of the young airmen, was only four at the time but has distinct memories.

> I can remember the family assembling in the farmhouse, and the gloom that descended. The effect upon the whole family was profound . . . the poignant point to me as the years rolled by was the fact that two young men from a remote but beautiful New Zealand valley met their deaths over a far and distant land which they had never even visited or had any association with.

John Mee, known to his family as Jack, was a vastly experienced pathfinder pilot when his 7 Squadron Lancaster was shot down over Berlin on the night of 24–25 March 1944. None of the crew survived. Mee had done a full tour with 75 Squadron in 1943 and gone straight to 7 without a break. By the time he was killed he was on his 45th op and had done 19 with 7. He had been to Berlin 12 times. It was the worst of bad luck that he was lost on the very last raid of the series on that city.

George Mee, a talented piano player who had his own dance band in Wellington, enlisted in July 1941. After 10 months flying with a squadron in Canada, he was only on his fifth op on the night of 26–27 April when his 57 Squadron Lancaster was shot down by a night fighter north of Schweinfurt.

James and Myra Mee had five sons, with George and John the oldest. When his wife died, James married her sister and had four girls and a boy. Eric Mee, youngest of the first five, says he believes losing two sons shortened his father's life. 'It was a very big blow to him; two boys in a month.' Two of George's crew — the navigator and bomb aimer — survived, and the family knew fairly quickly that George was dead, but it was months before John was presumed dead.

George Mee was the only New Zealander on his aircraft, but two other New Zealanders died with John Mee — navigator David Bain, 33 (Auckland), and bomb aimer David Luxton, 30 (Hamilton). The three had also flown together on 75 Squadron. Their bomber fell in a northeastern suburb of Berlin, and they and their crewmates were buried locally in an area that became part of East Berlin after the war. Soviet authorities denied RAF teams access to search for the graves, and all seven crewmen are therefore remembered at Runnymede.

Fifty-six years later the Mee family learned through a remarkable coincidence what had happened the night George was killed. The flyers' cousin — Dunedin woman Pat Martin — and her husband were holidaying in Britain in 2000, and on 12 July that year stood at a bus stop on the outskirts of Edinburgh. Pat Martin tells the story:

> The only other person at the stop was an elderly man, and we asked him which bus to take into the city. He told us and also took the same bus. We got off together and talked and it came out that we were New Zealanders. Then he told us, 'I was a navigator in the RAF during the war and my pilot was a New Zealander. He had an unusual name — Mee, M double E.' I asked what his first name was and he said, 'George.' I told him I was George's cousin.

Of all the millions of people in Britain, Pat Martin had bumped into George Mee's wartime navigator, Tommy Garry — the last person to see Mee alive. Although Mee had been commissioned and Garry a flight sergeant, the two men had become friends and Garry had taken the New Zealander to his home in Edinburgh. 'Poor old Tommy, he was just blown away that day. He'd felt badly about not contacting the family after the war but didn't have an address. We spent the whole day with him next day. We had drinks, we had lunch, we had more drinks.'

Garry wrote later to Eric Mee: 'My Mum and everyone who met George thought the world of him and were really saddened he hadn't survived.' Garry said he remembered their Lancaster being hit by a fighter and Mee saying, 'Bale out, quick.' He knelt by Mee waiting for flight engineer Bert Pollard and bomb aimer Joe Connor to go. Then he followed. 'George was trying to pull the plane up; we gave each other the thumbs up, daft I know, but true. I saw a puff of smoke from the rear, then I was falling; pulled the cord and hit the trees.' Garry, captured a few days later, and Connor were the only survivors.

Some families bore a disproportionate share of suffering in World War II casualty lists. *For Your Tomorrow* identifies four sets of three brothers and more than 100 sets of two who died serving in the RNZAF or Allied air forces between 1915 and 1998. Most pairs were lost in World War II.

Of the parents who lost three boys, only Herbert and Fanny McFarlane of Dunedin had a son killed in Bomber Command. Laurence McFarlane, 25, second pilot on a Whitley, was killed attacking the battle cruiser *Scharnhorst* at Kiel on 1–2 July 1940. His death was the second hammer blow, for less than three weeks earlier Frank McFarlane, 24, had died when his Oxford crashed in Akaroa. The family was devastated again, in December 1943, when John McFarlane, 23, was killed flying a fighter in the Pacific.

The authorities sometimes acted to save families from further anguish. Pilot Allan Black was repatriated in 1943 after his two younger brothers, also pilots, were killed in Bomber Command. He himself had a close shave in the Middle East flying Wellingtons when engine failure forced a night ditching followed by 12 hours in a dinghy. He was back in England after his Middle East tour and serving at 11 OTU, Westcott, when the second of his brothers, Norman, 21, was killed. His first, John, 27, and known to the family as Jack, had already perished with all his crew in November 1941 when his 75 Squadron Wellington crashed in Holland while homebound from Berlin. Now, 14 months later, on 1 March 1943,

Norman, with 23 ops to his credit, was dead, his 76 Squadron Halifax lost without trace, also on a Berlin raid.

Norman and Allan had a brief reunion when the latter reached England in December 1942. Norman wrote to a friend in Christchurch on 5 January 1943:

> Allan returned . . . a few days ago and I went down to my aunt's place in Bedford to spend Christmas with him. My other brother Jack has been listed as killed in action but yesterday [a New Zealand representative in London] told my aunt his aircraft had been found in Holland. No bodies were found so I am hoping he was able to escape and is now in hiding. With a piece of luck he will turn up some day or else get out after the war is over — let's hope so anyhow.

In fact the Dutch Red Cross had reported the aircraft as having 'penetrated so deeply into the ground that it was not possible to extricate any bodies'. Its visible remains had been covered with earth and a cross erected on the mound to mark it as a consecrated grave. The bodies were recovered later and now lie in Bergen-op-Zoom War Cemetery. Black's crew included two fellow countrymen — second pilot Trevor Gray, 27 (New Plymouth), a married man, and navigator Eric Lloyd, 28 (Fordell, Wanganui). Samuel and Lillian Lloyd were another couple destined to lose two sons. Five months later Raymond Lloyd, also a navigator, was killed on a Wellington in the Middle East.

The Blacks — Irish-born 'Pop', his wife Margaret, and their three sons and two daughters — lived before the war in Bromley, Christchurch. Shirley Bool, then Shirley Caldwell and unofficially engaged to Norman when he left New Zealand, remembers the tragedy-struck family. The parents were already dealing with Jack's loss and worrying about Allan, then overseas too, when Norman was about to sail. 'Mrs Black, a plump motherly woman, was very upset that Norman, her youngest, her "baby", was going,' Mrs Bool says. 'In fact, she died just before Norman sailed.' She adds that Pop Black was almost unhinged by his wife's death and the loss of two sons and talked of taking his own life. She helped him survive. 'He was a lovely chap and he liked me to go over and have a meal with him. He kept chooks and always killed one when I was going and wanted me to eat almost all of it. I couldn't eat chicken for years.'

Leonard Cheshire, the most distinguished bomber pilot of World War II, was 76 Squadron CO when Norman Black was lost. He wrote to his father:

> He appears to have been attacked by a fighter and suffered a certain amount of damage. As result of this he was forced to turn for home and for an hour remained in contact with us. As none of his messages were urgent or in any way out of the ordinary, I do not think he could at this stage have been in serious trouble. I am very much afraid, however, that for some reason or other he must have been forced down just off the Dutch coast. A search on the widest possible scale was immediately organised and continued for two days, extending right up to the enemy coast itself. But this, I fear, was unsuccessful.

It isn't known who ordered Allan Black's recall but clearly someone in authority had decided the loss of two of three sons was enough. Allan was home in May 1943 and instructed for a year before ending his service in September 1944. He died in 1985.

The RAF forbade brothers flying together but twins sometimes got away with it, refusing to be split up. Canadians Robert and Richard Tod flew and died together in 75 (NZ) Squadron. On 10–11 April 1943 their Stirling, captained by another Canadian, was shot up during a raid on Frankfurt and ditched three miles off the English coast. The entire crew was rescued, but the Tods were killed two months later during the Battle of the Ruhr when a night fighter shot their bomber into the Ijsselmeer. The bodies of five of the crew, including the twins, were recovered. The Canadians, so close in life, lie side by side in a Dutch cemetery.

Peter and Tony Singer, twin sons of a popular Gisborne doctor, never flew together but both captained 57 Squadron Lancasters in attacks on Germany's most heavily defended cities — Hamburg, Cologne, Essen, Berlin — in late 1942 and early 1943. Both survived the war. They enlisted the same day, had consecutive service numbers, trained together, were often over the same targets at the same time, and finished their tours by bombing Dortmund. 'We never asked to be together,' they told a reporter. 'It just seemed automatic.' Awarded the DFC the same day, they went to Buckingham Palace together to receive their medals.

Brothers Bob and Nelson Renner flew together but not until they'd finished ops. Bob flew a tour with 15 Squadron in 1943 and then instructed before being posted in January 1945 to 511 Squadron, RAF Transport Command. At 511, flying Avro Yorks — unarmed long-range passenger and cargo transports based on the Lancaster — he was able to nominate his navigator and promptly suggested his brother. The RAF approved. Nelson, four years younger, had finished a quick tour of 30 ops with 75 Squadron a few days before Christmas 1944 and joined his brother at Lyneham, Wiltshire. By chance the brothers' service numbers ended in the same three digits and both flew the majority of their ops on U (Uncle) aircraft. Bob wrote later he knew of no other case in the RAF of two brothers flying in the same aircraft as pilot and navigator. Also in the crew was Bob's 15 Squadron wireless operator, fellow countryman Norm Southern.

Few, if any, families matched the record of the Cowans of Hastings. Four of Lily Cowan's five sons joined the RNZAF, and three — Jim, Bruce and Neville — won the DFC. John, the fourth, who served in the Pacific, was mentioned in dispatches in 1946. Jim, killed in 1943, and Bruce won their decorations at different times flying Lancasters with 9 Squadron. Neville's DFC was awarded for 42 ops, most of them with 148 Squadron on Wellingtons in the Middle East. Bruce, Neville and John all survived the war to return to Hastings, where Mrs Cowan had brought up her five sons and one daughter alone after the death of her husband in 1921.

Jim completed a tour with 9 Squadron but was killed in a training accident on 12 March 1943. Instructing at 1661 HCU, his Lancaster crashed near his Nottinghamshire airfield after an engine caught fire. All 10 airmen and ground crew aboard died. Bruce was due to fly the last op of his tour the next night but his CO said, 'No, you're finished right now.'

Will you marry me?

It wasn't surprising pilot Don Boon fell in love the moment he first saw Acting Sergeant Tina Moore. She was tall, blonde and strikingly attractive. Especially in uniform. She was not quite so impressed with Boon. He was at a table in the New Zealand Services Club in London with a group of buddies. They'd been there most of the day drinking beer, and empties littered the table. Moore had been to the cinema in Leicester Square with a friend from her barrage-balloon section, and the two women had chosen the club for a cheap meal. The place was crowded, and they asked Boon and his friends to keep an eye on two chairs while they got their food.

'They didn't, they were keeping an eye on us. They invited us to sit with them and of course they wouldn't let us go home on our own and took us back to our camp.' Boon then surprised Moore by turning up at the balloon site when he was on leave and watching the WAAFs working. More than once, Moore talked to her elder sister about this young man from the other side of the world and was told 'He'll be lonely. Bring him home.' 'He arrived carrying a biscuit tin full of coffee, chocolate and toffees — goodies we didn't see. And cigarettes. He became very popular with my sister, and whenever I visited on leave he'd be there.'

Moore had been writing to a naval officer — 'very prim and proper; wanted to be a bank manager after the war'. But she soon decided she quite liked 'this mad New Zealand pilot', and when he proposed over a drink in a pub on the way back to London after they'd visited her mother in Southsea, she accepted. They were married in England on 3 October 1945. Boon went home while she impatiently waited six months for a ship to New Zealand. They raised a family and milked cows for 33 years on a farm outside Whakatane, Moore loving every minute of it.

Boon flew his first op, to distant Konisberg, on 28 August 1944 and came home a flight lieutenant, surviving a tour of 35 ops with 61 Squadron, flying Lancasters. He was one of hundreds of New Zealand airmen who courted and married British women. Wartime Britain, despite moments of horror, death and destruction, was an exciting place to be. Young men and women, thrown together in tension-filled circumstances, fell in love in droves — especially on RAF stations, where countless WAAFs worked. New Zealand aircrew married WAAFs who packed parachutes, worked in admin and in the messes, and drove the trucks that delivered them to the planes waiting to take off for Germany.

Owen Foster, shot down over Amsterdam and captured in May 1943, married Olive Williams after the war. She was a WAAF at 487 Squadron, a telephone operator and waitress in the officers' mess. She was dark, very pretty — and unsmiling. Foster said something that made her smile one day, winning £4 from the others at his table, who bet that he couldn't. 'It was the most beautiful smile and I fell in love with her right away.' She was not amused when she learned what had gone on but, just the same, after that she always met Foster with a smile, a cup of tea and a 'Glad to see you made it back, sir' when he returned from ops.

Officers were not permitted to fraternize with WAAFs on station, but Foster sent a note to Williams one day, passed on by a helpful batwoman. That night there was a reply under his pillow with a copy of her roster, her days off marked. Wearing civilian clothes, they met in a park in Ely. Romance blossomed. His batwoman became their go-between, notes flying backwards and forwards. They thought no one else knew. The whole station knew.

The day he didn't come back from Amsterdam, Williams stood by the debrief room until midnight, waiting, praying. They had an emotional reunion at her parents' home in Felixstowe, Suffolk, when he got back to England in May 1945, and were married the following month.

Land girl Elsie Taylor met RNZAF pilot John Young at a Wings for Victory gala in the grounds of Blenheim Palace, Oxfordshire. She was participating in a sports event, he was demonstrating flying equipment. He told someone he wanted to meet her and was introduced. They were married in London on 13 June 1945 after he had been repatriated from Germany.

Young was shot down raiding Schweinfurt on the night of 26–27 April 1944, an only survivor. Elsie Taylor: 'He sailed to New Zealand on the *Andes*, arriving in October 1945. I followed on the *Akaroa* and arrived on 8 March 1946. There were three other war brides in my cabin; we became firm friends and have remained so all these years. We are all widows now and have reunions every two to three years.'

Pilot Bill Dashwood and Eileen Wilson met each other in the late autumn of 1941 at a dance in Boston, a Lincolnshire town near Coningsby, where his squadron was stationed. He was barely 20, she 16, not long out of school and working in the town clerk's office. They courted for three or four months until he parachuted over Denmark in mid-January 1942 where he was captured, fated to spend more than three years in a POW camp. 'We wrote to each other and I sent him food parcels and cigarettes and we got married when he came back,' she says.

Dashwood was among the many prisoners whose return was held up by the Russians, and he didn't reach England until late May 1945. He then made a beeline for Boston and married Eileen there on 3 July in St Botolph's, England's biggest parish church with its landmark 272-foot-high tower, known as The Stump.

Mick Cullen, a wireless operator on 15 Squadron, was served by barmaid Brenda Jaggard at the Bird in Hand on the edge of Mildenhall airfield, near the sergeants' mess, and she became his wife. Brenda Cullen remembers aircrew banging on the door for a drink late at night.

> We'd yell out that we were closed but the boss thought a lot of the boys and would always say, 'Go on, girls. Open the door and give them a drink.' We didn't mind. Being on the camp, they used to look after us well. It was a marvellous life. Wartime, it was sad, but it was the best time of our lives really.

The couple married in October 1944 and had their first child in England. Mrs Cullen, an only child, remembers her parents 'not being at all impressed that I was going to New Zealand'. So they also came out, in 1951, and stayed 15 years.

Many British parents watched with mixed emotions as their daughters sailed off on ships to New Zealand, a country on the other side of the world. A few families 'lost' two daughters. Laurie and Nora Adams, farmers near the village of Seagrave, Leicestershire, did. First Jeanette, or Nettie, to bomb aimer Rod Hoffman of Invercargill, then Jessie to navigator Trevor Dill. Jeanette, a land girl, met Hoffman, training at Wymeswold, also in Leicestershire, at a dance on 4 May 1944. She partnered various airmen until she was introduced to the New Zealander and that was that. 'All night our eyes did not seem to leave each other [and] as we danced there was magic between us.' Hoffman spent every available moment of leave with Jeanette and her family, pitching in when needed to harvest crops. Then he was posted to 625 Squadron at Kelstern, Lincolnshire, and they became engaged. She 'flew' his tour with him, flight after flight, night after night, petrified he would be killed. They set a wedding day, 10 February 1945, but didn't mail invitations until he came home safely from his last op, a six-hour trip to Wiesbaden on 2 February. Then, from Kelstern, he sent her a telegram: 'One week to go.' In her engaging 1997 book, *With the Down Wind*, the story of their lives, she wrote: 'I remember . . . going into the barn and sitting there with tears running down my face because . . . Rod and the crew had made it through 30 ops . . . I thanked the Lord.' The top tier of their wedding cake went to Invercargill.

Dill met his future wife in March 1945 when he was driving south through Leicestershire with Aucklander Roy Hathaway after both had finished a course. Hathaway had been the navigator in Hoffman's crew, and when Dill's little Morris 8 ran short of fuel, he said, 'I know where we can get some petrol.' He had often been to the Adams' farm with Hoffman, and both Jeanette and Jessie were home when they arrived. The two New Zealanders were invited to stay the weekend. When they left, Dill asked if he might come again. He did, three or four times.

The new Mrs Hoffman wrote of the initial meeting: 'I think Jess could have fallen in love with Flt/Lt Trevor Dill.' She had. But Dill was suddenly ordered on to a New Zealand-bound ship in September 1945 and left without proposing to the crestfallen young woman. But just before sailing he wrote and asked her to marry him. They were wed in the Anglican church in Warkworth on 18 September 1946. Rod Hoffman gave the bride away and his wife was matron of honour. Dill wrote years later of the wonderful welcome he'd received from the Adams family — parents and five children — in their farm environment. 'Jessie had just turned eighteen, a very beautiful, full-of-life young woman. Everything so peaceful, so different from service life. No wonder I fell in love. I knew she was for me pretty early, but because the war still went on I did not want to make commitments till my war at least was over.'

Hoffman died in 1982, his wife in 2002. The Dills live in Warkworth.

Some English war brides promised early return visits to England to see Mum and Dad — Muriel Merchant, only daughter of an Essex couple, for one. She met Norm Southern, the wireless operator on *Te Kooti*, after he had finished his tour and was instructing at Woolfox Lodge in the county of Rutland. She was on the same station, serving as a WAAF shorthand-typist in the orderly room. 'I remember the WAAFs put on a dance and we had to invite someone on the camp. The girl in the bed next to me also had her eye on Norman, but I must have won.'

Southern and Merchant were married on 10 May 1944, having been given a week's leave to organise the event. They managed a four-day honeymoon in the Lake District. When she sailed for New Zealand in late 1945, after a tearful parting from her parents, she had her eight-month-old son with her. 'It's all right, Mum and Dad,' she said. 'I'll be back in a couple of years to see you and it'll go very quickly.' Three more babies and 27 years later she finally managed it.

The three New Zealanders on *Te Kooti* all married English women. Bomb aimer Ian McColl met Barbara Oxbrow one day when he went into the London branch of the Bank of New Zealand, where she worked. They were married in a London church on 24 November 1944. Their son Tony says the first time his father visited his prospective wife's parents he took a large suitcase. 'Barbara's mother was not impressed. She thought he planned to move in. But when he opened the suitcase it was full of goodies. He went to the top of the list real quick.' He adds: 'It must have been a hell of a shock to my mother to go from London to the back blocks of Taihape, with gravel roads, no electricity or flush toilet and a resident father-in-law with a fairly short fuse.'

Skipper Bob Renner married a daughter of the owner of a 1000-acre Rutland farm she helped to run. He met her after a church service in a village not far from his airfield. He and fellow countryman Bob Scott, handsome young officers, were invited back to the farm for lunch. They married the farmer's only children, Mary and Elizabeth Wakefield. The Renners came to New Zealand after the war but returned to England to run the farm. Scott, a wing commander at the end of the war, switched from the RNZAF to the RAF in 1947 and served another 11 years. He remained in England.

Davenport Brown, an early gunnery leader on 75 Squadron, knocked down an Me 110 that attacked his Wellington when he was homebound from Brest one night in April 1941. Minutes later, the plane collided with a Blenheim, which went straight down. The Wimpy — port wing damaged, half the port tailplane gone and the floor ripped out of Brown's rear turret — struggled to a safe landing. Brown survived all that and married Victoria Judd in St Martin-in-the-Fields, Trafalgar Square, on 12 January 1942.

He met his wife at his then girlfriend's flash 21st birthday party at the Mayfair Hotel. They played games. 'I was the spider and had to go and find Miss Muffett. She turned out to be my wife. Soon after meeting her I was posted [as an instructor at a gunnery school] to Australia. I phoned her up and proposed. She accepted.' The wedding at St Martin's went well but the expensive Bond Street photographer Brown organised turned up without film in his camera. New Zealand Press Association correspondent Alan Mitchell was there with his Box Brownie and one snapshot from that is the only photograph Brown has of the important day. Why did he choose the famous St Martin's? 'I didn't; I did what I was told. I think Vicky was taken with the idea it was the king's parish church, and her father was prepared to pay for it.'

Brown, scheduled to sail on a packed troopship, confronted the Air Ministry with the information he had a wife. 'You bastard,' said the ministry man. The Browns sailed in comfort a bit later from Liverpool, two of just 12 passengers on a fast supply ship. Her holds were packed with mines, torpedoes and ammunition. There was no boat drill. 'If we're hit, no one will know anything about it,' an officer told Brown. 'No point in drills.'

Pilot Jim Holdaway knew and liked his mother-in-law a long time before he met his wife. He often visited Ann Mellersh's parents' home in Surrey, one of those many pleasant places where Britons hosted Commonwealth airmen. Holdaway, a tour in the Middle East behind him and a DFC to show for it, got to England in late 1942 and after instructing for a year joined 139 Squadron, a multipurpose night-bomber Mosquito squadron. He flew 50 ops with 139, 11 of them to Berlin, for another DFC and a niche in Mosquito history as the first pilot to take the Mark XVI on operations — with a 4000-pound bomb to the German capital on 10 February 1944.

Ann Mellersh came home in 1944 from Canada, where she had been at university. Fluent in French, she got a job in MI5 translating reports from secret agents in France. She also met Jim Holdaway when he came visiting her mother. They became engaged in January 1945 and married later in the year. Holdaway distinguished himself in civilian life after the war and garnered more honours for his role in conservation and in Auckland local-body and community affairs.

In the movies nurses marry their patients. They do so in real life too. Mid-upper gunner Jack Marshall (Tauranga) was one of two survivors when his 218 Squadron Stirling crashed and burned on return from Wilhelmshaven at 1.00 a.m. on 15 September 1942. Trapped, he was rescued in the nick of time, badly burned and grievously injured. He lost both legs above the knee and was in hospital for two years. But on 6 January 1945 Flight Sergeant Marshall walked on artificial limbs and a stick down the aisle of St Etheldreda's Church, Ely, Cambridgeshire, to marry Pat Walthew from Dublin, the woman who nursed him for six months.

His best man was fellow New Zealander Squadron Leader Arthur Colville (Methven), who had also been badly injured in a bomber. His 75 Squadron Wellington crashed during an air test in February 1942. Colville survived by the slimmest margin — feet almost wrenched off, 14 breaks in one leg, four in the other. His back was broken in two places, his skull fractured and he had severe facial injuries. An indomitable will helped him recover, and he and Marshall became firm friends in Ely RAF hospital.

The Marshalls came home to New Zealand, Jack to work for the Railways in Tauranga. But he spent a lot of time in hospital and died in October 1953, his death the direct result of his war injuries.

New Zealanders training in Canada fell for local girls too. Some married before going on to England and operations, leaving wives to worry about them flying ops and often to become widows. Others waited until the end of the war to marry.

Hec Frew had hardly arrived in Winnipeg a few weeks before Christmas 1942 before he was introduced to his future wife. He admits his courting of June Callaghan contributed to his failure to master Morse code at wireless school. He was remustered as a gunner, which suited him fine. After graduating from gunnery school in far-off Quebec in the summer of 1943, he returned to Winnipeg on leave to see Callaghan before sailing to England.

Frew survived a terrible training crash in April 1944 and didn't fly again. He sailed for Canada on the first troopship out of Portsmouth after the war, joining other New Zealanders headed for joyous reunions with fiancees and wives. He arrived in Winnipeg on a Tuesday and was married on the Saturday. The couple honeymooned at the family cottage on Lake Winnipeg and were then separated again, he to return to New Zealand, she to follow with other war brides before the end of the year.

Wireless operator Maurice Robison, in hospital in Germany in late 1942 after being shot down on an anti-submarine patrol in the Atlantic, was befriended by two young nurses who paid for a barber to cut his hair. They also sneaked into his room before Christmas and gave him two postcards showing Christmas trees and snow. Robison mailed one to his parents in Tolaga Bay, the other to fiancee Edith Kelly in Winnipeg. Both arrived at their destinations.

Robison suffered dreadfully on the winter march west from a POW camp in early 1945 and was in hospital for weeks when he got back to England. He tried without success to get a ship to Canada and eventually returned to New Zealand on the *Andes* in October 1945. Kelly came out three months later with other Canadian war brides and the couple married on 22 February 1946. They raised four daughters and had 45 years together. Mrs Robison died in 1991. Despite his wartime privations Robison was in good shape at 84 when this book was written.

Pilot Leicester Kingsbury and Joy Brocherie were engaged before he left New Zealand to join the RAF on a short-service commission to train as a pilot in 1938. At some stage they decided they didn't want to wait until the end of the war to marry, perhaps because his chances of survival were slim. In February 1940 Brocherie sailed for England on the *Rangitane* and the couple wed in Cirencester soon after the ship docked. 'I always thought it was brave of her to sail into a war zone to marry him,' son Tony says.

Kingsbury was then sent to Southern Rhodesia as an instructor under the Commonwealth training scheme. His wife was pregnant when they arrived in late 1940 and Tony was born there in January 1941. The family returned to England in 1943 and Kingsbury began ops on 218 Squadron's Stirlings. Then he was tapped for the pathfinders, transferring to 7 Squadron on Lancasters. He was shot down raiding Berlin on 1–2 January 1944, surviving to become a POW. His wife endured anxious weeks before learning he was alive, then moved with her young son to Torquay, working there while she waited for the end of the war and her husband's return. The three Kingsburys returned home in 1946.

David Clark's New Zealand wife-to-be also sailed to England during the war. Pat Laird caught a ship in March 1944, acting as nurse/nanny to two children and their sick mother, the wife of a VIP engineer. Clark and Laird, who had known each other before the war, were married at 4.30 p.m. on 19 July 1944 in a civil ceremony in the village of Downham Market, the base from which he was then flying with 635, a pathfinder squadron.

It was a close-run thing but the newlyweds were able to go off afterwards to the Lake District on honeymoon. The bridegroom was on the battle order for that night but bad weather intervened on their behalf and the operation was scrubbed.

They returned to New Zealand in early 1945 and bought a farm near Otorohanga, where they remained for the rest of their working lives before moving into the town.

When pilot Ralph Martin got back to his farm at Ruatangata, outside Whangarei, after the war he was straight back into milking cows and soon it seemed as if he'd never been away. In 1950, unsettled, still young and unattached, he decided to go back to England for a couple of years. On the ship he met a young woman. She'd been a war bride, married to a New Zealander in the Fleet Air Arm. Now she was going home to Scotland with a year-old daughter, a failed marriage behind her.

The inevitable happened. Martin and Wilhelmina, or Billy as she was known, fell in love. He got a job in Glasgow and every weekend went up to see her in the Highlands where she was living with her parents. After two years in Britain Martin returned to New Zealand, Billy and her little girl with him. 'I was quite happy to come back, marry and settle down,' he says. Martin is a widower now but his married step-daughter still lives on the farm.

75 Squadron navigator Ted Anderson met his future wife, a Wren, when he walked into a sergeants' party at 11 OTU, Westcott, just before Christmas 1943. Magda Orczy-Barstow was sitting with an empty glass in the crowded room. 'So I filled it and we started chatting' — and fell in love, there and then.

Anderson promptly accepted an invitation to a party where the young woman was based — 10 miles from Mepal, 75 Squadron's station. He was puzzled about what Wrens were doing so far inland but getting to the party was a more immediate problem. 'We couldn't arrange transport so two or three of us "borrowed" bikes and rode to the party. The signposts were all gone because of the war and country lanes branched off all over the place. It was one of my more difficult pieces of navigation; a masterpiece to get there and back in the blackout.'

Orczy-Barstow, a granddaughter of novelist Baroness Orczy, was bound by the Official Secrets Act and couldn't tell Anderson what she was doing in the Wrens. It was only years later he learned the full story. His wife worked at Bletchley Park with the people who cracked the Enigma code.

Anderson and Orczy-Barstow began writing to each other regularly as 1944 began and were engaged 10 weeks later even though they'd only spent a few hours together. They were married in a London church on 3 January 1945 and sailed for New Zealand the following month. They had been together for more than 56 years when Mrs Anderson died in 2002.

Frances Berger was distraught when New Zealander Keith Neilson didn't come home from a Ruhr raid the night of 25–26 June 1943. She had joined the WAAFs in November 1940 after serving as an air-raid warden in London and was posted to Stradishall, a big Bomber Command base in Suffolk. A year or so later she met Neilson after he arrived on the station to join 214 Squadron. Romance blossomed. Berger was a sergeant, secretary to the engineer wing commander. She and Neilson spent their off-duty hours together — precious time in an era when so many bomber crew had such short lives.

The morning after each of Neilson's ops the English WAAF, heart thumping, rushed to the base headquarters to check the list of aircraft that had returned safely. On that late June morning in 1943 Neilson was posted missing on the ops board at nearby Chedburgh, a Stradishall satellite where 214 had moved when it had opened in October 1942. But Neilson had come down safely by parachute and it wasn't long before Berger learned her sweetheart was safe in a prison camp.

Neilson was among the last POWs to get back to Britain, arriving at Southampton on 29 May 1945. Berger got word in a telegram; given leave, she dashed onto the road outside Stradishall and thumbed lifts to Southampton in her frantic haste to get there. Four days after his homecoming they wed in Paddington registry office, London, before spending a joyous honeymoon in Devon. Neilson went home alone, followed a few months later by his wife, one of 100 war brides on the *Dominion Monarch*.

English woman Nicky Nicholson and New Zealander Jim Boag fell in love at Bardney, 9 Squadron's Lincolnshire base, where both were posted in the autumn of 1944. She joined the WAAFs as a driver in September 1939 and during the Battle of Britain was stationed at North Weald, a sector field.

She was in the Motor Transport section at Bardney and soon met Boag, a bomb aimer who came from Christchurch. Both were sergeants. She often drove him and the rest of his crew, including fellow New Zealanders Dave Coster (pilot) and Cliff Black (navigator), to their Lancaster for ops and watched the planes take off. She remembers: 'It was all right going out but picking them up [on return] was a different matter. I'd say "Where is S-Sugar or L-Love?" and they hated saying "It went down in flames" or "We don't know."'

Nicholson and Boag often went into Lincoln for a meal, and a movie or a drink in a quiet pub. 'Jimmy asked me to marry him and I laughed and said "No" as I was six years older than he was. People would say I was cradle snatching.' But as the war wound down, 9 Squadron was told it would be going to India and that all Commonwealth personnel would be sent home.

So I said 'Yes', and we were married in the lovely little church in Bardney in July 1945. All Jimmy's crew were there. We had to catch a slow train to Nottingham to meet the express to Edinburgh for our honeymoon. It had very dirty windows and no corridors and the crew wrote 'Just Married' in the dirt. At every stop people would get on and ask if it were true and then get off and leave us alone.

9 Squadron didn't go to India and Boag didn't go home immediately. He was permitted to stay because his wife was pregnant. They had twin daughters with them when they sailed for New Zealand in May 1946.

Few New Zealand airmen went to such lengths as rear gunner Max Dowman to remain in England. He volunteered for a third tour so he could stay to marry WAAF Kathleen Kerr.

Dowman was working on his father's Opunake dairy farm when he enlisted in March 1941. He flew his first tour with the pathfinders of 156 Squadron (29 ops), his second with 617 Squadron, the Dambusters (20 ops), and his third with 75 (NZ) Squadron (25 ops), for a remarkable tally of 74 ops and 832 operational flying hours.

'Lofty' Dowman, almost six feet tall, did his first 617 trip with legendary Australian pilot Dave Shannon on the disastrous 15–16 September 1943 low-level attack on the Dortmund–Ems Canal, in which five of the eight participating Lancasters were lost. Dowman won the DFM for his shooting that night, the recommendation for the award noting his aircraft had been faced with severe and accurate fire from light flak of all calibres. 'It was due in large measure to his resolute and effective return fire that [Shannon] was able to complete a very protracted search for the target at a height of only 100 feet.'

Dowman flew the rest of his 617 tour with New Zealand pilot Terry Kearns and his able navigator, fellow countryman John Barclay. Dowman had flown with Kearns at 156 and joined up with him again when Shannon was sick and grounded.

When he finished at 617 Dowman was told he was being sent home. But he had met and fallen in love with Kerr, a sergeant servicing aircraft batteries at Coningsby, then 617's base. So that they might continue their courtship and get married, Dowman announced he would do a third tour. 75 Squadron was happy to have a man whose logbook assessment said he had had 'an exceptionally distinguished 2nd operational tour'.

His third tour finished, Dowman married Kerr in St James the Greater, the parish church in the village of Birstall, Leicestershire, where she had grown up. They had two or three months together before Dowman sailed for home. His wife followed on the *Dominion Monarch*, on the same sailing as Frances Neilson.

This is one story that doesn't have a happy ending. Dowman, back on the farm, died without warning from a brain haemorrhage on 2 January 1948, leaving a wife and three-months-old son Richard. Mrs Dowman went home to England with her child but four-and-a-half years later they returned. 'I thought he would have better chance in New Zealand, a better life,' she says. 'And having made the decision I wanted him to start school in New Zealand, so we came back in time for that.' She settled in Opunake, eventually remarried and raised a new family. Kathleen McKie now lives with her retired second husband in New Plymouth.

Graveyards

They lie in graves in small communities on the Dutch coast, in English village churchyards, in beautiful cemeteries in Denmark, alongside fjords in Norway, in public burial grounds and Catholic churchyards in France and Belgium, and in all the big war cemeteries created in Germany after the war by the Commonwealth War Graves Commission. A few lie in Poland, Czechoslovakia and Italy, killed over the most distant targets raided by Bomber Command. All lie in some corner of a foreign field that is forever New Zealand — 1450 of them. Another 400 New Zealand bomber aircrew with no known graves are remembered on the panels at Runnymede, in England.

Few New Zealanders have any idea of the deep veneration in which the RAF war dead, especially Bomber Command crew, are held by people who lived in the occupied countries. Night after night they heard the bombers on their way to Germany and exulted. They devotedly tended the fresh graves of Allied airmen and covered them with flowers. They defied the Germans and held funeral processions and church services. After the war they erected monuments and memorials — and continue to do so, in many cases to individual crews. It isn't only those who lived through the war years that remember. New generations are also involved.

Pilot Leslie Lissette, a young man from Hastings killed on the Mailly-le-Camp raid in May 1944, was buried with his rear gunner in the shadow of a high brick wall in the cemetery of the town of Chaintreaux, southeast of Nemours. An elderly woman still takes a school class to the cemetery to spruce up the flyers' joint grave and headstones every Friday afternoon. She was a young pupil at the school when Lissette's Lancaster crashed nearby.

Many Bomber Command dead were reinterred when hostilities ceased, their remains being moved to war cemeteries. Kiel War Cemetery, established in 1954, is the last resting place of men lost in raids over northern Europe. Their bodies were brought in from cemeteries and churchyards throughout Schleswig-Holstein, the Frisian Islands and other parts of northwest Germany.

Thirty-seven New Zealanders lie in Kiel, among them Maurice Bell of 75 Squadron, lost raiding Lubeck on 28–29 March 1942. In 2002 Thelma Good of Wanganui, who was engaged to Bell when he was killed, contacted German Horst Ahrens after he offered in a Bomber Command (UK) newsletter to take photographs, without charge, of headstones of airmen buried in Kiel. Ahrens, who lives near the cemetery, was a schoolboy in Kiel during the war, his family blasted out of their home three times by British bombs and a brother-in-law lost in a U-boat. Ahrens holds no grudges. 'It is an honour to take these photographs.' In the autumn of 2002 he planted a cherry-red rose at Bell's gravesite. 'I have watered the rose and gave her special dung. Now I think she will be under blossoms next summer.' She was.

Eight New Zealanders lie beneath the manicured lawn sloping away from Svino Evangelical Lutheran Church (Denmark's national church), eight of 62 in the British plot. Three of them are from a 75 Squadron Lancaster captained by Wilson Hadley, 30 (Christchurch), shot down on 11 September 1944. Save English engineer Colin Fowler, the crew were all New Zealanders: Hadley (known as Joe), navigator John Gudgeon, 23 (Christchurch), bomb aimer Jack Wilcox, 24 (Matamata), wireless operator Paddy Giles, 21 (Christchurch), mid-upper gunner Vic Boyd, 20 (Nelson), and rear gunner Jock Biggar, 22 (Wanganui). Wilcox and Fowler were the only survivors.

The aircraft had dropped mines in Danzig Bay and was homebound when attacked by a fighter over Vordingborg at about 11.45 p.m. In 1990, Wilcox, a dairy farmer, wrote about what happened for a Danish researcher. He said they had been on track and just about to cross the coast at 20,000 feet when they were hit by cannon fire. 'The plane became an inferno ... the heat was horrific.' He jettisoned the hatch cover but the heat was so unbearable he only had time to snap his chute onto one harness clip before throwing himself out. He hurt his right shoulder landing and found himself covered in blood. He woke an elderly farm couple to get help. 'They were darlings and most helpful bathing my face and giving me a drink.' Wilcox was taken to the local hospital, where he was picked up by Germans. Fowler escaped the clutches of the Germans, was spirited to Sweden and got back to England.

Gudgeon, Giles and Boyd apparently jumped from the Lancaster but too low for their parachutes to open. Their bodies were taken to Svino for burial. Hadley and Biggar were still on the bomber when it crashed — on a farmhouse at Orslev, 10 miles from Svino. The gasoline-fuelled explosion and fire burned the house to the ground, incinerating the flyers and five Danes, members of one family — the farmer, his wife and three of their grown children. Despite the devastation and tragedy, surviving children insisted Hadley and Biggar be buried in the village churchyard alongside their parents and siblings. 'They died together, so they belonged together,' one Dane wrote years later.

Another New Zealander buried at Svino is John Henry, who grew up in Christchurch. A rear gunner on a 9 Squadron Lancaster shot down over Denmark during a raid on Germany in September 1942, he was one of no fewer than five New Zealanders onboard. But his body was the only one of the five recovered after the aircraft plunged into the sea north of the Baltic island of Lolland.

Eight of the 32 New Zealanders in Danish cemeteries are buried in Fourfelt Cemetery in Esjberg, a port on the west coast of mainland Jutland. One of them is pilot Jack Sligo, a Wellingtonian, 24 when he was killed in May 1942. What exactly happened is not known but his 57 Squadron Wellington, on a mine-laying mission, was probably caught by a fighter and is thought to have crashed off Fano Island, near Esjberg. The bodies of all five crew were eventually recovered and buried in Fourfelt. Sligo had married Marie Peters in February 1941 and she was pregnant when he sailed for England six months later. She gave birth to their daughter, Anne, on 3 February 1942 but sadly he never saw photographs of the baby. 'I sent photographs to Jack but he hadn't received them because the mails were slow . . . they were all returned to me . . . he knew about her but he didn't get the photos.'

Just one New Zealander is buried in the Grand Duchy of Luxembourg. Forrest Thompson, known to his friends as Tommy, died the night of 20–21 March 1945 when the 161 Squadron Hudson on which he was flying as gunner was shot down and crashed on a steep wooded hill in the Ardennes on the northern tip of Luxembourg. Three Belgian agents and three members of the crew died, the pilot the only survivor. Thompson had flown a tour with 218 Squadron prior to joining the secret-operations squadron.

The dead were buried where they fell, among the trees high above the village of Maulesmuhle. After the war the Commonwealth War Graves Commission proposed removing the bodies to a war cemetery in Belgium. The people of Maulesmuhle refused to countenance the shift, declaring, 'We will care for them.' The CWGC relented. Six headstones stand amid the trees, the wreckage and a memorial dedicated in August 1970.

Thompson's death, just before the end of the war, was doubly poignant because he left an English wife, a tall attractive woman. Olive Thompson was pregnant when her husband was killed. Anne Thompson, now Anne Thoday, was born on 5 May 1945, the day the Germans surrendered in northwest Europe. 'My mother never remarried,' she says. 'She maintained that "Forrest was the only man for me" and that was it. And she didn't want any other man involved in my upbringing.'

When Anne Thompson was two her mother brought her to New Zealand to meet her grandparents, Waldo and Ethel Thompson, who lived at Waipiro Bay, on the East Coast. The Thompsons had lost both their sons in the European air war. Onslow, a Bomber Command Mosquito pilot, was killed on 1 May 1943 when his aircraft crashed at Marham, Suffolk, his 105 Squadron airfield, and is buried there. He was married but had no children, so Anne was precious. She and her mother stayed for a year then returned to England.

Every year on 25 April Thompson's widow pinned a New Zealand silver-fern brooch on her coat and took her daughter up to London from her home in Bedford to attend the Anzac Day ceremony. She died in 1988, still grieving for the New Zealander to whom she had been married a bare 10 months.